Engaging Coloniality

The Global Story of Christianity Series
History, Context, and Communities

Seven One-Volume Books

SERIES EDITORS
Emma Wild-Wood & Mark A. Lamport

SERIES ASSISTANT EDITOR
Gina A. Zurlo

SERIES INTRODUCTION
Dana L. Robert

BOOK EDITORS
Mitri Raheb *(Middle East)* | Amos Yong *(Asia)* | Wanjiru Gitau *(Africa)*
Alex Ryrie *(Europe)* | Raimundo Barreto Jr. *(Latin America)*
Upolu Lumā Vaai *(Oceania)* | Christopher Evans *(North America)*

SERIES EDITORIAL ADVISORY BOARD
Edwin Aponte *(Louisville Institute)*
Elias Bongmba *(Rice University)*
Arun Jones *(Candler School of Theology/Emory University)*
Brett Knowles *(University of Otago)*
David Maxwell *(University of Cambridge, UK)*
Elizabeth Monier *(University of Cambridge, UK)*
Dana L. Robert *(Center for Global Christianity and Mission/Boston University)*
Nelly van Doorn-Harder *(Wake Forest University)*
Stephanie Wong *(Valparaiso University)*

SENIOR EDITORIAL CONSULTANT
Joshua Erb

Series Concept

The Global Story of Christianity Series is designed as a set of accessible introductions for those who wish to understand the emergence of the Christian faith and its global church presence today. The concept of "story" will be the featured motif and is reflected in fifteen chapters spread over three main subheadings in each book:

Section One: The Story of Christianity Narrated in Historical Context

Section Two: The Story of Christianity Expressed in a Grand Church Family Mosaic

Section Three: The Story of Christianity Encounters Twenty-First-Century Issues

The Global Story of Christianity Series

Book Title	Year of Release	Editors
Surviving Jewel: The Enduring Story of Christianity in the Middle East	Book 1: 2022	Mitri Raheb *(Dar al-Kalima University College, Bethlehem)* & Mark A. Lamport
Uncovering the Pearl: The Hidden Story of Christianity in Asia	Book 2: 2023	Amos Yong *(Fuller Theological Seminary)* & Mark A. Lamport
Globalizing Legacies: The Intermingling Story of Christianity in Africa	Book 3: 2024	Wanjiru M. Gitau *(Palm Beach Atlantic University, Florida)* & Mark A. Lamport
Entangling Web: The Fractious Story of Christianity in Europe	Book 4: 2024	Alec Ryrie *(University of Durham, UK)* & Mark A. Lamport
Engaging Coloniality: The Liberative Story of Christianity in Latin America	Book 5: 2025	Raimundo C. Barreto Jr. *(Princeton Theological Seminary)* & Mark A. Lamport
Restoring Identities: The Contextualizing Story of Christianity in Oceania	Book 6: 2023	Upolu Vaai *(Pacific Theological College, Fiji)* & Mark A. Lamport
Expanding Energy: The Dynamic Story of Christianity in North America	Book 7: 2024	Christopher H. Evans *(Boston University)* & Mark A. Lamport

Engaging Coloniality

The Liberative Story of Christianity in Latin America

Edited by
Raimundo C. Barreto Jr.
and Mark A. Lamport

CASCADE *Books* • Eugene, Oregon

ENGAGING COLONIALITY
The Liberative Story of Christianity in Latin America
Global Story of Christianity Series 5

Copyright © 2025 Wipf and Stock Publishers. All rights reserved. Except for brief quotations in critical publications or reviews, no part of this book may be reproduced in any manner without prior written permission from the publisher. Write: Permissions, Wipf and Stock Publishers, 199 W. 8th Ave., Suite 3, Eugene, OR 97401.

Cascade Books
An Imprint of Wipf and Stock Publishers
199 W. 8th Ave., Suite 3
Eugene, OR 97401

www.wipfandstock.com

PAPERBACK ISBN: 978-1-6667-3000-5
HARDCOVER ISBN: 978-1-6667-2098-3
EBOOK ISBN: 978-1-6667-2099-0

Cataloguing-in-Publication data:

Names: Barreto, Raimundo C., Jr., editor. | Lamport, Mark A., editor.
Title: Engaging coloniality : The liberative story of Christianity in Latin America / edited by Raimundo C. Barreto Jr. and Mark A. Lamport.
Description: Eugene, OR: Cascade Books, 2025. | The Global Story of Christianity Series 5. | Includes bibliographical references and indexes.
Identifiers: ISBN: 978-1-6667-3000-5 (paperback). | ISBN: 978-1-6667-2098-3 (hardcover). | ISBN: 978-1-6667-2099-0 (ebook).
Subjects: LCSH: Latin America—Church history.
Classification: BR600 E67 2025 (print). | BR600 (epub).

Scripture quotations are from the Holy Bible, New International Version®, NIV®, copyright © 2011 by Biblica, Inc.® Used by permission of Zondervan. All rights reserved worldwide.

Dedication

For *Raimundo*—To *M. Richard Shaull* (in memoriam) and *Nancy Johns*

For *Mark*—To *Francisco Garcia de Padilla*, OFM (one of the first three Roman Catholic bishops in the New World), *Antonio de Montesinos* (Spanish Dominican friar-missionary on the island of Hispaniola [now the Dominican Republic and Haiti], 1475–1540), *Manuel da Nóbrega* (Portuguese Jesuit, founder of several cities, such as Recife, Salvador, Rio de Janeiro, and São Paulo, as well as many Jesuit colleges and seminaries, 1517–70), and *Erasmo de Carvalho Braga* (Protestant educator, writer, and thinker, 1877–1932)

Contents

Series Introduction by Dana L. Robert xi
About the Editors and Introducers xxi
Preface: Latin America by Gina A. Zurlo and Mark A. Lamport xxiii
Acknowledgments xxix
About the Contributors xxxi
Introduction by Raimundo C. Barreto Jr. xxxv

SECTION ONE
The Story of Christianity Narrated in Historical Context: Colonial Encounters, Negotiations, and Contestations

Chapter 1—The Christianization of the Nahuas and the Nahuatilization of Christianity / Nadia Marín-Guadarrama 3

Chapter 2—Women's Religiosity in New Spain Colonial Catholicism / Jessica Delgado 18

Chapter 3—Sor Juana Inés de la Cruz: A Seventeenth-Century Mexican Nun and Poet Through the Lenses of Ecofeminism / Theresa A. Yugar 34

Chapter 4—Afro-Latin American Religious Practices in the Iberian Colonies / Joan Cameron Bristol 50

SECTION TWO
The Story of Christianity Expressed in a Grand Church Family Mosaic: National States and the Rise of Modern Christianity

Chapter 5—Christianity, Nationalism, and Anticlericalism in Nineteenth-Century Latin America / Francisco J. Peláez-Díaz 65

Chapter 6—The Making of Protestantism in Latin America / Pedro Feitoza 79

Chapter 7—Christianity and Social Movements in Latin America / Nicolás Panotto 95
Chapter 8—Hierarchy and Ritual: A Comparative Study of Candomblé, Umbanda, and Neo-Pentecostal Churches / Luiz C. Nascimento 111
Chapter 9—Theoquilombism: Perspectives for an Afro-Brazilian Christianity / Cleusa Caldeira 126

SECTION THREE
The Story of Christianity Encounters Twenty-First-Century Issues

Chapter 10—Christian Unity and Reconciliation: A Latin American Decolonial Contribution / Raimundo C. Barreto Jr. 145
Chapter 11—The Indigenous Church: The Changing Face of Liberation Christianity in Latin America / Graciela Chamorro 167
Chapter 12—Latin American Pentecostalism as Popular Religion / Ángel D. Santiago-Vendrell 187
Chapter 13—Christianity, Gender, and Ecology in Abya Yala / Sandra Duarte de Souza 202
Chapter 14—Christianity on the Move: Migratory Christianity in and from Latin America / João B. Chaves 216

Timeline—Latin America and the Caribbean / Brett Knowles 232

Index of Names and Subjects 247

Series Introduction

The Global Story of Christianity: History, Contexts, and Communities

DANA L. ROBERT

WHAT DOES IT MEAN *to tell the story* of global Christianity? Storytelling is important for personal identity, for community life, and for shared humanity. When people tell their own stories, both individually and as communities of faith, they share who they are and who they hope to become. When people make friends, they swap stories. They introduce themselves. They discuss their work, or where they went to school. They might talk about the sports teams they support, or what activities they enjoy. As people get to know each other better, they exchange stories about their families, or politics, or other important issues. Friends do things together—and the being together creates memories that launch new stories they recall when they see each other again. In listening to each other, people's stories merge and create a common basis for relationships—even across boundaries or divisions.

Global Christianity is the story of a huge extended family. Christians are rooted in a common ancestor, Jesus Christ. For two thousand years, the followers of Jesus of Nazareth have traced their spiritual lineage through him to the God of ancient Israel, as spoken through the prophets and written in the Bible and celebrated in worship and outreach. Christianity is now the world's largest religion, encompassing one-third of the world's peoples. During the twentieth century, the family of faith burst out of European frameworks and began growing rapidly in Africa, Asia, and Latin America. By 2018, Africa had become the continent with the largest number of Christians, followed by Latin America, and Europe, with Asia soon to become second in numbers.[1] Christianity as a global story reminds me of the chatter at a giant family reunion, where the relatives get together and reminisce about their distant family history, and the departed saints that they remember—and the old family arguments that never seem to end. For better or worse, whether or not they know each other personally, the people who call themselves Christians are spiritual brothers, sisters, and long-lost cousins. Shared family history connects them.

And yet, nobody has only *one* story. This book series on the global story of Christianity embodies many stories that have unfolded across two thousand years of time, and which inhabit wide-ranging geographic and cultural spaces. The sheer size and complexity of the global Christian family means that a shared history is composed of multiple memories, from thousands of contexts. Being part of a community means organizing the stories into a convincing whole and claiming a common identity through them. Communities can be direct sets of relationships, such as families, neighborhoods, sports clubs, therapy groups, and local churches. They can also be "imagined" and thus composed of people who may never meet in person, but whose groups—including ethnicities, cities, political parties, and even nations—share common interpretations of experiences. For Christians, both personal and imagined faith communities use shared narratives to organize their spiritual realities. And yet, the meaning and identity of faith communities also changes over time, depending on the context. Depending on one's purpose or needs, different parts of one's story become more important than others. I am reminded of a friend who was the new pastor of a small church. Each week, no matter how hard he tried to get the old-timers to move, nobody would sit in the front section of the church. Finally, in frustration he asked one old man why he wouldn't move toward the front of the church. "I've been sitting in this pew for forty years," he replied. "It is not my fault that the people who used to sit in front of me have died or moved away." In his mind, the old man was still sitting in his imagined community made up of previous generations of friends and neighbors who had composed his church. But the new minister, looking out every week, saw nothing but empty front pews, waiting to be filled with new faces and new stories. Because the context had changed, the church community had changed; and because the community had changed, the context had changed—even though the old man had not moved anywhere at all. And yet, until the old man shared his story, the history of his community, the new minister couldn't understand the old man's resistance to his request.

---

1. Zurlo, "Who Owns Global Christianity?"

History, contexts, and communities—all these pieces are important frameworks for organizing the many stories that together paint a global picture of Christianity. The connection among history, contexts, and communities was beautifully expressed by the late Andrew Walls, Scottish historian and expert on African Christianity, and a founder of the field of "world Christianity."[2] Walls asked his readers to imagine a visitor from outer space, a professor of comparative religions, who visits Earth for fieldwork every few centuries, to observe the practices and beliefs of representative Christians. First the space man visits the original Christians in Jerusalem, a few years after the death of Jesus. He finds that they are Jewish and follow Jewish customs, including offering animal sacrifices, worshiping on the seventh day, and reading old scrolls in Hebrew. They identify the Messiah, Son of Man and Suffering Servant, with their teacher who just died, Jesus of Nazareth. They live in close-knit families and eat meals together in each other's homes. When the visitor from space next returns to earth, he observes a big church meeting of church leaders around 325 CE, in Nicaea (now in Turkey). Hardly any are Jewish and most are unmarried. To them, sacrifice means a ritual meal of bread and wine and they worship God on the first day of the week, not the seventh. They talk about Jesus, but they are debating whether the Greek words *homoousios* or *homoiousios* better characterize his nature. They argue a lot about theology.

Walls goes on to describe the space visitor's next field visit, Ireland in the 600s. There monks are gathered on a rocky coastline reciting the psalms. Some are going into a small boat with a box of beautiful manuscripts heading toward nearby islands to ask the inhabitants to give up worship of multiple nature divinities. Other monks sit alone in caves, denying themselves food. Upon examining the manuscripts, he finds they are the same writings he saw on his last visit, and he hears the monks recite the same basic statement of belief or creed he heard at Nicaea in 325. Yet these monks seem much more interested in being holy than in debating theology.

Next the space visitor returns to earth in 1840s London. He finds a convention of mostly white Christians hearing speeches about the desirability of promoting Christianity and trade in Africa. To eliminate the slave trade, they are planning to send missionaries, lobby the government, and promote the education of black Africans. He sees many people carrying printed Bibles and finds out they accept the creed of Nicaea. They talk about

---

2. Walls preferred the term "world Christianity" to what this book series is calling "global Christianity." On the use of the terms "world" versus "global," see Robert, "World Christianity"; Sanneh and McClymond, "Introduction," 4–6; Johnson and Kim, "Describing the Worldwide Christian Phenomenon."

holiness but would be shocked at the thought of praying alone in a cave. Rather, they are well fed and committed to political activism.

Finally, the space visitor returns in the 1980s to Lagos, Nigeria, in time to see a white-robed procession of people dancing and chanting through the streets. They are inviting people to come with them and experience the power of God. They talk about healing and driving out evil spirits. They say they accept the creed of Nicaea, but they are not really interested in theological creeds or in political activism. They do care passionately about personal empowerment through prayer, preaching, and healing. Back on his own planet, the professor must figure out what it all means. He notes that the location of the Christian heartland has shifted each time he has visited. How does he conclude what it means to be a Christian? Is there any coherence across time? What do Christians around the world have in common, despite the visible differences in culture, race, locations, ethnicities, and practices that he observed?

Andrew Walls's fantasy about the space visitor illustrates the complexities of telling the global story of Christianity. What each era had in common was its historical connection. Like links in a chain, history connected the different communities to each other. Jews from Jerusalem preached to Greeks and led to the events of Nicaea in 325. Emissaries from the Mediterranean planted the seeds that became Irish Christianity. Celtic missionaries launched what became the religion of London in the 1840s, and the British evangelical lobby sent the messengers who energized churches in Africa. To bring the story up to the present, today Nigerian churches send missionaries around the world, including to London. In fact, some of the largest churches in Europe have African pastors. Other historical connections involve a "continuity of consciousness" across time.[3] In each group's story, Jesus Christ "has ultimate significance." They use the "same sacred writings," though in different formats and languages. Writes Walls, "Each group thinks of itself as having some community with the others," continuous with ancient Israel, even though they are no longer Jews.[4] These elements of continuity, however, are embedded in very different contexts, ranging from the Middle East to West Asia, to Europe, Africa, and beyond. In each context, the space visitor found worshipping communities, ranging in form from house churches to bishops' gatherings, from monasteries to conferences and popular processions. The shape of the Christian communities and what they do differs according to their local cultures, politics, and historical period.

---

3. Walls, "Gospel as Prisoner," 6.
4. Walls, "Gospel as Prisoner," 6–7.

And yet, taken together, the many stories echo the shared memory of Jesus Christ, passed down through the ages.

About This Book Series

To tell the global story of Christianity, each book in this series is organized into a common format. If we think about what goes into telling our stories, the elements are common to the books in the series. The *first* thing to notice is that the books each cover a different *geographic region*. In other words, they are organized by "neighborhood." This organization allows the editors, who come from each region, to explore the "historical context" and to answer the questions: Where are we from and how did we get here? Who are the people who brought Christianity? How did the Christian story change in each part of the globe, and what difference did it make? How are the followers of Jesus in that region anchored in his heritage? What is the testimony of the people of each region about their Christian identity, and how did they become part of the global story of Christianity? There are a range of answers to questions like "Where are we from and how did we get here?," including stories of migration and mission, slavery and coercion, violence and resistance, joy and struggle. Analyzing where they have come from also allows the editors to build toward where they think their region might be going.

The *second* section of each book in the series talks about the kind of *faith communities* found in each geographic region, and the issues they face. Communities reflect group identities shaped by such factors as theology, ethnicity, language, or persecution. In the case of the volume on Asia, a vast continent with thousands of different ethnic groups, the communities described are organized by subregion. The North America volume discusses some of the fundamental theological and organizational issues behind different groups of North American Christians. In Christian parlance, faith communities shaped by shared theologies and histories are often called "denominations," organized groups of Christians that recognize each other as brothers and sisters but have different stories to tell about how they got to be where they are today. Some faith communities are rather like private clubs, with high membership fees and strict rules as to who can belong. Others are more like groups of sports fans, open to anyone who feels like supporting the team and participating in its activities. In all cases, the discussion of different communities shows how their identity reflects both its local context and its participation in the global story of Christianity. Communities each have their own special saints, prophets, and leaders—people who have guided them and symbolize their identity to the world. They have their own favorite religious practices. Conversations internal to each community spill into the outside world, and sometimes attract others to join them. Contexts shape communities, and communities shape contexts. Faith communities are where the global story of Christianity forms church families and creates spaces in which they build a home.

The *third* section of each volume discusses *global issues* that are important to each region today. This is where the urgency behind each volume becomes clear. What are the passions that drive the communities in context? What problems do they face? What political and social issues are vital to their well-being? Some of the volumes explicitly discuss what churches call "ecumenism," churches cooperating and joining together to pursue shared ideals and common goals. Important twenty-first-century issues such as climate change, racism, interfaith relations, war and peace, gender, church-state relations, and religious persecution are global issues that affect people on every continent. It is often these pressing issues that connect Christians in solidarity with others across geographic boundaries.

Elements of a Global Story

Although each book in the series stands alone, putting them into dialogue with each other paints a bigger picture of what is called "global (or world) Christianity." As already mentioned, Christianity in the twenty-first century has become a multicultural religion practiced by one third of the world. The fact that it exists nearly everywhere means that to tell the story of Christianity in one region affects the story of Christianity in another region. To think of Christianity as a global story requires seeing each region as connected. In scholarly terms, this idea is called "entanglement," an important concept in global history. The idea of historical entanglement means that each region is shaped by its relationship to the others. To think of Christianity as a global story means looking for ways in which the local and the global are entangled—all mixed up together, influencing each other, and not easily separated. As people in each region embrace what they see as the universal story of Jesus Christ, the way they practice their faith affects the nature of the religion as a whole. To be "global" means that regional stories are linked, with and through their Christian faiths.

Looking for interconnections among the regions is a way to trace how the assumption of entanglement creates a global story out of what are usually thought of as separate stories. As you read the different books in this series, also zoom out and look for common themes that bind the regions together to create a global story, though from different perspectives and angles. What follows are three major themes that intersect all the volumes—movement, translation, and public theologies:

- *Movement* is central to the global story of Christianity. Without new people entering old spaces, or people on the move, Christianity could not spread from one place to another. The New Testament journeys of Paul throughout the Mediterranean modeled how Christians moved from place to place in spreading their faith. Migration and "global diaspora" are features of the global Christian story, especially today when more people are on the move than ever before. When people deliberately cross boundaries to spread their faith, they are often called missionaries. During the era of colonialism, Europeans sent missionaries around the world. Today missionaries go from everywhere to everywhere, including especially from Korea, Brazil, Nigeria, and North America.[5] Sometimes movement to new areas causes migrants to embrace Christianity as a new way of life. Although migrants typically seek economic security over religious change, sometimes the act of moving to a new place can inspire them to launch missions of their own: Central Americans moving to North American cities, and Africans moving to Eastern Europe, have started numerous churches. Forced migration can also spread Christianity. In a monstrous crime against humanity, over ten million Africans were sent to the Americas as slaves. Many of their descendants became Christians and reshaped the faith into a vehicle of resistance. Migrating people—whether forced or by choice—bind together their places of origin with their destinations and change both places in the process.[6]

- *Translation* is another theme that makes Christianity a global story. In literal terms, translation of the Bible into thousands of languages has been the foundation of Protestant missions for centuries, and the basis for faith-sharing across linguistic and cultural boundaries. Once people have the Bible in their own language, they interpret it according to their own cultural norms and needs.[7] During the twentieth century, many indigenous prophets—equipped with the Bible in their own language and inspired by dreams and visions—launched new Christian movements in Africa, Asia, and Latin America. Studies of conversion show how new Christians translate the Christian faith into their own

---

5. Robert, *Christian Mission*.

6. See Frederiks and Nagy, *Religion, Migration, and Identity*; see also Hanciles: *Migration and the Making*; *Beyond Christendom*.

7. Sanneh, *Translating the Message*.

personal contexts, or use it to revitalize their surroundings.⁸ At a more theoretical level, translation can refer to cultural processes of hybridization, of adopting the Christian message and reframing it to fit new contexts and to energize Christian communities.⁹ Since all communication comes packaged in particular cultural forms, the process of translation is necessary for sharing the Christian faith across all kinds of ethnic, cultural, and geographic barriers. As Christians encounter other cultures and live alongside persons of other religions, their faith is often stimulated into renewed life. The translation process, both on personal and social levels, is an endlessly rich source of innovation that feeds into the global story of Christianity.

- *Public theologies* also shape the global story of Christianity. In the modern West, people often think of faith as a private matter, separate from politics or social life. But the idea that religion is a matter of personal choice, irrelevant to community life, is a fairly recent cultural innovation that itself assumes a public theology of secularism.¹⁰ In most of the world, in most periods of history, religion carries practical implications for how people live in community. Christianity shapes people's attitudes toward authority, power, nature, gender relations, and human rights. Such ideas as "the doctrine of discovery," or the "priesthood of all believers," or "one nation under God" express the relationship of Christianity to peoples, politics, and land. The global story of Christianity consists of theological flows that spread around the world through migration and social media.¹¹ Public theologies require analyzing flows of power, including the supernatural and spiritual power embedded in Christian belief itself, the unequal political and economic power of Christians who use faith to justify control of others, and the tenacious power of resilience by Christians who are suffering or persecuted. By the late 1900s, evangelicalism, liberation theologies, and Pentecostal practices were all vehicles for political power, especially in Africa and the Americas. Christian charitable outreach through nongovernmental organizations remains a major social factor throughout the world, especially in poor communities. Half of all Christians are Roman Catholics, a worldwide faith network with a

---

8. Kling, *History of Christian Conversion*.

9. For a postcolonial analysis and typology of historical religious encounters, including syncretism and selection, see Lindenfeld, *World Christianity and Indigenous Experience*, 1–30. See also Jones, *Christian Interculture*; Gruber, *Intercultural Theology*.

10. Casanova, *Public Religions in the Modern World*.

11. Schreiter, *New Catholicity*.

central teaching authority lodged in the pope and the Vatican. Public theologies—the globalization of religious ideas, institutions, power, and practices—are a key feature of Christianity as a world religion.

Conclusion: From Local Stories to Global Story and Back Again

To tell the global story of Christianity requires reconstructing the entangled histories of communities down through the ages, in different regions. It requires retracing their historical contexts and learning how communities respond to the urgent issues of the day. As this series shows, only as different Christian communities tell their own stories—and listen to the stories of others—can the global story of Christianity be glimpsed in all its fullness.

For Further Reading

Casanova, José. *Public Religions in the Modern World.* Chicago: University of Chicago Press, 2011.
Frederiks, Martha, and Dorottya Nagy, eds. *Religion, Migration, and Identity: Methodological and Theological Explorations.* Theology and Mission in World Christianity 2. Leiden: Brill, 2016.
Gruber, Judith. *Intercultural Theology: Exploring World Christianity After the Cultural Turn.* Research in Contemporary Religion 25. Göttingen: Vandenhoeck & Ruprecht, 2018.
Hanciles, Jehu J. *Beyond Christendom: Globalization, African Migration, and the Transformation of the West.* Maryknoll, NY: Orbis, 2008.
———. *Migration and the Making of Global Christianity.* Grand Rapids: Eerdmans, 2021.
Johnson, Todd M., and Sandra S. Kim. "Describing the Worldwide Christian Phenomenon." *International Bulletin of Missionary Research* 29 (2005) 80–84.
Johnson, Todd M., and Gina A. Zurlo. *World Christian Encyclopedia.* 3rd ed. Edinburgh: Edinburgh University Press, 2019.
Jones, Arun W., ed. *Christian Interculture: Texts and Voices from Colonial and Postcolonial Worlds.* University Park: Pennsylvania State University Press, 2021.
Kling, David W. *A History of Christian Conversion.* New York: Oxford University Press, 2020.
Lindenfeld, David. *World Christianity and Indigenous Experience: A Global History, 1500–2000.* Cambridge: Cambridge University Press, 2021.
Robert, Dana L. *Christian Mission: How Christianity Became a World Religion.* Hoboken, NJ: Wiley-Blackwell, 2009.
———. "World Christianity as a Revitalization Movement." In *World Christianity: History, Methodologies, Horizons,* edited by Jehu J. Hanciles, 17–18. Maryknoll, NY: Orbis, 2021.

Sanneh, Lamin, and Michael J. McClymond. "Introduction." In *The Wiley Blackwell Companion to World Christianity*, edited by Lamin Sanneh and Michael J. McClymond, 1–18. Malden, MA: Wiley-Blackwell, 2016.

Sanneh, Lamin O. *Translating the Message: The Missionary Impact on Culture*. American Society of Missiology Series 13. Mary-knoll, NY: Orbis, 2009.

Schreiter, Robert J. *The New Catholicity: Theology Between the Global and the Local*. Maryknoll, NY: Orbis, 2004.

Walls, Andrew F. "The Gospel as Prisoner and Liberator of Culture." In *The Missionary Movement in Christian History: Studies in the Transmission of Faith*, 3–15. Mary-knoll, NY: Orbis, 1996.

Zurlo, Gina A. "Who Owns Global Christianity?" Gordon-Conwell Theological Seminary, Dec. 11, 2019. https://www.gordonconwell.edu/blog/who-owns-global-christianity.

About the Editors and Introducers

Series Editors

Emma Wild-Wood (PhD, University of Edinburgh) is director of the Centre for the Study of World Christianity, University of Edinburgh School of Divinity, and senior lecturer of African Christianity and African Indigenous Religions. She is the former director of the Cambridge Centre for Christianity Worldwide and lecturer in World Christianities in the Faculty of Divinity of the University of Cambridge. Wild-Wood is the editor of *Studies in World Christianity* journal and a fellow of the Royal Historical Society.

Mark A. Lamport (PhD, Michigan State University) has been a professor for forty years at graduate theological schools in the United States and Europe. He is author of *Nurturing Faith: A Practical Theology for Educating Christians* (2021); and editor of *Emerging Theologies from the Global South* (2022); *Christianity in the Middle East* (2 vols., 2020); *Encyclopedia of Christianity in the Global South* (2 vols., 2018); *Encyclopedia of Martin Luther and the Reformation* (2 vols., 2017); *Encyclopedia of Christianity in the United States* (5 vols., 2016); *Encyclopedia of Christian Education* (3 vols., 2015).

Gina A. Zurlo (PhD, Boston University) is visiting lecturer in world Christianity at Harvard Divinity School. She is co-author of the *World Christian Encyclopedia*, 3rd edition, and co-editor of the World Christian Database.

Volume Editors

Raimundo C. Barreto Jr. (PhD, Princeton Theological Seminary) is associate professor of world Christianity at Princeton Theological Seminary and one of the conveners of the World Christianity Conference at Princeton. A

Brazilian-American scholar, his work spans different disciplines, including world Christianity, ecumenics, and Latin American religions. He is general editor of the series World Christianity and Public Religion and co-editor of *Journal of World Christianity*. He is author of *Protesting Poverty: Protestants, Social Ethics and the Poor in Brazil* (2023) and of the forthcoming *Base Ecumenism: A Latin American Contribution to Ecumenical Praxis and Theology* (Series: Shapers of Ecumenical Theology).

Mark A. Lamport—see above

Series Introduction

Dana L. Robert (PhD, Yale University) is Truman Collins Professor of World Christianity and History of Mission, and director of the Center for Global Christianity and Mission at Boston University School of Theology. She is a member of the American Academy of Arts and Sciences and in 2017, she received the Lifetime Achievement Award from the American Society of Missiology. Recent books include *Faithful Friendships: Embracing Diversity in Christian Community* (2019); *African Christian Biography: Stories, Lives, and Challenges* (2018). An active lay United Methodist, in 2019 Roberts spoke at the 150th anniversary of the United Methodist Women.

Book Introduction

Raimundo C. Barreto Jr.—see above

Preface: Latin America

GINA A. ZURLO AND MARK A. LAMPORT

IN WORLD CHRISTIANITY DISCOURSE, the global South consists of Africa, Asia, Latin America, and Oceania. While these continents are often lumped together for convenience of describing generalized trends, the history of Christianity in Latin America and the Caribbean is, quite obviously, much different from that in Africa, Asia, and Oceania. The region has been shaped by five hundred years of Catholic dominance, and not just in terms of religion, but also in culture and politics. Christianity arrived in fifteenth-century Latin America alongside colonization, violence, and decimation of indigenous populations. Local peoples reconciled the Catholic faith with their own indigenous beliefs and practices to create forms of popular religion, illustrating the strength of faith beyond formal institutions. The Virgin Mary had a particularly important role in the indigenization of Catholicism in Latin America and the Caribbean, especially her appearance to Cuauhtlatoatzin (Juan Diego, his Christian name) in what is now Mexico in 1531. The Virgin of Guadalupe became a symbol of Latin American Catholicism and remains so today. The arrival of *evangélico* faith in the nineteenth and twentieth centuries—Protestantism, Evangelicalism, Pentecostalism—changed the face of Christianity in Latin America and the Caribbean by introducing more religious choice. While many people decided to switch to these newer churches, just as many held fast to their Catholic faith, and in particular, a charismatic version of it. Christianity in Latin America and the Caribbean is by no means monolithic and continues its great theological, linguistic, and ethnic diversity today.

Figure 1. North/South Distribution of Christianity

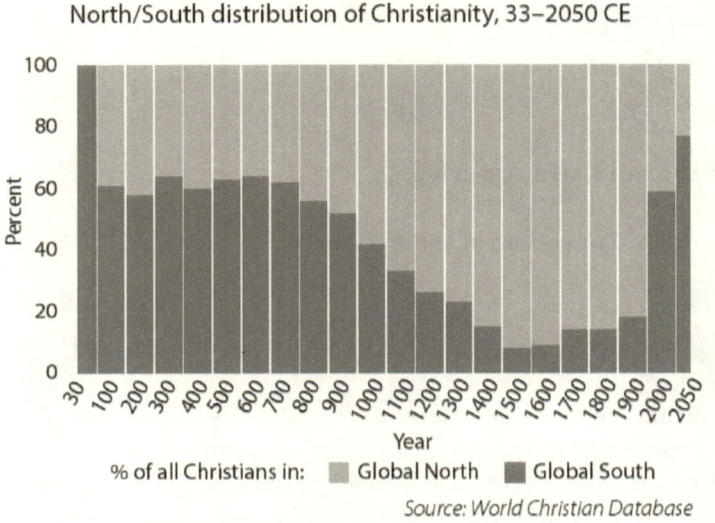

Source: Todd M. Johnson and Gina A. Zurlo, *World Christian Encyclopedia*, 3rd ed. (Edinburgh: Edinburgh University Press, 2019), 4.
Used by permission of the authors.

Table 1 shows trends in religion and non-religion in Latin America from 1900 to 2020, with projections to 2050. In 1900, Latin America was nearly entirely religious (99 percent), mostly Christian, but with small populations of ethnic religionists (3 percent) and spiritists (<1 percent). By the turn of the twenty-first century, religious affiliation in Latin America had dropped only to 97 percent, illustrating a remarkable resilience against potential secularizing trends seen elsewhere in the world. The Christian share of Latin America's population has decreased only slightly, from 95 percent in 1900 to 92 percent in 2020, despite an increase of nonreligious (atheists and agnostics together) from less than 1 percent to nearly 4 percent over the same period. Those practicing exclusively traditional religions declined dramatically, down to less than 1 percent in 2020. Looking toward 2050, it is likely Christians will remain the largest tradition by far, but perhaps dropping to 90 percent of the population. The nonreligious are expected to make the most gains to perhaps 6 percent of Latin America's population in 2050.

Table 1. Religions over 1 percent in Latin America, 1900–2050

Year	1900	%	2000	%	1900–2000 % p.a.	2020	%	2000–2020 % p.a.	2050	%
Religious	64,760,000	99.4	503,396,000	96.5	2.07	628,166,000	96.1	1.11	714,819,000	93.8
Christians	62,002,000	95.2	482,355,000	92.4	2.07	602,892,000	92.2	1.12	685,870,000	90.0
Catholics	58,567,000	89.9	439,879,000	84.3	2.04	504,199,000	77.1	0.68	528,678,000	69.3
Protestants	1,659,000	2.5	44,544,000	8.5	3.35	63,398,000	9.7	1.78	88,332,000	11.6
Independents	33,200	0.1	36,353,000	7.0	7.25	58,045,000	8.9	2.37	84,463,000	11.1
Doubly Affiliated	-240,000	-0.4	-44,681,000	-8.6	5.37	-31,175,000	-4.8	-1.78	-26,275,000	-3.4
Unaffiliated Christians	1,976,000	3.0	5,339,000	1.0	1.00	7,061,000	1.1	1.41	8,459,000	1.1
Spiritists	257,000	0.4	12,143,000	2.3	3.93	14,352,000	2.2	0.84	15,235,000	2.0
Ethnic Religionists	2,245,000	3.4	3,237,000	0.6	0.37	3,980,000	0.6	1.04	3,889,000	0.5
Nonreligious	382,000	0.6	18,440,000	3.5	3.95	25,796,000	3.9	1.69	47,613,000	6.2
Agnostics	372,000	0.6	15,922,000	3.1	3.83	22,594,000	3.5	1.77	43,154,000	5.7
Total Population	65,142,000	100.0	521,836,000	100.0	2.10	653,962,000	100.0	1.13	762,432,000	100.0

Data source: Gina A. Zurlo, ed., World Religion Database
(https://www.worldreligiondatabase.org)

Within Christianity, Catholics were the largest tradition in 1900 (91 percent of all Christians), followed by Protestants (9 percent), then independents (8 percent). While there are Orthodox in the region, they make up a very small share of all Christians. The internal makeup of Christianity in Latin America changed somewhat dramatically since 1900: 84 percent Catholic, 11 percent Protestant, and 10 percent independent in 2020. Indeed, the growth of Protestant, independent, evangelical, and Pentecostal Christianity is the major story of religious change in Latin America from 1900 to 2020, and it is likely these trends will continue into the future. By 2050, if current trends continue, Christians in Latin America could be 77 percent Catholic, 13 percent Protestant, and 12 percent independent.

Some of the largest Protestant denominations in Latin America are Pentecostal/charismatic in history, worship, practice, and theology, such as the Assemblies of God (Brazil, Argentina, Mexico) and the International Church of the Foursquare Gospel (Brazil). Other large Christian families include Baptists (Brazil), Seventh-day Adventists (Brazil), and Reformed Presbyterians (Mexico). Among independents is a mixture of nineteenth-century restorationist movements such as Jehovah's Witnesses and the Church of Jesus Christ of Latter-day Saints in Mexico and Brazil. However, the bigger story is the growth of independent charismatic megachurches such as the Universal Church of the Kingdom of God in Brazil (Igreja Universal do Reino de Deus), the God is Love Pentecostal Church in Brazil (Igreja Pentecostal Deus é Amor), and the Light of the World Church in Mexico (Iglesia La Luz del Mundo). These churches are not only growing within Latin America but are spreading all around the world through robust missionary activity and diasporic movements. Latin America is increasingly important for the global Pentecostal/charismatic movement. The continent is 30 percent Pentecostal/charismatic, Christians there are 32 percent Pentecostal/charismatic, and Latin America is home to 30 percent of all Pentecostal/charismatics in the world. It is expected all of these figures will increase moving toward 2050.

Table 2. Christianity in Latin America by Region, 1900–2050

Country	Pop. 1900	% Christian 1900	Pop. 2020	% Christian 2020	Pop. 2050	% Christian 2050
Caribbean	6,715,000	97.7	36,616,000	84.1	39,963,000	84.3
Central America	17772000	99.0	171979000	95.7	209112000	93.5
South America	37515000	93.1	394297000	91.5	436795000	88.9
Latin America	62,002,000	95.2	602,892,000	92.2	685,870,000	90.0

Data source: Gina A. Zurlo, ed., World Christian Database (https://www.worldchristiandatabase.org)

Historical, geographic, political, and numerous other factors in Latin America have shaped religious trends differently in each of its three regions—the Caribbean, Central America, and South America (table 2). Each region was majority Christian in 1900. By 2020, their Christian populations had each dropped only slightly, with the largest decrease in the Caribbean from nearly 98 percent to 84 percent. Part of the explanation is the Communist takeover in Cuba in 1959, during which Christians faced severe persecution and repression. In 1900, Cuba was 99 percent Christian; by 1970, it was just 46 percent. Cuban Christianity has grown again since the 1990s, especially newer Pentecostal/charismatic churches.

Table 3. Christianity in Latin America by Country, 1900–2050

Country	Pop. 1900	% Christian 1900	Pop. 2020	% Christian 2020	Pop. 2050	% Christian 2050	% Change 1900–2020
Colombia	3,055,000	79.9	48,543,000	95.4	52,208,000	93.3	15.5
Ecuador	1,430,000	87.7	16,843,000	95.5	21,822,000	93.6	7.7
Suriname	35,100	46.2	299,000	51.0	356,000	52.3	4.8
Peru	3,589,000	94.7	31,809,000	96.5	38,574,000	95.5	1.8
Uruguay	575,000	62.7	2,209,000	63.6	2,200,000	60.5	0.9
Venezuela	2,298,000	93.0	26,343,000	92.6	32,150,000	86.8	-0.4
Bolivia	1,456,000	93.6	10,836,000	92.8	14,472,000	91.4	-0.7
Paraguay	580,000	96.7	6,810,000	95.5	8,505,000	93.4	-1.2
Honduras	524,000	97.0	9,485,000	95.8	12,907,000	93.3	-1.3
El Salvador	1,029,000	98.0	6,271,000	96.7	6,523,000	94.0	-1.3
Saint Lucia	48,700	97.7	176,000	95.9	172,000	94.3	-1.8
Guatemala	1,690,000	99.4	17,441,000	97.4	25,883,000	96.1	-2.0
Belize	35,000	94.5	367,000	92.3	526,000	92.1	-2.2
Guadeloupe	179,000	98.4	430,000	95.9	416,000	92.8	-2.5
Nicaragua	489,000	97.8	6,297,000	95.1	7,940,000	93.1	-2.7
Latin America	62,002,000	95.2	602,892,000	92.2	685,870,000	90.0	-3.0
Grenada	63,200	99.6	109,000	96.6	110,000	95.3	-3.0
Dominican Republic	588,000	98.0	10,296,000	94.9	11,810,000	92.3	-3.1
Mexico	13,494,000	99.2	123,370,000	95.7	144,882,000	93.4	-3.5
Martinique	208,000	99.8	360,000	96.0	309,000	93.1	-3.7
Aruba	14,000	100.0	103,000	96.3	101,000	92.5	-3.7
Puerto Rico	952,000	99.9	2,740,000	95.8	2,230,000	91.2	-4.1
Costa Rica	319,000	99.6	4,860,000	95.4	5,253,000	91.0	-4.2
Guyana	167,000	58.7	425,000	54.0	459,000	55.7	-4.7
Bahamas	51,900	97.9	366,000	93.0	418,000	90.2	-4.9
Barbados	196,000	100.0	273,000	94.9	257,000	92.9	-5.1
Saint Kitts & Nevis	42,300	100.0	50,300	94.6	51,400	91.5	-5.4
United States Virgin Is	30,500	100.0	98,700	94.5	79,200	91.9	-5.5
Brazil	17,319,000	96.3	192,939,000	90.8	201,934,000	88.2	-5.5
Dominica	28,800	100.0	68,000	94.4	65,700	92.7	-5.6
Haiti	1,499,000	99.9	10,748,000	94.3	13,650,000	91.7	-5.7
Panama	193,000	96.5	3,888,000	90.1	5,198,000	88.8	-6.4
Curaçao	30,000	100.0	153,000	93.5	161,000	91.5	-6.5

Trinidad & Tobago	194,000	70.7	888,000	63.4	854,000	63.6	-7.3
Antigua & Barbuda	35,000	100.0	90,800	92.7	101,000	91.0	-7.3
Caribbean Netherlands	1,700	100.0	24,200	92.1	26,300	88.5	-7.9
Chile	2,863,000	96.8	16,869,000	88.2	17,074,000	84.0	-8.5
Turks & Caicos Is	5,100	100.0	35,400	91.5	45,600	90.7	-8.5
Montserrat	12,200	100.0	4,600	91.4	3,300	80.0	-8.6
French Guiana	19,500	92.9	251,000	84.2	462,000	84.7	-8.7
Anguilla	4,200	100.0	13,600	90.6	14,100	85.5	-9.4
Argentina	4,127,000	98.3	40,118,000	88.8	46,578,000	84.9	-9.5
Jamaica	680,000	94.4	2,504,000	84.5	2,482,000	83.8	-9.9
Saint Vincent	46,500	98.9	98,300	88.6	92,600	84.8	-10.3
Sint Maarten	300	100.0	38,300	89.3	48,300	87.8	-10.7
Falkland Islands	2,200	98.0	2,900	82.7	2,400	75.3	-15.2
British Virgin Islands	4,900	100.0	24,700	81.7	24,400	77.4	-18.3
Cayman Islands	4,800	100.0	53,600	81.6	69,600	82.2	-18.4
Cuba	1,796,000	99.1	6,870,000	60.7	6,373,000	62.7	-38.4

Data source: Gina A. Zurlo, ed., World Christian Database (https://www.worldchristiandatabase.org)

The countries with the most Christians in Latin America are Brazil (213 million), Mexico (123 million), and Colombia (49 million) (table 3). Brazil is increasingly important in global Christianity as the country with the most Catholics (150 million), the most independents (26 million), the most Protestants (32 million), and the most Pentecostals/charismatics (108 million). Brazil is also a major hub of missionary sending of all kinds: direct sending from churches, para-church organizational sending, and diaspora sending.

Although Christianity in Latin America remains demographically robust, forty-two of the forty-seven countries on the continent experienced proportional decline of its Christian population between 1900 and 2020. Colombia, Ecuador, Suriname, Peru, and Uruguay experienced growth (ranging between 16 percentage points and less than 1 percentage point). Of those in decline, the largest were in Cuba (99 percent to 61 percent), Cayman Islands (100 percent to 82 percent), British Virgin Islands (100 percent to 82 percent), Falkland Islands (98 percent to 83 percent), and Sint

Maarten (100 percent to 89 percent). The practical reality is that 100 percent Christian affiliation is difficult to maintain.

Figure 2. Christianity in Latin America

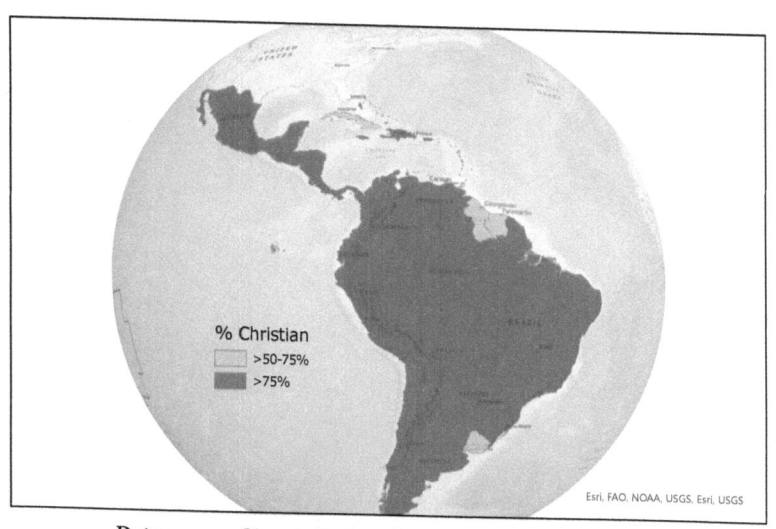

Data source: Gina A. Zurlo, ed., *World Christian Database* (https://www.worldchristiandatabase.org)

For many hundreds of years, Europe was the continent with the most Christians. However, Latin America claimed that title in 2014, surpassing Europe's Christian population for the first time (four years later, Africa became the continent with the most Christians). One trend to watch is the increasing influence of Pentecostal/charismatic churches, including the Catholic charismatic movement, which in Latin America is the largest in the world. Issues facing Latin American Christians are wide ranging, including corruption, drug and gang violence, migration, theological education for leaders, *mashismo* and patriarchy, and the increased intertwinement of Christianity and politics. Christians in Latin America and the Caribbean are wrestling with these, and other issues, in contextually appropriate ways. In doing so, they are carving out a central role in global Christian discourse for generations to come.

Gina A. Zurlo and Mark A. Lamport

Acknowledgments

THE GERM OF AN idea pollinated into a book-length treatment of the history, plight, and experiences of the multifaceted expressions of Christianity celebrated in the Church. We have been more than a little assisted by the comments, guidance, and perspective of sensational scholars Philip Jenkins, Erica Hunter, Wafik Wahba, Harold Suerman, Akram Khater, Jonathan Swift, Deanna Ferree Womack, and Michael Ghiz. Thanks one and all for your friendship and collegiality in the spirit of collaboration. Thanks also to Michael Hahn for smoothing out the voices in the preface.

Conceptualizing on the angle for the book titles and their intended appealing splash came from the fertile minds of Rachel Baker, Jean Van Horn, Gary Camlin, Bill Engvall, Alayna Baker, Aaron Lamport, Jay Ellis, Amy Grubbs, Zachary Grubbs, and Michelle Lamport.

The following were instrumental in shepherding the contents of the book into production-worthy copy—Joshua Erb (senior editorial consultant), Philip Bustrum, Mel Wilhoit, Jean Van Horn, and Heidi Herbruck for tremendous skill and detail in indexing the contents.

Further, we are beholden to Michael Thomson, acquisitions and development editor for Wipf & Stock Publishers. Michael tracked Mark down in the produce aisle of a large grocery chain in Grand Rapids and proposed the first book in the series to him! Emma Wild-Wood and Gina A. Zurlo filled out the team nicely. Soon thereafter Mark came back to Michael and pitched *this* book (and the remaining five) to complete this seven-book series: *to tell the global story of Christianity*. Michael is at once analytical and spontaneous, perceptive and intelligent, exacting and gracious. We are pleased that an additional large international edited book was just released under Michael's guidance describing "emerging theologies from the global South" (Cascade Books, 2023). Thank you for cheering on our vision.

Finally, we feel great respect for Christians in Latin America and wish to tell their historic, unique, and inspiring story of Christianity. There is good evidence that the most dynamic growth and creative trends will be revealed in the coming years from Latin America, and particularly Brazil, the largest country.

About the Contributors

Joan Cameron Bristol (PhD, University of Pennsylvania) is associate professor of history at George Mason University. She is the author of *Christians Blasphemers, and Witches: Afro-Mexican Religious Practice in the Seventeenth Century*.

Cleusa Caldeira (PhD, Jesuit Faculty of Philosophy and Theology, Brazil) is an Afro-Brazilian theologian who has dedicated herself to thinking theologically about black resistance in Latin America. She is a pastor in the Independent Presbyterian Church of Brazil.

Graciela Chamorro is a theologian in the Igreja Evangélica de Confissão Luterana in Brazil. She is a retired professor of indigenous history at the Universidade Federal da Grande Dourados. She has actively worked among the Kaiowá and Guarani people since 1983.

João B. Chaves (PhD, Baylor University) is assistant professor of the history of religion in the Americas at Baylor University. He is an award-winning author of several books, including *Evangelicals and Liberation Revisited* (2013), *Migrational Religion* (2021), and *The Global Mission of the Jim Crow South* (2022).

Jessica Delgado (PhD, UC Berkeley) teaches at The Ohio State University in the departments of History and Women's, Gender, and Sexuality Studies. She is author of *Troubling Devotion: Laywomen and the Church in Colonial Mexico, 1630–1770*.

Sandra Duarte de Souza (PhD, Universidade Metodista de São Paulo) is professor of gender and religion at Pontifícia Universidade Católica de Goiás. Her most recent publication is *Religious Sciences and Theology: Epistemology, Identity and Relations* (2022).

Pedro Feitoza (PhD, Emmanuel College, University of Cambridge) is lecturer in Latin American Christianity at the School of Divinity, University of Edinburgh. Prior to that he was a postdoctoral research fellow at the Brazilian Center of Analysis and Planning, São Paulo. His monograph *Propagandists of the Book: Protestant Missions, Christian Literacy, and the Making of Brazilian Evangelicalism, 1860–1930* is forthcoming.

Brett Knowles (PhD, University of Otago) recently retired as associate professor of church history at Sydney College of Divinity, Australia, and teaching fellow in church history at the University of Otago, Dunedin, New Zealand. His most recent publication is *A Timeline of Global Christianity* (2020).

Nadia Marín-Guadarrama (PhD, University at Albany, State University of New York) is visiting professor at Skidmore College and research associate at the University at Albany. Her most recent publication is a chapter about Nahua baby religious rituals that were part of the colonial negotiations held by friars and Nahuas during the sixteenth century in Central Mexico.

Luiz C. Nascimento (PhD, Princeton Theological Seminary) is academic director and professor at Seminário Teológico Batista do Nordeste (Brazil). His most recent publication is *The Future Shape of Christian Proclamation: What the Global South Can Teach Us About Preaching*.

Nicolás Panotto (PhD, Latin American Faculty of Social Sciences, Argentina) is assistant professor and postdoctoral researcher at Arturo Prat University, Chile. He is author of several books on religious studies and postcolonial and political theology in Latin America, his most recent edited book being *Decolonizing Liberation Theologies: Past, Present, and Future* (with Luis Andrade, 2024).

Francisco J. Peláez-Díaz (PhD, Princeton Theological Seminary) is assistant teacher professor in Latinx studies and ministries at Drew University. His most recent publication is "*La Santa Muerte*—Saint Death," in *Latin American and US Latino Religions in North America: An Introduction* (2024).

Ángel D. Santiago-Vendrell (ThD, Boston University) is associate professor of world Christianity at George W. Truett Theological Seminary, Baylor University. His most recent book is *Ríos de agua viva: Teologías de la misión pentecostal* (2023).

Theresa A. Yugar (PhD, Claremont Graduate University) is a Peruvian American scholar in Latin American feminism and ecology. She teaches at California State University, Los Angeles, in the Chicana/o & Latina/o Studies Department. Yugar is chief editor for *Valuing Lives, Healing Earth: Religion, Gender, and Life on Earth* (2021).

Introduction

RAIMUNDO C. BARRETO JR.

LATIN AMERICA WAS THE first region of the colonized world to be considered Christianized. Distinct from Africa and Asia, Christianity first formed in Latin America within the broader context of a colonial enterprise. While Africa and Asia can trace Christianity back to premodern times, in Latin America, the first contact the native peoples of Abya Yala had with Christianity coincided with the arrival of European conquistadores. Christianity arrived along with European explorers and colonizers as part of a watershed violent event that would change the future of the entire world.

The colonial process that began in the sixteenth century also coincided with the early origins of what would be later known as modernity. This is the reason Latin American decolonial thinkers affirm that modernity and coloniality are two faces of the same coin. According to that view, modernity cannot be adequately understood as an exclusively European phenomenon. Its formation and development were intrinsically linked to the violent encounter between the European colonizers and the Indigenous peoples whose lands were invaded, conquered, and colonized since the sixteenth century. As Walter Mignolo and Catherine Walsh underscore, the rhetoric of modernity invented globally hierarchized designs that continue to inform our lives nowadays, thus keeping the colonial wound open and unhealed.[1]

The invention of Latin America is, therefore, a key feature of modernity/coloniality, as the creation of a new world in the image of the European civilization, which demanded the eclipse of the Indigenous and the African others. As Dussel correctly puts it, "By controlling, conquering, and violating the Other, Europe defined itself as the discoverer, conquistador, and colonizer of an alterity likewise constitutive of modernity. Europe never

---

1. Mignolo and Walsh, *On Decoloniality*, 10, 140.

discovered this Other as Other but covered over the Other as part of the Same."[2]

The coloniality of power, knowledge, and being that stems from that original violent encounter has shaped many Latin American Christian institutions. However, neither colonization nor its derivative coloniality has succeeded in extinguishing Indigenous agency. Consequently, over the centuries, Latin American Christianity has taken multiple shapes and forms, as this volume shows. On the one hand, a hegemonic colonial Christianity has often served to justify the status quo and the systemic violence perpetrated against the people of the land—Indigenous peoples and all Black and Brown peoples brought to the region as enslaved persons or indentured workers.[3] On the other hand, the peoples targeted by systemic violence were never merely passive colonial victims. They continued to resist death and reinvent themselves, even through the very lenses of Christianity, thus creating what is known in the region as popular Christianity, a reinterpretation of Eurocentric Christian narratives through popular culture and Indigenous traditions. That is one of the reasons Latin American Christianity remains a vibrant force permeating the very essence of the region's cultural, social, and political fabric.

Thus, while traditional readings of Latin American Christianity tend to underscore the influence of colonial powers and institutionalized churches, in recent decades, renewed emphasis has been placed on the equally significant story that emerges from the bottom up among poor and marginalized communities, unveiling a trajectory of resilience and resistance, in particular among grassroots movements that have increasingly contributed to shape Latin American Christianity, turning it, despite its violent origins, into a significant force for social change.

This volume reflects these contrasting experiences, offering a critical view of colonial Christendom and neocolonial forms of Christianity while also pointing to instances in which Christianity has been relocated and reinvented among the poor either by taking the shape of a hybrid faith or as the fuel for liberation movements in the grassroots struggle for justice and freedom. Looking at the history of Latin American Christianity through

2. Dussel, *Invention of the Americas*, 10.

3. The two main atrocities, the genocide of Indigenous peoples and African slavery, went hand in hand as both aimed at the end of the day at destroying nonconforming bodies and cultures, often darker-skinned people, and their cultural and religious traditions. Prominent twentieth-century Brazilian Black scholar, politician, and artist Abdias do Nascimento underscored what he described as "the genocide of the black Brazilian population," the creation of a systemic and permanent racist structure to erase Brazilian blackness—both culturally and demographically (*Genocídio do negro brasileiro*).

this paradoxical lens, this book highlights what Enrique Dussel calls the inversion of the inversions Christianity experienced over the centuries as an initial messianic grassroots movement, which later took the shape of Christendom and, starting in the late fifteenth century, was closely associated with the European colonial enterprise.[4] In the popular forms it has taken in Latin America, Christianity is reclaimed by the victims of modernity/coloniality, who are determined to "be the agents of their own destiny."[5] This book invites the reader, then, to a transformative journey exploring often-overlooked stories of Latin American Christians who have been moved by their faith to engage in the pursuit of solidarity, justice, liberation, and community building without ignoring the paradoxical instances in which Christian institutions and individuals have stood in the way of such a pursuit, reinforcing and reenacting colonial legacies. Through the eyes of Indigenous peoples, Afro-Latin Americans, women, Pentecostals, and migrants, this volume delves into the diverse tapestry of Latin American Christianity and its encounter with various expressions of faith, including Indigenous and African-derived spiritualities. The contributors to this volume themselves are scholars representing a variety of nationalities and academic disciplines, combining historical and ethnographic methodologies and showing how different Christian movements in the region have addressed pressing issues such as socioeconomic disparities, race and racism, land rights, environmental concerns, Indigenous rights, gender equality, and sexuality, and exploring how faith has informed Latin American communities as they navigate the tensions and complexities emerging from their encounters with religious and political hierarchical institutions, colonial legacies, and global capitalism, among others.

Although not exhaustively or exclusively, this volume contributes to amplifying often-neglected and marginalized Christian voices in Latin America, providing a platform for the lived experiences of people and grassroots communities who have embraced their faith as a catalyst for social

---

4. The first inversion, starting in the fourth century, reaches its apex when the emperor of the newly formed Holy Roman Germanic Empire is crowned by the pope, turning what he describes as an early messianic Christianity into a triumphant one, which ceased to be critical of empire, becoming, instead, its supporter and legitimator. The second inversion takes place with the transformation of Christendom into a world system, a self-proclaimed center of incipient global geopolitics, a radical change in geopolitics that would relocate Europe from its peripheral status to the center of global commerce and politics. Through this second inversion, Christendom becomes imperial Christendom as it expands its reach to dominate "oppressed colonies in the name of the gospel of the Crucified One" (Dussel, "Epistemological Decolonization of Theology," 32).

5. Gutiérrez, *Theology of Liberation*, xiv.

change and the construction of more just and equitable societies, while also serving as a reminder of the many instances in which religion—Christianity, in the case of Latin America—has been used to delay or even prevent that very pursuit of justice, equality, and liberation.

The Context for the Study of Latin American Christianity

Despite the significant demographic changes in the region in the past fifty years, Latin America remains the most Christianized continent in the world, with around 90 percent of its population still identifying as Christian. Simultaneously, Latin Americans are increasingly aware of the region's rich cultural diversity and vibrant spiritual traditions, contributing to the increasing diversity of Christian expressions in the region. Beneath its surface, Latin American Christianity is shaped by a complex web of historical, cultural, and sociopolitical developments and struggles. By approaching Latin American Christianity from an explicit decolonial perspective, this volume unravels the intricate intersection of faith, culture, and power dynamics in the region, critically exploring Christian identities and roles in the region's history and self-perception.

As a theoretical framework, decoloniality challenges dominant narratives, structures, and systems that perpetuate colonial legacies. Concomitantly, it unveils hidden stories, knowledge, and ways of knowing, amplifying the perspectives and voices of those pushed to the margins. Not only that, but, as Nelson Maldonado-Torres puts it, decoloniality also helps to "making visible the invisible" and to "analyzing the mechanisms that produce such invisibility or distorted visibility in light of a large stock of ideas that must necessarily include the critical reflections of the 'invisible' people themselves."[6] By adopting such a theoretical framework, this volume seeks to shed light on Christianity's entanglement with colonialism, imperialism, and cultural hegemony, while also lifting suppressed grassroots narratives of resistance, syncretism, and liberation struggles, as materialized in diverse Christian communities as they navigate the complexities of living their faith vis-à-vis their daily encounters with unjust and oppressive structures of power. Consequently, this volume explores how Christianity has concomitantly perpetuated and challenged social, racial, and gender inequalities in the region, past and present, inviting its readers to reflect on the entangled relationship between religion, power, and decolonization in an increasingly interconnected world.

---

6. Maldonado-Torres, "On the Coloniality of Being," 262.

Purpose of the Book

Many recent developments in the study of religion in Latin America—mostly produced in Spanish or Portuguese—still need to be made available to the Anglophone reader. The task of introducing college and seminary students to Latin American Christianity in a way that is more representative of its diversity continues to be hampered by the limited resources available in English. Some existing introductory texts present the story of Latin American Christianity linearly, sometimes perpetuating distorted understandings of it, as they reinforce a view of Latin American churches as extensions of European and North American Christianities. Others import analytical frameworks such as the Protestant-Catholic binary, which leaves out imbricated contexts and other cultural, political, and religious factors in their interpretation of a reality whose complexity can no longer be adequately represented that way.

The purpose of this volume is to expose the reader to various expressions of Latin American Christianity using a recognizably Latin American tool kit for that task. Aiming to reach the nonspecialist reader, this resource mainly targets students in academic coursework, furnishing basic information about different faces of Latin American Christianity while also paying attention to the relationships among them and between them and the broader cultural, political, and religious environment in the region. While particular historical, geographical, doctrinal, and liturgical contexts are accounted for in the several chapters of this book, priority is given to understanding Christian experiences in the region through the metaphor of encounters. While the volume focuses on the development of Christianity south of the Mexican-US border, it also hopes to inform the Latinx experience with Christianity in the US and Canada and its impact on the current demographic changes within North American Christianity. Considering the history of Latin America as a mission field but also its recent rise as a sending missionary hub, this book highlights transnational connections vital to the broader understanding of Christianity in the Americas.

Telling the Story of Latin American Christianity Otherwise

Many stories of Latin American Christianity are still told from a Eurocentric perspective as a progressive development of events in continuity with the history of European and North American Christianities. One of the most critical historiographical turns in the final quarter of the twentieth century can be noted in Andrew Walls's realization that the history of world

Christianity is not a progressive tale but a serial one. While Latin America was not the primary context he had in mind when he came up with that insight, such an approach applies to the story of Latin American Christianity.

Most expressions of the Christian faith that can be found today in Latin American result from encounters—both pacific and violent—between representatives of foreign powers—Spanish, Portuguese, French, British, Dutch, and North American—and both Latin American Indigenous peoples and the millions of enslaved Africans brought to the continent. Therefore, the story of Christianity in Latin America involves ongoing encounters, conversions, resistance, resilience, survival strategies, the formation of new identities, and the liberation struggle.

This is a five-hundred-year tale, which can be fully understood only when put in conversation with the ancestral experiences of the people of Abya Yala, the African peoples forcibly brought to the region and the Caribbean for three centuries, and European and North American missionaries, migrants, and military incursions, which have all contributed to shape what we currently identify as Latin America. The premodern European history that also impacts this story includes the Ottoman Empire's occupation of the Iberian Peninsula and how the centuries of Muslim-Jewish-Christian relations in occupied Europe influenced the expansionist turn to the Americas after the fall of Granada, in 1492, with a shift from a focus on the reconquest to the early conquest and colonization of the Americas, the pre-Columbus Indigenous history in the region, and African religious traditions and encounters with Christianity prior to the transatlantic slave trade.

Centuries of slavery, genocide, expropriation of lands, impoverishment of the local populations, and destruction of their forests and rivers have produced a region with one of the most unjust distributions in the world, forming a massive gap between a tiny, wealthy, and powerful elite and a vast, impoverished mass living below the line of poverty, often subjected to the brutal rule of authoritarian governments and corporative greed. In that context, towards the end of the twentieth century, a generation of Latin American liberation theologians emerged, developing an autochthonous theology focused on economic justice and transformative political action. Since then, concerns with cultural, epistemic, racial, gender, and sexual justice have been added to that agenda to create more just conditions of life, especially for the vulnerable and often forsaken masses.

In the late 1980s, Latin American scholarship underwent a cultural turn, bringing increased attention to the greater complexity of the colonial matrix of power formed during the years of colonization, which continues to inform a hierarchized order of society in Latin America that remains operative in church and society. At the time of the commemoration of the fifth centenary of the first evangelization, in 1992, the Indigenous peoples of the continent rose to remind the church of the genocide they continued experiencing, not only through the force of the weapons that are still murdering many of them but also through what they called cultural genocide, a cultural hierarchization aimed at devaluing and erasing their traditions, knowledge, and ways of being, including their religion.

While the administrative domination of colonialism is largely gone, the social, racial, ethnic, and gendered hierarchies it created continue to exist, although in different forms. The contemporary struggle for justice and liberation cannot be limited, therefore, to the political and economic spheres of power. Decolonial thinkers have identified those spheres of coloniality as the coloniality of power (political, economic injustice), the coloniality of being (ontological, cultural injustice), and the coloniality of knowledge (epistemological injustice). In order to be politically efficient, liberation must include an epistemic and ontological dimension. Modern/colonial racialized hierarchies materialized into the political and economic realms after forming a view of the world marked by the illusion of white superiority. By contrast, emerging Afro-Latin American and Indigenous theologies are articulating Latin American Christianity and theology through an intercultural lens that dislodges whiteness and white supremacy. While still a numerical minority, the decolonial liberating Christianity that stems from such efforts is becoming increasingly important in the region.

Finally, side by side with the official Catholicism of the church hierarchy and the prophetic face often associated with the work of religious orders, priests/pastors, catechists, and theologians, Latin American Christianity has also been a fertile soil for popular religious movements and devotions like Our Lady of Guadalupe in Mexico or Blessed Anastacia in Brazil. This popular face of Latin American Christianity, also presented in the Pentecostal experience, still tends to be neglected in some scholarly works, often debased through accusations of syncretism.

This volume sees these popular religious expressions as bridges and articulations of the borderlands, spaces where people standing at different ends of what Mignolo calls "colonial difference" meet.[7] Borderland is a place where, as Gloria Anzaldúa indicates, identities and spirituality are rewritten.[8] The borderlands are not only geographical spaces where migrants cross physical borders. They are also symbolic spaces where cultural, gender, racial, and epistemological border crossing occurs.

---

7. Mignolo, "Prophets Facing Sidewise."
8. Anzaldúa, *Borderlands*.

A focus on the multiple popular faces of Christianity in Latin America allows us to hear often-neglected voices and to understand the shaping of Latin American Christianity through narratives that magnify the persistence and resilience of Indigenous and African-derived spiritualities (which refuse to die) and their influence upon the formation of popular Christianity (both popular Catholicism and Pentecostalism). In this book, Pentecostalism is seen as the most prominent expression of popular Christianity among Protestants and as a transnational, border-crossing movement that also includes a significant fraction of the Latin American Catholic Church. Thus, Pentecostalism—the charismatic face of Latin American Christianity—is essential, along with the poor's yearning for liberation, for the development of renewed understandings of the emerging forms of ecumenicity in the life of the Latin American churches.

Organization of the Book

Instead of emphasizing denominational branches, this volume is organized through the lenses of literature, decolonial, and intercultural movements mentioned above. On top of being a collection of cutting-edge scholarship on religion and theology in Latin America, this book puts together a selection of essays that seeks, to the extent that it is possible, to do justice to the geographic extension and cultural diversity of a continent where more than 650 million Christians live today. Moving between plurality and hybridity, this volume displays a vast combination of Christian spiritualities and practices resulting from continuous encounters, contestations (tensions), and negotiations (responses) in five centuries. Those encounters do not occur in a historical vacuum but as part of a broader history in which visible and invisible power disparities still impact the limits, challenges, and promises of the Christian experiment in the region.

To unveil that story, instead of pretending to produce a chronological sequence of tightly connected and coherent scenes, the editors of this book chose to show a series of snapshots, a collage of photos contextualized in time and space, stories that overlap with each other, expanding the perspectives and horizons through which they are explored while also highlighting their radical plurality, since no single element can turn them into a comprehensive script.[9] More than speaking of a single phenomenon, Latin American Christianity, this volume draws attention to multiple Latin American Christianities. The still-burgeoning field of world Christianity has taught us

---

9. I borrow this analogy from my colleague Edin Sued Abumanssur, "Enigma pentecostal."

that Christianity is not a ready-made commodity that can be transmitted from one context to another. Thus, it is never abstract, constantly emerging anew in concrete encounters between gospel and local communities and particular cultural contexts. That is why scholars such as John Mbiti have affirmed that Christianity is always Indigenous.[10] Those Indigenous stories, however, are always interconnected. They complement and expand one another. While the chapters that follow focus on particular Christian experiences, highlighting especially often-marginalized voices and perspectives, they also point to broader connections, networks, and relationships between those experiences and others beyond the region, allowing the reader to identify characteristics and patterns that make Latin American Christian experiences characteristically distinct and, at the same time, familiar and interwoven into a broader web of Christian expressions and experiences around the world.

Therefore, this volume is about multiple encounters between gospel and Latin American communities and the cultured memories and knowledges shaping those encounters. The fifteen chapters that follow tell this complex and multifaceted story in a way and from perspectives that no other volume available in the English language, as far as the editors are aware, has done. The stories depicted in these pages alternate between continuity and change, portraying the diverse faces of the Christian experiment in Latin America primarily through non-Eurocentric lenses.

Bibliography

Abumanssur, Edin Sued. "O enigma pentecostal." Academia, 2016. https://www.academia.edu/36761409/O_enigma_pentecostal.
Anzaldúa, Gloria. *Borderlands/La Frontera: The New Mestiza*. 25th anniv. 4th ed. San Francisco: Aunt Lute, 2012.
Dussel, Enrique. "Epistemological Decolonization of Theology." In *Decolonial Christianities: Latinx and Latin American Perspectives*, edited by Raimundo Barreto and Roberto Sirvent, 25–42. New Approaches to Religion and Power. Cham, Switz.: Palgrave Macmillan, 2019.
———. *The Invention of the Americas: Eclipse of "the Other" and the Myth of Modernity*. New York: Continuum, 1995.
Gutiérrez, Gustavo. *A Theology of Liberation: History, Politics, and Salvation*. Rev. ed. Maryknoll, NY: Orbis, 1988.
Kinney, John W. "The Theology of John Mbiti: His Sources, Norms, and Methods." *Occasional Bulletin of Missionary Research* 3 (1979) 65–68.

---

10. See John Mbiti's response to John W. Kinney's paper "The Contribution of John Mbiti to the Development of Christian Theology in Africa: An Overview and a Critique," quoted in Kinney, "Theology of John Mbiti," 66.

Maldonado-Torres, Nelson. "On the Coloniality of Being: Contributions to the Development of a Concept." *Cultural Studies* 21 (2007) 240–70.

Mignolo, Walter D. "Prophets Facing Sidewise: The Geopolitics of Knowledge and the Colonial Difference." *Social Epistemology* 19 (2005) 111–27.

Mignolo, Walter D., and Catherine E. Walsh. *On Decoloniality: Concepts, Analytics, Praxis*. Durham: Duke University Press, 2018.

Nascimento, Abdias do. *O genocídio do negro brasileiro: Processo de um racismo mascarado*. Rio de Janeiro: Paz e Terra, 2016.

Section One

The Story of Christianity Narrated in Historical Context: Colonial Encounters, Negotiations, and Contestations

1

The Christianization of the Nahuas and the Nahuatilization of Christianity

NADIA MARÍN-GUADARRAMA

IT HAS BEEN APPROXIMATELY four decades since scholars started perusing sources written in Nahuatl, the language of the Aztecs, to understand the processes of spiritual colonization experienced by Nahua communities in central Mexico. Through the study of these type of indigenous sources, we have found that, in contrast to what Robert Ricard wrongly proposed, colonization did not bring the annihilation of the Nahua religion and the instauration of European Christianity.[1] Instead, ethnohistorical, historical, anthropological, and linguistic studies have shown that the imposition of Christianity was merely a desire of the colonial apparatus because the indigenous appropriated the Western religion on their own terms. The conquest and its consequent colonization of the territory decimated the indigenous population and reconfigured the daily life of Mesoamerican communities. However, they learned, negotiated, and created a different way of living within the colonial structure.

Academics from different parts of the world have pored over texts written in Nahuatl and are discovering highly complex processes for the construction of religiosity among the Nahuas and other Mesoamerican indigenous groups. The work of Louise M. Burkhart is the cornerstone for the study of Nahua Christianity in colonial times. Burkhart's introduction to the book *Words and Worlds Turned Around* reconstructs the history of the study of indigenous Christianity. This chapter is based on her academic production and her reflection on this area of study. It also incorporates some

1. Ricard, *Spiritual Conquest of Mexico*.

of the more recent literature in order to provide an overview of the past and current scholarship that has delved into the intricate origins of indigenous colonial Christianities in Mesoamerica.

The Studies of Indigenous Christianity

In 1959, the Mexican historian and anthropologist Miguel León-Portilla published *La vision de los vencidos:* the first academic monograph attempting to write a history of the conquest from the indigenous perspective using Nahuatl sources. Years later, Eric Wolf urged scholars to document the history of peoples without history; it was an appeal for specialists to document the history of the world's colonized societies who had been written out of history and excluded from national projects around the world.[2]

Such invitation resonated among Mesoamericanists interested in the study of religion in colonial times. As in example, Klor de Alba proposed the existence of a spiritual warfare in colonial Mexico,[3] and Dibble stated that instead of being Christianized, the Nahuas Nahuatlized Christianity.[4] With these antecedents, Louise M. Burkhart's work opened the window to the study of that Christianism in which indigenous, rather than being passive or receptive, have shown a continuous negotiation of their beliefs with the colonizers. Her copious body of work has inspired decades of research to reconstruct those colonial processes that Nahuas and clerics experienced in creating a different way of believing and of understanding the indigenous world. Burkhart states that Nahuas were not living a cultural *nepantlism*.[5] This term, coined by León-Portilla, derives from the Nahuatl word *nepantla*, which suggested an indigenous existence where they experienced a state of confusion due to their beliefs and their ancient ways of living along with the unassimilated new European culture. Burkhart proposes that it is not about the quantity of Christian beliefs incorporated in the lives of the indigenous. Instead,

> we have come to speak of indigenous Christianities, nativized and multitudinous recreations of Christianity by indigenous people, who took the imported ideas, texts, and images and recast them for their own use. Sometimes their versions align closely with European models, sometimes they are radically

2. Wolf, *Europe and the People*.
3. Burkhart, "Introduction," 5; Klor de Alba, "Spiritual Warfare in Mexico."
4. Dibble, "Nahuatlization of Christianity."
5. Burkhart, "Introduction," 5.

different and both extremes can coexist within the same community and even within the same text.⁶

Thus, indigenous Christianity is a sociocultural sphere where we can learn about human agency under colonization. We can imagine indigenous Christian religion in colonial times as a continuum where indigenous peoples (not only Nahuas) gave different hues to their Christianity or, in terms of Christensen, different versions of Catholicism.⁷

Based on a Boasian cultural relativistic perspective that sought to understand cultures in their own terms, Burkhart assertively proposed that the Nahuatl sources that academics used to study the pre-Columbian era were written in colonial times, hence, they are a window to understand the processes of Mesoamerican indigenous colonization. They are written sources that let scholars understand Christianities in the context of indigenous cultures, languages, and histories, preventing universalistic ideas that misdirect scholars to find explanations of religion in the Old World.⁸ And I would add, those sources help us understand how indigenous cultures survived in a context where colonial or neocolonial systems of power fortunately failed to restrain their agency.

Sources to Explore Nahuatl Catholicism

Studying Nahua, or any indigenous culture, has led researchers to examine the written sources left behind by indigenous scholars and religious authorities. There are numerous religious, civil, and ethnographic sources, mainly in Nahuatl using the Latin alphabet. But how have these texts survived? How have researchers gained access to them?

Answering those questions takes us to pre-Hispanic times. According to Whittaker, Nahuas already possessed a fascinating writing system before the conquest,⁹ one that was based on a hieroglyphic structure that survived the conquest and can be found in the early pictorial catechisms.¹⁰ However, colonization brought a transformation in their writing, which was progressively substituted by the European alphabet. The process of adoption of this new system started when the first friars arrived in the Americas and saw communities devoted to worshipping their gods and goddesses. For the

---

6. Burkhart, "Introduction," 5.
7. Christensen, *Nahua and Maya Catholicisms*.
8. Burkhart, "Introduction," 5.
9. Whittaker, *Deciphering Aztec Hieroglyphs*.
10. Boone et al., *Painted Words*; Gaillemin, "Art ingénieux de peindre."

friars, the ascetic way of living that they observed among the indigenous and their spiritual devotion was the utopistic society they wished to have in Europe; the only problems were the indigenous deities and worship practices. Thus, they decided to construct bridges of communication on their own terms and started a project to preserve the austere life of the indigenous while converting them to Christianism. With the support of the indigenous communities, they learned Nahuatl and other languages spoken in Mesoamerica. The friars taught the sons of elite Aztec families to read and write in Nahuatl, Spanish, and Latin at El Colegio de Santa Cruz de Tlatelolco (The Holy Cross of Tlatelolco College), founded on January 6, 1536. In this boarding school, boys were enculturated into European traditions and cosmovision. Those children later became the Nahua scholars who, along with the friars, created a corpus of Christian documents written in their native language using the alphabetic writing. Most important, the Nahua boys were equipped with the required knowledge to negotiate what and how to write those religious texts.[11]

During that epoch, there was an abundant production of Christian doctrinal documents in the form of manuscripts and printed books where we can find sermons, catechisms, hymns, and plays, among other genres. It has been almost impossible to find a religious text authored by an indigenous writer due to colonial restrictions. The indigenous were authorized to write texts or help to write texts, but they were not acknowledged as authors of the texts. Most of the sources are attributed to friars. However, in a few sources, we can trace the name of some of the Nahua scholars who participated in writing some of the documents. Friar Juan Bautista's sermonary lists the names of Juan Berardo, Esteban Bravo, Antonio Valeriano, Francisco Baptista de Contreras, Pedro de Gante, Hernando de Rivas, Diego Adriano, and Agustín de la Fuente.[12] They were outstanding indigenous scholars who wrote Nahuatl Christian documents and taught the indigenous language to friars. As in example, Nahua scholar Hernando de Rivas helped Friar Alonso de Molina write the *Arte y vocabulario mexicano* (A Nahuatl vocabulary). He also helped Father Juan de Gaona write *Diálogos de la paz y tranquilidad del alma* (Dialogues of peace and tranquility for the soul). Agustín de la Fuente became a teacher at El Colegio de Santa Cruz de Tlatelolco and worked with Franciscan friars Juan Bautista and Bernardino de Sahagún and with Augustinian friars Pedro de Oros and Juan de Mijangos. With Mijangos, Fuente wrote *Espejo divino* (Divine mirror), a book written with the most elegant Nahuatl speech where the indigenous scholar and

---

11. Burkhart, *Slippery Earth*; Marín-Guadarrama, "Childrearing."
12. Bautista, *A Jesu Christo*, prologue.

the friar redacted the longest known Nahuatl dialogue, in which a father taught his son the Christian doctrine.[13] Interestingly, they used their own names for the characters: Agustín was the father, and Juan was the son. In this game, we can see a playful negotiation between a friar and a Nahua scholar.[14]

Those Nahua men raised by the friars were immersed in two cultural systems, and in different degrees, they had the ability to socialize within those systems.[15] There were cases of nonindigenous men raised near the Nahua communities who grasped the culture and later became friars capable of writing texts in Nahuatl, always with support of a native speaker. Nahua scholars were not able to have ecclesiastic titles or even claim authorship of the manuscripts and books they wrote. However, they found a way to exert influence on some aspects of the colonial religious and civil spheres. Some of them became governors of their towns, and they were able to marry and become fathers, which were highly desired male roles in Mesoamerican societies. And while participating in the life of their communities in important ways, they were able to shape the Christianism that ecclesiastic authorities had introduced.

With the decline of El Colegio de Santa Cruz de Tlatelolco at the end of the sixteenth century, the friars' aspirations of creating an indigenous utopistic society also came to an end. The use of indigenous languages to write ecclesiastic texts waned down as well. Mexico became independent from Spain in 1821 after a war that lasted eleven years. This war was followed by a reform movement that tried to separate the religious institutions from the civil government, and later, a civil war known as the Mexican Revolution (1910–21) paved the way to a national project that, in the new government's desire to homogenize cultures, precipitated a crisis for indigenous groups who tended to hide their ethnic identities in the following decades. Fortunately, such a task did not completely succeed. There are still indigenous communities speaking their language, and more importantly, some of them are revitalizing their mother tongues by themselves or by working with other academic institutions.[16] Furthermore, there is a generation of Nahua scholars who have embraced the task of not only revitalizing their language but using linguistic, historical, and anthropological theories and methodologies to study their own culture. That is the case of anthropologist

---

13. Mijangos, *Espejo divino*.
14. Marín-Guadarrama, "Childrearing," 56.
15. Marín-Guadarrama, "Childrearing."
16. Olko and Sullivan, "Empire, Colony, and Globalization."

Abelardo de la Cruz, who is studying Nahua devotion from precolonial times to the present.[17]

Countless documents written in Nahuatl and other indigenous languages such as Mixtec, Zapotec, Purépecha, Mazahua, and Otomi, among others, were taken from Mexico by collectors. Through time, some of them ended up in libraries, archives, ecclesiastic institutions, and houses inside or outside Mexico. Scholars interested in consulting indigenous documents used to visit repositories in Mexico, Europe, and the United States, but with advancement in technology and the internet, libraries and archives that have the resources and time to preserve and digitize the documents are making them available to anyone with access to internet.[18] Nowadays, whenever an unknown colonial document is located, scholars use it to reevaluate their research because such documents can be of great relevance to the continuation of the reconstruction of the colonial processes that indigenous communities experienced while incorporating Christian doctrine in their own terms.

Current Research Methods of Studying Indigenous Christianity

Researchers have applied James Lockhart's new philology studies to colonial sources written in Nahuatl.[19] Lockhart's method is considered by Terraciano a tool that changed the course of ethnohistorical studies.[20] Rather than trying to understand colonial indigenous accounts by studying institutions, it proposed to understand indigenous cultural change by focusing on the analysis of the indigenous language used in the texts. Thus, it was important to register how the texts incorporated Spanish words or how Nahuatl terms were preserved.

Lockhart focused on any document written in Nahuatl, but Burkhart opened the door to investigate Nahua Christianity by analyzing a corpus of Christian Nahuatl documents where she found that friars tended to teach Christian morality to Nahuas through the use of Nahuatl terms and indigenous rhetorical figures that sometimes did not find correspondence with

17. De la Cruz, "Value of *El costumbre.*"

18. Some of the most relevant repositories in Mexico are Archivo General de la Nación, Biblioteca Nacional de México, and Biblioteca Nacional de Antropología e Historia. Outside Mexico, some of the most important repositories are the Bancroft Library, the John Carter Brown Library, the Newberry Library, Dumbarton Oak Library, Princeton University Library, the Tulane Library, Bibliothèque National de France, and the Medicea Laurenziana Library.

19. Lockhart, "Introduction."

20. Terraciano, "Native Expressions of Piety," 126.

the Spanish terminology.[21] Her method of translation favors preserving the original meaning of a Nahuatl word instead of finding its English (or Spanish) equivalence. This type of translation has been successful to explore Nahua colonial cosmovision because it gives the opportunity to find cultural descriptions in the etymology of the Nahuatl word.

Even though Mesoamerica had a diversity of indigenous languages, Nahuatl became the precolonial lingua franca during the Aztec territorial expansion. After the conquest, friars focused on working with Nahuatl. For this reason, Nahuatl colonial religious texts outnumber all others in the region. Researchers have been perusing, translating, and analyzing these documents to hear the voices of the Nahuas and to reconstruct the processes that reconfigured indigenous religiosity in the colonial era.

Studies of Colonial Indigenous Christianism in the Twenty-First Century

Current studies of indigenous Christianities take us to the twentieth century, when George Baudot and John Leddy Phelan studied Nahua Christianism using the versions left behind by the first Franciscans in the Americas.[22] Arthur J. O. Anderson translated the *Psalmodia christiana*, a group of songs written in Nahuatl for Christian calendric celebrations from Jesus's circumcision on January 1 to Christmas.[23] This text was of great academic interest. Anderson, Suarez Roca, and Alcántara Rojas translated the text.[24] Burkhart and Alcántara Rojas conducted a deep analysis of the songs and found elements of Nahuatlized Christianity.[25] Researchers are continuing the study of the appropriation of Christianism by indigenous communities by concentrating on specific religious genres, some of which are discussed in the next section.

Indoctrination Through Sermons

Nowadays, the study of sermons has been of high academic interest due to the information we can find in regard to religion, but it also opens a

21. Burkhart: "Moral Deviance"; *Slippery Earth*.
22. Burkhart, "Introduction."
23. Burkhart, "Doctrine for Dancing."
24. Sahagún: *Bernardino de Sahagún's "Psalmodia christiana"*; *Psalmodia christiana*; Alcántara Rojas, "Cantos para bailar."
25. Burkhart, "Doctrine for Dancing"; Alcántara Rojas, "Cantos para bailar."

window to ethnographic information about the life of the Nahuas during colonial times. In sermons, we can observe negotiations between friars and Nahuas about the way the indigenous should experience Christianism. Alcántara Rojas mentions three printings from the sixteenth century and ten manuscripts that together contain around five hundred sermons. They are thought to have been read to the Nahuas after Sunday Masses and on the main Christian holidays. The sermons were meant for an indigenous community whose members were in different stages of conversion; some were about to be catechized, and others, mainly the nobility, had already converted.[26]

An ongoing open access research project that just finished the translation and analysis of two corpora of sermons is *Sermones en mexicano* (Sermons in Mexicano). Alcántara Rojas led an international team of historians and anthropologists to transcribe, translate, and analyze of one of the oldest corpora of sermons written in Nahuatl.[27] It is attributed to Friars Bernardino de Sahagún and Alonso de Escalona, as well as to other unknown authors. The document has been named *Manuscrito 1492* (Manuscript 1492) for its location in the National Library in Mexico City. This corpus of sermons presented a diversity of devotional topics, some of them already analyzed by the research team. For example, Dávila Montoya compares pain and death in Christian martyrdom to the Nahua perspective that considers suffering as precious.[28] Marín-Guadarrama demonstrates that the most mundane practices, such as baby rituals, were a contested terrain where friars and Nahuas were discussing, resisting, and reconfiguring religious practices.[29] Leeming compares one of the sermons in the manuscript (attributed to Friar Escalona) with a play written by Nahua scholar Fabian de Aquino and shows how a sermon was written in a context of vigilantism while Fabian de Aquino wrote the play by his own will.[30] Dehouve finds lexicological and conceptual changes when comparing Nahua terms about the reincarnation of Jesus.[31] Sanchez Aguilera compares Solomon's proverbs with *Huehuetlatolli*, Nahuatl discourses historically attributed to indigenous elders. However, Sanchez Aguilera proposes that *Huehuetlatolli* were most likely Nahuatl translations of the proverbs, to be used by noble parents to

---

26. Alcántara Rojas, "Mala nueva," 81.
27. See https://sermonesenmexicano.unam.mx/.
28. Dávila Montoya, "Cuix Oquiçopelicama in Tetl."
29. Marín-Guadarrama, "Rituales de bebés."
30. Leeming, "Del centro a la periferia."
31. Dehouve, "Dios se hizo hombre."

indoctrinate their children.³² Sánchez Aguilera continued the project by working on the paleography, translation, and analysis of Manuscript 1488, a corpus of sermons attributed to Franciscan friar Bernardino de Sahagún.³³

Some sermons are still being translated; others have not even been touched or found. The work of contemporary scholars is to continue this labor to reconstruct the colonial interactions between the religious institutions and the indigenous communities. Besides the sermons in Nahuatl, there is a corpus of sermons written in other Mesoamerican languages. Some sermons in Otomi, attributed to Friar Pedro Oroz, possibly from the sixteenth century,³⁴ or the sermons in Purépecha written by Maturino Gilberti must be studied.³⁵

Making the Pictorial Sources Speak

Pictorial catechisms are small manuscripts, booklets, indigenous sources where scholars have found a complex pictorial Nahuatl writing.³⁶ In these sources, pictographers painted the words of the catechism.³⁷ Rather than a mere colonial instrument of conversion, they show pictographic traditions that contain information about power and indigenous religion.³⁸

During the 1980s, Galarza proposed a method to decipher the contents of the little manuscripts.³⁹ Gaillemin went deeper into the study of this genre of religious documents in her dissertation,⁴⁰ and Boone, Burkhart, and Tavárez published a comprehensive study of one of the sources known as the *Atzaqualco Pictorial Catechism*. They also analyzed its religious and political transcendence. The authors located thirty-six more manuscripts that are heterogeneous in "physical size, date, figural style, pictorial and ideographic conventions, and degree of phoneticism."⁴¹ Even when these sources have the same prayers, the order of texts differs. Few of them are written in other languages such as Otomi and Mazahua.

32. Sánchez Aguilera, "Huehuetlatolli del Viejo Mundo?"
33. Sahagún, *Siguense unos sermones*.
34. Oroz, *Sancturale hiemale*.
35. Gilberti, "Sermones."
36. Boone et al., *Painted Words*.
37. Burkhart, "Afterword."
38. Burkhart, "Introduction."
39. Galarza, *Estudios de escritura indígena*.
40. Gaillemin, "Images mémorables."
41. Boone et al., *Painted Words*, 20.

Nahua Drama

In colonial times, Spaniards used plays for conversion. They expected the translation of the plays from Spanish or Latin to Nahuatl to be easy. However, the linguistic complexities found in the analysis of such dramas are another way of understanding the indigenous colonial struggles with religion.

The study of Nahua plays started in 1890 with Francisco del Paso y Troncoso. Then, in 1974 Fernando Horcasitas translated into Spanish a corpus of plays.[42] To continue his work, Burkhart translated the Nahua play *Holy Wednesday*.[43] Then, by comparing two plays, one in Spanish and the other in Nahuatl, she traced cultural particularities in, for instance, the depictions of Mary and Christ. Her work contributed to the study of gender in indigenous Christianism.

Sell and Burkhart later published four volumes of Nahuatl plays. The first one covers topics of life and death among colonial Nahuas. They published the plays of the three kings, the sacrifice of Isaac, and the final judgment.[44] Along with Stafford Poole, they devoted the second volume to the Virgin of Guadalupe.[45] They published the third volume with Wright and worked on Nahua plays from the Golden Age of Spanish Theater (1580–1680) and published the complete dramas of Bartolome de Alva.[46] Sell and Burkhart titled their fourth volume *Nahuatl Christianity in Performance*. Some of the included plays were *Start Sign*, the *San Simón Tlatlauhquitepec*, and the Tepaltzingo passion plays.

Burkhart and Mosquera launched an open access project where they show how Nahuatl and Spanish passion plays from eighteenth-century central Mexico ended up confiscated by the inquisitors.[47] A file in the Archivo General de la Nación was found containing four confiscated Spanish passion plays. The inquisitorial case explained the ecclesiastical authorities' rationale. Beyond the state's desire to regulate the ways in which indigenous communities practiced Christian devotion, there was desperation, because they had failed to teach indigenous people the "right way" to perform the plays, to believe in God without falling into sin, or because of prejudices that prevented the indigenous from embodying Jesus.

42. Horcasitas, *Teatro náhuatl*.
43. Burkhart, *Holy Wednesday*.
44. Sell and Burkhart, *Death and Life*.
45. Sell et al., *Our Lady of Guadalupe*.
46. Sell et al., *Spanish Golden Age Drama*.
47. Abelardo de la Cruz, Rebecca Dufendach, and Nadia Marín-Guadarrama are participating in this project in different capacities. See https://passionplaysofeighteenthcenturymexico.omeka.net.

Based on this open access project, Burkhart published a book about the plays and inquisitorial documents found in the archives, which currently is the most recent study of this religious genre.[48] Another recent study is Schwaller's book *Via crucis en mexicano*.[49] This is not a Nahuatl drama but a little prayer book and devotional guide published by Friar Agustín de Vetancurt at the end of the seventeenth century. The author uses the document to explore the origins of devotion in Europe and its application in the Nahua territories. Leeming also published a translation and study of two sixteenth-century Nahuatl dramas by Nahua Fabian de Aquino, who addressed the topics of human sacrifice and ritual divination.[50] Leeming used his work to explore a Nahua interpretation of Christianity that still made space for the Mesoamerican pantheon.

Beyond the Nahuatlization of Christianism

Libraries around the world have repositories of Christian documents written in indigenous languages from colonial times. David Tavárez, Mark Christensen, Dora Pellicer, and Christina Monzon have used some of those documents to incorporate other indigenous languages into the study of Christianism. Pellicer's translation of a Christian doctrine written in Mazahua explores the depiction of gender roles in the text.[51] Monzon explores the concept of sin in a seventeenth-century Christian doctrine written in Purépecha, attributed to Friar Angel Serra.[52] Both Pellicer and Monzon concentrate on the study of a specific language but do not compare their sources with the work already done on Nahuatl sources. Tavárez and Christensen take their analysis to a higher level by using at least two indigenous languages. While Christensen's work on Yucatec Maya proposes the existence of diverse indigenous forms of Christianism,[53] Tavárez explores how friars and indigenous scholars used the Zapotec language to build a conceptual common ground between Spanish and Zapotec.[54] In this religious perspective, they tried to make room for Christianism in the Zapotec cosmovision.

---

48. Burkhart, *Staging Christ's Passion*.
49. Schwaller, *Stations of the Cross*.
50. Leeming, *Aztec Antichrist*.
51. Pellicer, "Confesión y conversación."
52. Monzon, "Pecado."
53. Christensen, *Nahua and Maya Catholicism*.
54. Tavárez: "Performing the Zaachila Word"; *Invisible War*.

Conclusion

Although the religious studies in colonial Mesoamerica started with the study of the Nahuas, there is a clear tendency of incorporating texts written in other indigenous languages while using sacred documents in Nahuatl to study postconquest Nahua everyday life.[55] The paleography and translation of these sources deepen the understanding of the way indigenous communities used an imposed religion in their own way. They also gave information about the daily religious accounts observed among the colonial communities in topics of gender, class, ethnicity, and material culture, among other topics.

The academic contributions to the understanding of indigenous Christianity are already vast, and I want to end this chapter by mentioning Madajczak's study on the deconstruction of the Nahua Christian confession, where she concludes that the sources we use to study indigenous Christianity were produced by a culture of coercion.[56] Even though Mesoamericanists have tried to decolonize the discourse, scholars keep returning to the use of cultural calques that friars used in their descriptions of Nahua religious activities. Thus, our work remains unfinished. While we have some outstanding work on the Mesoamericanization of Christianity, as well as numerous documents useful to studying particular topics in colonial indigenous devotion, and even though we keep incorporating new sources into our analysis, we need to be always willing to challenge our understanding of colonial indigenous devotion while we incorporate new discoveries in our analysis.

Bibliography

Alcántara Rojas, Berenice. "Cantos para bailar un cristianismo reinventado: La nahuatlización del discurso de evangelización en la psalmodia christiana de Fray Bernardino de Sahagún." PhD diss., Universidad Nacional Autónoma de México, 2008.

———. "La mala nueva: La llegada del cristianismo en sermones en lengua náhuatl de la primera mitad del siglo XVI." *Iberoamericana* 19 (2019) 77–98.

Bautista, Juan. *A Jesu Christo S. N. ofrece este sermonario en lengua mexicana su indigno siervo Fr. Ioan Baptista de la Orden del Seraphico Padre Sanct Francisco de la Provincia del Santo Evangelio*. Mexico City: López Dávalos, 1606. https://archive.org/details/iesuchristosnofroojuan/page/n7/mode/2up.

Boone, Elizabeth Hill, et al. *Painted Words: Nahua Catholicism, Politics, and Memory in the Atzaqualco Pictorial Catechism*. Dumbarton Oaks Pre-Columbian Art and

---

55. Truitt, *Sustaining the Divine*.
56. Madajczak, "Towards a Deconstruction," 78.

Archaeology Studies. Washington, DC: Dumbarton Oak Research Library and Collection, 2016.

Burkhart, Louise M. "Afterword: Painting Piety and Politics." In *Painted Words: Nahua Catholicism, Politics, and Memory in the Atzaqualco Pictorial Catechism*, by Elizabeth Hill Boone et al, 383–89. Dumbarton Oaks Pre-Columbian Art and Archaeology Studies. Washington, DC: Dumbarton Oak Research Library and Collection, 2016.

———. "A Doctrine for Dancing: The Prologue to the *Psalmodia christiana*." *Latin American Indian Literatures Journal* 11 (1995) 21–23.

———. *Holy Wednesday: A Nahua Drama from Early Colonial Mexico*. New Cultural Studies. Philadelphia: University of Pennsylvania Press, 1996.

———. "Introduction." In *Words and Worlds Turned Around: Indigenous Christianities in Colonial Latin America*, edited by David Tavárez, 4–26. Boulder: University of Colorado Press, 2017.

———. "Moral Deviance in Sixteenth Century Nahua and Christian Thought: The Rabbit and the Deer." *Journal of Latin American Lore* 12 (1986) 107–39.

———. *The Slippery Earth: Nahua-Christian Moral Dialogue in Sixteenth-Century Mexico*. Tucson: University of Arizona Press, 1989.

———. *Staging Christ's Passion in Eighteenth Century Nahua Mexico*. Denver: University Press of Colorado, 2023.

Christensen, Mark Z. *Nahua and Maya Catholicisms: Texts and Religion in Colonial Central Mexico and Yucatan*. Stanford, CA: Stanford University Press, 2013.

Dávila Montoya, Alejandra. "Cuix Oquiçopelicama in Tetl: San Esteban protomártir en el Manuscrito 1482 de la Biblioteca Nacional de México." In *Vestigios manuscritos de una nueva cristiandad*, edited by Berenice Alcántara Rojas et al., 43–59. Mexico City: Universidad Nacional Autónoma de México, 2022.

Dehouve, Danièle. "Dios se hizo hombre: ¿Oquichtli o Tlacatl? Simbolismo de género y encarnación en los sermones en náhuatl." In *Vestigios manuscritos de una nueva cristiandad*, edited by Berenice Alcántara Rojas et al., 109–29. Mexico City: Universidad Nacional Autónoma de México, 2022.

De la Cruz, Abelardo. "The Value of *El costumbre* and Christianity in the Discourse of Nahua Catechisms from the Huasteca Region in Veracruz, Mexico, 1970–2010." In *Words and Worlds Turned Around: Indigenous Christianities in Colonial Latin America*, edited by David Tavárez, 267–88. Boulder: University of Colorado Press, 2017.

Dibble, Charles E. "The Nahuatlization of Christianity." In *Sixteenth-Century Mexico: The Work of Sahagún*, edited by Munro S. Edmondson, 225–33. Albuquerque: University of New Mexico Press.

Gaillemin, Bérénice. "L'art ingénieux de peindre la parole et de parler aux yeux: Élaboration et usages des catéchismes en images du Mexique (XVIe–XIXe siècles)." PhD diss., Université Paris-Ouest Nanterre, 2013.

———. "Images mémorables pour un texte immuable: Les catéchismes pictographiques testériens (Mexique, XVIe–XIXe siècles)." *Gradhiva: Revue d'Anthropologie et d'Historie des Arts* 13 (2011) 204–25.

Galarza, Joaquín. *Estudios de escritura indígena tradicional azteca-náhuatl*. Mexico City: Centro de Estudios Mexicanos y Centroamericanos, 2019.

Gilberti, Maturino. "Sermones en lengua de michuacan para cada domingo del año: Fundados sobre un tema aunque por diversas materias." Handwritten manuscript, ca. 1559. https://archive.org/details/siguenseunosbrevo2gilb.

Horcasitas, Fernando. *Teatro náhuatl: Épocas novohispana y moderna*. Mexico City: Universidad Nacional Autónoma de México, 2004.

Klor de Alba, J. Jorge. "Spiritual Warfare in Mexico: Christianity and the Aztecs." PhD diss., University of California at Santa Cruz, 1980.

Leeming, Ben. *Aztec Antichrist: Performing the Apocalypse in Early Colonial Mexico*. Institute for Mesoamerican Studies. Denver: University Press of Colorado and Institute for Mesoamerican Studies, 2022.

———. "Del centro a la periferia: La (de)construcción de un simbolismo nahua-cristiano." In *Vestigios manuscritos de una nueva cristiandad*, edited by Berenice Alcántara Rojas et al., 85–107. Mexico City: Universidad Nacional Autónoma de México, 2022.

León-Portilla, Miguel. "Testimonios nahuas sobre la conquista espiritual." *Estudios de Cultura Náhuatl* 11 (1974) 11–36.

———. *La visión de los vencidos: Relaciones indígenas de la conquista*. Mexico City: Universidad Autónoma del Estado de México, 1959.

Lockhart, James. "Introduction: Background and Course of the New Philology." WPMUCDN, 2007. https://bpb-us-e1.wpmucdn.com/blogs.uoregon.edu/dist/7/5151/files/2022/01/Intro.pdf.

Madajczak, Julia. "Towards a Deconstruction of the Notion of Nahua Confession." In *Words and Worlds Turned Around: Indigenous Christianities in Colonial Latin America*, edited by David Tavárez, 63–81. Boulder: University of Colorado Press, 2017.

Marín-Guadarrama, Nadia. "Childrearing in the Discourse of Nahuas and Friars in Early Colonial Central Mexico." PhD diss., SUNY: University at Albany, 2012.

———. "Los rituales de bebés en textos en lengua náhuatl: Espacios de negociación colonial." In *Vestigios manuscritos de una nueva cristiandad*, edited by Berenice Alcántara Rojas et al., 61–84. Mexico City: Universidad Nacional Autónoma de México, 2022.

Mijangos, Juan de. *Espejo divino en lengva mexicana, en que pveden verse los padres y tomar documento para acertar a doctrinar bien a sus hijos y aficionarlos a las virtudes*. Mexico: López Daualos, 1607. https://archive.org/details/espeiodivinoenleoomija.

Monzon, Cristina. "El pecado en la lengua tarasca (purépecha): Conceptos para la confesión en el sexto mandamiento del confesionario de Fray Ángel Serra (1697)." *Indiana* 35 (2018) 151–73.

Olko, Justina, and John Sullivan. "Empire, Colony, and Globalization: A Brief History of the Nahuatl Language." *Colloquia Humanistica* 2 (2013) 181–216.

Oroz, Pedro. *Sancturale hiemale*. Mexico: N.p., ca. 1560–79.

Pellicer, Dora. "Confesión y conversación en la doctrina y enseñanza de la lengua mazahua de Diego de Nágera Yanguas." *Estudios de Cultura Otopame* 5 (2006) 13–52.

Ricard, Robert. *The Spiritual Conquest of Mexico: An Essay on the Apostolate and the Evangelizing Methods of the Mendicant Order in New Spain, 1523-1572*. Translated by Lesley Byrd Simpson. Berkeley: University of California Press, 1966.

Sahagún, Bernardino de. *Bernardino de Sahagún's "Psalmodia christiana."* Edited and translated by Arthur J. O. Anderson. Salt Lake City: University of Utah Press, 1993.

———. *Florentine Codex: General History of the Things of New Spain*. Edited and translated by Arthur J. O. Anderson and Charles E. Dibble. 12 vols. Santa Fe: School of American Research and University of Utah Press, 1953–82.

———. *Psalmodia christiana y sermonario de los sanctos del año, en lengua mexicana*. Edited and translated by José Luis Suarez Roca. León, Spain: Diputación Provincial de León and Instituto Leonés de Cultura, 1999.

———. *Siguense unos sermones de dominicas y de sanctos en lengua mexicana: Ms. 1485, Ayer Collection, the New Berry Library*. Translated by Mario Alberto Sánchez Aguilera. Mexico City: Universidad Nacional Autónoma de México, 2022.

Sánchez, Aguilera. "Huehuetlatolli del Viejo Mundo? Los proverbios de Salomón en los sermones sahaguntinos." In *Vestigios manuscritos de una nueva cristiandad*, edited by Berenice Alcántara Rojas et al., 195–223. Mexico City: Universidad Nacional Autónoma de México, 2022.

Schwaller, John F. *Church and Clergy in Sixteen-Century Mexico*. Albuquerque: University of New Mexico Press, 1987.

———. *The Stations of the Cross in Colonial Mexico: "Via crucis en mexicano" by Fray Agustín de Vetancurt, and the Spread of a Devotion*. Norman: University of Oklahoma Press, 2021.

Sell, Barry D., and Louise M. Burkhart, eds. *Death and Life in Colonial Nahua Mexico*. Vol. 1 of *Nahuatl Theater*. Norman: University of Oklahoma Press, 2004.

———. *Nahuatl Christianity in Performance*. Vol. 4 of *Nahuatl Theater*. Norman: University of Oklahoma Press, 2009.

Sell, Barry D., et al., eds. *Our Lady of Guadalupe*. Vol. 2 of *Nahuatl Theater*. Norman: University of Oklahoma Press, 2006.

———. *Spanish Golden Age Drama in Mexican Translation*. Vol. 3 of *Nahuatl Theater*. Norman: University of Oklahoma Press, 2008.

Tavárez, David. *The Invisible War: Indigenous Devotions, Discipline, and Dissent in Colonial Mexico*. Stanford: Stanford University Press, 2011.

———. "Performing the Zaachila Word: The Dominican Invention of Zapotec Christianity." In *Words and Worlds Turned Around: Indigenous Christianities in Colonial Latin America*, edited by David Tavárez, 29–62. Boulder: University of Colorado Press, 2017.

Terraciano, Kevin. "Native Expressions of Piety in Mixtec Testaments." In *Dead Giveaways: Indigenous Testaments of Colonial Mesoamerica and the Andes*, edited by Susan Kellogg and Matthew Restall, 115–40. Salt Lake City: University of Utah Press, 1998.

Truitt, Jonathan. *Sustaining the Divine in Mexico Tenochtitlan: Nahuas and Catholicism, 1523–1700*. Norman: University of Oklahoma, 2018.

Whittaker, Gordon. *Deciphering Aztec Hieroglyphs: A Guide to Nahuatl Writing*. Oakland: University of California Press, 2021.

Wolf, Eric. *Europe and the People Without History*. Berkeley: University of California Press, 1982.

2

Women's Religiosity in New Spain Colonial Catholicism

JESSICA DELGADO

THERE IS A CURRENT of misogyny in the nationalist anticlericalism in late nineteenth and early twentieth-century Mexican political discourse; as symbol and supposed coconspirators, women were linked to legacies of colonial power through their relationship to the Catholic Church.[1] Scholarship tracing a historical process of "feminization of piety" in the early national era does seem to confirm a special link between women and the church that grew in inverse relationship to the conflict between church and state. However, as these scholars make clear, the reasons for this are complex and have less to do with women clinging to colonial-era ideas than with women responding to new opportunities the national church offered.[2] The image of unbroken, monolithic female piety within anticlerical nationalist narratives contradicts the reality of dynamism in Mexican women's relationship to church and state in the postcolonial era, but it also misunderstands the history of women's engagement with the colonial church. In some ways, Mexican women in the early national era were simply doing what they had always done: finding within the church ways to solve problems, protect themselves and their families, and participate in both ordinary and extraordinary ways in the creation of culture and society.

---

1. Wright-Rios, *Searching for Madre Matiana*; Fallaw, "Seduction of Revolution"; Wies, "Pious Delinquents."

2. Chowning, *Catholic Women and Mexican Politics*; Chowning, "Catholic Church and the Ladies"; Olcott, *Revolutionary Women in Postrevolutionary Mexico*, 241–27.

Women's Religiosity in Political and Historical Perspective

Women's engagements with the church in New Spain were complex and paradoxical. Differences in geography, racial, social, sexual, religious, and economic status make it difficult to generalize about women's religiosity, but two strong patterns do emerge. The church represented both powerful constraints and important opportunities for women, and women's engagement with the church was shaped by both devotion and survival strategies in ways that always coexisted and comingled. Church doctrine and institutions produced and supported ideologies of misogyny and policies of colonial patriarchy, and yet women found and forged theological and structural resources within the church that they did not find or forge to the same degree within other colonial institutions and authorities.

While historians of the last decade have expanded our understanding of laywomen's religiosity in colonial society, nuns are still overrepresented because of the disproportionate imprint they left in the historical record.[3] The visibility of cloistered religious women, combined with what we know about official doctrine and law related to sexuality, marriage, and women's legal status, can create the impression that women had two viable life options: marriage, through which they relinquished authority to their husbands and their lives were shaped by the economic realities of their families; or the convent, which required obedience and devotion but paradoxically afforded a kind of independence and access to education that most women did not have and, in all cases, was available only to racially, socially, and economically privileged women. However, this "marriage or convent" hides the fact that consensual cohabitation, illegitimate children, and economically independent women were not unusual, and that single, childless women participated in devotional culture in unique and important ways.[4]

Overall, the well-developed scholarship on nuns and convents as well as the emerging work on laywomen illustrates that women's relationship to the church in New Spain is not accurately described through binaries of resistance versus accommodation or oppression versus empowerment. Rather, it included gradually forged networks; collectively learned problem-solving practices; and cumulative knowledge garnered over time through ordinary, daily interactions. These interactions were expressions of faith as well as the need for survival strategies, and both were important parts of

---

3. Leavitt-Alcantara, *Alone at the Altar*; Delgado, *Laywomen*; Chowning, "Convents and Nuns."

4. Lavrin, "Sexuality in Colonial Mexico"; Gonzalbo Aizpuru, "Mujeres novohispanos"; Leavitt-Alcantara, *Alone at the Altar.*

women's participation in colonial religious culture and colonial society in general.

Elsewhere I have written about the combination of devotion and survival visible in laywomen's relationships to sacraments, clergy, cloisters, and ecclesiastical courts, and what follows is largely drawn from that work.[5] But for the remainder of this essay, I will explore women's religiosity through two concepts that apply equally to nuns and laywomen. The first is what I have called "spiritual status," defined as a historically specific category of difference and power. The second is a gendered and racialized theology of containment represented in the values, institutions, and practices expressed by the colonial usage of the word *recogimiento*.[6] I will first discuss each of these concepts theoretically. Then I will examine an example of both concepts in action—namely, women's informal movement between institutional cloisters officially designed for very different women and purposes.

Spiritual Status and Its Material Consequences

I use the term *spiritual status* to name the aspects of women's social status shaped by religious proscriptions and values. Specifically, women's spiritual status was shaped by public perception of their sexual virtue and piety. Like race or *casta* and economic class, the public perception of a woman's spiritual status was based on a combination of visual cues, community knowledge, and social relationships—like family, lineage, and social networks and connections. And like these other markers of identity, spiritual status existed in co-constitutive relation to other categories of power that made up colonial social hierarchies.

The intersectional entanglement of spiritual, racial, and economic status had clear material expressions. For example, a professed nun automatically possessed a high level of spiritual status, but reaching this position almost always required economic and racial privilege as well. Professing in a convent required a large dowry and proof of racial and genealogical purity (*limpieza de sangre*) and "legitimate" birth (married parents).[7] A similar dynamic existed for laywomen as well. Wealthy women of Spanish descent were more likely to have the kind of family connections, living situations, and social networks that facilitated an unreproachable public reputation

---

5. Delgado, *Laywomen*.

6. For an excellent definition of the colonial usage of *recogimiento*, see Van Deusen, *Between Sacred and Worldly*.

7. For a discussion of *limpieza de sangre* and genealogical "stains" in Spain and Mexico, see Martínez, *Genealogical Fictions*.

for sexual purity and orthodox piety than did poor women of Indigenous, African, and mixed descent women.

Nonetheless, spiritual status could also raise or lower women's place on the social hierarchy. Poor women, women of Indigenous, African, and mixed descent, and women born of unmarried unions sometimes managed to accumulate spiritual status in spite of the obstacles through extraordinary acts of piety, cultivating relationships with clergy or religious women, and maintaining a public reputation for sexual purity and modesty. This spiritual status could then in turn improve their material and social possibilities. Conversely, wealthy, racially privileged women could lose their elite social and material status if they suffered damage to their reputations due to sexual scandal or rumors of religious deviance.

Occasionally the accumulation of spiritual status counteracted racial and economic factors enough to allow women to achieve higher-status marriages, enter lay cloisters meant for more socially privileged women, or more rarely, against all odds, even become a nun. Some of the most famous examples of this "exception that proves the rule" possibility became celebrated and widely regarded as examples worthy of hagiographic commemoration.[8] More common examples, of women's spiritual status mitigating their lower social status, but ones that are easy to miss in the historic record, are the strategies women utilized to gain access to and move between the range of institutional cloisters in New Spain.

Officially the boundaries between these institutions should have been clear: prestigious cloisters were meant to elevate and protect prestigious women; cloisters of mercy and reform were designed to educate and transform repentant women; and cloisters of punishment were built to isolate and discipline women who posed a threat to the social order.[9] However, in practice, women found ways to move between these cloisters, engaging with them at different moments for different reasons. These strategies often bent the rules, stretched the intentions of founders, or even outright defied official policies of these cloisters, but they worked because they rested on the underlying logic of these institutions—namely, *recogimiento*. Through their strategic engagement with the logic of *recogimiento*, women created relationships, negotiated their spiritual and social status, and participated actively in the construction of colonial religious culture.

---

8. Benoist, "Estefania de San Joseph"; Brewer-Garcia, "Hierarchy and Holiness"; Lavrin, *Brides of Christ*, ch. 1, "The Path to the Convent."

9. Delgado, *Laywomen*, chs. 4–6.

Recogimiento: A Racialized and Gendered Theology of Containment

To contextualize women's engagement with these institutional cloisters, it is important to understand the historically specific concept of *recogimiento* that animated them.[10] In some ways, the word *recogimiento*, when referring to a quality that a woman either possessed or lacked, could be used interchangeably with spiritual status. However, distinguishing between the two concepts is important for several reasons. First, "spiritual status" is not a term anyone living in New Spain would have recognized; rather it is merely an analytical lens I have proposed to aid historians in identifying the ways that gendered perceptions of sexual and religious purity operated to shape women's position in colonial social hierarchies. But more importantly, *recogimiento* was a highly contested category in colonial Latin America. In addition to sexual virtue, it also implied obedience, modesty, and having a quiet, retiring manner, and women asserted these qualities even when they had suffered a public loss of sexual purity—sometimes as a way of combating the harm that this loss caused. This counter discourse was not generally sufficient to repair their damaged spiritual status, but it could aid them in convincing ecclesiastical authorities and institutions to provide them help and support. In addition, *recogimiento* referred not only to a set of gendered personal qualities but also to a practice and a type of institution. And finally, *recogimiento* operated as a comprehensive gendered and racialized theology of containment that was larger than the sum of its parts. It transcended the common usages of the word and infused the church's doctrines, practices, and ideas related to women—as well as most civil colonial laws and policies about women.

Underlying the significance of *recogimiento* was the cultural and theological understanding that sin and scandal were contagious and that women were particularly dangerous vectors of that contagion.[11] This idea led to beliefs about women's potential impact on collective spiritual health. Virtuous women who were effectively contained and protected by male authorities or in an institutional cloister had the opportunity to accumulate a level of personal virtue that could eventually benefit society as a whole. Convents of nuns carried a particular mystique about them and were thought to sanctify the cities they were in. And laywomen whose virtue was properly protected could help maintain order in families and communities. But there was a great deal of fear about the large number of *mujeres desamparadas* (unsupported

---

10. Van Deusen, *Between Sacred and Worldly*; Delgado, *Laywomen*, 141–44.
11. Delgado: *Laywomen*; "Contagious Women."

women). Women without fathers, unmarried women, even widows were imagined as particularly vulnerable to falling prey to forces of temptation and ruin. And once they "fell" in a way that became visible to others around them, they became sources of contagious scandal that threatened to cause harm to society and, ultimately, to the colonial social order. Where women found themselves on this spectrum shaped their spiritual status, and this had a significant impact on their material possibilities. But this very spectrum, and the gendered and racialized theology of containment that created it, was also something women actively engaged with—both in their faith and in their strategies for survival.

Josephina Muriel has described the widespread practice of institutional and informal *recogimiento* as a solution to the social problem of unprotected women.[12] This "social problem" was indeed one that caused a great deal of concern for religious and civil authorities. In response, these men, together with large numbers of wealthy and pious individuals, developed a range of legal practices, institutions, and resources to contain and quarantine dangerous women, protect virtuous and vulnerable women, redeem repentant women, and maximize the sanctifying power of exceptionally virtuous women. Confraternities and pious donors raised funds and created endowments to support these endeavors. Religious and civil authorities contributed money, regulations, and oversight. Poor, virtuous, and—increasingly over time—racially pure women became the beneficiaries of lotteries, receiving money from *obras pías* (good works) to be used as dowries for marriage or profession or to pay for room and board in prestigious lay cloisters where they could be sequestered until they "took state" as a wife or nun.

In other contexts, ecclesiastical judges made sure that wayward or disorderly wives were placed in appropriate institutions or under the custody of a private households licensed to serve as *casas de depósito* (houses of "deposit") for women who needed protection and supervision. These same judges also responded to women's own requests to be placed in such locations when their husbands abandoned them, mistreated them, or were absent because of work, travel, or death.

In related practices of spiritual inversion, the *recogimiento* of some women was compromised to facilitate that of others; in the hierarchical economy of female piety, some women worked as servants or were enslaved in convents so that nuns could avoid the labor and contact with the outside world that would have threatened their complete seclusion and the highest protection of their *recogimiento*. And from the perspective of this racialized,

---

12. Muriel, *Recogimientos de mujeres*.

hierarchical theology of female containment, this in turn benefitted all of society by allowing the most virtuous women to concentrate their sanctifying power.

From an elite perspective, only women living in institutional cloisters or homes in which it was possible to refrain from contact with men outside their family were truly *recogida* (literally cloistered and thus possessing the true quality of *recogimiento*). Yet women outside of these circumstances claimed and interpreted these terms for themselves. For poor women and those who worked in the marketplace or as domestic servants, being *muy recogida* meant being modest, obedient, and chaste within the constraints and possibilities of their lives. Unmarried women living in monogamous, consensual unions claimed that they lived with *mucho recogimiento* to signal that they lived free of scandal, behaved according to their place in the gender and social hierarchy, and comported themselves with humility and obedience. In testimonies and petitions, these women regularly claimed to "be very *recogida*" (*estar muy recogida*) or to "have a great deal of *recogimiento*" (*tener mucho regimimiento*) as reasons they deserved protection from ecclesiastical judges or were credible witnesses.[13]

Over time, reading the range of meanings *recogimiento* held in religious and civil sources of all kinds, and the wide variety of contexts in which people deployed and contested this term, I came to understand it as representing a colonial ideology of gender—or more accurately, as a gendered and racialized *theology* of containment. I stress that it is a theology, not merely an ideology, because it was linked to eschatological concerns, not only for individuals but for colonial society in general. Since sin and scandal were understood as contagious, and doctrinally and theologically, God could not be in the physical presence of sin, a soul troubled by the tainting caused by participation in or exposure (via scandal and rumor) to sin was without God's grace until this absence was rectified through the practice of confession. Individuals in this state of being, named as *en hora mala* (in a bad or unhealthy time), were a vulnerable part of society, susceptible to diabolical forces. Thus collective spiritual health depended on effective containment of societies' most vulnerable individuals, who were also the most likely to become contaminated and infect others.

Emerging out of the nexus of the idea of spiritual contagion and the gendered and racialized hierarchy of presumed spiritual, emotional, and physical capacity, the theology of female containment linked the seemingly distinct institutions of convent, lay cloister, and asylum, together with practices of *depósito* in private homes, as practices aimed at women but thought

---

13. Delgado, *Laywomen*, ch. 2.

necessary for society as a whole. Furthermore, *recogimiento* informed women's interactions with confessors, ecclesiastical judges, and other religious authorities. In a multitude of ways, *recogimiento* shaped women's life possibilities. Understanding the significance of *recogimiento* is crucial for understanding women's religiosity in New Spain.

The remainder of this essay looks at one of the concrete ways women directly engaged with *recogimiento*: namely, how they utilized—and in particular, moved between—institutional cloisters in an effort to navigate and change their spiritual status. Institutional cloisters are by no means the most important aspect of women's religiosity in New Spain. Elsewhere I have explored laywomen's relationships to sacraments, clergy, ecclesiastical courts, sacred images, and other aspects of the church. Women's devotional lives were rich and varied, and there is a great deal left out in the particular approach I have taken in this essay. However, all aspects of women's religiosity existed *within* the theological and social context of *recogimiento*, the concept of spiritual contagion, and the reality of spiritual status. And the example of laywomen's movement between institutional cloisters in which they also interacted with cloistered nuns affords a concentrated way, in a brief essay, to provide a concrete example of how women in general—both professed religious and lay—navigated *recogimiento* and attempted to improve their spiritual status. And as such, this example highlights what I find to be the core pattern within women's religiosity: namely, a balance of devotional and strategic impulses, motivations, and practices.

Moving Between Cloisters: A Religiosity of Faith and Strategy

On the nineteenth of August in 1720, a group of men belonging to the one of the most illustrious confraternities in New Spain, the Archicofradia del Santísimo Sacramento y Caridad, met in the cathedral of Mexico City. The first order of business was a petition from a young woman, Doña Margarita Yturri, a woman of Spanish descent whose parents had died and left her destitute. She asked the religious brotherhood for entrance into the school and shelter it had established for poor, virtuous girls of Spanish descent, the Colegio de las Niñas de Nuestra Señora de la Caridad, known colloquially as "la Caridad."

The men agreed. As a new *colegiala*, Yturri would be given protection, room and board, education, and a five-hundred-peso dowry for her future marriage or profession in a convent. Her entrance would be marked by a ceremonial appearance in the choir balcony of the colegio's church, announcing to the public the importance of her new status. She would be seated with the other residents, separated from the rest of the parishioners by a gate symbolizing her entrance into a cloistered life, wearing a special blue mantle and holding a lighted candle in her hands.

Yturri had previously resided in another institution designed for the protection and seclusion of women: the less prestigious but also reputable Recogimiento de San Miguel de Belém. Belém was under the authority of the archbishop, and his office had paid for Yturri's room and board out of the funds set aside for girls and women with no other source of support. A man described as "her countryman" had petitioned for her entrance when Yturri's parents died, but in doing so he had not relinquished authority over her destiny. A few months prior to presenting her petition to enter Colegio de Caridad, Yturri's "countryman" had pulled her out of Belém so she could "provide company" for his wife—a phrase that generally meant help with domestic labor if not outright servitude. Resisting this new arrangement, Yturri sought the protection of the religious brotherhood. In doing so, she was placing herself under the authority of powerful men who would claim her as their adopted daughter. No countryman, guardian, relative, or even parent could remove her from their colegio without their permission, which they would not give unless she herself chose to leave.

Nine years later, this same group of men responded to a different kind of petition: that of a woman who sought license to *leave* their Colegio de Caridad. Doña Ana Margarita de Casterón y Trigo's petition expressed a mix of regret and gratitude as she thanked the brotherhood for the years of shelter and protection but explained that several doctors had advised her to leave the colegio for health reasons. She assured her surrogate fathers she would continue to honor the ideals of *recogimiento* by taking up residence in the nearby convent of San Bernardo where she would live with her relative, Madre Francisca María.

In spite of her tone, Casterón's petition infuriated the brotherhood. In their response they stated that by leaving without "taking state"—either through marriage or profession as a nun—Casterón was betraying her benefactors and undermining their intentions for the Colegio de Caridad. Since they could not keep her there against her will, they decided to make a public example of her to dissuade other *colegialas* from following in her footsteps. Gathering together all of the residents, member of the brotherhood Don Nicolás de Uría announced that Casterón was no longer a *colegiala*, could never return, and would be stripped of all rights and privileges, including the five-hundred-peso dowry she would have received had she remained under their protection until taking state. After that he delivered her to the convent of San Bernardo.

Stories like these, of entrances into and exits from institutions where women lived under the supervision, protection, and control of religious organizations or authorities, represent the experience of hundreds of women in New Spain. The social backgrounds and circumstance of these women varied greatly, as did the kinds of institutions they were entering or leaving. These institutions were collectively referred to as *recogimientos de mujeres* and were part of a continuum of institutions meant to protect, control, and sometimes correct women. While theoretically they housed very different kinds of women, they all responded to the ideology of *recogimiento*. Protecting vulnerable women from the dangers of society and protecting society from the dangers of vulnerable women were two sides of the same coin.

Recogimientos were formally divided between voluntary and involuntary cloisters. "Voluntary" cloisters included prestigious *colegios de niñas* (schools for girls) like the Colegio de Caridad, lay cloisters designed for either repentant women or unprotected but virtuous women, as well as convents of nuns, and *beaterios*, which were cloisters for laywomen taking religious vows similar to nuns but not permanently binding. Involuntary cloisters were correctional institutions that nonetheless had a religious purpose and were supported by the church and religious organizations.

Theoretically, these different types of cloisters had different purposes and housed different populations, but in practice, these distinctions often broke down. Even the difference between "voluntary" and "involuntary" cloister was not as clear as it sounds. Ecclesiastical judges often placed women in what was known as *deposito* during marital disputes—either in a private home or institutional cloister. Sometimes women sought this out when their husbands had abandoned or mistreated them. Other times, husbands asked judges to place their wives in *deposito* as a way controlling their wives' behavior and movements. So, even when women were placed in a prestigious "voluntary" cloister rather than one designed as a place of punishment, they might not have chosen to be there. Differences between voluntary cloisters also tended to blur. For instance, *colegios de niñas* were intended to be literally "schools for girls," but in reality they sheltered women of all ages—many of whom arrived as girls but then never left. Even entrance requirements intended to uphold social hierarchies and distinctions could be navigated. The more prestigious voluntary *recogimientos* required permanent residents to virgins from "good" families and who were able to prove *limpieza de sangre* and legitimate birth. However, these standards were often overlooked for temporary residents—including both in the *depositadas* (women "deposited" by judges or family members) or servants. This was true to an even greater extent for convents, where laywomen of varying social backgrounds often lived as servants, dependents, and temporary *depositadas*. And finally, though the ideal of all these institutions was stability—semi-permanent or indefinite enclosure broken by a few sanctioned reasons—the practice of *deposito* and the presence of servants and dependents challenged this ideal. Contrary to the goals of founders and supervisors, many laywomen moved between these types of institutions to negotiate economic or social difficulties and to improve their spiritual status.

The reality of overlap, blurring of boundaries, and informal movement between these supposedly different kinds of cloisters should not obscure the material differences between them in terms of access and experience. The stories of Margarita Yturri and Ana Margarita de Casterón y Trigo above reflect the concerns of men supervising the more restrictive and prestigious voluntary *recogimientos*. Other places, like the large and more permeable colegio and *recogimiento* of Belém, and cloisters known as *casas de magdelena* (Magdalena houses), built to house and reform repentant prostitutes and other women whose sexual reputation was less than pure, operated with different entrance requirements and different expectations, constraints, and opportunities for residents.

The details of individual institutions lie outside the bounds of this essay, but general patterns can be identified.[14] The colegio and *recogimiento* of Caridad was founded in the early sixteenth century primarily to shelter and protect the mestizo daughters of wealthy Spaniards, housing them alongside virtuous *españolas* in order that the latter could provide an example to the former. But by the early seventeenth century, all of the permanent residents at Caridad were listed as *españolas doncellas* (maidens whose virginity remained intact.) A similar evolution over time occurred for almost all of the prestigious voluntary *recogimientos* and colegios in New Spain. Magdalena houses and other voluntary *recogimientos* designed for reform tended to evolve up or down over time. Some became popular recipients of religious donation, which led to increased prestige until they too were employing strict entrance requirements and no longer serving the originally intended population. Others became involuntary correctional institutions where ecclesiastical judges or family members might send women against their will.

By the mid-seventeenth century, racial requirements probably constituted the most difficult obstacles to overcome for women who attempted to use these institutions as places of shelter or ways to improve their spiritual status. As this took place, *deposito* or working as a servant were officially the only point of access to cloisters for most nonwhite women. But for those women who could at least pass for *españolas* but who lacked other

14. Delgado, *Laywomen*, chs. 4–6.

requirements for the most prestigious voluntary cloisters, moving between these institutions—perhaps first as a convent servant and then later to a more reputable *recogimiento*—could sometimes allow them to bypass the economic and social restrictions that might have barred their entrance into the latter.

Many women undertook this extra-official movement by seeking employment as servants in convents or in the more prestigious *recogimientos*. This could be seen as either a step up or a step down in terms of status and possibilities, depending where they were coming from and why they were leaving. Residents of institutions like the *recogimiento* of Belém, for instance—a large voluntary cloister run by the archbishop and supported by donations, which was chronically low on resources to support its residents—often gave up the honored status of living as a permanent resident there for the far less prestigious status of convent servant, chosen for economic reasons. Other women living as permanent residents in places like Belém, Caridad, or other convent-like *recogimientos* might choose to become a convent servant because of waves of stringent reforms that limited their choices, activities, and movements within these institutions. Moving the other direction, it was also possible for women who had been placed in involuntary *recogimientos*—a situation of disgrace rather than honor—to request transfer to a convent or voluntary *recogimiento* where they would work as servants. After a few years in this position, such women might then seek entrance into a voluntary *recogimiento*—probably not one of the most prestigious places like Caridad but perhaps a place like Belém or a former Magdalena house.

It is easy to see this movement as purely strategic—women negotiating social, economic, and material realities, but the quasi-monastic context of these cloisters and the underlying theological framework of *recogimiento* makes it impossible to separate survival strategies from devotional practices and desires. Within the gendered, racialized, and economic hierarchies these women navigated, seeking a cloister, seeking to leave one cloister for another, and arguing for changes in the terms of their cloister were methods of improving spiritual status and practices and processes that both strengthened and challenged aspects of colonial religious patriarchy. Women's spirituality within colonial religious patriarchy was equally shaped by the need for survival strategies and the desire to respond to devotional mandates and impulses.

Final Reflections: Women's Religiosity in Colonial Catholic Culture

I offer one final story of movement that is unlike those above as final reflections. These reflections are meant to raise questions and inspire new directions of inquiry rather than to provide clear conclusions. Spiritual status, *recogimiento*, and the example of women's informal, extra-official engagement with religious cloisters is but one avenue into the large and complex subject of women's religiosity in New Spain. I hope it is one provocative enough to encourage scholars interested in the complicated story of Christianity's role in colonial power in Latin America to expand our understanding of colonial religious patriarchy and women's participation in colonial religious culture.

Despite the many similarities between prestigious colegios and *recogimientos* and convents—and the hopes of these institutions' founders that many of their *colegialas* would eventually profess as nuns in the latter—some former residents of *recogimientos* found this path too difficult. The founders kept track of the *colegialas* who had left their cloisters to profess as nuns and noted with disappointment when they had not completed their novitiate period—usually going to live with relatives. It is not clear what happened to these women's dowries in these instances—whether they had been absorbed by the convent or were returned to the *cofradía* when the former *colegiala* failed to profess. According to the constitutions of many of these colegios, a *colegiala* had to profess as a nun or be married in order to have her dowry applied and therefore keep it, so presumably the *cofradía* would attempt to recollect it. And since these women were no longer living in the colegio but had not succeeded in taking state, they would have forfeited their *colegiala* status—and with it any future access to their dowry. Certainly their time in these cloisters might have increased their spiritual status and with it their marital possibilities, but these "failures" to maintain this ideal form of *recogimiento* might have also constituted a stain on their reputations and thus a loss of spiritual and social status.

At least one woman avoided these potential pitfalls by petitioning to return to her original cloister. In 1731, the *cofradía* who governed the Colegio de Caridad received a letter from Catarina de San Pedro, the *presidenta* of the convent of Santa Ynez. She said that former *colegiala* Doña María de Pevedilla suffered from constant fatigue and illness and could not complete the novitiate process. Pevedilla, who had taken the name of Sor Maria de Guadalupe, was apparently physically unable to fulfill her responsibilities in spite of efforts to cure her. Pevedilla had risen to the position of *maestra* (teacher) at Caridad, yet perhaps her life at Santa Ynez was more strenuous, or perhaps her health had simply deteriorated. Whatever the case, according to the petition, María de Pevedilla now wanted nothing more than to return to "her colegio." After extensive discussion, the *cofradía* decided that her illness warranted compassion and welcomed her back, restoring her collegial status. However, in doing so, they made every effort to minimize the visibility of her return, writing in their notes that the situation was exceptional and could set a bad example. Once back in the colegio, María de Pevedilla's health must have stabilized, because eleven years later in 1748, she was once again serving as *maestra*, and by 1751 had advanced to the prestigious head office of *vicaria*. By then, she was past marriageable age, but she also probably knew that the increased intensity of monastic life in convents was beyond her. Presumably, María de Pevedilla had decided to stay indefinitely at the Colegio de la Caridad.

María de Pevedilla's story of an exit, entrance, and then return, though unusual, highlights the ways that these institutions were understood as options for the women who inhabited them. Against the grain of their official constitutions, women without other means of support, or with varying degrees of religious vocation and capabilities, or who hoped to change their spiritual and social status navigated the boundaries of the institutional landscape of female cloister. This kind of navigation was not easy to do by any means, but it was possible and made up part of the survival and life improvement strategies of women in New Spain. Like women's explicit references to gendered theologies in the petitions they presented to ecclesiastical courts to seek protection, or the ways women navigated the threat of clerical sexual abuse in order to complete confession and avoid being seen as skipping the more public sacrament of communion, women's devotional practices related to these cloisters cannot be separated from their strategic engagements with church institutions, authorities, and rituals. Nor can these strategic engagements be separated from their devotional impulses and desires to respond to religious expectations. These equally strategic and devotional practices were in turn central to the ways women participated in the making of colonial Catholic culture.

Bibliography

Benoist, Valérie. "Estefania de San Joseph and Esperanza de San Alberto: The Dual Discourse in the Lives of Two Exemplary Afro-Women Religious in Early Modern Spanish America." In *Women Religious Crossing Between Cloister and the World: Nunneries in Europe and the Americas, ca. 1200–1700*, edited by Mercedes Pérez Vidal, 131–44. Spirituality and Monasticism, East and West. Yorkshire: Arc Humanities, 2022.

Brewer-Garcia, Larisa. "Hierarchy and Holiness in the Earliest Colonial Black Hagiographies: Alonso de Sandoval and His Sources." *William and Mary Quarterly* 76 (2019) 477–508.

Chowning, Margaret. "The Catholic Church and the Ladies of the Vela Perpetua: Gender and Devotional Change in Nineteenth-Century Mexico." *Past and Present* 221 (2013) 197–237.

———. *Catholic Women and Mexican Politics, 1750–1940*. Princeton: Princeton University Press, 2023.

———. "Convents and Nuns: New Approaches to the Study of Female Religious Institutions in Colonial Mexico." *History Compass* 6 (2008) 1279–303.

Delgado, Jessica L. "Contagious Women and Spiritual Status in Colonial Latin America: A Theoretical Proposal." In *Religion in the Américas: Trans-Hemispheric and Transcultural Approaches*, edited by Christopher D. Tirres and Jessica L. Delgado, 281–306. Religions of the Americas. Albuquerque: University of New Mexico Press, 2025.

———. *Laywomen and the Making of Colonial Catholicism in New Spain, 1630–1790*. Cambridge Latin American Studies 110. Cambridge: Cambridge University Press, 2018.

Fallaw, Ben. "The Seduction of Revolution: Anticlerical Campaigns Against Confession in Mexico, 1914–1935." *Journal of Latin American Studies* 45 (2013) 91–120

Gonzalbo Aizpuru, Pilar. "Las mujeres novohispanos y las contradicciónes de una sociedad patriarchal." In *Las mujeres en la construccíon de las sociedades iberoamericanas*, edited by Pilar Gonzalbo Aizpuru and Berta Aires Queija, 184–203. Mexico: Colegio de México, 2004.

Lavrin, Asunción. *The Brides of Christ: Conventual Life in Colonial Mexico*. Stanford, CA: Stanford University Press, 2008.

———. "Sexuality in Colonial Mexico: A Church Dilemma." In *Sexuality and Marriage in Colonial Latin America*, edited by Asunción Larvin, 61–89. Lincoln: University of Nebraska, 2014.

Leavitt-Alcantara, Briana. *Alone at the Altar: Single Women and Devotion in Guatemala, 1670–1870*. Stanford: Stanford University Press, 2018.

Martínez, María Elena. *Genealogical Fictions: Colonial Mexico*. Stanford: Stanford University Press, 2008.

Muriel, Josefina. *Los recogimientos de mujeres: Una respuesta de una problemática social novohispana*. Mexico City: Instituto de Investigaciones Históricas, 1974.

Olcott, Jocelyn. *Revolutionary Women in Postrevolutionary Mexico*. Next Wave: New Directions in Women's Studies. Durham: Duke University Press, 2005.

Olcott, Jocelyn, et al., eds. *Sex in Revolution: Gender, Politics, and Power in Modern Mexico*. Durham: Duke University Press, 2006.

Van Deusen, Nancy. *Between the Sacred and the Worldly: The Institutional and Cultural Practice of Recogimiento in Colonial Lima.* Stanford: Stanford University Press, 2001.

Wies, Robert. "Pious Delinquents: Anticlericalism and Crime in Postrevolutionary Mexico." *Americas* 73 (2016) 185–210.

Wright-Rios, Edward. "La Madre Matiana: Prophetess and Nation in Mexican Satire." *Americas* 68 (2011) 241–27.

———. *Searching for Madre Matiana: Prophecy and Popular Culture in Modern Mexico.* Diálogos. Albuquerque: University of New Mexico Press, 2014.

3

Sor Juana Inés de la Cruz: A Seventeenth-Century Mexican Nun and Poet Through the Lens of Ecofeminism

Theresa A. Yugar

I am a Peruvian American Catholic scholar of religion and an ecofeminist liberation theologian. My positioning is South America's contemporary Andean-based *buen vivir* (good way of living), a social philosophy that gives primacy to "harmony with Nature, respect for the values and principles of Indigenous peoples, satisfaction of basic needs, social justice and equality as a responsibility of the state and democracy."[1] This philosophy is rooted in the Quechua Indigenous cosmovision of the people of the Andes who value equilibrium, interdependence, communal living, respect for human life and biodiversity. In Sor Juana's seventeenth-century New Spain, modern-Mexican world, the values of the Mexica Indigenous people embodied these principles.

My ancestry and expertise in twenty-first-century Latin American ecofeminist theology inform my reflections on one of Mexico's most famous historical figures, the colonial era poet, scholar, philosopher, theologian and nun Sor (Sister) Juana Inés de la Cruz (1648/51–95). As a prolific writer, she was read throughout the Western Hemisphere, including Spain, the Spanish Empire, Colombia, Ecuador, Peru, the Philippines, and Sweden.[2] In the Americas, she is remembered for having the largest library with an estimated

---

1. Caria and Domínguez, "Ecuador's *Buen vivir*," 30.
2. Pamela Kirk Rappaport, in Juana, *Selected Writings*, 6; Margaret Sayers Peden, in Juana, *Poems, Protest, and Dream*, xi.

1500 to 4000 books.[3] In the Catholic Church, Sor Juana's prophetic voice has yet to fully be recognized. Her sex and her vocation as a writer were a threat to church hierarchy. In her patriarchal world, Sor Juana's opinions on gender and clericalism in the Catholic Church were met with resistance by clerical leaders. Still, Sor Juana used her literary genius and talent as a writer-scholar to create a new narrative of Mexican identity in her colonial New Spain world. Her dream was harmony between the east (Spain) and the west (New Spain).[4] Secular and religious texts, along with her faith in God, enabled her to envision a united multicultural Catholic Church that valued both Spanish and Indigenous religious practices.

In 1693, Sor Juana was found guilty of heresy by the Catholic Church and was ordered to renounce her literary and intellectual activities.[5] As her punishment, her most prized books were confiscated. The church did not kill Sor Juana physically, but they broke her spirit by taking her vast corpus of books.[6] In 1974, Sor Juana was recognized in Mexico City as "the first feminist in the New World."[7] The challenges Sor Juana endured in advocating for her human rights—and those of all women—to study, read, and write needs to be understood in the context of her colonial, clerical, and patriarchal New Spain world.

In the twenty-first century, Sor Juana should be recognized as a Doctor of the Roman Catholic Church because her importance is equivalent to that of Hildegard de Bingen, Teresa of Ávila, and Thérèse of Lisieux—all of whom have been given the title. Like her sisters in Europe, Sor Juana served the church she loved by writing devotionals to the Blessed Virgin Mary, poems for religious celebrations, and *villancicos* (songs) for major feasts, which were set to music and performed in the cathedrals of Mexico City, Puebla, and Oaxaca.[8] Personally, I believe that Sor Juana's writings planted the seeds for a Mexican identity that embraced diverse ethnic, religious, and linguistic backgrounds of her colonial world. Additionally, Sor Juana would be the first non-European woman religious to be recognized as a Doctor of the Church.

3. Margaret Sayers Peden, in Juana, *Poems, Protest, and Dream*, xii.
4. Yugar, *Sor Juana*, 93.
5. Kirk, *Sor Juana*, 25.
6. Kirk, *Sor Juana*, 31.
7. Yugar, *Sor Juana*, xii.
8. Pamela Kirk Rappaport, in Juana, *Selected Writings*, 9.

Sor Juana Inés de la Cruz: Precursor Feminist and Ecofeminist

This chapter argues that Sor Juana Inés de la Cruz is both a precursor feminist and an ecofeminist in the spirit of these contemporary terms. Feminism critiques patriarchal assumptions that women are inferior to men by virtue of their sex, while at the same time advocates for the full humanity of both sexes. *Ecofeminism*, a term coined by Françoise d'Eaubonne in 1974, is a philosophical approach that examines the shared exploitation of women and the natural world. It advocates for the interrelatedness of all life-forms. In the twenty-first century, Sor Juana's life and writings reflect a Latina ecofeminist perspective because of her high valuation of women, nature (in Spanish, *naturaleza*), and Indigenous wisdom. To support my argument, I identify feminist and ecofeminist themes in Sor Juana's primary texts: *La respuesta* (The answer) and "El primero sueño" (First I dream/First dream).[9] In *La respuesta*, a feminist perspective is evident because Sor Juana critiques prescribed gender roles for women, and she advocates for women to be able to read, study, and write. In "El primero sueño," an ecofeminist perspective is manifest in the way Sor Juana blends Indigenous and Christian knowledge systems.

Sor Juana embraces three principles of a Latin American ecofeminist perspective, which privileges (1) women's experiences, (2) the natural world, and (3) Indigenous wisdom. In *La respuesta*, Sor Juana privileges women's experiences, while in "El primero sueño" she identifies the natural world and Indigenous wisdom. Together, both texts reflect a Latina ecofeminist perspective. There are challenges in reclaiming Sor Juana as a precursor Latina ecofeminist. First, Sor Juana's text *La respuesta* is the only document that contains biographical information. Second, though Sor Juana had the largest library in the Americas, sadly, there is no index. Third, the Indigenous Mexica influence on Sor Juana has been neglected or disregarded to date.

Feminism and Ecofeminism in Latin America

In Latin America, North American ecofeminist Judy Ress articulates that a contemporary Latin American ecofeminism *groans* "for a new definition of ourselves that perceives us as part of the Earth community rather than

---

9. In my analysis, I use two primary texts, *The Answer/La respuesta* (trans. Arenal and Powell) and "El primero sueño" in *Poems, Protest, and Dream* (trans. Peden). For accuracy, I cite verse numbers, not page numbers, when referencing quotations in both texts.

somehow apart from it or over it."[10] It seeks a post-patriarchal mindset and worldview that values women, the Earth, and the interdependence of all life-forms.[11] It yearns for more just relationships between men and women, God and creation, people and land. In the 1970s, a "feminist consciousness" emerged in the Latin American liberation theology movement. It focused on reclaiming the historical subjectivity of poor individuals. In the 1980s, an awareness of the lack of attention given to the unique constraints that oppress poor women emerged. This awareness was that an option for the poor did not necessarily include an option for women. In the 1990s, the ecofeminist movement emerged, and it aimed at the "total reconstruction of [Christian] theology from a feminist perspective."[12] Today, a Brazilian Catholic nun, Ivone Gebara, is the foremost ecofeminist theologian. She states that ecofeminism as a social philosophy desires a "different understanding of ourselves, our work in the world and in our relationships with other living beings, anthropology, cosmology and ethics."[13] Gebara comments that though ecofeminism "is not a flower of Latin America," it takes on the "region's specific identities and context," meaning that in various regions it looks different.[14]

In Sor Juana's seventeenth-century New Spain world, there were two competing ideological frameworks for prescribed gender roles for women. First, there were Roman Catholic and Spanish gender roles for women. Second, there were gender roles for women in the traditional Mesoamerican culture. Both the church and Spanish culture sought to restrict women's agency to the private sphere. Greek philosophies and church doctrine overlapped and created a cultural universe for women that included dualisms and hierarchies. Religious constructs elevated men to the transcendent rational mind, while women were relegated to a lower status, associated with body, matter, and nature.[15] For the church, this meant that maidens and respectable women lived under the custody of a male figure, whether it was a husband, father, or brother.[16]

Sylvia Marcos, a Mexican anthropologist and ethnographer, describes the Mesoamerican traditional Indigenous worldview as a cosmovision that valued parity between the sexes, gods and goddesses. Though this world

---

10. Ress, *Ecofeminism in Latin America*, ix.
11. Ress, *Ecofeminism in Latin America*, 1–3.
12. Ress, *Ecofeminism in Latin America*, 9; see also 7, 8–19.
13. Gebara, *Intuiciones ecofeministas*, 111.
14. Ress, *Ecofeminism in Latin America*, 123.
15. Ruether, *Sexism and God-Talk*, 93–94.
16. Socolow, *Women of Colonial Latin America*, 11–12.

was completely gendered, binary oppositions were nonexistent. Rather, the world was governed by unity between the feminine and the masculine, which was fused into one bipolar principle. A dual divinity created the cosmos as well as regenerating and sustaining it. Concepts such as fluidity, equilibrium, and complementarity infused all aspects of this worldview.[17] The sexes were characterized by gender fluidity and the concept of "complementarity," which privileges equilibrium among humans, nature, and gods. Gender was not fixed nor static but rather was fluid and constantly changing.[18]

In Sor Juana's text "El primero sueño," her feminist and ecofeminist perspectives reflect a Mesoamerican religious thought regarding gender roles for women. In this worldview there was freedom for Sor Juana to reclaim her voice and affirm her sex in the process—although, at this time, the understandings of feminism and ecofeminism were nonexistent.

Sor Juana's Heritage: Tenochtitlan-Mexico

Sor Juana's perspective on women and *naturaleza* was informed by her mid-seventeenth-century New Spain world. It was a patriarchal society governed by Spain's viceroyalty and the Roman Catholic Church. The Mexica Empire and their capital city, Tenochtitlan, were destroyed by Spanish conquerors during the years 1519-21. The Spanish invasion of the capital resulted in the deaths of about 100,000 Mexica Indigenous people from European epidemic diseases and military violence. Sor Juana was born less than a century and a half after the destruction of this ancient civilization. She grew up in a rural agricultural setting outside Mexico City. In her lifetime, Sor Juana navigated varied Mexican identities of her day, including Spaniards from Spain (*peninsulares*); native-born Spaniards (*criolla/os* like herself); European and Indigenous (*mestizo*); Spaniard and African (*mulato*); and African, Indigenous (*zambo*), and other ethnic mixtures of Indians and Africans.[19]

Sor Juana's mother, Doña Isabel Ramírez de Santillana, and her grandfather, Pedro Ramírez de Santillana, were proprietors of two land estates outside Mexico City. The first was in Nepantla, where Sor Juana was born. The other was in Panoáyan, where she studied as a young girl in her grandfather's private library. As a *criolla*, Sor Juana's daily needs would have been attended to by the Mexica Indigenous and Black laborers who lived on the haciendas. As a young girl, she would have been exposed to their languages—Nahuatl and the Afro-Spanish Bazal—and their related religious

17. Marcos, "Embodied Religious Thought."
18. Marcos, "*Otroa compañeroa.*"
19. Burkholder and Johnson, *Colonial Latin America*, 196.

practices.²⁰ As a nun in the convent of San Jerónimo, Sor Juana would also have heard both languages from servants. Sor Juana's ability to write *villancicos* (songs) using both Nahuatl and Afro-Bazal terms demonstrates her value and competency in their language and belief systems.²¹

Like the Mexica Indigenous people, Sor Juana valued the natural world. In a poem, she described the foothills where she lived. From her view, she could see two prominent mountains. The first was Popocatépetl (in Nahuatl, Smoking mountain). The second was Iztaccíhuatl (in Nahuatl, White woman). In Spanish, this mountain is sometimes referred to as Mujer Dormida (Sleeping woman). Sor Juana says, "I was born where solar rays stared down at me from overhead, not squint-eyed, as in other climes."²² These mountains embodied a Mexica myth with which Sor Juana would have been familiar. It is:

> Iztaccíhuatl was a princess who fell in love with one of her father's warriors, Popocatépetl. The emperor sent Popocatépetl to a war in Oaxaca, promising him Iztaccíhuatl as his wife when he returned (which Iztaccíhuatl's father presumed he would not). Iztaccíhuatl was falsely told that Popocatépetl had died in battle, and believing this news, she died of grief. When Popocatépetl returned to find his love dead, he took her body to a spot outside Tenochtitlan and kneeled by her grave. The gods covered them with snow and changed them into mountains.²³

It is likely that Sor Juana learned Indigenous language and history from servants on her family's haciendas. The primacy of oral tradition in the Indigenous worldview would have enabled Sor Juana to learn more about their cosmocentric worldview. In Indigenous schools (called *calmécac* and *telpochcalli*), children were educated about their history through myths, stories, and songs—*villancicos*.²⁴ They employed a memorization system, which was instrumental for them to preserve their ancient hymns, myths, epic narratives, and other literary compositions.²⁵ In *La respuesta*, Sor Juana testifies to her capacity to easily memorize information. She states, "When I did go to Mexico City, people marveled not so much at my intelligence as at my memory and the facts I knew at an age when it seemed I had scarcely

---

20. Pamela Kirk Rappaport, in Juana, *Selected Writings*, 13.

21. Margaret Sayers Peden, in Juana, *Poems, Protest, and Dream*, xxxii; Pamela Kirk Rappaport, in Juana, *Selected Writings*, 13.

22. Paz, *Sor Juana*, 64.

23. Wikipedia, "Iztaccíhuatl," s.vv. "The Legend of Iztaccíhuatl and Popocatépetl."

24. León-Portilla, *Aztec Thought and Culture*, xxi.

25. León-Portilla, *Aztec Thought and Culture*, xvi.

had time to learn to speak" (243–46). Indigenous schools predated the conquest. Ferdinand Anton explains:

> One of the most important achievements [of the Mexica people] was the introduction of compulsory education. The date when this was done cannot be ascertained exactly; that it happened was a tremendous achievement for that time. In the Medieval Ages, when in Europe school education was a privilege of the upper classes, there was in Aztec society not a single child, of whatever origin, who grew up without it. The state took care of the education of children. With immense solicitude it tried to further civilization, to uphold morals, and to train useful subjects.[26]

By contrast, in Spanish culture, compulsory education for all children was not a requirement. In *La respuesta*, Sor Juana said that at nearly three years of age, she secretly followed her older sister to a girls' school for privileged Spanish youth called *Amigas* (214). She told the teacher that her mother "wanted her to teach [her] also," but this was not true (216). Sor Juana learned how to read before her mother found out. At six or seven years of age she pleaded with her mother to "dress [her] in men's clothes" so she could go to Mexico City to study "the sciences" (236, 238). Her mother "refused" (240). To quench Sor Juana's "desire" to learn, she read "a great variety of books that belonged to [her] grandfather" (241–42). Sor Juana comments that with "no teacher," she learned about the world "through earthly methods" (84–85, 93–94). It is highly likely that she learned these methods from the Indigenous people.

There is a question as to whether Sor Juana drank the hallucinogenic mushroom wine used in Mexica Indigenous religious rituals while she engaged in her own scholarly writing. Sor Juana's familiarity with such rituals is assumed in a sacramental drama called *El divino Narciso* (The divine Narcissus). In the prelude (*loa*) to this drama-play, an elegant Indigenous couple celebrate the tocatin dance. Both wear festive Indigenous garb, holding "feathers and bells in their hands."[27] In it, Sor Juana creatively crafts a conversation between Spanish and Indigenous people in New Spain. She highlights similarities in how each honors their gods and the "true God."[28] Sor Juana believed both peoples came from an "ancient" and "noble" heritage.[29]

26. Anton, *Women in Pre-Columbian America*, 48.
27. Juana, *Selected Writings*, 69.
28. Juana, *Selected Writings*, 81.
29. Juana, *Selected Writings*, 69.

Sor Juana's library had Indigenous books and folklore.³⁰ It is safe to assume that she had access to Indigenous and Spanish perspectives on the conquest. Though Spaniards did burn Indigenous centers of education in the Central Valley of Mexico, Miguel León-Portilla states that the Indigenous people retained linguistic competency in codices, pictographic resources, and the written word.³¹ It is hard to conceive that Sor Juana did not have access to Franciscan friar Bernadino de Sahagún's twelve-volume book collection called *The Florentine Codex*, or *General History of the Things of New Spain*, which documents Indigenous history, ritual practices, religious cosmology, culture, society, and economics. It was written in both Nahuatl and Latin. Sor Juana was versed in both languages.

The Mexica Indigenous Empire had a rich ecological legacy. Martin Medina argues that Tenochtitlan, their glorious capital city, was the first ecological city in the Americas.³² He elaborates that the Mexica people had a high regard for their natural habitat. They used all their natural resources sustainably and enacted strict consequences for those who used them wastefully. If an individual was caught exploiting the environment—especially if the person were in a leadership position—the punishment could be death. Bernal Díaz del Castillo, one of Hernán Cortés's men, describes Tenochtitlan: "When we saw so many cities and villages built in the water and the other great towns on dry land and that straight and level causeway going towards Mexico, we were amazed. And some of the soldiers even asked whether the things that we saw were not a *dream*."³³

The Mexica Indigenous people have also been recognized as the first engineers in the Americas for their innovative waste management systems, which included canals, aqueducts, and *chinampas* (floating gardens), which made it possible for them to live on land.³⁴ In *Religions of Mesoamerica*, Davíd Carrasco cites Díaz del Castillo's description of Tenochtitlan's ecological beauty:

> When we had looked well at all of this, we went to the orchard and garden, which was such a wonderful thing to see and walk in, that I was never tired of looking at the diversity of the trees, and noting the scent which each one had, and the paths full of roses and flowers, and the many fruit trees and native roses, and the pond of fresh water. There was another thing to observe,

---

30. Margaret Sayers Peden, in Juana, *Poems, Protest, and Dream*, xii.
31. León-Portilla, *Aztec Thought and Culture*, xvi.
32. Medina, "Aztecs of Mexico."
33. Carrasco, *Religions of Mesoamerica*, xiii; emphasis added.
34. Medina, "Aztecs of Mexico"; History Channel, "Engineering an Empire."

the great canoes were able to pass into the garden from the lake through an opening that had been made so that there was no need for their occupants to land. Of all these wonders that I then beheld today all is overthrown and lost, nothing left standing.[35]

Undoubtedly, Sor Juana's high valuation of the natural world was influenced by the legacy of the Mexica Indigenous people and their cosmocentric worldview.

Sor Juana's *La respuesta* (The answer), March 1691

La respuesta is Sor Juana's response to the Jesuit bishop of Puebla, Manuel Fernández de Santa Cruz. In 1690, the bishop circulated two documents relating to Sor Juana. The first document was titled *Carta atenagórica* (Letter worthy of Athena). It was a letter condemning Sor Juana for a theological treatise she wrote that criticized a sermon written by the well-known Portuguese Jesuit Antonio Vieira (1608–97). The second document was the theological treatise itself that Sor Juana had written. In *Carta atenagórica*, Fernández de Santa Cruz signed the letter using the female pseudonym Sor Filotea de la Cruz (Sister Lover of the Cross). In it, the cowardly bishop, or nun, chastised Sor Juana for spending too much time studying secular rather than sacred texts. *She*/he argued that secular study was a vain and presumptuous activity inappropriate for a professed religious. *She*/he recommended that Sor Juana focus on wisdom from above in contrast to "earthbound knowledge," which could result in her going to "hell."[36] In Sor Juana's theological treatise, she criticized Vieira's sermon, which argued that Christ's greatest *fineza* (demonstration of love) was his "encouragement of the love of human beings for each other." By contrast, Sor Juana argued that Christ's greatest *fineza* was "withholding his love in order to allow for the exercise of effort and will."[37] Sor Juana's interpretation was problematic because it allowed for free will, which gave women a voice. This interpretation threatened the church's prescription for female behavior. Ultimately, Sor Juana had a choice whether to respond to Sor Filotea's accusations of her or not. She responded: "And therefore I had nearly resolved to leave the matter in silence; yet although silence explains much by the emphasis of leaving all unexplained, because it is a negative thing, one must name the silence, so

---

35. Carrasco, *Religions of Mesoamerica*, xiv.
36. Juana, *Sor Juana Anthology*, 200.
37. Juana, *Answer*, 108.

that what it signifies may be understood. Failing that, silence will say nothing, for that is its proper function: to say nothing" (68–73).

La respuesta demonstrates characteristics of a twenty-first-century Latin American ecofeminist perspective because Sor Juana privileges women's experiences. Sor Juana challenges the argument that women are not equal to men in their capacity to reason. I believe Sor Juana's experience living in three communities of women—from her youth with a single mother and four sisters, to life in the viceroyal court as a protégé of the *virreinas* (queens), and twenty-five plus years in the convent of San Jerónimo— proved to her that women were not inferior to men because of their sex. Sor Juana disputes Sor Filotea's argument that women are incapable of reason. She also refutes the assumption of men "who simply because they are men think themselves wise" (905–6). Sor Juana critiques St. Paul's assertion that "women should be silent in the churches." Rather, she argues that the apostle's assertion "Let [them] keep silence" was meant not only for women but for all individuals "who are not competent" (944–46). Sor Juana cites the "venerable Dr. Arce," a Mexican philosopher and "Scholar of the Bible," who supported women being educated (885–86).[38] He raised the question:

> Is it permissible for women to apply themselves to the study, and indeed the interpretation, of the Holy Bible? And in opposition he presents the verdicts passed by many saints, particularly the words of [Paul] the Apostle: "*Let women keep silence in the churches: for it is not permitted them to speak,*" etc. Arce then presents differing verdicts, including this passage addressed to Titus, again spoken by the Apostle: "*The aged women, in like manner, in holy attire . . . teaching well*"; and he gives other interpretations from the Fathers of the Church. Arce at last resolves, in his prudent way, that women are not allowed to lecture publicly in the universities or to preach from the pulpits, but that studying, writing, and teaching privately is not only permitted but most beneficial and useful to them. (887–99)

Sor Juana clarifies Dr. Arce's assertion by saying that all individuals who are incompetent, whether they are a man or a woman, should be "prohibited from the interpretation of the Sacred Word" (906–7). The result, if they are permitted to interpret, is "numerous heresies" (910).

Dr. Arce comments

> that he knew two nuns in this City, one of them in the Convent of Regina, who had so thoroughly committed to memory the Divine Office that with the greatest alacrity and propriety she

---

38. Juan Díaz de Arce (d. 1653).

would apply its verses, psalms, and maxims from the homilies of the saints to all her conversations. The other, in the Convent of the Conception, was so adept in reading the Epistles of my father St. Jerome . . . that Arce says: "*I thought that I heard Jerome himself, speaking in Spanish.*" (1169–77)

Sor Juana recounts, "Of the second nun, Arce says that he learned, after her death, that she had translated those very Epistles into the Spanish language; and he grieves that such talents should not have been set to higher studies, guided by the principles of science" (1177–81).

Sor Juana identifies men who misused knowledge and points out that neither sex is exempt from abusive practices. She writes, "This is what the Divine Letters became in the hands of that wicked Pelagius and of the perverse Arius, of that wicked Luther, and all the other heretics like our own Dr. Cazalla (who was never either our own nor a doctor). Learning harmed them all" (928–32). Sor Juana declares, "To such men, I repeat, study does harm, because it is like putting a sword in the hands of a madman: though the sword be the noblest of instruments for defense, in his hands it becomes his own death and that of many others (925–28).

To support her argument that women are equal to men in their capacity to reason, Sor Juana records a "vast throng" of pagan and Christian women who were equal to or surpassed men in knowledge (855). In her litany, Sor Juana lists Christian and pagan women who "merited titles" for using their knowledge well for the advancement of their people (855). She celebrates Deborah, one of the Israelite judges, for exercising military and political leadership, while at the same time "governing the people among whom there were so many learned men" (828–29). She remembers the queen of Sheba, who used her knowledge exceedingly well and "dare[d] to test the wisdom of the wisest of all men with riddles without being rebuked for it" (831–33). She highlights Abigail for "the gift of Christian prophecy," Rahab for "piety," and Anna, who possessed the gift of "perseverance" (835–37).

Sor Juana cites pagan women such as the Sibyls who were chosen by God "to prophesy the essential mysteries of our Faith" (839–40). She includes Minerva, "the daughter of the great Jupiter," who was "adored . . . as goddess of the sciences" (842–44); Zenobia, "queen of the Palmyrians," who was recognized for her courage and wisdom; and Aspasia Miletia, who was professor in the disciplines of "philosophy and rhetoric" and teacher to the great legislator Pericles (847, 850–51). She recalls Nicostrata, well known for her mastery of Latin and Greek wisdom; Hypatia, who "taught astrology and lectured for many years in Alexandria"; and Leontium, who "won over the philosopher Theophrastus and proved him wrong" (849, 851–54). Sor

Juana concludes by declaring, "Oh, how many abuses would be avoided in our land if the older women were as well instructed" (990–91).

Sor Juana's capacity to reason is further demonstrated in her knowledge of individuals in the Bible and in the Christian tradition. They include church fathers and mothers such as St. Thomas Aquinas (8, 376–77); Mary, "the Mother of the Word" (27, 1114); St. Jerome (141, 297, 969, 1395); St. Paula (297); St. Teresa of Ávila (556, 1109); St. Augustine (947); Mary of Jesus of Ágreda (1109, 1119); Martha (1114); Mary, "the mother of Jacob" (1114–15); St. Cyprian (1127); and St. John Chrysostom (1287). Sor Juana's conversation partners included contemporary Jesuits. Her conversation partners were Athanasius Kircher from Germany (1602–80); Baltasar Gracián y Morales from Spain (1601–58); Antonio Vieira from Portugal (1608–97); Manuel Fernández de Santa Cruz (1637–99); Carlos de Sigüenza y Gongora (1645–1700); and Antonio Núñez de Miranda from New Spain (1618–95). Like the Jesuit motto, Sor Juana saw God in all things. Sor Juana concludes, "In sum, we see how this Book [the Bible] contains all books, and this Science includes all sciences, all of which serve that She may be understood" (368–70).

"El primero sueño" (First I dream/First dream), 1685

The poem "El primero sueño" reflects characteristics of a twenty-first-century Latin American ecofeminist perspective because Sor Juana privileges Indigenous thought and their cosmocentric worldview. It is an epic 975-line poem, which is estimated to have been written in 1685.[39] The Spanish word *sueño* literally translates as "sleep." It can also be used to describe a person's dreams or ambitions in life. In Sor Juana's poem, these three meanings converge in her intellectual quest for ultimate truth. Sor Juana refers to her poem as "El Sueño," a "trifle" of a text (1127). In Spain, her poem was recognized as a literary masterpiece, comparable to Spanish Baroque poet and Catholic priest Luis de Góngora's poem "Soledades" (Solitudes). In New Spain, it generated animosity between her and the ecclesiastical leaders who were envious of the recognition she was receiving in both hemispheres.[40]

In the Mexica Indigenous tradition there were esteemed poets and philosophers. In Nahuatl, these male sages were called *tlamatinimes*. León-Portilla comments that they reflected on life beyond earthly existence. In their quest to understand ultimate "truth," they wrote poetry.[41] The dream

---

39. Paz, *Sor Juana*, 357.
40. Paz, *Sor Juana*, 357.
41. León-Portilla, *Aztec Thought and Culture*, 77, 79.

metaphor was integral to their understanding of god and the universe.⁴²
In their dreams, they pondered if they could understand more about their
supreme gods and goddesses. Octavio Paz describes Sor Juana's poem as
"poetry of the intellect confronting the cosmos."⁴³ Like Nahua sages, in Sor
Juana's "El sueño," she is also a poet (*poeta*) in an intellectual quest for ultimate truth (383). In her poem, Sor Juana is a non-gendered soul. In the
Christian tradition, her soul is on a spiritual journey (*peregrinaje*), while
in the Mesoamerican tradition she is the *tonalli* (soul) that travels at night
during dreams.⁴⁴ Like the Nahua sages, Sor Juana's poem-dream "El sueño"
is an intellectual quest for ultimate truth. The natural world is prominent in
Sor Juana's poem. For example, she names *naturaleza* (108, 110, 160, 240,
420, 661, 780, 842); the sun (88, 332, 326, 372, 460, 503), the sky (2, 331,
347, 353, 357, 405, 678), and the stars (4, 287, 682) are frequently referenced.

In "El sueño," Sor Juana's soul "thrust[s] toward the Heavens, attempting to ascend and touch the Stars" (3–4). Her non-gendered soul is looking
over Sor Juana's New Spain world with markers of its pre-Columbian heritage, which included pyramids, obelisks, and goddesses (1, 3, 13). Sor Juana
narrates the history of the encounter between the Mexica Indigenous people
and Spain. In Sor Juana's dream, the people of the region are "mocked from
afar" (7). Ill omens attest to a pending "war" in the region (8). Though not
named Montezuma, the ancient Mexica Indigenous leader had an ill omen
prior to the arrival of Spaniards and the demise of Tenochtitlan.⁴⁵ Sor Juana
sees mass destruction in the form of shadows (1, 11), black vapors (9), and
darkness (18).⁴⁶ The air has been colonized (16). It is likely that Sor Juana
was familiar with the sixteenth-century text *Cantares mexicano*, which contains Nahuatl songs and poems which document the tribulations the Mexica
Indigenous people endured as a result of the encounter. The people record:

> The Aztecs are besieged in the city;
> The walls are black,
> The air is black with smoke . . .
> Our cries of grief rise up . . .
> And our tears rain down . . .
> Weep, my people:
> Know that with these disasters
> We have lost the Mexican nation.⁴⁷

42. León-Portilla, *Aztec Thought and Culture*, 71–75.
43. Paz, *Sor Juana*, 358.
44. Paz, *Sor Juana*, 360; Marcos, *Taken From the Lips*, 6.
45. Schwartz, *Victors and Vanquished*, 29–31.
46. Juana, *Poems, Protest, and Dream*, 79.
47. León-Portilla, *Broken Spears*, 211.

Before the encounter, it was a "quiet" and "silent kingdom" (19-20). The Roman goddess of the moon, Diana, illuminates the region with her beauty (13-15). Her light outshines the darkness, and Sor Juana continues to move "toward the Heavens" and sees the glorious pyramids, over and against "muted voices" and "silence" (3, 21, 24).

Sor Juana's "soul" (*Alma*) is a "beauteous essence and disincarnate being . . . made in His image . . . the Divine she bears within" (540, 293, 295-96). Her "Soul [is] dazed by the enormity of all that lay before her eyes, regained her concentration, although, embracing such diversity, unable still to rid herself of the prodigious awe that had paralyzed her reason" (540-46).[48]

> The Soul's aspiring flight,
> ever higher through the atmosphere,
> consigned of its own mind a portion
> to heaven's farthest heights,
> ascending so far above itself, it
> fancied it soared to some new region.[49] (429-34)

Unlike the Christian tradition, which elevates one male God, Sor Juana's dream, like the Indigenous tradition, is polytheistic and includes many gods and goddesses. In it, she narrates the challenges of women. For example, the Roman and Greek goddess Nyctímene—a princess and the daughter of Epopeus, a king of Lesbos—is raped by her father and is "humiliated" (27). She hides at the crevice of the "sacred doors" (27). Like Sor Juana, Nyctímene engaged in "sacrilegious" behavior by drawing near to the "holy lamps" in the church (32-33). The goddess Minerva takes pity on Nyctímene, turning her into an owl and keeping her as a companion (38). The "three . . . audacious Sisters," daughters of Minyas, who were disobedient to the Roman god, Bacchus, are dishonored and "hideously transformed" (41, 43, 48).

Sor Juana's poem "El sueño," like the Mexica Indigenous Nahua sages, sought ultimate truth. Her dream concludes with the presence of the planet Venus, who is also the Roman goddess of love (744). Venus is the brightest star to shine over the whole universe. It is my belief that the goddess Venus for Sor Juana would bring the east (Spain) and the west (New Spain)

---

48. In Spanish, "Alma, que asombrada de la vista quedó de objecto tanto, la atención regió, que derramada en diversidad tanta, aun no sabía recobrarse a sí misma del espanto que portentoso había su discurso calmado."

49. In Spanish, "Ambicioso anhelo, hacienda cumbre de su propio vuelo, en las más eminente la encumbró parte de su propia mente, de sí tan remontada, que creía que a otra nueva región de sí salía."

together in harmony. In this harmonious world, Huitzilopochtli, the Aztec sun god, and Jesus, the Son of God, would be equally respected for the ancient wisdom that each held in their respective traditions. At the end of her *sueño*, Sor Juana wakes up surrounded by light, presumably that of Venus. I suggest that this light, for Sor Juana, indicates the possibility of an authentic and real harmony between Spaniards and non-Spaniards. Sadly, Sor Juana did not see this *sueño* actualized in her lifetime.

Conclusion

In the twenty-first century, Sor Juana Inés de la Cruz is a precursor Latina feminist and ecofeminist in the spirit of these contemporary terms for her high esteem for the importance and worth of women, *naturaleza*, and Indigenous wisdom. In her era, Sor Juana was bold in her valuation of Mexica Indigenous knowledge systems as a means of understanding the world around her. At the time, there was antagonism between the Amerindians and Europeans.[50] Distinct from her male peers, Sor Juana's primary texts, *La respuesta* and "El primero sueño," affirmed the rich legacies of both peoples. In the process, like Latina ecofeminists today, she engaged in the practice of reimagining Judeo-Christian history and theology from both a feminist and an Indigenous perspective. Moreover, Sor Juana *yearned* for more just relationships among women, God, creation, people, and land. In our time, Sor Juana's contribution to Latina ecofeminism was her desire for harmony between the Spanish and the Indigenous peoples in her New Spain world. She is also a resource for Indigenous environmental resisters in Mexico, many of whom have been martyred for their efforts to safeguard the environment.[51] Tomás Rojo, *presenté*!

Bibliography

Anton, Ferdinand. *Women in Pre-Columbian America*. New York: Schram, 1973.
Associated Press. "A New Report Labels Mexico as the World's Deadliest Spot for Environmental Activists." NPR, Sept. 29, 2022. https://www.npr.org/2022/09/29/1125854118/a-new-report-labels-mexico-as-the-worlds-deadliest-spot-for-environmental-activi.
Burkholder, Mark A., and Lyman L. Johnson. *Colonial Latin American History*. 6th ed. Oxford: Oxford University Press, 2007.
Caria, Sara, and Rafael Domínguez. "Ecuador's *Buen vivir*: A New Ideology of Development." *Latin American Perspectives* 43 (2016) 18–33.

50. Kirk, *Sor Juana*, 17.
51. Associated Press, "New Report Labels Mexico."

Carrasco, David. *Religions of Mesoamerica: Cosmovision and Ceremonial Centers.* Chicago: Waveland, 1990.
Gebara, Ivone. *Intuiciones ecofeministas: Ensayo para repensar el conocimiento y la religión.* Montivedeo: Trotta, 2000.
History Channel. "Engineering an Empire: The Aztecs (S1, E3)." YouTube, July 25, 2020. https://www.youtube.com/watch?v=bK4ypIfEkjg.
Juana Inés de la Cruz. *The Answer/La respuesta.* Edited and translated by Electa Arenal and Amanda Powell. 2nd ed. New York: Feminist, 2009.
——. *Poems, Protest, and a Dream: Selected Writings.* Translated by Margaret Sayers Peden. Penguin Classics. New York: Penguin, 1997.
——. *Selected Writings.* Edited by Pamela Kirk Rappaport. Classics in Western Spirituality. Mahwah, NJ: Paulist, 2005.
——. *A Sor Juana Anthology.* Translated by Alan S. Trueblood. Cambridge: Harvard University Press, 1988.
Kirk, Stephanie. *Sor Juana Inés de la Cruz and the Politics of Knowledge in Colonial Mexico.* New Hispanisms: Cultural and Literary Studies. London: Routledge, 2016.
León-Portilla, Miguel. *Aztec Thought and Culture: A Study of the Ancient Nahuatl Mind.* Norman: University of Oklahoma, 1990.
——. *The Broken Spears: The Aztec Account of the Conquest.* Boston: Beacon, 2007.
Magaloni Kerpel, Diana. *The Colors of the New World: Artists, Materials, and the Creation of the Florentine Codex.* Los Angeles: Getty Trust, 2014.
Marcos, Sylvia. "Embodied Religious Thought." In *Gender/Bodies/Religions,* edited by Sylvia Marcos, 69–83. Mexico City: ALER, 2000.
——. "*Otroa compañeroa*: A Contemporary Gender Identity in Mexico, Based on Ancestral Mesoamerican Legacy." YouTube, Apr. 21, 2022. https://www.youtube.com/watch?v=1M5XnOqfPVU.
——. *Taken from the Lips: Gender and Eros in Mesoamerican Religions.* Religion in the Americas 5. Leiden: Brill, 2006.
Medina, Martin. "The Aztecs of Mexico: A Zero Waste Society." Our World, Apr. 21, 2014. https://ourworld.unu.edu/en/the-aztecs-of-mexico-a-zero-waste-society.
Merrim, Stephanie. *Feminist Perspectives on Sor Juana Inés de la Cruz.* Detroit: Wayne State University Press, 1991.
Paz, Octavio. *Sor Juana, or, The Traps of Faith.* Cambridge, MA: Belknap, 1988.
Ruether, Rosemary Radford. *Sexism and God-Talk: Toward a Feminist Theology.* Boston: Beacon, 1983.
Ress, Mary Judy. *Ecofeminism in Latin America.* Women from the Margins. Maryknoll, NY: Orbis, 2006.
Schwartz, Stuart B. *Victors and Vanquished: Spanish and Nahua Views of the Conquest of Mexico.* Boston: Bedford, 2000.
Scott, Nina M., ed. *Madres del verbo/Mothers of the Word: Early Spanish American Women Writers.* Albuquerque: University of New Mexico, 1999.
Socolow, Susan Migden. *The Women of Colonial Latin America.* New Approaches to the Americas. Cambridge: Cambridge University Press, 2000.
Wikipedia. "Iztaccihuatl." Wikipedia, last edited Feb. 9, 2025. https://en.wikipedia.org/wiki/Iztaccihuatl.
Yugar, Theresa A. *Sor Juana Inés de la Cruz: Feminist Reconstruction of Biography and Text.* Eugene, OR: Wipf & Stock, 2014.

4

Afro-Latin American Religious Practices in the Iberian Colonies

JOAN CAMERON BRISTOL

AFRO-LATIN AMERICAN RITUAL PRACTICES in the Spanish and Portuguese American colonies were as varied as the Afro-Latin American people who participated in religious life during more than three centuries of colonial rule. West and West Central Africans brought deities and knowledge about healing methods to the Americas and adapted them for their new lives in the Iberian colonies. Africans and their American descendants adopted practices and ritual materials from Indigenous Americans and Spaniards. Afro-Latin Americans created specific practices to help them deal with the difficulties associated with enslavement and the racism that affected many aspects of their lives. Africans and their descendants practiced Catholicism in both orthodox and unorthodox forms. Afro-Latin Americans joined colonial residents of all races and classes to practice syncretic rituals that helped them deal with the often difficult material and ideological conditions of life in the Iberian colonies. Religious practice was an arena in which people of African descent created communities and formed individual relationships outside of communities, created and maintained identities, and shaped life in Iberian America during the colonial period and after.

The experiences and ritual lives of Africans and people of African descent were affected by many factors, including location, gender, time period, class and caste, and status as enslaved or free. West and West Central Africans, most but not all enslaved, first arrived in the Americas in the early 1500s with Spanish and Portuguese colonizers and continued to arrive throughout the colonial period and after; between 1501 and 1857, about 12.5 million

Africans were forcibly transported to the Americas. The Atlantic slave trade peaked in the eighteenth century but continued well into the nineteenth century, long past the abolition of the legal slave trade. Of the over 10 million captives who survived the brutal transatlantic journey, the majority went to Iberian American colonies: more than 5.5 million African captives were forcibly transported to Brazil, and over a million Africans were trafficked to Spanish America.[1] The bulk of the remaining numbers went to the British, French, and Dutch Caribbean plantation islands. Enslaved Africans embarked on European slave ships from West and West Central African ports, although many were captured from interior regions and suffered long journeys before arriving at the coast. Both men and women were trafficked across the Atlantic. The gender ratio of captives varied by time and place, although overall more African men than women were transported across to the Americas. This imbalance occurred because the demand for female slaves was greater in Africa and thus fewer women than men were sold into the transatlantic trade, and also because European enslavers preferred male workers over female. European enslavers also showed a preference for youth over age.

Colonial Afro-Latin Americans were a diverse group for reasons other than geography, gender, and time period. Afro-Latin Americans occupied different class statuses and racial categories in the Iberian colonies. They were not all enslaved: sizable populations of free people of African descent lived in the Iberian colonies, and their numbers grew over time. A few Africans arrived as free people, and more Africans and African-descent people became free in the Americas. Enslaved people earned money to buy their freedom by hiring out their services and selling agricultural products, and enslavers also manumitted enslaved people, often in their wills. Maroon communities of formerly enslaved people who had escaped bondage also lived freely and at times created small empires, like the famous example of Palmares in northeastern Brazil. Smaller maroon communities existed in Mexico, Ecuador, Hispaniola, Colombia, and elsewhere. Afro-Latin Americans, enslaved and free, occupied a variety of racial categories: while Africans, particularly those who were recently arrived, were identified as "Black," *negro* in Spanish America and Brazil, those with Afro-European and Afro-Indigenous parentage were identified through a number of labels, including *mulato* in Spanish America and *pardo* in Brazil. Spanish and Portuguese authorities developed complicated systems of caste labels that, while not always used on a daily basis, reflected the degree of racial diversity in the Iberian colonies. These caste or racial labels also testified

---

1. See https://www.slavevoyages.org/assessment/estimates.

to the anxieties of colonial authorities; faced with increasingly mixed and fluidly defined populations of subjugated people, elites and imperial officials tried to control the population by labeling, stereotyping, and restricting non-Europeans' opportunities. Thus Afro-Latin Americans had varied life experiences, cultural practices, and social roles, and they had diverse identities. This diversity is reflected in the variety of ritual practices in which Afro-Latin Americans engaged.

Sources for Understanding Afro-Latin American Practice

When examining the ritual lives of Afro-Latin Americans it is important to consider the sources historians use to understand the past, and this is particularly pressing when thinking about the past of non-elite people who did not leave many first-person accounts. Scholars use colonial sources to understand colonial practices, and these sources often have particular viewpoints. Records such as legislation, catechisms, prayer books, chronicles, ecclesiastical accounts, Inquisition records, and criminal records are essential for understanding the lives of ordinary colonial residents, but these texts give us a limited view of religious practice, only in part because a large gulf of time separates us from the people we study. More importantly, such sources were produced for specific reasons: the Iberian colonial authorities who created these records were charged with maintaining order, enforcing Catholic mores, and ensuring that social hierarchies based on white supremacy prevailed. When describing Afro-Latin Americans' Catholic practice, colonial officials tried to create a picture of orthodox compliance in which Indigenous and African-descent people practiced orderly forms of Catholicism, although in most places Iberian religious leaders were more interested in evangelizing Indigenous people than African-descent people. Thus ecclesiastical records, descriptions of Masses and religious plays, and confession manuals give us a sense of Afro-Latin Americans' normative Catholic practice. For less orthodox practices we often rely on records that were produced in a more punitive setting, such as trial records, particularly those from the Inquisition, in which colonizers recorded information about religious practices that they found problematic, such as practices that they labeled "witchcraft," as well as blasphemy, bigamy, and other crimes. Sources that sought to reveal heretical behavior, such as Inquisition records, may give us a sense of Afro-Latin Americans' voices and ideas because they record the testimonies of witnesses and accused people. However, such sources are not transparent; they were still produced in courtrooms controlled by colonial officials, the words recorded by colonial scribes. These records still leave us with questions about participants' motivations and activities. Thus we must read all historical sources with an understanding of the reasons these texts were produced and the arguments authorities were making through these records, while also paying attention to the actions of non-elite subjects.

The remainder of this essay discusses specific religious practices. The first section discusses the practices that colonial Afro-Latin Americans engaged in outside of church control and sometimes in defiance of colonial authorities. The second part examines Afro-Latin American participation in state-sanctioned Catholic practices. There are two points to keep in mind while thinking about these religious practices. First, a discussion of Afro-Latin American religion is necessarily a discussion of more general colonial Latin American ritual practice. Afro-Latin Americans practiced religious rituals alongside people of all races and classes, sharing knowledge and engaging in collective activities. A second point to keep in mind is that the categories used in this essay are heuristic and somewhat schematic. In reality, colonial residents practiced Catholic and non-Catholic rituals simultaneously. Those suffering an illness might consult a ritual healer to investigate possible witchcraft possession while also praying to the Virgin Mary and at the same time consulting a licensed physician. Ritual healers themselves might use Christian prayers or images, along with herbs and their knowledge of witchcraft, in their attempts to cure their patients. African-based religious practices grew in Catholic organizations like confraternities, brotherhoods, and cabildos. Colonial Afro-Latin Americans and other colonial residents often did not see any contradiction between what we might now see as the two separate categories of sanctioned Catholic practices and the unsanctioned ritual practices that the church fought to suppress.

Religious Practice Outside the Catholic Church

Afro-Latin Americans and others engaged in a variety of ritual practices that were often outside church control. Many of these unorthodox practices involved healing bodies, emotions, and social imbalances, and they drew on African, Indigenous American, and European ritual traditions. As mentioned above, much of our information about non-Catholic practices comes from Inquisition and criminal cases that investigated potentially heretical practices that colonial officials labeled "magic" or "witchcraft." In addition to worrying that unorthodox practices might be heretical, colonial officials were suspicious of practitioners who asserted authority that challenged the power that European colonial officials claimed by virtue of their race and class.

Afro-Latin American and other healers drew on knowledge about the visible material world as well as the unseen, spiritual world of deities and supernatural power to cure a variety of maladies. One set of rituals involved curing physical ills. Most colonial residents believed that while disease could originate in the physical body, caused by an imbalance in Galenic humors, illness and misfortune could be caused by forces outside the body as well. Such outside forces included demonic possession and the ill will of other humans or spirits; people could harm each other inadvertently through jealous thoughts and angry feelings. People could also cause each other harm on purpose, using objects or incantations that invited diabolic forces. These kinds of illness and problems could be cured by supernatural means. Because an illness could be caused by the actions and desires of other people, healing one person's misfortune could mean causing problems for another.

Afro-Latin American and Indigenous healers used many tools, including materials like herbs, roots, and plants, the bones, hair, nails, body fluids, and the bodily secretions and parts of humans and animals. Healers also availed themselves of Christian, Indigenous, and African images and invocations. Healers' knowledge was based in an understanding of the properties of these materials as well as an understanding of the rituals that made the materials powerful. We see this in the curing practices of the eighteenth-century West African Gbe-speaking healer Domingos Álvares in Brazil. When Álvares cut the feet of enslaved people and rubbed herbs in the wounds in order to protect them from illness caused by the evil of others, he did not expect the herbs to work because of the physical properties of the plants themselves. Instead, Álvares was able to activate the protective power of these herbs through his knowledge of how to administer them and his connection to the deities of the spiritual world.[2] When the seventeenth-century Mexican Eurafrican (labeled *mulata*) healer Ana de Vega treated an ailing Spanish woman, she administered purgatives, but the purgatives were not the healing mechanism. Instead, when Vega found a worm in the woman's feces, the healer was able to diagnose her patient's illness, which Vega claimed was caused by the witchcraft of a relative. She prescribed powders to kill the relative who had used the witchcraft to cause the illness. Thus, although Vega used medicines on her patient's body, the healer did not cure her by expelling the worm. Rather Vega cured her patient by divining the cause of her illness and by trying to put an end to the witchcraft that was harming her.[3] We see here that materials such as herbs, purgatives, and other objects could heal only when administered by a knowledgeable

---

2. Sweet, *Domingos Álvares*, 101.
3. Bristol, *Christians, Blasphemers, and Witches*, 183.

practitioner who understood the rituals that made the materials powerful. Afro-Latin Americans like Álvares, Vega, and many others earned money and gained authority and reputation through such knowledge. Given that we know about both Álvares and Vega through their Inquisition trail records, these healing practices, and the authority they accrued, could also put ritual curers in the path of colonial authorities and invite punishment.

Colonial Afro-Latin Americans and others also cured social ills with ritual practice. For example, a set of practices sometimes called "love magic" was designed to attract and control romantic partners. Colonial residents of all races and classes consulted Indigenous and African-descent curers for medicines that would bind lovers to them or punish romantic partners if they strayed; such cures often involved women adding substances such as menstrual blood or herbs into men's food and drink. While the use of these techniques was widespread, enslaved Afro-Latin Americans had a special use for such rituals, linked to their conditions of servitude. In Mexico enslaved people bought powders from Native American sellers and put them in their owners' chocolate and clothing to make their owners kinder to them. Enslaved Afro-Brazilians and others also used amulets containing objects, including written prayers, hair, feathers, and seeds, to protect themselves from their masters. These amulets had connections to West and West Central African customs of wearing pouches containing herbs, beads, and shells to protect wearers from evil and to prevent specific illnesses: in West Africa Muslims wore *grigri* containing Koranic verses, and in West Central Africa Kongo ritual specialists sold protective charms or amulets *(minkisi)*. Such amulets were meant to protect their wearers from harm caused by the ill will and witchcraft of people or spirits. Iberians also had traditions of wearing protective bags with papers containing prayers and other objects. Thus Afro-Latin Americans drew on the array of tools and knowledge at their disposal to cure their patients of a variety of ills.

As we see in these examples, enslaved and free Afro-Latin Americans did not merely use these curing methods when they suffered their own misfortunes. Afro-Latin Americans also acted as practitioners along with Indigenous curers, dispensing medicines and enacting the rituals surrounding them. Their patients came from all social groups; Europeans of all classes often consulted Afro-Latin American and Indigenous practitioners in time of need, paying them and submitting their bodies to them. Afro-Latin American and other healers' ritual practices brought people comfort and healed them, but this work reverberated beyond individual experiences. Through their ideas and techniques, healers contributed important elements to Latin American cultural and religious traditions.

In some parts of Latin America, African-based ritual practices continue to play a role in healing bodies and relationships and in building communities. In the eighteenth and nineteenth centuries Brazil and the Spanish Caribbean had larger and more recently arrived African populations than other parts of Iberian America, and in these areas Afro-Latin Americans developed established African-based religions, such as Santería or Lucumí in Cuba, Candomblé in Brazil (especially associated with Salvador de Bahia), and the closely related vodoun in the French colony of San Domingue, later Haiti. Such African-based religious practices are closely connected to West Africa, particularly the Yoruba and Fon areas (present-day Nigeria and Benin), as well as West Central Africa, particularly the Congo-Angola region. African captives from these regions arrived in large numbers in Brazil and the Caribbean in the eighteenth and nineteenth centuries and brought their deities with them. Yoruba and other deities, called orishas, orixás, *nkisi* (from Kongo), and vodun in different areas, as well as ancestors, became central to the African-based religions in these areas, and they continue to be important today. For example, Ogun, the god of iron and metal work in West Africa, is venerated in Brazilian Candomblé as well as Cuban santería (as Oggun) and Haitian vodoun. At times West African deities became fused with Catholic saints, so that Ogun is variously identified with St. George, St. Anthony, and St. Michael in different areas.[4] Deities and adherents relate to each other in these African-based religions through possession; powerful followers, women as well as men, can become possessed by the deity during collective ceremonies characterized by drumming and other music, dancing, and movement; all the senses are engaged during these ceremonies. While the initiates are in this state, devotees can approach them as if they are the deity and ask for aid, be healed, and communicate in other ways. These religious practices gave enslaved and exploited colonial Afro-Latin Americans power and helped them form communities.

West and West Central African practices were not transplanted to the Americas wholesale. Practices changed through contact with Africans from different regions, through contact with Indigenous Americans and Europeans, and because of the new environment of the Americas. Enslaved Africans from different areas contributed practices to these African American religions, so that Kongo as well as Fon and Yoruba elements are strong in Haitian vodoun and Brazilian Candomblé. Africans and their descendants also combined elements of Catholic practices with African practices. They did this by incorporating Catholic prayers and images of saints into healing practices, as well as through participation in Catholic institutions. In Cuba

---

4. Lawuyi, "Ogun," 127.

slaves venerated their deities in *cabildos*, mutual aid societies based around specific African ethnic identities. Worshippers combined ideas about African deities with Catholic saints. Confraternities, discussed below, also served as sites of incorporation of African and Catholic deities. African-based practices continue to be widely important in Brazil and the Caribbean and no longer have to be concealed as they were under colonial rule.

Officially Sanctioned Catholic Practice

Iberian Americans of every group were required to practice Catholicism, which was central to Latin American colonialism and to the Atlantic slave trade that initially brought most Africans to the region. Christian practice provided a justification for the Atlantic exploration that led to the Atlantic slave trade and to Iberian colonization; theoretically Iberians explored the Atlantic in order to spread Christianity, receiving this right in a series of late fifteenth-century papal bulls. In the 1494 Treaty of Tordesillas Pope Alexander gave Spain jurisdiction over the area to the west of the line of Tordesillas, an imaginary line in the Atlantic Ocean 370 leagues west of Iberia. He gave Portugal the right to trade and rule the lands to the east. In exchange, Iberian monarchs agreed to convert any inhabitants they encountered, even if by force. While many nonclerical explorers and traders did not prioritize Christianization, some Europeans took seriously the mission to spread Christianity. Catholic missionaries, eventually including Jesuits after their sixteenth-century founding, evangelized African nobles. Catholic missionaries were particularly successful in the kingdom of Kongo, where the king adopted Catholicism as the state religion in the 1490s, and in neighboring regions in West Central Africa. French Capuchins and others worked to spread Christianity in West Africa as well, beginning in the seventeenth century, with varying results. Most Spanish and Portuguese ecclesiastics accepted that the enslavement of Africans was justified although some questioned its legality. Even the famous Alonso de Sandoval, a seventeenth-century Jesuit who cared for newly arrived enslaved Africans in Cartagena and argued that they should be treated better and taught about Christianity, accepted that Africans were meant to be enslaved, in part so that they could be exposed to Christian teachings.[5]

Conversion within the context of the slave trade was less effective. By the end of the fifteenth century Portuguese merchants were trading for enslaved people in forts along the African coast, and by the mid-sixteenth century Portuguese missionaries were baptizing slaves in trading posts in

5. Sandoval, *Tratado sobre la esclavitud*.

Africa.[6] However, the exigencies of commerce took precedence over conversion. With little evangelization, and suffering emotional and physical distress, enslaved Africans often had no idea what was happening during ceremonies of mass baptism conducted in European languages that were foreign to them. Colonial Spanish American clerics acknowledged this, complaining that enslaved Africans arrived in the Americas unbaptized and without any knowledge of the Catholic practice they were expected to follow. Thus, enslaved Africans arriving in the Iberian colonies came with varying degrees of Catholic indoctrination: while people from certain regions might have been somewhat familiar with Christianity before capture, enslaved Africans whose first contact with Catholicism was through hasty baptism ceremonies in slave trading forts were usually Christian in name only.

Despite the ineffective nature of coastal baptisms, once African captives reached the colonies, Iberian authorities defined them as Christians; theoretically only Catholics were allowed to enter the Americas. This rule was meant to exclude Muslims and Jews as well as African ritual practitioners. Yet evangelization and education efforts aimed at Africans and their descendants in the Iberian colonies were uneven. Theoretically enslavers were responsible for the religious education of those they enslaved, although allowing workers time for education and fulfilling the sacraments ran counter to enslavers' desires to take advantage of their labor as much as possible. However, in some cases enslavers, as well as Jesuits, Dominicans, and members of other religious orders, undertook the responsibility for religious education. Experience was probably more effective than formal evangelization, however: Africans and their Latin American descendants learned about Christian practice by attending church services as well as the public religious events that were common spectacles in colonial Latin America, such as festivals, religious plays, religious processions during liturgical festivals, and inquisitorial autos de fé, ceremonies in which convicted heretics were punished in centrally located urban areas. Such public displays taught Afro-Latin Americans and their fellow colonial residents what was expected of them as Catholic imperial subjects.

Afro-Latin Americans, free and enslaved, practiced orthodox Christianity in much the same ways as their fellow colonial Latin Americans of other races and classes. Afro-Latin Americans attended church services and public festivals such as Corpus Christi; they observed the sacraments, baptizing their children and marrying within the church; they owned religious objects such as images of the saints and the Virgin Mary; and if they had

---

6. Miller, *Way of Death*, 402–4.

enough money they left funds for Masses to be said for their souls after death. Some Afro-Latin Americans devoted their lives to Christian practice; although non-Europeans were not permitted to become priests in Iberian America, free people of African descent and Indigenous men took minor orders, were tonsured, became lay brothers, and occasionally were able to profess as friars and even priests. The priest José Morelos y Pavón, an important figure in early nineteenth-century Mexican independence, is commonly understood to have been designated *mulato*, or Eurafrican, at birth.[7] African and Afro-Latin American women also participated in church institutions. While non-European women were restricted from taking holy orders as nuns, due to racist ideas as well as the difficulties of raising money for dowries, some enslaved women who worked in convents followed the customs of the nuns they served. A formerly enslaved Black woman named Úrsula de Jesús became a *donada*, or lay sister, in Lima's convent of Santa Clara in the seventeenth century. Because of Úrsula de Jesús's piety and mystical experiences, her confessor encouraged her to record her experiences, giving us a rare look at the life of a colonial Black woman in her own words.[8] In seventeenth-century Puebla, Discalced Carmelite nuns and male clerics urged an enslaved West African woman named Juana Esperanza de San Alberto to take orders as a nun on her deathbed. They took this unusual step because, over the decades that Juana Esperanza spent decades serving the convent's nuns, she had acquired a reputation for the piety, humility, and asceticism that were hallmarks of the order. Juana Esperanza's example enhanced the convent's reputation.[9] The fact that these Black women's experiences of taking holy orders were unusual reminds us that Catholic practices, like all colonial practices, were hierarchical and based in ideas of white supremacy. Úrsula and Juana Esperanza were exceptions, yet their stories remind us that Catholic practice played a significant role in the lives of Afro-Latin American women.

A more common way that enslaved and free Afro-Latin Americans participated in Catholic life was through membership in confraternities, lay organizations often based in parish churches and organized around devotion to particular saints and the chapels that housed them. Confraternity members' most public activities involved dressing the statues of the saints and parading with them on important days in the liturgical calendar, including Corpus Christi, Holy Week, and saints' days. Confraternities had other functions as well. They functioned as mutual aid societies, supporting

7. Leslie, *African Experience in Spanish America*, 139.
8. Ursula de Jesús, *Souls of Purgatory*.
9. Bristol, *Christians, Blasphemers, and Witches*, 23–24.

members when they were ill or suffering and paying for members' funerals. Africans and their descendants belonged to mixed confraternities and also formed their own groups restricted to those of African descent. In some cases, members of slave confraternities bought the freedom of enslaved members in addition to their more standard mutual aid functions. These organizations also gave enslaved and free Afro-Latin Americans opportunities for social enhancement by serving as officers of the group. In many areas these groups encouraged the maintenance or formation of identities based on African origin—in Mexico, Peru, Argentina, and Brazil confraternities were formed for people from specific African ethnic groups. In eighteenth-century Rio de Janeiro there were several confraternities for Minas, a West African identity group from present-day Benin.[10] In other cases confraternities were formed around racial identities, such as Black and Mulatto confraternities formed in Mexico.[11]

In some cases, elites and government officials suspected confraternities of being sites of rebellion. In early seventeenth-century Mexico City, rumors circulated that Black confraternities were conspiring to overthrow Spanish rule and put their own rulers in power. While these reports were likely false, officials responded by arresting and brutally executing the leaders of prominent Black confraternities in 1612, leaving their severed body parts on pikes to serve as a warning to others who might try to revolt.[12] While this rumor seems to have reflected Spanish fears more than reality, religious affiliation and organizations did in fact allow enslaved and free people to form communities, and at times community members conspired against colonial authorities. In 1835 enslaved West African Hausa and Yoruba Muslims led a revolt, known as the Malê uprising, in Salvador de Bahia. They sought to upend colonial society by taking power from Portuguese colonial leaders. The leaders of the uprising were influenced by Islamic ideas of equality and freedom, which circulated widely in Bahia at the time.[13] In response, Portuguese authorities suppressed the Muslim leadership and forbade Arabic writings. Their actions reflected the religious foundation of the movement. The revolutionary potential of slave religion was most fully realized in the French colony of Saint-Domingue, now Haiti, where in 1791 a slave revolt began with a vodoun ceremony and, after a long and bloody war involving many social classes, ended with Haitian independence. While vodoun is not central to the extended story of the Haitian Revolution, the story of the vodoun ceremony is a reminder that religion was connected to

10. Sweet, *Domingos Álvares*, 85.
11. Germeten, *Black Blood Brothers*.
12. Martinez, "Black Blood of New Spain."
13. Reis, *Slave Rebellion in Brazil*.

a feeling of African identity, a desire for justice, and a sense of action and purpose among enslaved people.

Conclusion

This essay has tried to provide a sense of the depth and breadth of Afro-Latin American religious practice in the Iberian colonies. Colonial Afro-Latin Americans themselves were a diverse group. Those whom we consider part of this group were born in many different locations in West and West Central Africa and across Spanish and Portuguese America. Depending on the time, place, and other conditions of their birth, Afro-Latin Americans were raised with different ideas about the methods and purposes of religious ritual. Class and material conditions affected religious practice as well—enslaved people had different religious needs than free people, rural people had different needs than urban people. Age and gender also affected how Afro-Latin Americans approached religious practice.

Religion played a variety of roles in the lives of Afro-Latin Americans. Religious ritual, including Catholic as well as other practices, provided solace and healing, both spiritual and physical, in times of trouble. Religion created communities, as devotees of various deities gathered together in groups to venerate their orishas and saints. At times these organizations were limited to Afro-Latin Americans, but often these groups included Indigenous, European, and other members of colonial society. Religion provided Afro-Latin Americans a way to resist the dehumanizing aspects of enslavement and colonial rule in multiple ways: individuals gained authority through their ritual knowledge and healing practices, and they formed independent communities around the veneration of specific orishas and saints. Just as religion always evolves to meet the changing needs of its devotees, Africans and their American descendants adapted their ritual lives to the conditions of life in the Americas, but they often retained their deities and cultural cohesion through their religious practices. Even while practicing church-sanctioned Catholicism this was true: confraternities, although monitored by Iberian clerics, allowed Africans and their descendants to form communities along ethnic lines that helped individuals navigate colonial life. Catholic practice was not just a screen to hide African practices, however; Catholicism itself was important to many Afro-Latin Americans, who fulfilled the sacraments and devoted themselves to Catholic practice. Colonial authorities at times feared that ritual practice could spur rebellion, and in places like Haiti and Rio de Janeiro, religion did play a role in uprisings, for the great number of colonial Afro-Latin Americans religion provided solace and community rather than the means or motivation to stage large scale revolts.

Several millions of Africans arrived in Iberia's American colonies over hundreds of years, and their descendants, many of whom fall under the category of Afro-Latin American, populated the region. The physical and ideological mixing that occurred in Iberian America under colonialism makes it difficult to draw distinct lines between Afro-Latin American colonial practices and the practices of other groups. This fluidity also suggests that colonial Latin American religious practice was shaped by Afro-Latin Americans to a large degree. We see clearly the religious influence of Afro-Latin Americans in the African-based practices of the Caribbean and Brazil, but we must remember the influence of Africans and their descendants when we look at religious practice, including Catholic practice, all over the region.

Bibliography

Bristol, Joan Cameron. *Christians, Blasphemers, and Witches: Afro-Mexican Ritual Practice in the Seventeenth Century*. Diálogos. Albuquerque: University of New Mexico Press, 2007.

Germeten, Nicole von. *Black Blood Brothers: Confraternities and Social Mobility for Afro-Mexicans*. History of African-American Religions. Gainesville: University of Florida Press, 2006.

Lawuyi, Olatunde Bayo. "Ogun: Diffusion Across Boundaries and Identity Constructions." *African Studies Review* 31 (1988) 127–39. https://doi.org/10.2307/524422.

Martínez, María Elena. "The Black Blood of New Spain: *Limpieza de sangre*, Racial Violence, and Gendered Power in Early Colonial Mexico." *William and Mary Quarterly* 61 (2004) 479–520.

Miller, Joseph C. *Way of Death: Merchant Capitalism and the Angolan Slave Trade, 1730–1830*. Madison: University of Wisconsin Press, 1988.

Reis, Joaõ José. *Slave Rebellion in Brazil: The Muslim Uprising of 1835 in Bahia*. Translated by Arthur Brakel. Baltimore: Johns Hopkins University Press, 1993.

Rout, Leslie B., Jr. *The African Experience in Spanish America, 1502 to the Present Day*. Cambridge Latin American Studies 23. Cambridge: Cambridge University Press, 1976.

Sandoval, Alonso de. *Un tratado sobre la esclavitud*. Translated by Enriqueta Vila Vilar. Madrid: Alianza, 1987.

Sweet, James H. *Domingos Álvares, African Healing, and the Intellectual History of the Atlantic World*. Chapel Hill: University of North Carolina Press, 2011.

Ursula de Jesús. *The Souls of Purgatory: The Spiritual Diary of a Seventeenth-Century Afro-Peruvian Mystic, Ursula de Jesús*. Translated by Nancy E. van Deusen. Diálogos. Albuquerque: University of New Mexico Press, 2004.

Section Two

The Story of Christianity Expressed in a Grand Church Family Mosaic: National States and the Rise of Modern Christianity

5

Christianity, Nationalism, and Anticlericalism in Nineteenth-Century Latin America

Francisco J. Peláez-Díaz

Latin America is a mosaic of experiences regarding the long and complicated relationship between national identity, political and economic paradigm changes, and Christianity, particularly Roman Catholicism. This chapter explains some of the central dynamics in the origin and development of clericalism and nationalism in Latin America in the nineteenth century. In this period, some defining events and ideological shifts brought profound reconfigurations politically, socially, culturally, and economically to the entire region. Despite the diverse ways each nation experienced those shifts, some common phenomena involving the Catholic Church and the formation process of national identity can be identified: First, the long-held socioeconomic and political power of the Catholic Church that was profoundly linked to the colonial enterprise faced formidable challenges before the winds of independence started to blow in the region. Second, those winds of independence were nurtured not only by the revolutions that took place toward the end of the previous century in France and the United States that inspired and laid down some of the principles of liberal democracy but also by domestic and international political events during the Napoleonic era in Europe. These events contributed significantly to the weakening of the Spanish and Portuguese empires, whose main colonial dominion was in the Americas. As a result of such a weakened position, most colonies and controlled territories started to seek self-governance forms, which led to a long process of reimagining their identity as less dependent or completely independent entities from the Spanish monarchy. Third, the Catholic

Church survived and thrived amid the major sociopolitical shifts that resulted from the independence struggles and revolutions that characterized this period, despite all the actions and efforts aimed at reducing its power and influence, including the introduction of Protestantism.

This chapter is divided into five main sections after a brief historical overview. The first four sections follow a chronological order, and the proposed periodization reflects, for the most part, the consensus in the literature on this period: First, early anticlericalism, initiated by the Bourbon Reforms; second, anticlericalism during the independence era, which saw some sectors of the Catholic Church involved in the independence movements and the crafting of foundational documents and at the same time the beginning of the abolishment of religious orders; third, mid-century clericalism, which sought formal separation between church and state and the intentional introduction of Protestantism; fourth, anticlericalism in the late nineteenth century, which took a positivist turn, leading to the complete secularization of public education. Finally, the fifth and last section reflects on the construction of national identity and nationalism, considering the main factors outlined in the previous four sections.

Historical Background

The nineteenth century marks a series of profound changes in the political and ideological configuration in the region primarily due to the independence movements. Between 1808 and 1826, all but two countries (Cuba and Puerto Rico) gained their independence from a three-century Spanish colonial rule. The various independence processes emerged from a series of factors that can be categorized as internal to the Spanish Empire and external to it, related to the expansion of the French dominion in Europe under the leadership of Napoleon Bonaparte. Regarding internal factors, some significant changes were made in the way the Spanish colonial powers ruled their colonies in the Americas. These changes, known as the Bourbon Reforms, intended to renovate and strengthen the Spanish Empire in all substantial areas, such as commerce, state finances, administrative and political operations, and the military. These reforms, however, negatively affected not only the colonizers' descendants, known as Creoles but, more notably, the clergy, who were very close to the indigenous and impoverished general populations. Creoles enjoyed a series of privileges derived from their role as the main connection between the peninsular center of power and the colonies. The Bourbon Reforms constituted a threat to the Creoles' social and political status and wealth, which created a sense of alienation between them and the Spanish Crown.[1] In turn, this alienation became fertile soil for the growth of a critical attitude and perspective toward the imperial rulers and authority in general. The Bourbon Reforms also included measures that negatively affected many priests and lower clergy who enjoyed a deep appreciation on the part of the majority of the population. Given this appreciation and closeness between the lower clergy and the people, the reforms were rightly perceived as an attack against the church by the Spanish rulers. The subversive ideological currents flowing from the French and American Revolutions later fueled this critical outlook. Regarding the external factors that contributed to the emergence of the independence movements in the Americas, some political decisions substantially limited Spain's control over its American colonies. When Spain allied with France to facilitate Portugal's invasion in the late 1700s, the relationship with England became antagonistic to the point that England effectively disrupted the trade that sustained Spain's dominion across the Atlantic Ocean. Eventually, Napoleon's invasion of Portugal included Spain, even though they were allies. This unsuspected invasion brought with it the neutralization of Spain's two central political figures, Charles IV and Ferdinand VII, creating a sort of power vacuum that debilitated Spain's ability to control its colonies even further. This power vacuum was seen as an opportunity to pursue self-governance by the Creoles, who already felt alienated from the Spanish and Portuguese monarchies due to the Bourbon Reforms.

Early Anticlericalism in Latin America

The Catholic Church was part of the colonial enterprise from the beginning. The evangelization process, regardless of any good intentions on the part of the various religious orders that conducted it, served the colonizers as a powerful tool to gain and maintain control of the population that already inhabited the continent: "The spiritual conquest . . . is actually the fundamental justification for the material conquest and the only excuse for the violence unleashed by some conquerors. . . . The Spanish State therefore justified its expansion and domination by the expansion and support of the church."[2] Most religious orders adopted a "modern business model" to fund their work. Such a model usually involved commercial enterprises and the establishment of "land states to produce goods for the market."[3]

---

1. See Brading, "Bourbon Spain."

2. Meyer, *Historia de los cristianos*, 23 (my trans.). Meyer references, among others, Hanke, *Lucha por la justicia*; see also Rivera, *Violent Evangelism*.

3. Schwaller, *History of Catholic Church*, 268.

This practice led to the acquisition of vast extensions of land, making the Catholic Church "the single largest landowner within the colony" with the consequent increase in political influence.[4] This power grew to the point that "even the crown saw the Catholic Church as a successful financial institution that could be used to further royal programs."[5] The power and presence of the Catholic Church, initially utilized by the Spanish Crown to advance its colonial dominance, was eventually considered excessive. This critical view on the part of the Spanish rulers shaped, to a degree, the Bourbon Reforms that, among other things, intended to curtail the power of the church[6] by limiting its ability to acquire more land and reducing the number of regular clergy, both male and female.[7] The roots of these actions on the part of the Spanish rulers can be traced to the established belief and practice of the civil authority's power over the church that, in this case, was linked to the Bourbon absolutism and more specifically to the royal patronage (i.e., control of the king of Spain over the church in the colonies). Given the fact that these actions involved the limitation of the church's influence, the Bourbon Reforms can be interpreted as either an antecedent of or a particular form of anticlericalism.[8] According to some interpretations, this form of anticlericalism took place from 1750 to 1850,[9] which means that it started almost sixty years before the independence revolutions in Latin America and before the introduction of the liberal democracy ideology.

Anticlericalism at the Beginning of the Independence Era

A different form of anticlericalism emerged as a result of the arrival of the liberal democracy ideology that was crafted in the context of the French and US revolutions and, more broadly speaking, as part of the Enlightenment. This ideological element, combined with the political rearrangements negatively affecting Portugal and Spain, were the main factors that led to the independence movements in the region. The Latin American independence processes started in 1808, right after the French invasion of Spain as part of the Peninsular War (1807–14), and the Latin American countries all shared the general conviction that in order to achieve liberation from colonial rule,

4. Schwaller, "Church in Colonial Latin America," s.v. "Introduction."
5. Schwaller, *History of Catholic Church*, 269.
6. Andrien, "Bourbon Reforms."
7. Klaiber, "Anticlericalism," 157.
8. Butler, "Liberalism, Anticlericalism," 251–52.
9. Meyer, *Historia de los cristianos*, 18. Cited in Butler, "Liberalism, Anticlericalism," 254. Butler adopts Meyer's periodization.

the Catholic Church's power and influence needed to be curtailed. On the one hand, this sentiment was understandable, considering the extremely close collaboration of the Catholic Church with the colonial enterprise. For most Creoles and those desiring self-governance, the Catholic Church was seen as an obstacle to the implementation of liberal democracies for several reasons, including the fact that the Spanish Crown appointed the Catholic hierarchy in the Americas. This fact implied that the church hierarchy owed loyalty to Spain, which represented a clear obstacle to the implementation of liberal principles and, ultimately, to achieving independence from Spain. On the other hand, the liberal project represented an entirely different approach to governance and social organization. It promoted a representative democratic form of government, including universal suffrage, the separation of powers, the rule of law, a market economy, and civil liberties, including freedom of religion and political freedoms. Under the colonial order, in contrast, the political power resided in the king's person. The rule of law excluded the kings and their families because their power was absolute, so they could not be held accountable. Freedom of religion was inexistent since it implied separation between church and state, which was practically inconceivable given their long and complicated alliance. These opposing worldviews were the essence of the contention between liberals and conservatives. Ultimately, both sides were striving for legitimacy.[10] It is important to note the complex relationship between these ideological convictions and the existential commitments of those who held them. While some clergy remained loyal to the Spanish rule—like in the case of most bishops—there were clergy who actively participated in or even initiated the independence movements and the shaping of the new republics. A clear example of this participation is Miguel Hidalgo y Costilla and Servando Teresa de Mier in Mexico. This latter phenomenon shows the degree of alienation Creoles, including clergy, experienced due to the Bourbon Reforms.

Additionally, the clergy were among the most educated of the population, which undoubtedly exposed them to Enlightenment ideas. One more element that complicated the clergy's choices was the chaos that characterized this period due to the forced abdication of Ferdinand VII, which left all the ecclesiastical leadership in the Americas without a guide. While for some, the king's absence represented the opportunity to seek independence, independence would mean chaos and uncertainty for others, particularly the bishops. These complex dynamics explain, to some degree, the anticlericalism that characterized this period.

---

10. Klaiber, "Anticlericalism," 157.

Another concrete expression of this complex anticlericalism was the hostility that religious orders experienced in some independent countries, such as Peru and Bolivia, which enacted decrees to suppress religious orders, including their dissolution, expulsion, and confiscation of their land and properties, among other measures.[11] All this means that while some sectors of the Catholic Church were seen as an obstacle to the construction of the new nations, other sectors were praised for their participation in the independence revolutions and their embracement of democratic principles.

Mid-Century Anticlericalism

The relatively moderate anticlericalism of the early nineteenth century evolved into a more aggressive one around the middle of the century. One of the first steps taken by the liberal governments that followed the declaration of independence was to change the mode of production. The Catholic Church had benefited for centuries from the mortmain. This land tenure system made all church property inalienable, owned in perpetuity, and free of taxes while allowing for its economic exploitation. This system was viewed as an obstacle to economic progress and the insertion of the nascent nations into a more global economy that required more freedom of circulation of products and labor. The confiscation of land and property, known as *secularization*, was perhaps the most significant measure toward the transformation of the economy and social organization of the region.[12]

Another set of measures taken by the liberal governments was the continuation of the abolishment the religious orders. The general perception was that religious life, as practiced by religious orders such as the Franciscans, Dominicans, Augustinians, and others, was "unproductive and useless for the life of the new nations."[13] Jesuits were the exception regarding this perception. They were perceived as having a strong alliance with conservative forces. This alliance's complicated history traces its roots to the suppression of the Jesuits in the eighteenth century, which led to their removal from most of Western Europe and their colonies. The Jesuit order was eventually abolished (1773) due to their tendency to act too independently, which was a threat, considering their great social influence and economic success. After some time, the order was reinstated (1814) and soon was seen as an ally of the Spanish Crown in countering liberalism and supporting the absolutist

11. See Tibesar, "Suppression of Religious Orders."

12. Uribe-Castro, "Expropriation of Church Wealth." See also Bazant, *Bienes de la iglesia*.

13. Klaiber, "Anticlericalism," 161.

aspirations of the Spanish monarchs, starting with Ferdinand VII.[14] This change in the Jesuit order, along with its closeness to the pope, prompted the liberal newly formed governments to expel them between 1843 and 1886 in Paraguay, Colombia, Argentina, Mexico, Uruguay, Ecuador, Peru, and Guatemala.[15]

All these measures pointed to the ultimate goal of separating church and state. Concrete examples of this goal were the reforms to the Colombian constitution of 1853 and the Mexican constitution of 1857. Additional anticlerical actions included other aspects of social life, such as the secularization of cemeteries, institutionalization of civil marriages (religious marriage ceremonies became legally insufficient), and laicization of public education, among others.

Liberal thinkers and political leaders also favored the establishment of Protestant churches, which were seen as allies in the effort to counter the culture of "obscurantism" and "fanaticism" believed to be a significant part of the culture created and promoted by the colonial church. This openness to other religious expressions signaled that anticlericalism at this historical stage was not antireligious. It recognized the role of religion in society toward the construction of a nation. Therefore, religious toleration was explicitly included in various constitutions during the second half of the nineteenth century and the first years of the twentieth century.

Anticlericalism in the Late Nineteenth Century

While the anticlericalism of the mid-century was deistic and sympathetic to Protestantism, a declared antireligious anticlericalism dominated the last part of the nineteenth century and the first years of the twentieth century. As French Mexican historian Jean Meyer has explained, this new form of anticlericalism was inspired by August Comte's positivism in combination with influences from Charles Darwin (theory of evolution), Herbert Spencer (social Darwinism), and Jeremy Bentham (utilitarianism). This amalgam embraced by intellectuals produced a "scientific culture" that sought to shape the economy, the social organization, and the political sphere of various Latin American countries, particularly in Mexico, Brazil, and Argentina.[16] According to this new approach, religion has no role in society, and science should replace it in order to achieve progress. In these liberals' opinion, the Catholic Church promoted fanaticism and intolerance,

14. Klaiber, "Anticlericalism," 158.
15. Klaiber, "Anticlericalism," 159.
16. Meyer, *Historia de los cristianos*, 89–90.

contrary to the project of modernity. Protestantism, in this regard, represented a step in the right direction, but the ultimate goal was to leave religion in the past. One of the concrete ways in which this anticlericalism took form was in the positivistic approach to public education. Two notable examples were Peru and Mexico, with Manuel González Prada and Gabino Barreda, respectively, who pushed for eliminating religious education in public schools.

The Emergence of Nationalism

The schematic overview of nineteenth-century anticlericalism above shows that the independence movements resulted from a complex convergence of political and ideological factors. After three centuries of dependence under an exploitative and acutely stratified social, political, and economic order, the notion of a unified national identity was either inexistent or vague, at least for most of the population. Even though national identity is an elusive concept, as Siekmeier explains, at a basic level, it can be defined as a "meta-narrative (a constructed collective memory of a nation) onto a space or place (the sovereign territory of the nation)."[17] Although this collective memory is not uniform or homogenous, because different segments of the population have different experiences, perspectives, and interests, in the end, the groups that hold control over mass means of communication have more influence in the process of shaping the meta-narrative. According to Siekmeier, this meta-narrative aims to provide a lasting collective meaning. The acquisition of such collective consciousness seems to have started with the independence revolutions, not before. As Colom González has put it, "National identity and sentiment were politically induced processes that extended throughout the nineteenth century and later."[18] It can be said that states preceded nations because the newly independent countries needed governing structures and institutions before anything else. The shared ideas that provided a cohesiveness to the people regarding a collective identity associated with a territory took longer to develop, in most cases over an entire century. Part of the reason for this long process was the fact that at least the first quarter of the eighteenth century was marked by struggle and, in most cases, chaos: "The patriot governments of Spanish America in the era of the wars of independence were usually too busy with military operations against the royalists, too much concerned with challenges from domestic

---

17. Siekmeier, *Latin American Nationalism*, 5.
18. Colom González, "Nationalism in Latin America," 1.

factions, too greatly handicapped by empty treasures and exhausted credit to do much more than maintain themselves precariously."[19]

Once this tumultuous stage was over, countries found themselves in the process of conceiving a form of government and creating the institutions that would allow them self-governance and sovereignty. It is at this stage that countries sought inspiration from Enlightenment ideals and the countries that embodied such ideals. For example, Griffin identifies countries in South America that intentionally tried to replicate some practices born from the Enlightenment, such as the idea that the government should procure, facilitate, and stimulate economic development. This is the case of Argentina, Chile, and Colombia, which sought to improve basic infrastructure and promote immigration from European countries to bring "skilled and industrious foreigners."[20] Also, around this time, there were consistent efforts to improve education and culture by founding universities in Argentina, Colombia, Venezuela, and Ecuador. The education provided in such institutions was inspired by the "secular viewpoint of the European Enlightenment,"[21] which explains in grand part the anticlerical sentiment that prevailed at this time in history.

Additional evidence that Latin American countries incorporated Enlightenment ideas was the inclusion of the concept of natural rights into their declarations of independence.[22] A good example of this is the Mexican Declaration of Independence signed on September 28, 1821, which "often echoes its American counterpart in themes and language, citing "unalienable" rights to be restored to the nation's citizens."[23] The influence of the American and French Revolutions is also palpable in the early constitutions of the region, such as the ones of Venezuela and Chile. Some topics and language used in those constitutions included a representative government and natural rights of liberty, equality, property, and security.[24] Enlightenment ideas, however, were not entirely uniform regarding political theory, and this created different interpretations as to how to achieve the core ideals in their collective life. An example of this was the disagreement among some leaders of the independence movements regarding the specifics of the form of government the new nations would adopt. This is the case, specifically, of José de San Martín and Simón Bolívar in South America, particularly in

19. Griffin, "Enlightenment and Latin American Independence," 131.
20. Griffin, "Enlightenment and Latin American Independence," 131–33.
21. Griffin, "Enlightenment and Latin American Independence," 133.
22. Griffin, "Enlightenment and Latin American Independence," 119.
23. New York Public Library, "Mexican Declaration of Independence."
24. Gargarella, "Constitution of Inequality."

Peru. Both leaders sought independence from Spain, but San Martín envisioned a constitutional monarchy, while Bolívar believed a republic would be best. Even though it is difficult to determine the extent of this influence in the shaping process of national identities, it is evident that some Enlightenment ideals were present at the starting point of the new nations.

Another factor involved in national identity formation in Latin America was the increased presence and intervention of Great Britain and the US in the region. Two of the most notable and consequential cases involving the US were the Mexican-American War (1846–48) and the Spanish-American War (1898). These wars represented the loss of one-third of the territory for Mexicans and the loss of sovereignty prospects for Puerto Rico and the Philippines. The backdrop of these military actions was the US policy toward Latin America, declared in 1823 by President James Monroe, who envisioned the American continent as a region where the US could expand its territory, influence, and dominance. Therefore, the US objected to the continuation or establishment of any European colonies and interventions. The early military enforcement of this policy soon morphed into measures geared to achieving economic American expansion and hegemony in the region. One of the first antecedents of this economic expansion was the acquisition of land to produce bananas for the American market. By the mid-1870s, three American corporations controlled banana cultivation, harvesting, and exploitation in Honduras. This trend continued in the early twentieth century and extended to other Central American countries. In the early 1900s, US corporations bought the British companies already exploiting Mexican oil. This action to control a major natural resource meant more decisive economic influence and dominance in the region. Also, in the early 1900s, the Panama Canal was built by the US, which kept absolute control of it until 1979. These interventions and an increasingly strong US presence in the region seeking to exploit and control many natural resources provoked a complex mixture of admiration and anti-US sentiment that also became part of the national identity in Latin American countries. A concrete expression of this complex mixture was the growing impulse to protect national resources and keep them out of reach of foreign interests. This impulse led to what some have called "economic nationalism," which took place in the early twentieth century in countries such as Argentina, Chile, Uruguay,[25] and Mexico, through the nationalization of means of production of raw materials and even expropriation of foreign companies' assets. This period (from 1870 to 1910) was known as neocolonialism, given its similarities with the colonial era, when the exploitation of raw materials by the Iberian

---

25. Siekmeier, *Latin American Nationalism*, 16.

colonial rule was commonplace. Much of this exploitation of resources was possible thanks to the collusion between foreign companies who enjoyed full support from their nations, especially the US, and local oligarchs and governments in Latin America. A case in point was Mexico, whose main leader and dictator at that time, Porfirio Díaz, not only allowed but promoted foreign investment and control of numerous natural resources to the point that the people crafted and applied to him the epithet *vendepatrias*, which means seller-out of his country. This sentiment of dispossession in favor of foreign interests created by Porfirio Díaz was one of the main factors that led to the Mexican Revolution, which started in 1910.

The efforts to build a nation proved difficult given the deep-rooted legacy of colonialism that, for generations, exerted exploitation and imposed hierarchical social and political relations. The successful independence processes in the nineteenth century were complex, challenging, and in many cases, marked by chaos, which made creating a sense of national identity slow and fragmentary. On the one hand, there were independence leaders who pushed for radical changes in governance, political and civic participation, economy, and culture, including religion. On the other hand, other leaders, acknowledging the monumental challenge before them, considered an approach that incorporated elements of the past, almost in the spirit of continuity with the legacy of the colonial era. An example of this tension is the complex role that the Catholic Church played in this process as a deeply ingrained institution in the social, political, cultural, and economic life of all the countries in the region.

The Catholic Church proved its resilience against the efforts of the newly formed governments to reduce and limit its influence but at the cost of internal tensions. On the one hand, as noted above, Catholic priests were involved in the independence movement and constituting new forms of government and institutions. On the other hand, the importance of the Catholic Church in the people's daily life was such that some in the leadership of the new governments believed that it would be counterproductive to ignore it or maintain a hostile relationship with it. An example of this viewpoint was Lucas Alamán in Mexico, who believed that "without the Catholic religion to cement its nationality and to fortify its virtues, Mexico was doomed to sink into civil discord, a prelude to foreign conquest. The order could not be established and maintained except in continuity, with the use of colonial elements."[26] The tension between those who viewed the Catholic Church as an obstacle to progress and true independence and those who recognized the depth of its importance for the people persisted

---

26. Meyer, *Historia de los cristianos*, 73–74.

for most of the nineteenth century and part of the twentieth. This tension became a significant part of the new nations' identity.

Another dimension of this tension relates to the status of the various segments of the population involved in the independence movements and the crafting and participating in governing structures and institutions and, therefore, in the configuration of national identity. Creoles played a central role in most countries in those processes. At the same time, mestizos (mixed race) and indigenous peoples were relegated and effectively marginalized from any positions of political and economic influence. This explains to a great degree the fact that except for the Mexican president from 1858 to 1872, Benito Juárez, who was Zapotec (one of the indigenous groups in Mexico), all the presidents in Latin America were Creoles until the late twentieth and early twenty-first centuries. The elitism that permeated the initial efforts to construct national identities was rooted in a deep wealth gap created by the alliance between foreign corporations, local landowners, and the new liberal governments to secure control of the natural resources, whose demand grew exponentially at the end of the nineteenth century due to the expansion of trade and commerce. According to Siekmeier, this arrangement helped local governments obtain resources to create state institutions, pay for infrastructure and educational systems, and ultimately promote national identity.[27] Besides its exclusionary nature, the problem with this approach is that it was imposed. In other words, it excluded mestizos and indigenous peoples from decision-making positions and imposed notions of private property, free-market economics, and political freedoms on everyone. Therefore, due to its top-down essence, it was not embraced by the majority of the population and soon became a source of conflict, as in the case of Porfirio Díaz's regime described above. It is in the twentieth century that a different form of nationalism emerged, one that was more grassroots based.

Conclusion

A complex relationship between anticlericalism and nationalism marked the nineteenth century in Latin America. Even though anticlericalism is generally understood as the opposition or hostility toward the influence and power of the clergy or religious institutions in society, this chapter has shown that anticlerical sentiments and impulses had various motivations and did not always have the goal of secularizing society. The various versions of anticlericalism evolved based on interacting social, political, and

---

27. Siekmeier, *Latin American Nationalism*, 80.

economic forces. One such force was the desire for independence and the pursuit of national identity. As time progressed, anticlerical movements aimed to establish a secular national identity, limit church power, and redefine the relationship between religion and the state. These developments profoundly impacted Latin American societies, shaping their cultural, political, and intellectual landscapes.

Bibliography

Andrien, Kenneth J. "The Bourbon Reforms." Oxford Bibliographies, May 24, 2018. https://doi.org/10.1093/OBO/9780199766581-0043.

Bazant, Jan. *Los bienes de la iglesia en México, 1856–1875: Aspectos económicos y sociales de la revolución liberal*. 2nd ed. Centro de estudios históricos, n.s., 13. Mexico City: Colegio de Mexico, 1977. https://doi.org/10.2307/j.ctv233mro.

Brading, D. A. "Bourbon Spain and Its American Empire." In *The Cambridge History of Latin America*, edited by Leslie Bethell, 1:389–440. Cambridge Histories—American History. Cambridge: Cambridge University Press, 1984.

Butler, Matthew. "Liberalism, Anticlericalism, and Antireligious Currents in the Nineteenth Century." In *The Cambridge History of Religions in Latin America*, edited by Virginia Garrard-Burnett et al., 251–68. Cambridge: Cambridge University Press, 2016. https://doi.org/10.1017/CHO9781139032698.017.

Colom González, Francisco. "Nationalism in Latin America." Wiley Online Library, 2016. From *The Encyclopedia of Postcolonial Studies*, edited by Sangeeta Ray et al., vol. 3. https://doi.org/10.1002/9781119076506.wbeps264.

Gargarella, Roberto. "The Constitution of Inequality: Constitutionalism in the Americas, 1776–1860." *International Journal of Constitutional Law* 3 (2005) 1–23. https://doi.org/10.1093/icon/moi001.

Griffin, Charles C. "The Enlightenment and the Latin American Independence." In *Latin America and the Enlightenment*, edited by Arthur P. Whitaker, 119–43. 2nd ed. Cornell Paperbacks. Ithaca, NY: Cornell University Press, 1961. https://catalog.hathitrust.org/Record/001446501.

Hanke, Lewis. *La lucha por la justicia en la conquista de América*. Buenos Aires: Sudamericana, 1949.

Klaiber, Jeffrey. "Anticlericalism in the Nineteenth and Early Twentieth Centuries." In *Religion and Society in Latin America: Interpretative Essays from Conquest to Present*, edited by Lee M. Penyak and Walter J. Petry, 157–74. Maryknoll, NY: Orbis, 2009.

Meyer, Jean A. *Historia de los cristianos en América Latina: Siglos XIX y XX*. Mexico City: Vuelta, 1989.

New York Public Library. "Mexican Declaration of Independence." New York Public Library, n.d. https://www.nypl.org/events/exhibitions/galleries/beginnings/item/3564.

Rivera, Luis N. *A Violent Evangelism: The Political and Religious Conquest of the Americas*. Louisville: Westminster John Knox, 1992.

Schwaller, John Frederick. "The Church in Colonial Latin America." Oxford Bibliographies, Mar. 31, 2016. https://doi.org/10.1093/OBO/9780199766581-0180.

———. *The History of the Catholic Church in Latin America: From Conquest to Revolution and Beyond*. New York: New York University Press, 2011.

Siekmeier, James F. *Latin American Nationalism: Identity in a Globalizing World*. War, Culture and Society. London: Bloomsbury Academic, 2017. https://doi.org/10.5040/9781474218672.

Tibesar, Antonine S. "The Suppression of the Religious Orders in Peru, 1826–1830, or the King Versus the Peruvian Friars: The King Won." *Americas* 39 (1982) 205–39. https://www.jstor.org/stable/981335.

Uribe-Castro, Mateo. "Expropriation of Church Wealth and Political Conflict in 19th Century Colombia." *Explorations in Economic History* 73 (2019) 101271. https://doi.org/10.1016/j.eeh.2019.03.001.

6

The Making of Protestantism in Latin America

Pedro Feitoza

For Brazilian Presbyterian minister, writer, and educator Erasmo Braga, isolation was one of the key hallmarks of Latin American spiritual life during the colonial era. Writing in 1929 as representative of a committee of Latin American Protestant churches at the Missionary Conference of Jerusalem (1928), Braga argued that for over "three centuries Spain and Portugal jealously guarded their western dominions from the inroads of foreign thought," labeling extraneous ideological and religious currents as heresy.[1] For him, the Protestant churches in the continent were witnessing an intensifying process of global integration that had begun with the first missionary incursions in the mid-nineteenth century and culminated with the inclusion of Latin America in the International Missionary Council. Braga claimed that now, after nearly a century of Protestant evangelization, the evangelical churches in the region felt that they were "no longer isolated, small congregations engaged in local or regional struggles, but a part of the great Christian world movement."[2]

To a certain extent, the history of Protestantism in Latin America is indeed a history of increasing global integration, with its resulting interactions, encounters, entanglements, frictions, and conflicts. The religion first entered the continent in a sustained and systematic manner in the context of the Napoleonic wars in Europe and the crisis of the Iberian colonial enterprise in the early nineteenth century, and was introduced by sailors, merchants, and immigrants. Later the region attracted considerable attention

---

1. Braga, "Jerusalem Meeting in Brazil," 261.
2. Braga, "Jerusalem Meeting in Brazil," 262.

from missionary organizations in Britain and the United States, becoming the destination of evangelical enthusiasts and recent graduates from Protestant seminaries and colleges. This chapter examines some of the religious and cultural transformations associated with the early history of evangelical religion in Latin America. It focuses on the migrant communities and missionary organizations that engineered and propagated new religious communities across the continent, and situates these experiences in the sociopolitical settings of the era. Catholic faith and practice were also revitalized in the process, as ecclesiastical authorities and laypeople devoted a good deal of zeal and energy to strengthen the church in the face of religious competition. Although the new religion was initially announced by foreign agents, the beliefs and practices of Evangelical Christianity were quickly picked up by local converts and ministers, who soon became the key agents of religious diffusion. This chapter focuses on the religious reforms, political transformations, and cultural interactions that enabled Protestantism to gain a foothold in Latin America and create roots.

Immigrants

The events that led to the Protestant Reformation coincided with the worldwide expansion of the Iberian empires in the sixteenth century. Responding to the rift in European Christendom caused by the likes of Luther, Zwingli, and Calvin, the Portuguese and Spanish monarchs, along with the Jesuits and other religious orders, set out to defend the Catholic faith from the assaults of Protestantism. Franciscan and Jesuit missionaries envisioned the newly discovered American lands as sacred spaces, stages in "which the great drama of salvation was played out" that offered the Catholic Church the opportunity to compensate for the losses caused by the Reformation in Europe.[3] In fact, despite the evangelistic energy of Catholic missionaries and the aggressive zeal of inquisitors, Lutheran and Calvinist "heresies" did circulate throughout the Iberian empires. Portuguese Jesuits encountered Protestant texts and ideas rejecting purgatory, the seven sacraments, auricular confession, and Mass in Goa and Rio de Janeiro as early as the mid-sixteenth century.[4] In the Spanish Indies, the Protestant assault on Catholic hierarchy, rituals, and symbols resonated with widespread criticism of the papacy, which gave a wider resonance to these ideas.[5] There were also organized attempts led by French Huguenots in Rio de Janeiro

---

3. Elliott, *Empires of the Atlantic World*, 184–85.
4. Paiva, "Impact of Luther."
5. Schwartz, *All Can Be Saved*, 143.

(1555–67) and Reformed Dutch in Pernambuco, Brazil (1630–54), to establish religious communities and experiments in religious toleration that were put to an end to the Iberian reconquest of these territories.[6] Although there long existed popular attitudes of religious tolerance in the Iberian-American world that conceived the possibility of universal salvation for Christian, Jews, and Muslims, ecclesiastical measures enforced at the local level by priests and colonial administrators ensured a fraught and uneven supremacy of Catholicism in the colonies.[7]

It was only in the context of the independence of Latin American states from the Iberian powers and the ensuing process of state building that the region was finally brought into the far-reaching networks of global Protestantism. Foreign immigration was one of the main vectors that contributed to this end. In the context of the Napoleonic invasion of the Iberian Peninsula in the early nineteenth century, the Spanish and Portuguese Crowns made a series of concessions to the British Empire in exchange for their military and naval support against the French. Some of these concessions related to the exercise of religious liberty for British citizens. The first recognizably Anglican and Presbyterian congregations in Latin America were composed mostly of English and Scottish merchants, sailors, and businessmen traveling through coastal cities.

Arguably the first Anglican chapel of South America was built in Rio de Janeiro in 1819. The papal nuncio in the city strongly opposed the plan, fearing that such compromise with British interests would undermine the Catholic faith. However, the liberal bishop of Rio de Janeiro, Dom José Caetano da Silva Coutinho, advocated the Anglican cause and, according to Anglican chaplain in Brazil Rev Robert Walsh, remarked that "the English... have really no religion; but they are a proud and obstinate people. If you oppose them, they will persist, and make it an affair of infinite importance; but if you concede to their wishes, the chapel will be built and nobody will ever go near it."[8] Although it is possible that this remark was apocryphal, the disagreement between the papal representative and the local bishop expressed a conflict that was played out in different ways throughout Latin America in the nineteenth century, involving the disparate attitudes of the orthodox, militant Romanized clergy and the liberal, reformist Catholic priests toward Protestantism. For some time in the eighteenth and nineteenth centuries, Catholic seminaries in the Iberian Peninsula and its American colonies espoused the reformist principles of Gallicanism and Jansenism, which upheld

---

6. Bastian, *Historia del protestantismo*, 46–57.
7. Schwartz, *All Can Be Saved*.
8. Walsh, *Notices of Brazil*, 1:322–24.

the autonomy of national churches and a reform of Catholic spirituality and religious practice respectively. In the age of revolutions this reformist clergy became intimately enmeshed in local and national political struggles, but more importantly for the purposes of this chapter, they facilitated the arrival and diffusion of Protestantism. The Jansenists' emphasis on the cultivation of an austere personal piety and their intimate attachment to the Bible resonated closely with Protestant practices.[9] Some of the most successful local evangelical ministers in Latin America had a close involvement with the liberal Catholic clergy, including people such as Manuel Águas in Mexico and José Manoel da Conceição in Brazil.[10] The ultramontane clergy, on the other hand, swore almost unconditional allegiance to Rome and the pope and strongly opposed evangelical diffusion by revitalizing Catholic institutions, promoting catechetical instruction, administering the sacraments to far-off communities, and encouraging Catholic missions.

A number of migratory waves further diversified and fragmented the religious landscape in the continent. Italian Waldensians settled Uruguay in the mid-nineteenth century and later on opened new religious communities in Argentina, on the other side of the River Plate. African American immigrants linked to the African Methodist Episcopal Church established Protestant congregations in Haiti and Santo Domingo. By the early twentieth century these communities had been absorbed into Haitian culture, holding services in French and Creole, but still had difficulties in communicating with the Spanish-speaking populations of Santo Domingo.[11] In the first decades of the twentieth century, large communities of Mennonite immigrants, who had fled Russia for Canada and were forced to military service in this country, then moved again to different parts of Latin America, including Mexico, Bolivia, and Argentina. Their main destination, however, was Paraguay, where they were given lands and granted exemption from military service. Throughout the twentieth century they created networks of schools, clinics, and centers of agricultural training that won the respect of the national community.[12]

The main destination of foreign immigrants in the region was Brazil. The country's vast and economically promising countryside, its booming coffee plantations, and the pressures to abolish slavery attracted communities in Europe and North America in contexts of conflict and economic

---

9. Vieira, *Protestantismo*, 29–31.

10. Bastian, *Disidentes*, 37–38; Ribeiro, *José Manoel*, 12–20.

11. González and González, *Christianity in Latin America*, 192–99; Davidson, "Redeeming Santo Domingo."

12. González and González, *Christianity in Latin America*, 200–203.

hardship. Apart from the aforementioned circulation of British merchants, sailors, professionals, and railroad workers, two other migratory currents contributed to the diversification of the religious landscape of the country. First was the large-scale German immigration to the coast and, more notably, the south of Brazil since the early nineteenth century. German immigration was so vast that by the 1930s Lutherans comprised the majority of the population of the state of Rio Grande do Sul in Brazil. Second, in the context of the American Civil War (1860–65) thousands of Confederate families relocated themselves to Brazil, especially to the province of São Paulo, attracted to the country's favorable economic prospects, cheap lands, and continued slavery. In smaller towns near the growing cities of Campinas and São Paulo, the Confederates founded Baptist, Presbyterian, and Methodist congregations with established pastors and elders.[13]

The settlement of these immigrant communities in Latin America responded to internal pressures following independence from the Iberian Peninsula and processes of state building. Most of the new nations had large and unoccupied swaths of land, and for some political thinkers of the era this situation created difficulties for the enforcement of power. Argentine diplomat, writer, and politician Juan Bautista Alberdi expressed the concerns of this generation with his oft-quoted mid-nineteenth-century adage "Gobernar es poblar" (To govern is to populate). The elites in power were interested in peopling thinly occupied areas of their nations' territories and transforming these spaces into productive lands. But the immigration policies that emerged in response to these demands were also informed by pseudo racial science. It was believed that the attraction of European immigrants would "civilize" the emerging nation states with large indigenous, black, and mestizo populations by whitening them. According to historian João José Reis, the policies of religious freedom and tolerance adopted in Brazil in the nineteenth century were conceived with white Protestant foreigners in mind, while the repression of African and indigenous rituals continued without restrain.[14] The same could be said of various other experiences in South America, particularly in the Southern Cone.[15]

Protestants, however, maintained an ambiguous relationship with these immigration policies and racialist thinking in general. Whereas medical anthropologists and other scientists throughout the region in the nineteenth and early twentieth centuries believed in innate differences between the human races, Evangelicals usually upheld the idea of the unity

---

13. Feitoza, "Historical Trajectories of Protestantism," 33–34.
14. Reis, *Divining Slavery and Freedom*, 126–27.
15. Míguez Bonino, *Rostros del protestantismo latinoamericano*, ch. 4.

of humankind as a foundational biblical principle.[16] For them, the disparities between human races were circumstantial, related to religious differences and other social impulses, not a fact of nature. They also placed great confidence in the "civilizing" power of conversion and education. Foreign missionaries and local ministers in places such as Guatemala and Brazil expressed these views in different ways, eschewing racial determinism and insisting on the idea that all human races possessed the same virtues and capacities.[17] In the late nineteenth and early twentieth centuries American missionaries and Brazilian Evangelicals were enthusiastic about the influx of immigrants from the Middle East, Eastern Europe, and Asia to São Paulo, claiming that converts from among these communities could then take the gospel elsewhere. For them, the evangelization of Brazil was a stage in the evangelization of the world.[18]

Missionaries, Colporteurs, and Local Converts

Apart from immigration, the other crucial vector shaping the early history of evangelical religion in Latin America was the missionary enterprise. Inspired by earlier models set by the Moravian Brethren, Anglo-American Methodism, and waves of religious revival on both sides of the Anglophone Atlantic, the Protestant missionary movement emerged almost simultaneously in Britain and the US. The revivals boosted an evangelical variety of "activist" religion, encouraging the zealous dedication and enthusiastic participation of laypeople in evangelistic affairs at home and abroad. To a certain extent, the movement's success depended upon the religious commitment of a multitude of believers who contributed to missionary organizations and Bible societies in local churches and received information about the ordeals and successes of missionaries and booksellers around the world. Initially, missionaries and colporteurs, what these itinerant booksellers were called, went to Latin America to attend to the religious needs of Protestant migrants. American Methodist missionaries in Argentina and Brazil, as well as English and Scottish chaplains and colporteurs in Chile, Peru, and Colombia targeted immigrant communities first, before turning to the local population of these countries.[19]

16. Stanley, "Christian Missions and Enlightenment."
17. Feitoza, "Middle Line of Truth"; Garrard-Burnett, *Protestantism in Guatemala*, 50.
18. See, e.g., *Brazilian Missions* 1.3 (1888).
19. Hempton, *Methodism*, 157–58; González and González, *Christianity in Latin America*, 209–16.

Colporteurs usually feature prominently in the histories of Protestant diffusion in modern Latin America for at least a couple of reasons. First, one of the earliest examples of successful Protestant evangelization in the continent came from the actions of Scottish colporteur James "Diego" Thomson (1788–1854). Working for the British and Foreign Bible Society, Thomson traveled widely across the region. He was first appointed to Argentina in 1818, but after a promising start there Thomson eventually moved to Chile, Peru, and then to Gran Colombia, holding temporary posts in present-day Colombia, Bolivia, and Ecuador up until his return to Britain in 1826. In the Southern Cone Thomson attracted considerable attention from notorious political leaders on account of his promotion of the Lancasterian method of mutual education, in which advanced pupils assisted teachers in classes by supporting the development of their peers. This method addressed the needs of emerging Latin American nation-states: Lancasterian schools relied on unpaid monitor students and were thus cheaper and easier to manage, enabling a wider expansion of educational institutions. Additionally, liberal political elites in the continent viewed state-sponsored public education as a way of taking cultural and educational institutions away from the hands of the Catholic Church.[20] In nineteenth-century Mexico, the efforts of the American Bible Society were also closely connected to the establishment of missionary schools, reinforcing the links between Protestantism and literacy in Latin America.[21]

Second, colporteurs played a crucial role in the evangelistic enterprise by reaching villages and rural communities inaccessible to foreign missionaries and local ministers. In Brazil, for instance, the majority of colporteurs were recruited either from among the newly established Protestant congregations of the country or from communities of Portuguese Protestant immigrants. Devoid of the usual linguistic and cultural barriers that curbed the successes of foreign missionaries, these agents communicated effectively with the Brazilian population and managed to circulate hundreds of thousands of Bibles or portions of the Bible in the last decades of the nineteenth century.[22] Additionally, local colporteurs crossed national boundaries united by language, and contributed to founding and deepening transnational religious networks of Portuguese- and Spanish-speaking communities across Latin America and the Iberian Peninsula. This was the case of Francisco Penzotti, the Italian Uruguayan colporteur who founded a successful mission in late nineteenth-century Peru, and the Portuguese immigrants from

---

20. González and González, *Christianity in Latin America*, 209–13.
21. Fea, *Bible Cause*, 120–30.
22. Feitoza, "British Missions."

the island of Madeira turned into successful colporteurs and evangelists in the Brazilian coast.[23] Missionaries, local ministers, colporteurs, and evangelists in modern Latin America sometimes operated within wider language zones, cutting across national frontiers in the Americas and reaching out to religious communities on the other side of the Atlantic.

Missionaries and missionary organizations in the field worked closely with the Bible societies in the nineteenth and twentieth centuries, aiming to obtain books for their evangelistic ventures and to supply missionary schools with reading matter. In some cases, the work of colporteurs and Bible societies preceded the arrival of missionaries. Francisco Penzotti's work as a colporteur in Peru evolved into an established Methodist congregation, while the legal conflicts around issues of religious liberty that his efforts sparked allowed for the expansion of missionary presence in the country.[24] In Brazil, too, it was a Presbyterian chaplain and representative of the American Bible Society named James Fletcher who called the attention of Portuguese-speaking Protestants to the country as a promising missionary field in the 1850s. For Fletcher, foreign immigration to the south and southeast of Brazil justified the need of an increasing missionary presence, while the existence of communities of Portuguese Protestant exiles in the US had the potential to facilitate the interaction between Portuguese evangelists and the Brazilian population.[25] As a result, Scottish Congregationalist medical missionary Robert Kalley settled in Rio de Janeiro in 1855, after years of a successful and turbulent ministry in Madeira. Initially, Kalley organized religious services for Anglophone communities in Rio de Janeiro and oversaw a team of Portuguese colporteurs. Kalley also had a close involvement with the British and Foreign Bible Society and encouraged their activities in Brazil.[26]

Evangelical Expansion and Its Consequences

In the nineteenth and early twentieth centuries, missionary Protestant progress was faster in the Southern Cone, Brazil, and parts of Central America than in the Andean region, including Peru and Bolivia. In Argentina, Chile, and Brazil, liberal political reforms since the era of independence deteriorated Catholic institutions that played a vital role in the church's

23. Santos, *Mascates da fé*, 60–69; Fonseca Ariza, *Misioneros y civilizadores*, 93–95.
24. Fonseca Ariza, *Misioneros y civilizadores*, 95–99.
25. Vieira, *Protestantismo*, 66.
26. On Fletcher, Kalley, and the Portuguese colporteurs, see Vieira, *Protestantismo*, 66, 116–19.

ecclesiastical reproduction and stability, including seminaries, dioceses, and confraternities. Lacking in human and material resources, the church in these places struggled to counter the evangelical missionary offensive. Protestant schools and congregations were usually seen as modernizing organizations, voluntary associations that spread the effects of literacy and met the demands of emerging nation states. Missionary schools, with their modern pedagogical methods, and evangelical churches, with their republican electoral systems, legitimized the aspirations of "people of the middling sort" such as urban professionals, civil servants, small farmers, and migrants in search of some degree of institutional participation and respectability.[27] Protestant proselytism had a similar appeal in Peru. Liberal and positivist political elites campaigned in favor of religious toleration in order to attract European immigrants, and a group of Methodist, Baptist, and Seventh-day Adventist missionaries tried to make the most of the existing legal breaches to carry out evangelism and built religious and educational institutions. However, the Catholic Church was able to put forward a consistent and elaborate plan to curb evangelical growth. Peruvian priests and bishops issued pastoral letters and catechisms warning the faithful against evangelical religion, pressure groups such as Unión Católica campaigned against laws of religious toleration in the 1890s, and the episcopate promoted the development of popular missions, spreading catechetical instruction and exposure to the sacraments as widely as possible.[28] In such a context, where the Catholic Church possessed the necessary institutional and intellectual resources to counter evangelical expansion, missionaries found it harder to make headway.

In Mexico and the Caribbean the arrival of Protestant missionaries and the diffusion of Evangelical Christianity took place amid complex struggles between competing imperial powers. According to historian Jean-Pierre Bastian's influential account, Mexican Protestantism was part of a broader culture of religious and political dissent. The agenda of Mexican converts and foreign missionaries demanding liberty of worship and religious tolerance resonated with the interests of liberal political elites in the secularization of the political and administrative machinery of the country. For Bastian, Protestant churches, associations, publishing houses, seminaries, and schools were part of a wider process of multiplication of spaces of sociability in Mexican society, along with the rise of Masonic lodges, secret associations, and the so-called "societies of thought."[29] As elsewhere in the

---

27. Mendonça, *Celeste porvir*; Willems, *Followers of the New Faith*.
28. Ramacciotti, *Politics of Religion*, 62–68.
29. Bastian, *Protestantes, liberales y francmasones*.

continent, Protestantism was seen as a modernizing force. However, in Mexico, reformist political programs took on different meanings and were deeply influenced by the conflicts with American expansionism toward the Pacific. Some political reformers in the nineteenth century, suspicious of the opening of the country to American interests, sought to modernize Mexican society by encouraging immigration from Catholic groups in Europe, instead of promoting full liberty of worship to accommodate non-Catholic populations.[30] In the nineteenth and twentieth centuries, Protestant evangelization in Mexico was in part carried out by missionaries and evangelists working on both sides of the Mexico-US border, which contributed to the politicization of religious identities in the country.[31]

Unlike Mexico, which managed to obtain independence from Spain and resist attempts at recolonization by the late 1820s, Cuba and Puerto Rico were caught in between the grip of Spanish colonialism and American intervention throughout most of the nineteenth century. The issue of religious tolerance divided opinions between *annexationists*, a group of mildly anti-Catholic and liberal individuals who defended the American annexation of Cuba, and the *assimilationists*, staunch Catholics who hoped that Cuba would become incorporated into the Spanish monarchy, instead of just remaining a colony. By the 1860s, when Spain started to lose control over the two colonies, Protestant evangelists and immigrants set out to circulate dissenting literature, which prompted immediate responses from conservative Catholics, who associated evangelical expansion to North American interests in the region. In this tense space under the grip of Spanish colonialism, Protestant clusters began to emerge in cities like Havana, Matanzas, Ponce, and Vieques, sites of greater economic dynamism linked to the sugar business that attracted foreign investment and trade.[32]

Throughout the nineteenth and twentieth centuries, denominational Protestant mission organizations became competent institution builders. Congregationalist, Presbyterian, Anglican, and Methodist evangelists entered Brazil, Peru, Mexico, and the countries of the Southern Cone as medical missionaries providing health care to local populations during outbreaks of cholera, yellow fever, and other diseases. Scottish missionaries associated with the Presbyterian Free Church opened small clinics in the Peruvian Andes in the first half of the twentieth century, which with the passing of time evolved into large and respectable institutions.[33] In most places mission-

30. Bastian, *Disidentes*, 27–28.
31. Francisco Martínez, *Story of Latino Protestants*, ch. 3.
32. Martínez-Fernández, *Protestantism and Political Conflict*.
33. Grigor, *Free Church in the Andes*.

ary organizations opened primary and secondary schools, which provided basic instruction and professional training to social sectors in the margins of the existing educational systems. Inspired by the belief that the ability to read the Bible was essential for Christians, Protestants championed the cause of universal literacy and supported educational reforms throughout the continent. Evangelical missionaries and educators in Guatemala started to codify indigenous languages and launch educational experiments among these communities since the 1890s.[34] In the twentieth century, these medical and educational institutions became closely involved in wider processes of social and political reform in Latin America, collaborating with local and national governments and projecting religious leaders into the realm of civil society as public actors.

Other missionaries, however, felt that these institutional bureaucracies wasted missionary resources and distracted evangelists from their primary task of preaching the gospel. These missionaries were in part inspired by the Plymouth Brethren, a movement originated in southwest England and Ireland in the nineteenth century that opposed denominational divisions, the rigid ecclesiastical hierarchies of established churches, and the mechanisms of fundraising of missionary societies.[35] Some of the Brethren's earliest proponents invited missionaries worldwide to "live by faith," relying on divine providence and dispensing with the complex and expensive bureaucratic apparatus of mission organizations. These "faith missions," as they were called, started to appear in Latin America in the second half of the nineteenth century and became increasingly important in the twentieth. In Brazil, faith missionaries extended the frontiers of evangelical religion widely, reaching out to the backlands of the Brazilian northeast and to the rural and indigenous populations of central Brazil. The engineer-turned-faith missionary Stuart McNair established his headquarters in the Livramento Hill, one of Rio de Janeiro's earliest favelas in the 1890s, carried out evangelistic tours throughout South America, and opened a publishing house with branches in Portugal and Madeira that circulated the ideas of the Christian Brethren across Lusophone religious networks.[36] Faith missionaries were particularly successful in Central America. Through organizations such as Wycliffe Bible Translators and the Texas-based Central American Mission they built an impressive technological infrastructure aimed at evangelizing

---

34. Garrard-Burnett, *Protestantism in Guatemala*, 80–83.

35. For a comprehensive and detailed study of the Christian Brethren, see Grass, *Gathering to His Name*.

36. McNair, *Round South America*.

indigenous communities of the region, which also sparked a good deal of anthropological controversy.[37]

Although conservative Catholics, nationalist writers, and Marxist intellectuals in modern Latin America depicted Evangelical Christianity as an alien and imperialistic religion, driven and funded by foreign agents and organizations, the new religion was in most cases propagated from below. Evangelical activism resonated closely with the participatory culture of folk Catholicism. Faithful Catholics played a key role in shaping the religious makeup of Latin America, taking an active part in brotherhoods and confraternities, and raising funds for religious festivals, local shrines, hospitals, charitable practices, and even for the Vatican and the pope. Additionally, the conversionist message of Protestant missionaries, the emphasis they placed on the regenerative quality of an individual encounter with God and the Bible, also resembled in some respects the message of Romanized Catholics and political elites. In the Río de la Plata region, Protestants and political reformers viewed traditional festivities and entertainments such as carnivals and cockfights with contempt, claiming that they threatened the social order and gave leeway to immoral, "uncivilized" behavior.[38] The revivalist enthusiasm of Evangelicals channeled these religious dispositions into the evangelistic enterprise and the emerging Protestant institutions. Small armies of local evangelists, acting as colporteurs, schoolteachers, Bible women, and church leaders, far outnumbered the foreign missionaries and contributed to spreading the new religion at grassroots level.[39] They also navigated between the cultural worlds of the missionaries and their communities, weaving the new religion into everyday life and lending local color to Evangelical Christianity.

Conclusion

In the nineteenth and twentieth centuries Protestantism was a force that dynamized, fragmented, and reconfigured the religious landscape of Latin America. Up until the 1950s, Protestants were still a tiny religious minority in the continent, even in places where immigrants, missionaries, and local preachers were able to make greater headway such as Guatemala, Chile, and Brazil. The impact of their evangelistic endeavors, however, lie elsewhere, in other religious and cultural spaces. They were part of a broader group

---

37. Dove, "Historical Protestantism in Latin America," 294–97.

38. Amestoy, "Festivals, Entertainment, and Pleasure."

39. On Brazil, see Feitoza, "Historical Trajectories," 38–42; Léonard, *Protestantismo brasileiro*, 94–106.

comprising Spiritists, practitioners of Afro-Caribbean and Afro-Brazilian religions, positivists, and others who were slowly but continuously undermining the fragile religious monopoly of the Catholic Church in the region. These groups, although interested in enlarging confessional frontiers or carving out autonomous spaces in which they could practice their faiths securely, ended up promoting a very specific form of secularization by challenging the normative authority of the Catholic Church after centuries of colonial control.

In the case of Protestants, the scale of their operations and the ideology of the missionary enterprise generated widespread potential for religious change. Bible and tract societies circulated hundreds of thousands, even millions, of books and tracts that were carried into innumerable households and assisted processes of religious change. Missionaries, colporteurs, ordained ministers, and itinerant evangelists moved in multiple directions throughout the continent. They established small religious congregations, mission stations, schools, clinics, and evangelical libraries in cities and the countryside that catered to the educational, medical, and religious needs of an increasing population. In the ideological camp, the evangelical idea of individual salvation and the principle of the free examination of the Scriptures destabilized hierarchical notions of religious authority and liberated converts from networks of kin and co-parenthood. Catholic authorities often found these ideological traits and the infrastructure of Protestant missions to be unpalatable, since they undermined principles of authority and tradition that could spread easily throughout the region.

To some extent, these challenges to the religious establishment pushed the Catholic Church to reorganize itself, revitalize its institutions, and try to reconquer its prestige and influence. On the one hand, this process involved a positive process of bureaucratic reconstruction and lay mobilization. In the twentieth century, after decades of bitter struggles with liberal regimes and some troublesome defeats, the church was able to strengthen its connections with Rome, replenish its seminaries with new teachers and students, boost its educational and missionary initiatives, and in places such as Brazil and Peru even make new alliances with the state. The church also managed to involve the laity in this process of ecclesiastical reconstruction, encouraging the creation of Catholic associations of students, workers, and intellectuals.[40] On the other hand, this process also accompanied the escalation of bitter and violent Catholic-Protestant conflicts in Latin America. In Brazil, for instance, the Catholic authorities involved in the *restoration* program

40. Ramacciotti, *Politics of Religion*; Andes, *Vatican and Catholic Activism*; Miceli, *A elite eclesiástica brasileira*.

sought to regain the prestige and power of the church lost since the liberal reforms of the nineteenth century and the advent of the republic in 1889. Some of the clergymen involved in this program adopted an aggressive, almost intolerance stance toward Protestants that when distilled at the local level in parishes and lay associations evolved into violent confrontations.[41]

Although Evangelical Christianity was depicted by early observers as an extraneous religious project, Protestantism fit into Latin American culture and society in different ways. The settlement of migrant communities, the promotion of religious tolerance, and the missionary educational apparatus fulfilled the modernizing aspirations of political reformers interested in economic and technical improvements in harmony with the changes in the global capitalist economy. More importantly, local converts, ministers, and evangelists delved deeply into the customs and culture of their respective contexts and weaved the new religion into them. They domesticated evangelical religion by penetrating the cultural and conceptual worlds of Latin American society and mixing the beliefs and practices of evangelical religion into them.

Bibliography

Amestoy, Norman Rúben. "Festivals, Entertainment, and Pleasure in the Protestantism of the Río de la Plata Region, 1875–1900." *Journal of Latin American Theology* 2 (2011) 187–210.

Andes, Stephen J. C. *The Vatican and Catholic Activism in Mexico and Chile: The Politics of Transnational Catholicism, 1920–1940*. Oxford Historical Monographs. New York: Oxford University Press, 2014.

Bastian, Jean-Pierre. *Los disidentes: Sociedades protestantes y revolución en México, 1872–1911*. Mexico City: Fondo de Cultura Económica, 1989.

———. *Historia del protestantismo en América Latina*. Mexico City: CUPSA, 1990.

———, ed. *Protestantes, liberales y francmasones: Sociedades de ideas y modernidad en América Latina, siglo XIX*. Mexico City: Fondo de Cultura Económica, 1990.

Braga, Erasmo. "Following up the Jerusalem Meeting in Brazil." *International Review of Missions* 18 (1929) 261–65.

Davidson, Christina Cecelia. "Redeeming Santo Domingo: North Atlantic Missionaries and the Racial Conversion of a Nation." *Church History* 89 (2020) 74–100.

Dove, Stephen C. "Historical Protestantism in Latin America." In *The Cambridge History of Religions in Latin America*, edited by Virginia Garrard-Burnett et al., 286–303. New York: Cambridge University Press, 2016.

Elliott, J. H. *Empires of the Atlantic World: Britain and Spain in America, 1492–1830*. New Haven: Yale University Press, 2006.

Fea, John. *The Bible Cause: A History of the American Bible Society*. New York: Oxford University Press, 2016.

---

41. Helgen, *Religious Conflict in Brazil*.

Feitoza, Pedro. "British Missions and the Making of a Brazilian Protestant Public." In *Relocating World Christianity: Interdisciplinary Studies in Universal and Local Expressions of the Christian Faith*, edited by Joel Cabrita et al., 70–92. Theology and Mission in World Christianity 7. Leiden: Brill, 2017.

———. "Historical Trajectories of Protestantism in Brazil, 1810–1960." In *Brazilian Evangelicalism in the Twenty First Century: An Inside and Outside Look*, edited by Eric Miller and Ronald J. Morgan, 31–63. Christianity and Renewal—Interdisciplinary Studies. Cham, Switzerland: Palgrave Macmillan, 2019.

———. "The Middle Line of Truth: Religious and Secular Ideologies in the Making of Brazilian Evangelical Thought, 1870–1930." *Modern Intellectual History* 19 (2022) 1033–57.

Fonseca Ariza, Juan. *Misioneros y civilizadores: Protestantismo y modernización en el Perú (1915–1930)*. Lima: Pontificia Universidad Católica del Perú Editorial, 2002.

Francisco Martínez, Juan. *The Story of Latino Protestants in the United States*. Grand Rapids: Eerdmans, 2018.

Garrard-Burnett, Virginia. *Protestantism in Guatemala: Living in the New Jerusalem*. Austin: University of Texas Press, 1998.

González, Ondina E., and Justo L. González. *Christianity in Latin America: A History*. New York: Cambridge University Press, 2008.

Grass, Tim. *Gathering to His Name: The Story of Open Brethren in Britain and Ireland*. Milton Keynes, UK: Paternoster, 2006.

Grigor, Iain Fraser, ed. *The Free Church in the Andes: Scottish Missionaries in the Mountains of Twentieth-Century Peru*. Tarland, Scotland: Lumphanan, 2020.

Helgen, Erika. *Religious Conflict in Brazil: Protestants, Catholics, and the Rise of Religious Pluralism in the Early Twentieth Century*. New Haven: Yale University Press, 2020.

Hempton, David. *Methodism: Empire of the Spirit*. New Haven: Yale University Press, 2005.

Léonard, Émile G. *O protestantismo brasileiro: Estudo de eclesiologia e história social*. 3rd ed. São Paulo: ASTE, 2002.

Martínez-Fernández, Luis. *Protestantism and Political Conflict in the Nineteenth-Century Hispanic Caribbean*. Latin American Studies. New Brunswick, NJ: Rutgers University Press, 2002.

McNair, Stuart. *Round South America in the King's Business*. London: Marshall, 1913.

Mendonça, Antonio Gouvea. *O celeste porvir: A introdução do protestantismo no Brasil*. São Paulo: Editora USP, 2008.

Miceli, Sérgio. *A elite eclesiástica brasileira: 1890–1930*. 2nd ed. São Paulo: Letras, 2009.

Míguez Bonino, José. *Rostros del protestantismo latinoamericano*. Buenos Aires: Nueva Creación, 1995.

Paiva, José Pedro. "The Impact of Luther and the Reformation in the Portuguese Seaborne Empire: Asia and Brazil, 1520–1580." *Journal of Ecclesiastical History* 70 (2019) 283–303.

Ramacciotti, Ricardo D. Cubas. *The Politics of Religion and the Rise of Social Catholicism in Peru (1884–1935): Faith, Workers, and Race Before Liberation Theology*. Religion in the Americas 18. Leiden: Brill, 2018.

Reis, João José. *Divining Slavery and Freedom: The Story of Domingos Sodré, an African Priest in Nineteenth-Century Brazil*. Translated by H. Sabrina Gledhill. New Approaches to the Americas. New York: Cambridge University Press, 2015.

Ribeiro, Boanerges. *José Manoel da conceição e a reforma evangélica*. São Paulo: Semeador, 1995.
Santos, Lyndon de Araújo. *Os mascates da fé: História dos evangélicos no Brasil, 1855 a 1900*. Curitiba, Brazil: CRV, 2017.
Schwartz, Stuart B. *All Can Be Saved: Religious Tolerance and Salvation in the Iberian Atlantic World*. New Haven: Yale University Press, 2008.
Stanley, Brian. "Christian Missions and the Enlightenment: A Reevaluation." In *Christian Missions and the Enlightenment*, edited by Brian Stanley, 1–21. Studies in the History of Christian Missions. Gand Rapids: Eerdmans, 2001.
Vieira, David Gueiros. *O protestantismo, a maçonaria e a questão religiosa no Brasil*. Brasília: Editora Universidade de Brasília, 1980.
Walsh, Robert. *Notices of Brazil in 1828 and 1829*. 2 vols. London: Westley & Davies, 1830.
Willems, Emilio. *Followers of the New Faith: Culture Change and the Rise of Protestantism in Brazil and Chile*. Nashville: Vanderbilt University Press, 1967.

7

Christianity and Social Movements in Latin America

NICOLÁS PANOTTO

SOCIAL MOVEMENTS (HEREAFTER SM) are part of the modern political matrix, although they have had a paradoxical function, depending on contexts and times. On the one hand, they are a natural response to the diversification and pluralization of the modern postcolonial social field, in its expansionist, capitalist, and industrial nature. We speak of SM as both reactive and constitutive expressions of the processes of modern social differentiation, even as replies to demands born of this process. However, on the other hand, this emergence also expresses a symptom of structural crisis. The pretensions of cohesion in the state machinery, the sense of national sovereignty or the impact of certain abstractions in the modern liberal narrative, acted as alienating, hierarchizing, and excluding grounds, functional to the various hegemonic power dynamics. This gave rise to the birth of diverse SM as resistance to these logics.

In other words, SM are a reaction to the limits on three elements of modern politics: the agglutinating dimension of sociopolitical narratives, the performance of political identities, and the limitations of the scope of political-state institutionality. Although we will develop them throughout this chapter, we can summarize these three elements as follows. The first one accounts for the inability of mobilization and social legitimization that various ideologies aspired to, such as representative democracy, party machinery, or the boundless ideological labels—such as right and left, conservatism and progressivism—as homogeneous fields of political consciousness.[1] The second has to do with the restrictions on the spaces of political practice,

---

1. See Spivak's critique of the issue of conscience: *En otras palabras*, 327–61.

which have tended to a process of differentiation where "the political" has become an object of control of a type of knowledge, exercise, belonging, and institutionality by a particular and elitist sector, which is differentiated from "the social," almost as a passive mass. Finally, the political-state institutionality is far from being a space of plural representativeness, constitutive for any society, becoming not only a framework of legitimization of power of particular groups but also of a certain pretension of sovereign-nationalist homogenization.[2]

The emergence of SM responds to these three elements: being a field of pluralization of demands and processes of political/representative identification, and as an instance of diversification of performances that go beyond the modern-colonial institutionality of the political class or state bureaucracy. Rather, SM project themselves into fields such as the aesthetic, the popular, the religious, the artistic, among others, as alternative epistemic-political frameworks. Finally, they act as a collective of groups that not only respond to demands neglected by the state but also press the state's limits and boundaries for the creation of public policies and instances of recognition before society as a whole.

It is important to inscribe these processes from the distinction that Jean-Pierre Reed and Warren Goldstein identify between rebellions, revolutions, and social movements.[3] *Rebellions* represent a rather spontaneous phenomenon, as a conjuncture born of a crisis that puts a particular demand on the public table, which in turn mobilizes another set of demands. Rebellions do not respond—at least initially—to an organized or systematized process (the authors even define them as "pre-political" phenomenons) but are rather a reactive mobilization that shakes up the normalized political chessboard. *Revolutions*, on the other hand, are born of rebellions but from more organized configurations and with the objective of "seizing power" for its reformulation and replacement. Finally, *social movements* are a type of civil society organization that responds to this type of transforming hiatus in politics by addressing specific demands, although with more autonomous organizational processes and with a relationship that marks a distance from the state structure, albeit at different levels, depending on the context, the demand, and the intentions of the groups.

When speaking of the relationship between religion and these phenomena, we find that it has always been part of their development and evolution. On the one hand, there has been a pragmatic relationship—or

---

2. Bhabha, *Nación y narración*.
3. Reed and Goldstein, *Religion in Rebellions*, 1–27.

what sociologist Oscar Soto calls the *prefigurative dimension*[4]—where the religious has served as a platform for the creation of popular and social movements. On the other hand, the religious is inscribed as a *source of utopian inspiration*, where the senses of mysticism and political-historical transcendentality act as stages for mobilization and construction of identities. Finally, we could also identify that there is a relationship from *the very configuration of the religious as a social movement*, which touches on elements of both internal constitution and external articulations with social phenomena and agents.[5]

In this chapter we intend—almost as a medium-term research itinerary—to expand and link these aspects from a Latin American perspective. First, we will focus on defining the singularity of the category of SM, especially from its development in the history of the continent. Second, we will link it to its religious dimension, especially from the place occupied by liberation theologies. We will end with some theological notes that will allow us to think about the processes developed in this key.

What Is a Social Movement? Latin American Perspectives

Histories and Regional Origins of SM

The emergence of SM in Latin America responds, at the global level, to the whole process of postwar transformations, especially at four particular junctures: (1) the emergence of liberation movements between the '50s and '70s, (2) the resistance to dictatorial regimes—especially in South America—between the '70s and the '80s, (3) the implementation of neoliberal policies since the late '80s and the '90s with their erosion of the State and the social, and finally, (4) the period of neoliberal crisis and the emergence of progressive governments from the late 1990s until 2010, a year in which we see a pendulum swing with the birth of a new ultra-right and libertarian anti-political thinking.

Mónica Bruckmann and Theotonio Dos Santos, in a classic historical study on the subject, divide the history of SM in four phases: the first is the origins of classic SM from the anarchist influence to the third international conference; the second is the populist phase and national-democratic struggles; the third is the autonomy of SM and the new forms of resistance;

---

4. Soto, "Teología de la liberación," 86.

5. See Matt Marostica's work on the evangelical as SM in Argentina: "Pentecostals and Politics."

and the fourth involves the period of globalization of social struggles from Seattle and the new progressive agenda in the World Social Forum.[6]

In the first stage, we see the anarchist influence from the late nineteenth and early twentieth centuries, from the Italian migration. The main movements were born between 1917 and 1919, closely linked to the unionization of workers' groups. There was also a manifestation of peasant movements, especially in the Mexican Revolution in 1910. In Central America we will see similar scenarios between 1920 and 1930. Nicaraguan Sandinismo is an example. These groups were also related from their origins to indigenous movements. Middle-class movements will also emerge, such as the *aprismo* or the student movement, which had several foci throughout the region, especially in Cordoba, Argentina, in 1918.

The second stage was related to various movements that would take root after the First World War. The phenomenon of the "new workers" that arose in Latin American cities would give rise to the emergence of "populist models," such as Peronism in Argentina, Varguismo in Brazil, or the Mexican case itself. In these years, the demand for land was at the center of popular struggles and of the worker-peasant alliance, with strong support from students and sectors of the urban middle class. This was the prelude to the emergence of the landless movement in Brazil. Finally, the strengthening of the peasant movement began to establish itself under two directions: peasant-indigenous and peasant-Afro-descendant groups. The first feminist movements also began to appear in the region, especially from the 1960s onwards.

The third stage comes hand in hand with the social precariousness of the neoliberal model that began to take shape in postwar and, especially, post-dictatorship times. The workers' movements multiplied in the face of the disarmament of the state and the unions. Memory, solidarity economy, discourses on anti-debt and anti-privatization, factory takeovers, and identity-cultural representation groups mark this stage.

Finally, the fourth stage is related to the post-Seattle phenomena in 1999 and the meetings of the World Social Forum in Porto Alegre, which represent a much deeper questioning of global political agendas and try to place the political relevance of SM no longer as a reactive effect of hegemonic politics, but as a new way of doing politics that is here to stay, under the slogan "Another world is possible." It is also the time of regionalization and globalization of activism, from the slow opening to the participation of MS in multilateral organisms such as Mercosur, Alianza Bolivariana para los Pueblos de Nuestra América, and Unión de Naciones Suramericanas, or the

---

6. See Bruckmann, "Movimientos sociales."

CHRISTIANITY AND SOCIAL MOVEMENTS IN LATIN AMERICA

spaces for dialogue with civil society in Comisión Económica para América Latina y el Caribe and the Organization of American States.[7]

However, it is important to emphasize that multilateral spaces have not only served to reconfigure movements in favor of progressive demands or rights but also neoconservative voices, which have begun to operate strongly from a reactionary, anti-rights position, championing pro-life and anti-"gender ideology" views, as a way of questioning the deepening of inclusive policies and human rights agendas.[8] Several neoconservative religious movements—or what we call religious political networks[9]—have a fundamental role to play.[10]

Approaches and Frameworks of SM as a Sociopolitical Category

When we delve into theoretical and philosophical approaches in Latin America related to SM, we can find five central—though not unique—approaches from which both their evolution and their political configuration have been analyzed:

1. *The question of development and dependency theory.* In these currents, SM represent sectors excluded by the power groups functional in postwar capitalist development. They are dominated by an economicist vision, which articulates under the name of "liberation" any identity movement as a particular expression of opposition to the prevailing economic system.[11]

2. *Philosophy of liberation and the problem of the people.* This philosophy was one of the main currents of thought at the beginning of the political transformations of the 1970s. Nourished from neo-Marxist and Althusserian perspectives, it deals with the need to redefine hegemonic sociological conceptions in the light of liberation. One of the most divisive debates within this current was around the notion of "people," which tried to give a sociological notion that somehow moved away from the Marxist tradition or at least tried to go in a broader direction. This discussion brought about a dispute also within liberation theology.[12]

---

7. Gutiérrez, *Globalización*, 55–64.
8. Pleyer, "Ascenso político."
9. Panotto, "Incidencia religiosa en clave multilateral."
10. Panotto, "Nuevas cartografías."
11. Touraine, *Actores sociales.*
12. Cerutti Guldberg, *Filosofía de la liberación latinoamericana.*

3. *The concept of interculturality and the emergence of the pluri-national state.* The arrival of Evo Morales from the MAS in Bolivia had a great impact on regional politics, precisely because Morales's arrival was a government born of a peasant-indigenous movement that redefined the figure of the state from what was called pluri-nationality. Ecuador and Venezuela subsequently followed the example.[13]

4. *Poststructuralist approach to populisms.* The arrival of new progressive governments in the region since the end of the 1990s, with the presence of strong charismatic political leaders, gave rise to a poststructuralist production that offered a rereading of the subject of populism, vindicating some fundamental elements linked to SM, especially with regard to the definition of the social as a diversified space based on specific popular demands that achieve articulations in the light of a signifier, be it a narrative or a leader.[14]

5. *Postcolonial/decolonial studies.* A final approach of study goes hand in hand with the proliferation of postcolonial and decolonial analyses, which have continued the legacy of the study of popular and social movements but from a more intersectional key and from a more extensive historical matrix.[15]

These analyses are extremely varied, but they make it clear that SM do not only emerge from a crisis of the social state—as Jürgen Habermas suggests[16]—but rather the identification of a set of multiple subordinations and exclusions that are part, in turn, of the various dimensions of exclusion and representativeness of the collectives.[17] The mechanisms of indirect formal submission of the capitalist system have shifted mobilizations from the capital/labor axis to elements more linked to the quality of life.[18] Undoubtedly, it is also related to the pluralization of the axes of imposition/exploitation within neoliberalism, which is directly linked to the diversification of forms of political reaction. Added to this is the crisis of the traditional political mechanisms of doing politics, which implies the search for new performances and public action.

---

13. Sousa Santos et al., *Estado plurinacional y democracias.*
14. Laclau, *Razón populista*; Arditi, *Política en los bordes*, 161–229; Panotto, "'Pueblo' en disputa."
15. Martínez, "Rebelión, descolonización del poder."
16. Habermas, *Facticidad y validez.*
17. Gadea, "Crítica pós-moderna," 72–73.
18. Hotuart, *Deslegitimar el capitalismo.*

Faith on the Move: Liberating Christianity and SM in Latin America

The relationship between SM and Christianity should be understood in two ways. First, many Christianisms assume a process of internal/identitarian reconfiguration as a movement, just as various movements within the church displace institutional matrices. This shows an intrinsically religious dynamic linked to the processes of deinstitutionalization.[19] On the other hand, diverse Christianities assume a substantial role within the framework of the emergence of SM focused on diverse sociopolitical demands. Hence, the pluralization of Christian movements goes hand in hand with the globalization of the SM from the 1970s onwards.[20] In this context, Raúl Zibechi affirms that the three great political-social currents born in this region and that make up the ethical and cultural framework of the most important SM are, precisely, the ecclesial base communities linked to liberation theology (LT hereafter), the indigenous insurgency as a bearer of a different worldview from the Western one, and Guevarism, inspirer of revolutionary militancy.[21]

Already from this period we find extensive analyses of this linkage. In a 1979 classic of the sociology of Latin American religion, Otto Maduro analyzes the autonomy of religion and its relationship with Latin American sociocultural processes, emphasizing that such autonomy possesses and promotes an intrinsic dynamic of social mobilization.[22] Another reference is Michael Löwy's *Guerra de dioses: Religión y política en América Latina* (War of Gods: Religion and Politics in Latin America) from 1996, in which Löwy rescues LT in the sense of critical Marxism, identifying several binding elements between both currents: its universalism, its ethical concern for the poor and social victims, its anti-individualist valuation of collective life, its critique of capitalism, and its projection toward a kingdom of justice, peace, and fraternity.[23] We can also see it in the work of Chilean sociologist Cristián Parker, a central reference in early studies of Latin American popular religiosity, where such religiosity is understood as a critique of both colonial and modernizing reconfigurations of the field.[24]

---

19. Esquivel and Mallimaci, "Políticas y religiones."
20. Marchetti, "Cristianismo revolucionario en Argentina."
21. Zibechi, *Movimientos sociales latinoamericanos*, 28.
22. Maduro, *Religion and Social Conflicts*.
23. Löwy, *Guerra de dioses*, 99–117.
24. Parker, *Popular Religion and Modernization*.

LT has been a fundamental agent in the relationship between Christianity and SM. We see it in the creation of the Pastoral Land Commission created in 1975, as a prelude to the grassroots education movement or one of the most important movements in Latin America: the landless movement (MST) in Brazil. It also played a fundamental role in Central America and the revolutionary movements of the 60s and 70s,[25] or with national actors such as the Third World priests' movement in Argentina.[26] The same can be said of its relationship with the origins of the Latin American ecumenical movement, be it with the Christian student movements or later the church and society movement in Latin America.[27]

As Robert Mackin analyzes it, these movements have diversified significantly, for example, in national and transnational indigenous movements, especially in Ecuador, Mexico, and Peru, where even an indigenous pastoral perspective was developed, or in the women's movement and the development of liberation feminist theologies.[28] For his part, Élio Gasda summarizes three contributions of LT to SM:

1. Reformulation of thinking and production
2. Elaboration of a different theology focused on the transformation of values and ways of thinking the work of critical reflection of the movements and in terms of political intervention
3. Active participation of members of communities and groups within the movements, civil society organizations, and international networks[29]

Now, as we mentioned earlier, LT not only contributed to the origin and development of SM in the region, but we could even consider it as a movement itself. Christian Smith said in the early 1990s: "The liberation theology movement, however, is not only a set of theological ideas or beliefs, but an attempt to mobilize a previously unmobilized constituency for collective action against an antagonist to promote social change. The movement does articulate a specific set of ideas: liberation theology. But, as a movement, it consists of more than ideas. It is organization. It is action. It is social change."[30]

---

25. Spykman et al., *Let My People Live*; Vigil, *Entre lagos y volcanes*.
26. Morello, *Cristianismo y revolución*.
27. Tahar Chaouch, "Cristianismo y política."
28. Mackin, "Teología de la liberación."
29. Gasda, "Direitos humanos, movimientos sociais," 252.
30. Smith, *Emergence of Liberation Theology*, 25.

An example of the theological foundation of these convergences can be found in a text by Ignacio Ellacuría in 1978 on the relationship between the church and social organizations. Ellacuría starts from the fact that speaking of liberation in a theological key implies reading reality through the lens of God's kingdom. This means that the historical practice cannot be located only in the church but instead recognizes the role played by other agents in its manifestation. In other words, the church is not the only "mediation" of the kingdom in history. It must also commit itself to the promotion and defense of these other mediations. Moreover, the church must allow itself to be challenged by them.

Ellacuría argues that this vision represents not a dogmatic thesis but a *type of utopian ideal*. But as a utopian ideal, the role of social organizations must subvert any intention to establish themselves within hegemonic power structures. Ellacuría's words in this regard are very relevant for today:

> Popular organizations must be maintained as a utopian principle of power, but not as an effective principle, in order to occupy the real political power of the State. What this ideal means is that if it is true that without having as a goal the conquest of political power it is not possible to maintain an effective political organization, it is also true that by focusing the organization on the seizure of political power, the project of integral liberation, which the popular organizations could promote, is distorted. This is not intended to distort or weaken the social and political force of the organizations, but to place them where they can give more of themselves.[31]

Ellacuría makes this approach, moreover, as a way of questioning the division between the social and the political, making the concept of the kingdom of God a framework of divergence and at the same time a projection of everyday historical and micro-political practices in the horizon of a broader "project," but even beyond the institutionalization of the political, especially in its partisan or state scheme. Thus, the emergence of LT as a movement goes hand in hand with the counter-position of an essentialist reading of reality from a theological-Christian perspective.[32]

---

31. Ellacuría, "Iglesia y las organizaciones populares," 696.
32. Soto, "Teologias da libertação," 257.

Social and Political Mobilization as Disruption: Some Theological Conclusions

From all that has been said so far, we can draw two central conclusions. First, that the presence, mobilization, and existence of SM account for the paradoxical constituency of modern politics that frames Latin American societies. On the one hand, *they account for the very social diversification that characterizes modern politics*, in terms of the autonomy of social fields, the impact of the stratification of productive forces, the diversification of the processes of channeling social demands, and the influence of globalization on the extension of the territorialities of struggle, resistance, and mobilization. However, on the other hand, SM are also the symbol of the crisis produced by the failed utopias of modernity, not only with respect to the failure of their visions of social development but also in terms of their functionality in the processes of sociocultural homogenization, demobilization of the public sphere, and maintenance of central power groups, both political and economic.

Hence, SM represent a postcolonial/decolonial device that mimetically coexists and symptomatically resists the colonial mechanisms of modern politics with respect to the power of the political and business class, the totalitarianism that still survives in some models of state bureaucratization of the social, the naturalization of the effects of neoliberalism and its alienating instrumentalization of diversity as a result of methodological individualisms, and the constant crises of the hegemonic democratic paradigm. The distinctive feature of SM in this context is that they operate as spaces for the representation of plural demands based on political performances and types of institutionalities that operate singularly as multipolar, equivalent, articulated, and collective.

The second element to underline—without pretending to fall into generalizations and romanticism—is that SM possess *an intrinsic religious-theological potency*. This element does not arise only from the place occupied by religious groups in the practices of SM, as we have indicated. Rather, we could make a reverse reading and affirm that we find a relationship between the disruptive dimension of SM vis-à-vis modern political institutionality and the pluralization of social demands, with the articulating capacity that resides in the trans-immanence of the religious/spiritual as a sacredness that bursts into its utopian dimension.

The disruptive and pluralizing movement of contemporary politics is not an ad hoc phenomena but a constitutive condition. Collective dynamics always move in a tension between power and potency,[33] politics and police,[34] politics and the political,[35] and other forms of demarcation thought in contemporary political theory and practice, which show that the movement between segmentations—the constituted and the constituent—is far from being a phenomenological element but rather a condition of the political as an *event*.[36] The same condition deserves to be highlighted with respect to theological processes of reflection on political dynamics, as suggested by Mark Lewis Taylor with his distinction between *theology* as a "guild discipline" established by institutions, and *the theological* as a type of discourse that critically discerns the agonistic dynamics of the social. In his words: "More particularly, it traces and theorizes the ways that persons and groups rendered subordinate and vulnerable by agonistic politics and its systematic imposed social suffering nevertheless haunt, unsettle, and perhaps dissolve the structures of those systems."[37]

In other words, the political and the theological understood as disruptive movements find common ground in the following elements: (1) a utopian horizon as a historical projection that questions the established social and political forms that impede its effectiveness; (2) a trans-immanent vision of subjects, collectives, and contexts, where the notions of otherness and transcendence operate as devices of resignification of practices, places, and anthropological and social visions; (3) a critical stance toward the structures of power and social activity from a commitment to the concrete demands of the everyday life of the people, which not only operate as fields of action but also as hermeneutic frameworks of existential, social, and political reinterpretation from very diverse fields, practices, gestures, epistemes, and performances; and (4) instances of mystical inspiration, of channeling sensibilities outside (or marginal) to the traditional epistemes.

These elements were approached from different theological-religious fronts that we can identify in these shared crossings. One of them is *mysticism as nourishment for both faith and activism*. Frei Betto and Leonardo Boff have developed this theme,[38] where the sense of mysticism and militancy go hand in hand in the intrinsic relationship between mystery, originality, and utopia, which manifests itself as a mobilization that occurs in concrete reality but that goes beyond the limits that it has, through the

33. Maffesoli, *Transfiguración de lo político*.
34. Ranciere, *Disenso*.
35. Mouffe, *Agonística*.
36. Vatter and Ruiz, *Política y acontecimiento*.
37. Taylor, *Theological and Political*, 9.
38. Boff and Betto, *Mística y espiritualidad*.

mobilization of passions and affections.[39] According to João Pedro Stedile, one of the founders of the MST, "mysticism" is not conceived as a metaphysical or idealistic distraction but as a factor of unity of ideals, so there is no contradiction between faith and struggle. It is a struggle that is conceived as anti-static, anti-imperialist, and anti-capitalist. The "mystique" is expressed through symbols (flags, slogans, hymns, songs); it nourishes, forges, and affirms the identity of the movement. The symbolic-religious dimension becomes a source of inspiration for revolt and insubordination, and the "mystique" gives radical meaning to the sociopolitical horizon of the MST.[40]

Mysticism, then, serves not only as a kind of configuration of activism but even as an ontological framework around divine action in history. Here is the *trans-immanent notion of God* that several theologians have highlighted lately, as a critical approach to naturalized images of God, which in turn naturalize sociopolitical structures and practices. The immanence-transcendence tension means, in the words of Joerg Rieger, not to strive for a Manichean opposition but rather to see the possibility of transcending one kind of immanence for another, within the framework of the relationship between materialities and power relations.[41] "Transcendence, we might conclude, is not the otherworldly or the supernatural but the alternative immanence that totally reshapes dominant immanence."[42] Thus, we can say that the dimension of "movement" not only establishes a field of revelation but also a constitutive space of the divine as a theological notion. The disruptive dynamics movement/politics/power is conceived from the notion of history as a scenario where the trans-immanent tension of the divine and faith operate confronting the hegemonic forces of power.

This is why *we need to further develop a theology of the multitude,* where the tensions/conflicts are constituted as a process of political movement, based on the inscription of otherness as part of the collective. In the words of Joerg Rieger and Kwok Pui-lan, "The heart of the theology of the multitude is no religion in general but an experience of otherness and transcendence which can be mediated through religion as well as through other experiences."[43] This constitutive otherness is not an alien otherness, beyond borders but a representation of the power inherent in movement, where otherness is the sign of trans-immanence that mobilizes practices, mysticism, faith, projects. As Rieger and Pui-lan conclude,

39. Panotto, "Dimensión política de la espiritualidad"; González Gómez, *Dinamismo místico.*
40. See Matínez, "Religiosidad popular," 14.
41. Rieger, *Theology in the Capitalocene,* 79.
42. Rieger, *Theology in the Capitalocene,* 81.
43. Rieger and Pui-lan, *Occupy Religion,* 75.

In conclusion, a theology of the multitude offers a new perspective not only on transcendence but also on immanence. Immanence is changed in the encounter with transcendence in the sense that it becomes a space that provides both resistance and new opportunities for the multitude to become genuinely productive. Immanence is the new world—the anti-kingdom, or the reign of God—growing in the midst of the old. Understood in this way, both immanence and transcendence have a specific horizon: overcoming a status quo that does not allow alternatives and that exploits the agency and productivity of the multitude.[44]

Finally, this mystique from the theology of the multitude that reinscribes the mass-minority tension confers *the challenge of reimagining the utopian horizon that delimits mobilization*.[45] The question is: How can *the theological* regain its prefigurative dimension in popular struggles and SM, particularly as a mediation of the socioreligious utopia of the kingdom of God?[46] In this sense, the utopian in SM represents a horizon that must remain as such: as a remoteness that mobilizes the path to find "places" in its becoming and transit. Thus, the political in SM responds to this critical mobilization of the established structures. It is precisely the image of the kingdom of God. As Jung Mo Sung defines it,[47]

> What we long for is a utopian horizon of the Kingdom of God, always remembering that such a horizon, like every horizon, is barely attainable through the eyes of desires, but is impossible to be reached by our human steps. What we can and must build is a more just, more humane, more fraternal society . . . which will always coexist with the possibility of errors and problems, intentional or not.

We can conclude with a final reflection related to the link between the religious and the political in Latin America. We know that the relationship between these two fields in the region is a constitutive part of its history. It is an almost natural linkage of Latin American political development, which not infrequently played a negative role, through the legitimization of exclusionary power structures, the imposition of an alienating religiosity, or the limitation of rights. However, these are not the only faces of this relationship. The disruptive logic of religious groups and SM is the representation of

---

44. Rieger and Pui-lan, *Occupy Religion*, 76.
45. Houtart, *Mercado y religión*, 69–83.
46. Soto, "Teología de la liberación," 86.
47. Sung, *Sujeto y sociedades complejas*, 49.

a utopian-mystical logic that coexists mimetically and critically within the framework of the modern-centric matrices that limit social development. Hence the importance of highlighting this constitutive disruptive logic in the configuration of movements, not only as a passing or conjunctural symptom but as a hiatus that forms an inalienable part of our context, which we must collectively discern and channel.

References

Arditi, Benjamín. *La política en los bordes del liberalismo: Diferencia, populismo, revolución, emancipación*. Buenos Aires: Gedisa, 2009.
Bhabha, Homi K., ed. *Nación y narración: Entre la ilusión de una identidad y las diferencias culturales*. Buenos Aires: Siglo XXI, 2010.
Boff, Leonardo, and Frei Betto. *Mística y espiritualidad*. Buenos Aires: CEDEPO, 1995.
Bruckmann, Mónica. "Los movimientos sociales en America Latina: Un balance historico." Medelu, Apr. 15, 2008. From "Los movimientos sociales en America Latina: Un balance historico," by Mónica Bruckmann and Theotonio Dos Santos (*Prokla* 142). https://www.medelu.org/Los-movimientos-sociales-en.
Castells, Manuel. *Redes de indignación y esperanza*. Madrid: Alianza, 2015.
Cerutti Guldberg, Horacio. *Filosofía de la liberación latinoamericana*. Buenos Aires: Fondo Cultura Económica, 2006.
Cunha, Magali do Nascimento. "Limits and Possibilities for the Ecumenical Movement Today: A Latin American View." In *World Christianity and Public Religion*, edited by Raimundo Barreto et al, 33–48. Minneapolis: Fortress, 2017.
Ellacuría, Ignacio. "La iglesia y las organizaciones populares en El Salvador." In *Escritos teológicos*, 2:683–704. El Salvador: UCA, 2000.
Esquivel, Juan Cruz, and Fortunato Mallimaci. "Políticas y religiones en América Latina y el Caribe: Recomposiciones históricas, epistemológicas y conceptuales." *Anuario de Historia Regional y de las Fronteras* 23 (2018) 13–24.
Ferreyra, Julián. "Deleuze en América Latina: Hedor ontológico en la lucha y la organización." In *Luchas minoritarias y líneas de fuga en América Latina*, edited by Patricio Landaeta Mardones and José Ezcurdia Corona, 15–25. Santiago: Metales Pesados, 2023.
Gadea, Carlos. "A crítica pós-moderna e os movimentos sociais." In *Incluão social, identitdade e diferença: Perspectivas pós-estruturalistas de análise social*, edited by Aécio Amaral Jr. and Joanildo A. Burity, 67–84. São Paulo: Annablume, 2006.
Gasda, Élio. "Dereitos humanos, movimientos sociais e teologia da libertação." In *50 anos de teologias da libertação: Memória, revisã, perspectivas e desafio*, edited by Edward Guimarães et al, 239–56. São Paulo: Recriar, 2022.
González Gómez, Elías. *El dinamismo místico: Mística, resistencia epistémica y creación del mundo nuevo*. Mexico City: Alios Ventos, 2022.
Gutiérrez, German. *Globalización, caos y sujeto en América Latina: El impacto de las estrategias neoliberales y las alternativas*. San José: DEI, 2001.
Habermas, Jürgen. *Facticidad y validez: Sobre el derecho y el estado democrático de derecho en términos de teoría del discurso*. Translated by Manuel Jiménez Redondo. Colección estructuras y procesos. Madrid: Trotta, 2008.

Hinkelammert, Franz J., and Henry Mora Jiménez. *Hacia una economía de la vida: Preludio a una reconstrucción de la economía*. San José: DEI, 2005.
Hotuart, François. *Deslegitimar el capitalismo: Reconstruir la esperanza*. Panama:: CLACSO, 2009.
———. *Mercado y religión*. San José: DEI, 2001.
Laclau, Ernesto. *La razón populista*. Buenos Aires: Fondo Cultura Económica, 2005.
Longuini, Netom Luiz. *El nuevo rostro de la misión: Los movimientos ecuménico y evangelical en el protestantismo latinoamericano*. Quito: Sinodal, 2006.
Löwy, Michael. *Guerra de dioses: Religión y política en América Latina*. Translated by Josefina Anaya. Mexico City: Siglo XXI, 1996.
Mackin, Robert. "Teología de la liberación y movimientos sociales: Perspectivas, tendencias y casos." In *Movimientos sociales en América Latina: Perspectivas, tendencias y casos*, edited by Paul Almeida and Allen Cordero Ulate, 181–210. Colección democracias en movimiento. Buenos Aires: CLACSO, 2017.
Maduro, Otto. *Religion and Social Conflicts*. Maryknoll, NY: Orbis, 1982.
Maffesoli, Michael. *La transfiguración de lo político*. Barcelona: Herder, 2004.
Marchetti, María de la Paz. "Cristianismo revolucionario en Argentina en los 60's y 70's." *X Jornadas de Sociología* (2013). https://cdsa.aacademica.org/000-038/279.pdf.
Marostica, Matt. "Pentecostals and Politics: The Creation of the Evangelical Christian Movement in Argentina, 1983–1993." PhD diss., University of California, Berkeley, 2013.
Martínez, Luis. "Rebelión, descolonización del poder y movimientos anti-sistémicos en América Latina." *Revista de Ciencias Sociales* 17 (2011) 167–75.
———. "La religiosidad popular y el ecologismo de los pobres: Apuntes sobre el papel de la espiritualidad en los movimientos de resistencia." *Revista Sapiência: Sociedade, Saberes e Práticas Educacionais* 6 (2017) 7–27.
Míguez, Néstor, et al. *Beyond the Spirit of Empire: Theology and Politics in New Key. Reclaiming Liberation Theology*. London: SCM, 2009.
Morello, Gustavo. *Cristianismo y revolución: Los orígenes intelectuales de la guerrilla argentina*. Córdoba: Universidad Católica de Córdoba Editorial, 2003.
Mouffe, Chantal. *Agonística*. Buenos Aires: Fondo Cultura Económica, 2022.
Panotto, Nicolás. "La dimensión política de la espiritualidad como mística: Alteridad, lenguaje y hospitalidad radical en la construcción de lo público." *Hojas y Hablas* 20 (2020) 13–28.
———. "Incidencia religiosa en clave multilateral: La presencia de redes políticas evangélicas en las asambleas de la OEA." *Revista Cultura & Religión* 14 (2020) 100–120.
———. "Nuevas cartografías de la incidencia regional evangélica: Política local-multilateral desde y dentro del sistema interamericano de derechos humanos; Ejemplos del caso chileno." *Religião e Sociedade* 43 (2023) 125–50.
———. "El 'pueblo' en disputa: Nuevas (y viejas) coyunturas en los populismos de América Latina." *Cadernos de Estudos Sociais* 30 (2015) 1–15.
Parker, Cristián. *Popular Religion and Modernization in Latin America: A Different Logic*. Maryknoll, NY: Orbis, 1996.
Pleyer, Geoffrey. "El ascenso político de los actores religiosos conservadores: Cuatro lecciones del caso brasileño." *Encartes* 3 (2021) 65–84.

Pui-lan, Kwok. *Postcolonial Politics and Theology: Unraveling Empire for Global World*. Louisville: Westminster John Knox, 2021.

Ranciere, Jacques. *Disenso: Ensayos sobre estética y política*. Buenos Aires: Fondo Cultura Económica, 2019.

Reed, Jean-Pierre, and Warren S. Goldstein. *Religion in Rebellions, Revolutions, and Social Movements*. Routledge Studies in Religion and Politics. New York: Taylor Francis, 2022.

Rieger, Joerg. *Globalization and Theology*. Horizons in Theology. Nashville: Abingdon, 2010.

———. *Theology in the Capitalocene: Ecology, Identity, Class, and Solidarity*. Edited by Ashley John Moyse and Scott A. Kirkland. Dispatches. Minneapolis: Fortress, 2022.

Rieger, Joerg, and Kwok Pui-lan. *Occupy Religion: Theology and the Multitude*. Religion in the Modern World. Lanham, MD: Rowman & Littlefield, 2013.

Smith, Christian. *The Emergence of Liberation Theology: Radical Religion and Social Movement Theory*. Chicago: University Chicago Press, 1991.

Soto, Oscar. "Teologias da libertação e movimentos sociais: Matrizes de pensamento critico e articulações contrahegemônicas na América Latina recente, desde o processo social brasileiro." *MEMORIAS: Revista Digital de Historia y Arqueología Desde el Caribe Colombiano* 9 (2012) 248–71.

———. "Teología de la liberación y movimientos populares: Lucha por la tierra, educación popular y emancipación en América Latina." In *Re-encuentros & re-encantos: Caminos y desafíos actuales de las teologías de la liberación*, edited by Daylíns Rufín Pardo and Luis Carlos Marrero, 75–88. Buenos Aires: JuanUno, 2018.

Sousa Santos, Boaventura de, et al., eds. *Estado plurinacional y democracias*. Plural, Bol.: Paz, 2021.

Spivak, Gayartri. *En otras palabras, en otros mundos: Ensayos sobre política cultural*. Buenos Aires: Paidós, 2013.

Spykman, Gordon, et al. *Let My People Live: Faith and Struggle in Central America*. Grand Rapids: Eerdmans, 1988.

Sung, Jung Mo. *Sujeto y sociedades complejas: Para repensar los horizontes utópicos*. San José: DEI, 2005.

Tahar Chaouch, Malik. "Cristianismo y política en América Latina: El paradigma de la teología de la liberación." *Desafíos* 17 (2007) 157–99.

Taylor, Mark Lewis. *The Theological and the Political: On the Weight of the World*. Minneapolis: Fortress, 2010.

Touraine, Alain. *Actores sociales y sistemas políticos en América Latina*. Santiago: PREALC, 1987.

Vatter, Miguel, and Miguel Ruiz, eds. *Política y acontecimiento*. Buenos Aires: Fondo Cultura Económica, 2011.

Vigil, José María. *Entre lagos y volcanes: Práctica teológica en Nicaragua*. San José: DEI, 1990.

Zibechi, Raúl. *Los movimientos sociales latinoamericanos: Tendencias y desafíos*. Buenos Aires: CLACSO, 200

8

Hierarchy and Ritual: A Comparative Study of Candomblé, Umbanda, and Neo-Pentecostal Churches

Luiz C. Nascimento

In *Slavery and Social Death*, Orlando Patterson says that "slavery is one of the most extreme forms of the relation of domination, approaching the limits of total power of the master, and the total powerlessness from the viewpoint of the slave."[1] Patterson describes *power relation* as having three defining facets: the use of threat and violence; the capacity to persuade others to change the way they perceive their own interests and circumstances; and last, the ability to convert the use of force into a right, and the obedience of others into a duty.[2] He also says that power relations are built upon the concept of authority and states that they rely on forms of symbolic control. Patterson critiques those who explain authority by using Weber's theory of authority, which presents the law and charisma as the sources of authority. He disagrees with those who use this notion as a sufficient explanation because Weber himself understands that the law itself "begs" for authority; and that is true because no law has the authority to enforce itself.[3] He says that charisma cannot be taken as the source of authority in the case of slavery because most times slave masters were not more endowed with charisma than any other fellow citizens or even than their slaves could be. But he agrees with Weber that tradition, understood as a total complex of norms, values, ideas, and patterned behaviors that constitute what is known as culture, could be the source of authority. According to him, one would

---

1. Patterson, *Slavery and Social Death*, 1.
2. Patterson, *Slavery and Social Death*, 1–2.
3. Patterson, *Slavery and Social Death*, 36–37.

be able to use culture as a source of authority by making the situation of domain over the other seem something natural or inherent to the social order, so that it need not be questioned.[4]

The aforementioned theory of authority is essential to understand why the enslavement of African men and women, until not so long ago, was seen as a natural part of human experience and went unquestioned by the majority of people for centuries. And slavery was experienced by Africans in many parts of the world; in Brazil, it started being practiced not long after the discovery of Brazilian lands by the Portuguese navigator Pedro Alvares Cabral and was used there from the beginning of colonization. The forced labor of African men and women was practiced on Brazilian lands over a period of 356 years, commencing in 1532 and extending until it was eventually abolished on May 13th, 1888.

Enslavement usually involved some kind of social death of the slave. Patterson defines the meaning of *social death* as the state of no longer belonging to a community, as having no social existence. He says that in most slaveholding societies, slaves were required to go through some rituals by which they renounced their ancestry and identity; even their names were changed, and they were assimilated into the household of their master but at a status of the "domestic enemy," the totally other. This ritualized social death enforced the idea that the captive outsider or the dispossessed person who had to sell oneself belonged nowhere and had lost their personhood. Ritual death took different forms in different cultures, but the core meaning remained the same. No matter whether one would be a slave within one's own former milieu or elsewhere as a captive who had been taken away from their original community, one would come to the same sense of loss and humiliation.[5] In the context of Brazilian slavery Africans were ripped away from their original communities in Africa and brought overseas on the "black ships" or "slave ships." At arrival on continental Brazil, members of the same families and those who shared the same tribal identity were set apart from one another as a strategy to weaken their resistance to their condition and also to prevent rebellion. But despite all the efforts by slave masters and traders to deprive captive Africans of their identity and culture, some traces of them could not be taken away from their minds.[6]

My intent in the present work is to demonstrate that in the situation of degradation and complete objectification in which African slaves were placed in colonial Brazil, deprived of their native lands and cultures,

4. Patterson, *Slavery and Social Death*, 36–38.
5. Patterson, *Slavery and Social Death*, 38–45.
6. Dion, *Omindarewa*, 151–52.

HIERARCHY AND RITUAL 113

families and social structures, it was religion, especially the worship of the orixás in Candomblé with its highly ritualized and esoteric practices, as well as the more recently developed and less hierarchic religious practice of Umbanda, that permitted Africans to keep a sense of identity and community in Brazil, and particularly in the state of Bahia. I propose that the strict hierarchy, secretive rituals of initiation practices, and spirit possession played an important role in preserving the cultures, languages, and hope of those in the Brazilian experience of the African diaspora. In recent years, neo-Pentecostal churches in Brazil have been appropriating some of the ritual practices of popular language and symbols of those religions to incorporate them in their own services and worldview. These neo-Pentecostal churches, especially the Igreja Universal do Reino de Deus, have been among the fastest growing church bodies in Brazil. I contend that understanding how the traditions and structures of these religious groups work will help us realize why neo-Pentecostal churches find so much positive response among the middle class and working poor in Brazil. This present study will take the practices of the Igreja Universal do Reino de Deus as the Christian paradigm in the comparison with those practices of Candomblé and Umbanda.

A World of Rituals and Secrecy

Both Candomblé and Umbanda have a vocabulary of their own. It would be impossible to understand their practices and beliefs if one were not introduced to the particular terms and jargons used by followers in their rituals. For this reason I found it useful to define some of the essential vocabulary. There is some vocabulary that is shared by both traditions.

As the Brazilian Candomblé was formed by the junction of different tribal African traditions, some of the words may be spelled differently. For the sake of making it easier to the reader, I have decided to use the standard Brazilian spelling because it would probably be confusing to one not familiarized with the words to have to deal with the possible different spellings. I found it more useful to explain the meaning of the words as they are used for the first time in the text instead of only adding a glossary at the end of this work.

Candomblé is an esoteric religion, and knowledge of its secrets is granted only to those initiated in the religion. There is a strong sense of hierarchy, which is kept by strict discipline. The priestesses and priests of Candomblé are called either *mae de santo* or *pai de santo*, respectively. I find it interesting that even though Candomblé and Umbanda use distinct names to refer to male and female priests, this does not mean that they have problems in dealing with diverse sexual orientation among their priests and ordinary followers. In fact, Candomblé and Umbanda are well known for welcoming male and female homosexuals and bisexuals in their communities. I prefer to use the corresponding English words, which are "mother" for a female priest and "father" for a male priest. The usage of the words "mother" and "father" is explained by the fact that when Africans were brought to Brazil to work as slaves in coffee and sugar cane plantations, they were systematically separated from those of their own tribal tradition, and also members of the same family were not kept together in order to avoid closer interaction and the possibility of organization as individuals into groups of resistance. Slave traders and owners were concerned that if communication among enslaved Africans was made easier, the slaves could rebel against their masters. For that reason they tried to mingle Africans of different ethnic groups together to make communication more difficult, as their diversity of dialects and tribal backgrounds would then serve as a barrier.[7]

As tribal and family referentials were lost, Africans were forced to work toward finding other bonds to one another, and those were found in their religion. The efforts to keep slaves from gaining community proved to be not as effective as slave owners and traders expected, for despite the actual language barriers, Africans of different ethnic groups did not simply ignore other tribal dialects, and some of them were able to communicate to persons of other groups. The result of this interaction helped create a common ground of religious beliefs, and biological family ties were replaced by the relation to the sacred they found in the families of deities, called *orixás*, worshipped by the different groups. The resulting mixture of these traditions is a pantheon of orixás different than any other originally found among the ethnic groups in Africa. According to Johnson, most *terreiros* (temples of Candomblé) invoke between twelve and twenty orixás. Olorum, also known as Olorumaré, is the supreme god of Candomblé. Olorum is unreachable, untouchable. He lives in Orum, the heaven of Candomblé, where he lives in the company of the African ancestors. According to traditional knowledge, he does not relate to creation, cannot be reached directly by the prayers of believers, and is believed to have delegated the task of creation to his son Oxala, who is associated with Jesus Christ in the syncretism of popular Catholicism, Umbanda, and Candomblé.

The orixás are sometimes referred to as gods, but that is not the most appropriate term. They would be better identified as mediators between humanity and the Supreme Being. That's why they are popularly referred to as "saints" and have been for a long time associated with the names of saints

---

7. Dion, *Omindarewa*, 151–52.

of the Catholic tradition. That enabled the slaves to keep the worship of the orixás even when they were forbidden from having their own religious rituals and were forced to attend the Catholic Mass by their masters. Richard Fenn of Princeton Theological Seminary informs us that "the highlanders of Bolivia, not slaves, adopted a similar practice, of disguising the fact that in singing Christian hymns they were calling on their ancestors."[8] Slaves were taken to church and thought to have converted into Christianity, but in fact that was a strategy adopted by them to deceive their masters and provide the continuation of their expression of faith. More recently, some Candomblé priests, like Mother Stella, have been claiming the purity of orixás worship, thus denying any relation or influence of Afro-Catholic syncretism in Candomblé.[9]

In his book *Mitologia dos orixás*, Prandi collected the accounts of Candomblé's cosmogony and many other stories of how the orixás act and interact with humanity and the created world. These stories were until recently kept as part of the oral tradition of Candomblé and were accessible solely to Candomblé initiates. Harding poses that there are highly "pan-African syncretic formulations arising from the interactions of peoples of a variety of African rituals traditions."[10] According to Harding, historical evidence suggests that the emergence of Candomblé as a formalized and continuous religious tradition in Brazil took place in the nineteenth century, but Candomblé is in no way a unique Brazilian experience, because the practices, myths, families of orixás are the result of centuries of oral tradition, especially in the West African societies from which most of the African slaves were brought to Brazil and other parts of the world. Harding also suggests that the development of Candomblé in Brazil was made possible because of the growing number of freed Africans and the increase in the number of slaves who worked in the system named *de ganho*. Those slaves were permitted to work for other people and could eventually buy their freedom; they usually lived away from their masters and were less subject to their control. Those slaves were in closer contact and interaction with Blacks, and that enabled them to maintain and develop their language, culture, and religious practices.[11] In *Rituals of Blood*, Patterson works on the idea of the Christian bifocal narrative of sacrifice as a tradition that inconsistently symbolizes conflating aversion with purification. Patterson says that "Euro-Americans,

---

8. Professor Richard Fenn added this piece of information as a note when reading the first draft of this work.
9. Matory, *Black Atlantic Religion*, 22–23.
10. Harding, *Refuge in Thunder*, 39.
11. Harding, *Refuge in Thunder*, 41.

a people who considered themselves—all of them, including the lowliest—a triumphant superior race destined to create a master civilization built in the militaristic, honorific image of a chivalric, conquering 'white' Christ." He adds, "The humble Christ was dissociated from the triumphant Christ by virtue of being associated with the humble crucified Negro."[12] This may help explain the differences between the Brazilian slave-master relations and those of Southern plantation owners and their slaves in the US. Brazil was a Catholic country at the time of slavery and the fact that the emphasis in Catholic tradition lies on the suffering Christ, whereas in the US evangelical traditions focus on the triumphant Christ, might have shaped the sort of relation between masters and slaves and permitted slaves to have more freedom than they would have in the US. In Calvinist America, slaves were under much stricter control than in Brazil, especially because of the strong sense of moral superiority that white masters attributed to themselves in contrast to the moral degradation cast upon their "domestic enemies," the slaves. Apart from the aforementioned problem of the bifocal narrative of sacrifice as discussed by Patterson, one could add the contrast between the Protestant emphasis on the depravity of humankind and the understanding of the fundamental goodness of the human world in Catholic tradition as another element that might have influenced the levels of repression applied to slaves in the Protestant US and the officially Catholic imperial Brazil.[13]

A Geography of Secrecy

The temples of Candomblé are called *terreiros*, and there is a special geography to them that reflects this hierarchy. Johnson says that "as the initiate progresses in the hierarchy, he/she comes closer to the center of the *Terreiro*, into the most secretive rooms, where the initiate's heads are made and where *Orixás* are dispatched from possessed bodies."[14] One is granted access only to the knowledge of that level where they are and the levels they have already progressed through, but they are not even permitted to ask questions about anything related to knowledge pertaining to higher levels of hierarchy. When one asks a question that cannot be answered because one has not been initiated yet, that question may be answered, but that will be done in a way that never permits the secret to be revealed. Each secret of Candomblé is referred to as being a *fundamento*, and it cannot be shared with non-initiated persons. Johnson says that "the *fundamento* is kept secret

---

12. Patterson, *Rituals of Blood*, 218–23.
13. Curran, *Catholic Moral Tradition Today*, 34.
14. Johnson, *Secrets, Gossip, and Gods*, 32.

and questions regarding them by non-initiates are answered with silence or a cursory reply, and if an inattentive *Iaô* [initiate] begins to hazard an explanation he/she will be silenced by a look of the mother/father and a warning 'that's a *fundamento*.'"[15]

Johnson poses that "ritual or oral transmission preserves the bonds of the group by virtue of the necessity of long-term apprenticeship to a superior for acquisition of knowledge, whereas writing may allow secrets to be easily transmitted outside the boundary of the group."[16] This is true of Candomblé; not until recently did we have the first written accounts of their mythology, cosmogony, and ritual practices. And the unveiling of these secrets into the public life is not understood as positive; a good example of this concern is the Terreiro Ilé Axé Opô Afonjá, whose priestess, Mother Stella de Oxossi, will not permit the filming of ceremonies and festivals in honor of the orixás.[17]

On the other hand, Umbanda is a more recent development of religious life in Brazil. Most probably, the initial presence of Umbanda as an organized religion in the Brazilian scenario can be placed in between the 1920s and the 1930s. It all probably began with adepts of Kardecism, which consists of a body of doctrines created or codified, as they prefer to say, by a French man whose name was Léon Hippolyte Denizart Rivail. Reincarnation, communication between the living and the dead, and the evolution of the spirit through its many past life experiences are some of the basic doctrines of Kardecism. It is a religion practiced in Brazil mainly by upper- and middle-class followers who trace the origin of Kardecism to the second half of the nineteenth century. Umbanda came to exist when they started to use a syncretic form of Kardecism, borrowing some elements from the practices of Candomblé and also from several religious traditions of the native Brazilian populations.[18]

The body plays an important role in both Candomblé and Umbanda. It is through the body that followers experience the encounter with the sacred. In those religions the trance is the means by which the limited person breaks the boundaries between the immanence of physical life into the transcendent presence of the divine in their own bodies. Cunha says, "The body assumes, in these religions, the status of mediator through which the sacred manifests itself and acts in the world."[19]

15. Johnson, *Secrets, Gossip, and Gods*, 32.
16. Johnson, *Secrets, Gossip, and Gods*, 28.
17. Matory, *Black Atlantic Religion*, 22–23.
18. Silva, *Candomblé e umbanda*, 106–10.
19. Cunha, "Corpo nas religiões," 138–39.

In Candomblé the trance happens after a process of preparation of the devotee on whom the orixá or spirit is to come. There are special colors: clothing and objects of adornment that represent each of the orixás. The drums will be played at a specific cadence to call the spirit that will be honored with sacrifices fruit, animals, and the purest honey, or prepared foods like *vatapá*, *efó*, popcorn, and palm oil mixed in baked cassava flour. At the very beginning of the ceremony a sacrifice is offered to Exu, who is the orixá responsible for mediating between the material world and that in which the orixás and ancestors live. It is believed that if Exu is not satisfied first he will impede the normal communication between the two worlds. He is, then, satisfied and dispatched to bring the other orixás to the ceremony. Unlike the trance experiences described by Nabokov, the orixás of Candomblé do not speak through their possessed devotees, whereas spirit speech is a characteristic of the Tamil spirit possession described in Nabokov's work.[20] There is not any dialogue between the devotees and the orixás. All the manifestations and possible guidance offered by the orixás have to be mediated by the priest or priestess who will play divinatory games during consultations. Ifá is the spiritual being who is in charge of human destiny. The priest or priestess needs to play a game of sixteen small seashells, which are thrown on a specially prepared surface; the priest or priestess will study the positions of the shells on the surface and interpret what the orixás are telling through the game. Contrastingly, the spirits in Umbanda speak through the possessed devotees, different human types are represented in the spirit possession of Umbanda, and there is closer similarity with the possessions described in Nabokov's work. In Umbanda a diversity of different human characters is represented among the spirits that manifest in their rituals. They are spirits of children, men, women, former slaves, prostitutes, simple country people, and even deceased relatives of consultants and other devotees.

Even though Candomblé and Umbanda share some practices and beliefs, there is extreme difference in how the body is experienced as a medium of communication between the initiates and spiritual beings with which they come into contact. Cunha argues that "in Umbanda the medium has full control over their own corporality and, thus, can control the manifestations of spirits that happen through their bodies. Whereas in Candomblé, the body is consecrated, and must be purified, prepared for its function, and then 'given away' to the sacred that manifests through it."[21] Another difference is that in Candomblé the orixás come down on their sons and daughters—those are the terms to identify the initiates whose bodies are

20. I. Nabokov, *Religion Against the Self*, 86–89.
21. Cunha, "Corpo nas religiões," 139.

possessed by orixás—and dance to the sound of drums playing at a rhythm specific to each of the orixás. There is no direct communication between humans and the orixás, they do not speak or sing, and they do not give consultations or perform cures directly. The son or daughter is not free to let the orixá possess his or her body out of the temple or without the authorization of the Candomblé priest. Everything has to be interpreted and commanded by the priest. It is the priest who performs the divinations and prescribes the herbs to be used in ritual purification baths. This is not the same for those initiated in Umbanda; they learn to control possessions, and the spiritual entities that possess their bodies can communicate, not only by dancing to the sound of the drums but also by speaking, giving direct advice to petitioners. Possessions in Umbanda do not take place only under the supervision and authority of the priest; they can happen when and where the medium permits them to occur. In Umbanda the body is not consecrated, and even though the word used to name the medium in Umbanda, such as "horse" or "mule," carries depreciating meanings, the encounter with the sacred comes about more freely than in Candomblé.[22] Both rituals of possession require one's momentary loss of identity, but in the Candomblé experience this level of loss is more intense because one has to be subdued to two external forces, that of the orixás, demanding total surrender and exclusive possession over the body; and that of the priest, whose authority has to be recognized by the *iaô* (initiate).[23]

The circumstances in which initiation takes place in Candomblé and Umbanda resemble in some ways those presented by Nabokov in her study of Tamil rituals in India; Nabokov found a regular pattern that is applicable to the experiences of different people. All the examples of recruitment by the goddess that she describes involve some form of suffering or situation of conflict. Nabokov says that "the camis did not have much choice about their recruitment; the goddess ruthlessly penetrated their bodies in the guise of sickness, or actively lured them with the suggestion of sexual opportunity, until they could only surrender to her. There is a clear pattern of here of demands that are dangerously aggressive, particularly sexually violent."[24] This account of the recruitment by the goddess carries elements of ritual violence, which fits into the patterns found in recruitment by the orixás of Candomblé and Umbanda. Dion provides us with an illustrative example of how recruitment was similarly experienced by a French woman, married to a French ambassador who was serving in Brazil at the time. One day she

22. Cunha, "Corpo nas religiões," 140–41.
23. Cunha, "Corpo nas religiões," 141.
24. I. Nabokov, *Religion Against the Self*, 28.

started to feel sick for no apparent reason, and a friend of her looked after her. Some days later she was feeling better, but then she was invited by some friends to visit a *terreiro* in Rio de Janeiro for the parties in honor of Iansã, orixá that controls the winds and storms. Upon her visit to the *terreiro*, she came into a trance while they were singing and dancing to Iemanjá, and she only came around by the end of the party. The Candomblé priest who directed the *terreiro* told her that she had come into a trance because she was a daughter of Iemanjá. According to the priest, she had "killed" her and wanted her to become her (the orixá's) "horse"; she needed to be initiated to "have her head done"; this is the expression used to refer to the ritual of initiation in Candomblé and Umbanda. She initially refused to submit to initiation and decided to have only a remedial ritual called *bori*, which is intended to bring the person's energy into balance. She felt better for some time but eventually had to submit to initiation, and just then, after becoming an *iaô*, did she recover her complete well-being. In the vein of the examples of the Tamil Camis that Nabokov gave, the French woman had no other alternative but to become a servant of the orixá in order to regain her wholeness as a healthy person.[25] Nabokov compares the Tamil initiations by the goddess with marriage, as she says: "In Tamil society sexuality and marriage are connotative of unity, fusion, and incorporation and therefore become the perfect metaphor for understanding, experiencing, and internalizing those who, like the goddess, appear from the outside. Internalization of this sort is precisely the fundamental movement of these initiatic testimonies."[26] It is precisely the initiation that marks one as a member of the orixás' family, who comes under their authority and protection. As the orixás are divinized African ancestors and heroes, initiation rituals are intended to form the characteristics of the orixá in the initiate. That is the reason the initiation is known as "making the head" of the person under initiation. There is a sort of fusion between the personality of the initiate and that of the orixá or spirit to whom one is being consecrated. And the language used by Candomblé followers to describe the possession by an orixá is to say the medium *becomes* the orixá.

Initiation is a long ritual and lasts twenty-one days, usually. Johnson describes the ritual as beginning with the arrival of the *abiã* (prospective initiate) to the *terreiro* at the time prescribed by the priestess. An *ebomi* (one who has performed his/her seven-year obligatory rituals) comes to open the gates and admit the *abiã* to the *terreiro* grounds. As the *abiã* is coming in, the *ebomi* throws water behind her as a symbolic washing away of the

---

25. Dion, *Omindarewa*, 64–68.
26. I. Nabokov, *Religion Against the Self*, 27.

abiã's ties to her worries and occupations of daily life. The *abiã* is then taken to the large room where public ceremonies are carried out. There she will have to wait for long hours before other phases of the ritual are done. In that room there is no reference to chronological time, and no watches or clock are admitted. This is a time for relaxation and the marking of leaving street time and concerns behind. Nabokov describes a similar process of change that she calls "splits." In her description Nabokov talks of a split in identity. One would be divided, separated from a previous experience that could no longer be lived; there is no return, as Nabokov says. In the initiation ritual, the *abiã* ceremonially leaves her past behind to participate in a new reality, a new experience and community. Splittings are marked by one's abandonment of an experience in which one feels entrapped, and the beginning of a new life freed from the limitations of previous circumstances.[27] The evangelical experiences of conversion can possibly be a good comparison with this split. Especially those churches that do not practice infant baptism place special emphasis on the necessity of one's "turning away from sin" in order to begin a new life as a follower of Christ.

It is in the place where public ceremonies happen that the *abiã* will spend the first days of her initiation. Johnson says that over this period of cooling down the *abiã* will face the conflicting feelings of quiet and anxiety due to the sense of timelessness contrasted to what she experienced until not so long ago in her daily struggles for survival as a domestic worker. This is closely related to Bloch's ritual as providing the possibility of transcending time. When analyzing the Orokaiva children's initiation, Bloch says that during the ritual "All generations, past, present and future, are therefore involved in this oscillating processing spiral between bush and village, hunted and hunter, pig and spirit, both in the initiation ritual and always."[28] Peter Nabokov poses that "moments of symbolic manipulation intended to renew the world, sanctify rites of passage, restore distressed individuals, usurp the formal political or religious order, or steer community behavior in new directions require 'recentering' their fellowship into a credible cosmology; people often feel the need to move together,"[29] and he also says that ritualized reenactment of histories need to transport practitioners to a time before time in order to be effective.[30]

On the third day of her initiation, the *abiã* is driven to a stream and waterfall. She is made to enter the stream, and the priestess and her

---

27. I. Nabokov, *Religion Against the Self*, 108–13.
28. Bloch, *Prey into Hunter*, 17.
29. P. Nabokov, *Forest of Time*, 173.
30. P. Nabokov, *Forest of Time*, 177.

helpers pass dry food offerings on the *abiã*'s body, especially her head; this is done because they believe that the head eats as food is ritually offered to strengthen the *abiã*. Meanwhile the priestess sings Yoruba songs. The *abiã* then bathes under the waterfall. She is given some new white cotton clothes, and her former street clothes will be ceremonially disposed of in another river kilometers away from that spot. The *abiã* is transferred from the large room where she stayed the first three days of her initiation to a room near the priestess's quarter; she will again sleep on a straw mat, low, near the floor, where the ancestors are believed to be.

The young lady who is being initiated talks to the priestess about the strict Catholic upbringing that she had had and the mother responds by saying the Lord's Prayer in Yoruba and by telling the lady that it is present also in liturgy. The *abiã* is told that she is free to decide whether to proceed in her initiation or not. The next morning the *abiã* decides to proceed and is taken to another room, which will be the center of her initiation and where the social being that she was when she arrived at the *terreiro* will ritually die in order to be reborn as a new creature.

A Syncretic Conflict

In the last twenty years, Brazil has seen the rise of some neo-Pentecostal churches that characteristically grow fast as to the number of people attending to their services, and these churches emphasize prosperity as the sign of God's blessing upon one's life. This emphasis on the language of prosperity, along with the strongly syncretic rituals they adopt, have permitted them to reach the populations on the lower strata of the Brazilian social pyramid. I will focus on the Igreja Universal do Reino de Deus as I try to establish the relationship between the practices of this particular neo-Pentecostal church and its syncretism with Candomblé and Umbanda as Afro-Brazilian religions. In my analysis I will direct attention to one of their services that is characterized by rituals of spiritual cleansing, because in these sessions of spiritual cleansing several elements of common use in Candomblé and Umbanda rituals are appropriated and used by Igreja Universal do Reino de Deus.

The use of ritual plants, objects, and substances such as salt and the essence of plants have always been associated with the practices of Afro-Brazilian religious rituals. These ingredients are used in baths prepared for the purposes of spiritual wellness or for healing the body.[31] But the Igreja Universal do Reino de Deus makes use of those elements to symbolically

31. Voeks, *Sacred Leaves of Candomblé*.

HIERARCHY AND RITUAL 123

oppose the Afro-Brazilian religions, and here I can identify the concept of humiliation presented by Robbins in his work *Becoming Sinners*. In that book Robbins analyzes the influence of early contacts of the Urapmin in Papua New Guinea with colonial authorities and their introduction to Christianity. He describes how the colonial experience worked to convince the Urapmin of their moral backwardness and their need to adopt colonial laws for their superiority. Robbins mentions that the moralizing tone used by the Baptist Christianity to which the Urapmin were first exposed served to emphasize their sense of moral inadequacy, leading them to consider their traditional way of life as morally insufficient and to an eventual capitulation to Christianity as a way of gaining salvation.[32] One needs to understand that the use of plants and symbols believed to carry some sort of magical charm or power is deeply rooted in popular Brazilian religious practices, not only those of Candomblé and Umbanda but also in popular Catholicism. A large number of Brazilians from different religious backgrounds would probably be able to recollect memories of being taken to a *benzedeira* or a *rezadeira* when they were children.[33]

I see the concept of humiliation as motivation for change come into play when Christians in general, but neo-Pentecostals especially, depict other traditional faiths such as Candomblé, Umbanda, their deities and spirits as bad spirits or devils. In the view of churches like the Igreja Universal do Reino de Deus all sorts of suffering, whether social, economic, biological, or psychological are caused by the negative and evil influence of the deities or spirits worshipped in religions of African tradition or because of the practices of popular religious expressions, like the work of the *benzedeiras*, for instance. Every Friday, the day on which they hold the cleansing services, one will find their temples crowded with the people who go there in search of relief from their burdens.

The services I visited followed a preestablished pattern, which is used in their services all over Brazil. When the time to begin the service comes, a pastor will come into the sanctuary singing a song of power and victory. There are some moments of silence during the services, but most of the time there will be some background music, which changes in style and grows in intensity as the pastor starts quoting some Bible verses that tell of the glory

---

32. Robbins, *Becoming Sinners*, 15–34.

33. A *benzedeira* or *rezadeira* is a woman to whom people in Brazil go for consultation and to receive a blessing when they believe they are suffering spiritually or physically due to the influence of a bad spirit or bad energies from another person. Many times the woman does this kind of spiritual assistance without any payment. There are also men who do this sort of spiritual work, and in that case they are called *rezador* or *benzedor*.

of God and promises wellness and riches to those who serve Godself. People will be told that God wants them to have a plentiful life, and if they do not have it, it may be because of some sort of hereditary curse or bad spiritual influence, which they call *encosto*. According to them, this *encosto* might have been the result of personal or hereditary sin, or even result from a curse cast by an enemy. The text of Exod 9:18–27, which narrates the event when Ham saw his father's nakedness and had his descendants cursed with servanthood to his brothers, is used to explain the origin of suffering and poverty in Africa, among the Africans in the diaspora, and as an extension, anything related to African culture is depicted as essentially evil and sinful.[34] The services of spiritual cleansing and deliverance at Igreja Universal do Reino de Deus are performed in a way that is quite similar to descriptions of Tamil rituals of counter-sorcery and exorcism offered by Nabokov,[35] but unlike the Tamil exorcisms and counter-sorcery, where it is the goddess who replaces the *pey*, it is the Holy Spirit of the Christian God who comes into those under possession to cast away their evil spirits and the suffering they cause.

Bibliography

Bloch, Maurice. *Prey Into Hunter: The Politics of Religious Experience*. Lewis Henry Morgan Lectures. Cambridge: Cambridge University Press, 2004.
Cunha, Welthon R. "O corpo nas religiões de matriz umbandista: Fragmentos de cultura." *Goiania* 15 (2005) 137–54.
Curran, Charles E. *The Catholic Moral Tradition Today: A Synthesis*. Moral Traditions. Washington, DC: Georgetown University Press, 1999.
Dion, Michel. *Omindarewa: Uma francesa no candomblé, a busca de uma outra verdade*. Rio de Janeiro: Pallas, 2002.
Francisco, Luiz. "Mães-de-santo fazem manifestação em frente ao Tj." *Folha de S. Paulo*, May 4, 2005. http://www1.Folha.Uol.Com.Br/Folha/Brasil/Ult96u68783.shtml.
Harding, Rachel E. *A Refuge In Thunder: Candomblé and Alternative Spaces of Blackness*. Bloomington: Indiana University Press, 2000.
Johnson, Paul Christopher. *Secrets, Gossip, and Gods: The Transformation of Brazilian Candomblé*. New York: Oxford University Press, 2002.
Matory, J. Lorand. *Black Atlantic Religion: Tradition, Traditionalism, and Matriarchy in The Afro-Brazilian Candomblé*. Princeton: Princeton University Press, 2005.
Nabokov, Isabelle. *Religion Against the Self: An Ethnography of Tamil Rituals*. New York: Oxford University Press, 2000.
Nabokov, Peter. *A Forest of Time: American Indian Ways of History*. Cambridge: Cambridge University Press, 2002.

---

34. Prado, "Mae-de-santo acusa."
35. I. Nabokov, *Religion Against the Self*, 55–113.

Patterson, Orlando. *Rituals of Blood: Consequences of Slavery in Two American Centuries*. Frontiers of Science. New York: Basic Civitas, 1998.

———. *Slavery and Social Death: A Comparative Study*. Cambridge: Harvard University Press, 1982.

Prado, Gabriela. "Mae-de-santo acusa Bispo Edir Macedo." *Correio Braziliense*, Nov. 5, 2001. http://www2.Correioweb.Com.Br/Cw/2001-11-05/Mat_19429.Htm.

Prandi, Reginaldo. *Mitologia dos orixás*. São Paulo: Cia das Letras, 2001.

Robbins, Joel. *Becoming Sinners: Christianity and Moral Torment in a Papua New Guinea Society*. Ethnographic Studies in Subjectivity. Berkeley: University of California Press, 2004.

Silva, Vagner G. da. *Candomblé e umbanda: Caminhos da devocao brasileira*. São Paulo: Atica, 1994.

Voeks, Robert A. *Sacred Leaves of Candomblé: African Magic, Medicine, and Religion in Brazil*. Austin: University of Texas Press, 1997.

9

Theoquilombism:
Perspectives for an Afro-Brazilian Christianity[1]

CLEUSA CALDEIRA

MONOCULTURAL EUROCENTRIC THEOLOGY HISTORICALLY endorsed and prolonged the "Black Holocaust," reinforcing the societal denial of the divine image (*imago Dei*) to a substantial segment of humanity. Amid this holocaust, which systematically oppressed both the bodies and minds of those deemed inferior, Afro-diasporic communities tenaciously sought to reclaim and reconstruct their existence by developing new practices, spaces, and conditions that promote re-existence and humanization.

The emergence of black liberation theology in the mid-twentieth century exemplifies this Afro-diasporic resistance, functioning as a form of political theology vehemently opposing capitalism, imperialism, and Eurocentrism. Black liberation theology aims to liberate Afro-diasporic individuals from all white power structures, including the white church and its associated theology.

In the Brazilian context, black liberation theology, also known as Afro-Brazilian theology, has roots in liberation theology but places a strong emphasis on the racial dimension. This theological perspective emerged to expose the racial aspects of oppression and to advocate for the emancipation and dignity of Afro-diasporic communities, inherently taking a critical stance against the modern/colonial system and world. Constructing a contemporary black theology is imperative given coloniality's ability to adapt the *colonial* power structure and perpetuate racism. In Brazil and

---

1. Thank you to *Perspectiva Teologica* for permission to publish this chapter as a shorter version of Caldeira, "Theoquilombism."

Latin America, the challenge lies in developing a black theology centered on inculturation, integrating Afro-centric epistemologies without requiring black Christians to forfeit their African heritage. This approach, referred to as *theoquilombism*, seeks to reconcile Afro-Brazilian identity with its African cultural roots.[2]

Black Political Theology

Engaging in theological discourse with decolonial thought holds significance for two primary reasons. First, decolonial theory reveals the dominance of the modern/colonial system, where racism serves as the central axis.[3] Second, the examination of coloniality revitalizes theoretical and conceptual tools for addressing contemporary racism. This is crucial as conventional anti-racist ideologies face a crisis and require tool renewal.

Exploring the trajectory of coloniality examination revives the tradition of critical black thought, largely overlooked by the Latin American academy, particularly within theology. This neglect obscures the origins of critical theories developed by black Marxists, treating them as innovations. Ramón Grosfoguel underscores that concealing the black roots of critical theories perpetuates epistemic racism, reinforcing the perception of black thought as inferior and white thought as superior.[4] Consequently, critical black thought is recognized as a precursor to decolonial thinking, a means of achieving "epistemic justice" for this tradition.

Theology in Dialogue with Critical Black Thought

To grapple with the intricate reality of racism, interdisciplinary dialogue is indispensable. Critical black thought is pivotal in this discourse, facilitating theology's removal of Eurocentric lenses that obstruct its comprehension of the black experience in a structurally racist society. Authors of decolonial critique are integral to the genealogy of black critical thought, as black intellectuals were the first to expose the intrinsic connections between capitalism, colonialism, and racism.

Black political theology emerges from interdisciplinary dialogue with Afro-diasporic and African thinkers, rooted in an analysis of colonialism and coloniality as the principal fault line in modern civilization. This

---

2. Caldeira, "Decolonialidade," 255–60.
3. Quijano, "Colonialidade."
4. Grosfoguel, "Negros marxistas," 11.

perspective aligns with Aimé Césaire's condemnation of colonialism in "Discourse on Colonialism," where he emphasizes that colonialism seeks to dehumanize both the colonized and the colonizer, leading to moral degradation and a degradation of human worth.[5] This calls for a reevaluation of the colonial legacy and the urgent need to address its repercussions in the context of contemporary society.

Frantz Fanon, influenced by Césaire, emphasized that racism and colonialism are socially constructed worldviews and ways of existence. He argued that racism not only imposed a false image on Afro-diasporic individuals, created by the white perspective, but also ensnared both whites and blacks in a metaphysical and essentialist self-conception. Fanon contended that liberation must aspire to the universalism inherent in the human condition.[6] This necessitates transcending the hierarchical chromatic framework designed by coloniality for self-identification and identifying others.

It is remarkable that theological discourse rarely engages with critical black thought, given that theology seeks to address humanity's historical struggles with hope and redemption. Black intellectuals consistently assert that colonialism underlies intersubjective violence and represents, as Achille Mbembe notes, "the quintessential display of an impossible community."[7]

In this context, a crucial facet of black political theology is the exploration of the deontologization process among Afro-diasporic individuals, aiming to comprehend the roots and traumatic impacts of colonialism on Afro-diasporic subjectivity. These effects persist due to coloniality, concealed in Brazil under the guise of racial democracy. Fanon's analysis, particularly in "Black Skin, White Masks," becomes pivotal in understanding the detrimental consequences of the colonial situation on Afro-diasporic subjectivity and the ongoing necessity for decolonial struggle.[8]

Fanon's focus on the colonized body in Algeria extended beyond that French colony, shedding light on other regions and individuals subjected to colonial violence, as is the case in Brazil. His clinical perspective is significant, as it discerned that "colonialism influences the development of human senses and identities, alongside the individual and collective processes of historical re-signification."[9] Fanon exposed the fallacy of attributing complex characteristics to Afro-diasporic individuals as intrinsic traits, revealing

---

5. Césaire, *Discurso sobre o colonialismo*, 23–24.
6. Fanon, *Pele negra*, 26–28.
7. Mbembe, *Sair da grande noite*, 9.
8. Fanon, *Pele negra*.
9. Faustino, "Frantz Fanon," 148.

their social origins and the external causes of psychic distress among colonial subjects.

Fanon's diagnosis and prognosis hold vital significance for addressing global intersubjective violence rooted in the colonial legacy. Recognizing the "universality of Fanon" is crucial in contemplating the emergence of a new human condition.[10] It is worth noting that Christianity has long proposed the central idea of theosis/kenosis, as Saint Irenaeus pointed out.[11] In kenosis, there's a human-divine incarnation through self-emptying, while theosis signifies the transformation of life, culminating in a harmonious and innovative presence that transcends subjectivity, elevating it to a reconciled human state.

Achille Mbembe emphasizes that Fanon's work revolves around shouldering the suffering of the struggling individual, describing it, and comprehending it to give rise to a new human condition.[12] In other words, it seems difficult to understand the humanization process as an act of being fully human and divine (kenosis/theosis) outside the critique of the historical dehumanization produced by the colonial power matrix, which is perpetuated as the substratum of intersubjective relations.

Racism as Denial of the Humanity of the Other

Colonialism, operating through racism, is primarily a coordinated dehumanization endeavor characterized by its remarkable ability to adapt. Its core essence lies in negating the human status of the other based on racialization. Colonialism and racism perpetuate themselves by deontologizing Afro-diasporic individuals, relegating them to a "zone of nonbeing" where they are denied authentic existence, as Fanon observed.[13]

Building upon Fanon's insights, decolonial thought elucidates that the theoretical and historical construction of the racial subject occurred within the modern/colonial system/world, serving as a central axis of the enduring and effective colonial power matrix.[14] Racism, thus, transcends mere phenotypic and racial discrimination; it fundamentally constitutes a system of hierarchy that favors domination by establishing categories of inferiors and superiors.

---

10. Mbembe, "Universalidade de Frantz Fanon," 9.
11. Irenaeus, *Haer.*
12. Mbembe, "Universalidade de Frantz Fanon," 10.
13. Fanon, *Pele negra*, 26.
14. Quijano, "Colonialidade."

Regrettably, the foundation of this hierarchy of humanity can be traced back to the debate on the "rights of the peoples," where figures like Fray Francisco de Vitória and Fray Bartolomeu de Las Casas clashed with Gines de Sepúlveda. This debate revolved around whether indigenous peoples, in the eyes of Europeans, possessed full theological and legal rights, as the absence of religion in indigenous societies was equated with the absence of a soul and, consequently, relegation to the realm of animals. This theological uncertainty about the humanity of the other gave rise to the concept of "religious racism" as the initial racist discourse in modern history, preceding the emergence of color-based racism by nearly half a century.[15]

The historical debate concerning Amerindians' humanity, occurring within a Christian-theological context that served the imperial state, oscillated between acknowledging their potential humanity and asserting their animality. Ultimately, Amerindians were recognized as human beings, thus legitimizing their conversion to Christianity in the New World, as it was deemed impossible to evangelize beings deemed beasts. However, this recognition of Amerindians' humanity intensified the demand for enslaving Africans, who were deemed nonhuman and thus suitable for enslavement. Nelson Maldonado Torres termed this phenomenon *misanthropic skepticism*—the theological suspicion regarding the humanity of others—which played a pivotal role in the development of the coloniality of being and knowledge, intertwined with racism and ontological exclusion.[16]

Simultaneously, as African people were subjected to slavery for labor control, there emerged a symbiosis of racist religious discourse with color-based racism. Phenotypic racialization of humanity became a fundamental catalyst for the expansion and globalization of the modern/colonial system/world.[17] Aníbal Quijano defined racialization as the construction of identities based on the category of race, designed to express the hierarchical relations of global capitalism, forming the basis for new geo-cultural identities.[18] This racial line functioned to ontologically and epistemologically divide humanity into two groups: those above the line—recognized as human beings with subjectivity and access to human/citizen/civilian/labor rights—and those below, regarded as subhuman or nonhuman, subject to dehumanizing violence.[19]

---

15. Grosfoguel, "Negros marxistas," 18.
16. Maldonado-Torres, "Sobre la colonialidad," 145.
17. Grosfoguel, "Negros marxistas," 18.
18. Quijano, "Colonialidade," 119.
19. Grosfoguel, "Negros marxistas," 21.

Racism as an Existential Deviation

Neusa Santos Souza, an Afro-Brazilian psychiatrist, delineates the experience of Afro-Brazilians living under a dual injunction, one that requires them to embody the body and ideas of the white subject while simultaneously negating their own "black presence."[20] This predicament, observed particularly when analyzing Afro-Brazilian social ascent, results in a disconnection from their capacity to project an existential life. Afro-Brazilians find themselves confined within a false image crafted by whites to perpetuate dominance and dehumanization, leading to a state of "psychic annihilation."

Drawing inspiration from Fanon, Souza identifies in this dual injunction a desire for self-annihilation, as the "black," in their aspiration to whiten, seek nothing more than self-extinction. Their project becomes one of nonexistence in the future, reflecting an aspiration not to be or to have been.[21] This stems from colonial society convincing them, as Fanon notes, that their sole destiny as "black" (Afro-diasporic) individuals is to become white.[22] This phenomenon characterizes the "coloniality of being," marked by the imposition of an image that encompasses emotions, deities, beliefs, and language, all in service of Western civilization's humanism. Thus, Afro-Brazilians are condemned to dwell in the realm of nonbeing:

> It is, in fact, a life lived alienated from any possibility of cultivating an existential project and ontological affirmation, under the weight of dehumanization; a way of living expelled from the possibility of cultivating your own existential home. This means to exist not for oneself, but for another who lodges in the psyche, to whom one wants to conform or ends up living a depreciable existence.[23]

Racialization, colonization, and dehumanization are profoundly effective in inducing a level of alienation in colonized subjects that transforms them into nonbeings. They create an ontological fracture, a pivotal element for the operation of the colonial power matrix. The skepticism about one's own human nature, traditionally a feature of colonizers, begins to permeate Afro-diasporic individuals themselves as they internalize the false image imposed upon them.

Orlando Patterson terms this phenomenon in the context of African Americans as *social death*, a state induced by symbolic instruments

---

20. Souza, *Tornar-se negro*, 8.
21. Souza, *Tornar-se negro*, 5.
22. Fanon, *Pele negra*, 188.
23. Villa and Villa, "Sociogénesis en las víctimas," 176.

of domination, rendering enslaved Afro-diasporics as nameless, invisible entities within society.[24] This concept of social death prompts the colonized Afro-diasporic individuals to question "What am I?" rather than "Who am I?" since their human condition is not predefined.[25] This "existential deviation," as Fanon describes it, is a consequence of white civilization's imposition, where the notion of a "black soul" is merely a construct of the whites.[26] This deviation compels racialized colonized Afro-diasporic subjects to internalize their colonization, rendering them nonexistent.

Fanon advocates de-alienation and decolonization as the path to escaping both psychic annihilation and social death. This entails unlearning the impositions of colonialism and the dehumanization project and relearning how to be free individuals. Fanon's goal in the decolonial struggle is to assist black individuals in liberating themselves from the complex web woven during the colonial situation.[27] Employing "sociogeny" as a sociodiagnostic method, Fanon seeks to analyze and intervene in the lived experience of racialized and colonized subjects subjected to dehumanization. He recognizes that the issue of the fractured subject and their liberation is fundamentally a social problem. Sociogeny elucidates the reflexive relationship between capitalism, colonialism, and racism, offering a historical potential for an emancipatory anti-colonial praxis that encompasses both objective and subjective dimensions of human existence.[28]

Sociogenesis, at its core, seeks to reclaim humanity through "self-determination and self-liberation," fostering subjectivity, self-reflection, and liberation praxis. Its pedagogical mission involves empowering marginalized individuals to recognize and act independently.[29]

Understanding the behavior of colonized subjects enables the exploration of decolonization and the liberation of bodies long subjected to colonial domination. It also reveals the emergence of decolonization possibilities, such as innovative forms of existence that spring from the creation of a life detached from the model of dehumanization and Western domination.[30]

Only through de-alienation and decolonization can a political subject be born, capable of transcending "the desire to be and exist in a body that is not their natural habitat, especially when this results from an induction into

24. Patterson, *Slavery and Social Death*, 38.
25. Gordon, ed., *Existence in Black*, 104.
26. Fanon, *Pele negra*, 30.
27. Fanon, *Pele negra*, 44.
28. Faustino, "Frantz Fanon," 148.
29. Walsh, *Pedagogías decoloniales*, 1:46.
30. Villa and Villa, "Sociogénesis en las víctimas," 178.

the historical renunciation of the very ways of apprehending, affirming, and reaffirming a body schema blurred by the historical and structural power production."[31] This aspect, rooted in Fanon's sociogenesis, represents the "invention of existence," akin to "creation." It underscores the capacity for creation as a fundamental attribute of actively being, a facet of the practice of freedom, entailing creation, innovation, and communal living, thereby epitomizing radical humanity.[32]

Neglecting the significant rift in intersubjectivity engendered by ongoing colonialism not only blinds us to the reality of historical victims but also hinders the prospect of koinonia. Ignoring or denying the existence and impact of racism on subjectivity aligns one with oppression and, knowingly or not, makes one complicit in ontological-existential and epistemic racism. A political theology attuned to the struggles and resistances of the Afro-diasporic community must commit to dismantling the colonial power matrix and the Eurocentrism inherent in traditional theology while embracing silenced epistemologies.

Black Theology of Inculturation

Decolonial critique highlights epistemicide, a consequence of the historical war against indigenous peoples, particularly African cultures, branding them as primitive and uncivilized, thus rendering their ancestral knowledge invisible. To overcome Eurocentrism and the modern/colonial system, a black theology must pursue epistemic justice by incorporating African worldviews and Afrocentric epistemologies.

Traditional Christian theology, rooted in monocultural and Eurocentric Christianity, historically marginalized African cultures and spiritualities as primitive and diabolical. Theoquilombism implies a reconnection with African cultures, fostering intercultural dialogues, primarily preserved within Candomblé *terreiros* in Brazil, born from Afro-diasporic resistance.

Engaging in profound intercultural dialogue, as desired by figures like Bishop Dom José Maria Pires, recognizes that Afro-Brazilians can be disciples of Christ while preserving their Afro-Brazilian identity, culture, and orixá religion.[33] This process involves an ontological journey of becoming black and necessitates theological engagement with Africa and its epistemologies to transcend Eurocentrism and embrace decolonial approaches, including a brief exploration of African Christology.

31. Villa and Villa, "Sociogénesis en las víctimas," 178.
32. Walsh, *Pedagogías decoloniales*, 1:44.
33. Pires, "Deus da vida," 31.

South-South Dialogue: A Brief Approach to African Theology

African theology emerged as a contextual theology in the twentieth century, representing a theology created within Africa, reflecting African people's identity, employing African thought concepts, and addressing the African context.

African theology, predominantly focused on Christology, is characterized by two main approaches—liberation and inculturation—aligned with distinct schools.[34] The former, often referred to as "black theology," draws inspiration from African American and Latin American theologians, emphasizing political and sociological dimensions. With the principle of "contextualization," this approach earnestly considers the context of diverse human groups, encompassing cultural, religious, social, political, and economic aspects to discern the gospel's message within their context.

Its aim is to understand and address specific needs and aspirations. On the other hand, the inculturation approach, predominant in black Africa, revolves around an anthropological-cultural perspective. It employs the key concept of "indigenization" to Africanize Christianity, eliminating foreign elements and ensuring its relevance in the African context. This perspective fosters greater interaction between the gospel and culture.[35]

The inculturation perspective within African theology has faced criticism for potentially causing "confusion and distortion" of the Christian message and the spread of syncretism, particularly in Christology.[36] However, Mashau and Frederiks challenge the notion of who has the authority to determine what constitutes syncretism and authentic inculturation or contextualization of the gospel in Africa.[37]

African theology, guided by "reverse hermeneutics," is striving for an authentic inculturation of the Christian faith, respecting its unique characteristics and the transformations it has endured due to the Maafa, the Black Holocaust. This approach holds potential for redefining the one-sided relationship between Christianity and Afro-Brazilian cultures. Historically, evangelization has often been seen as a form of (neo-)colonization aimed at imposing a monocultural, Eurocentric version of Christianity, which often disregards the distinctive features of Afro-diasporic cultures. This has led to the marginalization of African cultures, seemingly devoid of contributions to our comprehension of the salvific mystery unveiled in Christ.

---

34. Nyamiti, "African Christologies Today," 3.
35. Mashau and Frederiks, "Coming of Age," 118–19.
36. Potgieter and Magezi, "Critical Assessment," 6–7.
37. Mashau and Frederiks, "Coming of Age," 120.

Inculturation remains an ongoing challenge, both in Africa and the black diaspora.[38]

Inculturation, apart from bolstering the self-esteem and dignity of Africans and Afro-diasporic individuals, should also unveil diverse facets of Christ, thus facilitating the development of various Christologies. This perspective acknowledges that while "the entire Revelation is already given . . . its meaning remains partially unexplored."[39] Although the incarnation signifies God's full revelation, our comprehension remains incomplete. Therefore, the significance of different cultures lies in accessing distinct expressions of the Loving Mystery, identified as God, allowing us to name him using alternative frameworks. As "every revelation is received and expressed according to the way of its recipients," diverse cultural interpretations enrich our understanding of God.

> The inculturation of the Gospel and the Church will be more authentic as each cultural expression of the Christian faith stands out for its uniqueness . . . In this process, it is essential to take into account that, although each culture appropriates the truths and values of Christianity in its own way, revealing a particular meaning in each one, none of them has them exclusively.[40]

In this sense, "reverse hermeneutics" can contribute to the rise of other expressions of the face of Christ that are totally unknown and even rejected by monocultural and Eurocentric Christianity. To this end, it briefly approaches the African theological aspect of inculturation, that is, the reception of revelation from African cultures, more specifically to the devotion to ancestors that so deeply marks the *homo africanus*.

Christology and Ancestral Devotion

The pursuit of a more embodied approach, emphasizing the recognition and essential role of traditional African cultures in contextualizing the gospel within Africa, has given rise to a controversial project employing the ancestral concept to expound Christology in an African context. This initiative, though contentious, offers valuable insights into the experiences of Afro-diasporic individuals in the process of "becoming black." It holds particular relevance within the context of religions grounded in African traditions, characterized by ancestor worship, much like in Africa itself.

---

38. Schreiter, *Faces of Jesus*.
39. Brighenti, *Por uma evangelização inculturada*, 53.
40. Brighenti, *Por uma evangelização inculturada*, 59.

Monocultural Christian theology posits an inherent incompatibility between Christian faith and African cultures, primarily due to the veneration of ancestors and orishas. This apparent paradox presents a dilemma in the construction of Afro-Brazilian identity, especially for Afro-Brazilian Christians, many of whom clandestinely practice "double belonging," eagerly anticipating the opportunity to openly embrace their Afro-Brazilian identity. However, from an African cultural perspective, including Afro-Brazilian culture, the notion of "double belonging" holds no relevance, as these cultures intrinsically embrace otherness, diversity, and relationality as integral aspects of their worldview.

Illustrating this inclusive human conception, Father François de l'Espinay's poignant account of his immersion in Candomblé reveals fragments of these principles. In his article "The Religion of the Orixás—Another Word of the One God?" he recounts the surprise he felt when women in the orixás cult declared themselves as "Catholic too." The most significant challenge in the encounter between Christianity and ancestral cults, as L'Espinay observed, lies in the introduction of Jesus Christ. It raises the question of whether "the Word would use the Orixás to speak to the Candomblé people." The relationship between Jesus Christ and the orixás remains a central issue in the inculturation of the Christian faith.

> The Afro-Brazilian believes that God speaks to him through the Orixá and above all through the whole tradition coming from the ancestors . . . Jesus the Son of God, God made man, Savior and Redeemer does not enter into Candomblé theology. In return, he is neither denied nor rejected nor despised; but in concrete we will say: "Jesus Christ is the way for Christians to talk about one of our Orixás."[41]

In fact, Father L'Espinay's observation highlights a significant dilemma at the intersection of Christ and the orixás, the veneration of ancestors. Christ, as the incarnate Word, has no place within the orixás. Conversely, if Christ is considered one among the orixás, it negates the concept of the incarnation of the Divine Word. In seeking to comprehend this complex relationship, Father l'Espinay suggests that "God speaks in very different ways that complement each other, and that each religion has a sacred deposit: the word that God told it."[42] How then does God communicate with African cultures? How can Christian faith be expressed in their unique expressions, thought patterns, and cultures?

---

39. L'Espinay, "Religião dos orixás," 646; emphasis added.
42. L'Espinay, "Religião dos orixás," 649.

In Africa, Christians have grappled with the same dilemma. For over forty years, they have been addressing this pivotal question through the development of a "Christology of the ancestors." This is significant due to the central role that ancestors play in African spirituality and the aspiration to acknowledge Christ within African cultures in his human-divine mystery. It's important to note that African religion, as well as Afro-Brazilian Candomblé, is monotheistic, believing in the existence of a Supreme God. In the African worldview, the authority of the ancestors serves as mediator between humans and God, not in opposition or conflict with the Creator.

African ancestors, distinct from European ones, are seen as living-dead individuals and supreme mediators of vital energy. They embody an "other presence" in African culture, invoked on significant occasions and integral to African life, participating in communal meals and rituals. This makes Jesus's proclamation, "Behold, I am with you every day" (see Matt 28:20b), profoundly meaningful for Africans.[43] Understanding the mediation of ancestors, their constant presence, is challenging without grasping the African worldview. In this hierarchized universe, particularly within the Bantu context, all entities partake in the Supreme Being's life at varying levels based on their nature, with humans occupying the center. However, this participation is indirect due to intermediaries in a hierarchy involving the Supreme Being, Spirit world, and human realm.[44]

> It was to the Ancestors that God first communicated the divine "life force." Thus they constitute the greatest link, after God, in the chain of human beings. In their passage through death, they became more powerful than other human beings—in their ability to exert influence, to increase or decrease the life force of earthly beings. In their present state, they behold both God and his subjects.[45]

Charles A. Wanamaker posits that the ancestors' mediating role between God and living humans appears to be influenced by Christianity, primarily among South African Bantus unfamiliar with the concept of a personal deity. Prior to the introduction of a personal God by Christianity, Wanamaker suggests that ancestors couldn't serve as intermediaries due to the absence of a personal God to mediate with. This rendered the ancestors omnipotent in the lives of their living families.[46] Nevertheless, the conviction prevails throughout black Africa that God interacts with his creatures

---

43. Kabasélé, "Christ as Ancestor," 120.
44. Kabasélé, "Christ as Ancestor," 123.
45. Kabasélé, "Christ as Ancestor," 117–18.
46. Wanamaker, "Jesus the Ancestor."

through ancestral mediation, informing ancestral Christologies in African theological thought.

The proposal for a Christology of the ancestors involves de-Hellenizing Christianity, synonymous with decolonizing Christology. "Decolonization necessitates the deconstruction of inherited monocultural theological frameworks that have constrained Christianity, hindering its creativity."[47] Given that Christ serves as the Messiah for Jews, Logos and Kyrios for Greeks, it is legitimate and essential to contemplate Christ from the unique vantage point of devotion to African ancestors.[48]

Christ, the Ancestor

In the realm of inculturation, Charles Nyamiti discerns two approaches to a Christology of the ancestors among African theologians. First, some theologians aim to construct an African Christology rooted in biblical teachings about Christ and seek relevant christological themes adaptable to the African cultural context. On the other hand, some theologians commence christological development from the perspective of African cultural heritage.

Those emphasizing tradition and culture include John S. Mbiti (1986) and Edward Fasholé-Luke (1974). Fasholé-Luke suggests that the Christology of ancestors should commence with the doctrine of the communion of saints, serving as a foundational theological premise for integrating the African cultural concept of ancestry.[49] Culture and its traditions predominate the vast majority of African Christologies.[50]

Nyamiti, a prominent figure in ancestral Christology, asserts that Christ achieved the full realization of ancestral mediation through the incarnation, making him the supreme Ancestor. In line with his ancestral Bantu tradition, Kabasélé posits that the Christology of ancestors should commence with Jesus's role as a mediator. He contends that Christ falls into the ancestor category because he embodies the synthesis of all mediations.[51] However, this doesn't imply that African Christians no longer require their ancestors. Rather, African Christology recognizes that the experience of ancestral mediation aligns with the Christian faith, acknowledging Jesus Christ as the supreme Ancestor.

47. Vasconcelos and Hurtado, "Descolonizar a cristologia," 480.
48. Okpaleke and Caldeira, "Ancestor Christology."
46. Fasholé-Luke, "Veneration."
50. Examples include "Christ, the Ancestor," in Nyamiti, *Christ as the Ancestor*; "Christ, the Proto-Ancestor," in Bujo, *African Theology*.
51. Kabasélé, "Christ as Ancestor," 123–24.

Adopting a similar perspective, Bujo elaborates on the notion of Christ as the Proto-Ancestor, granting it both transcendental and immanent attributes. Christ, as the Proto-Ancestor, not only consummates African veneration but also transcends and purifies it in light of biblical revelation.

> Jesus, the Christ, identified himself with humankind, so that he constitutes their explanation. From now on, Jesus makes his own all the striving of the ancestors after righteousness and all their history, in such a way that these have now become a meeting-place with God of salvation. Above all, Jesus Christ himself becomes the privileged locus for a full understanding of the ancestors. The African now has something to say about the mystery of the Incarnation, for after God has spoken to us at various times and in various places, including our ancestors, in these last days God speaks to us through the Son, whom God has established as unique Ancestor, as Proto-Ancestor, from whom all life flows for God's descendants (cf. Heb 1:1–2).[52]

The African concept of the divine, rooted in the ancestors, finds its most profound expression in Christ. The contextualization of Christ as the Proto-Ancestor is intrinsically linked to the biblical notion of the incarnation of the Word (John 1:14). By taking on human form and immersing himself in the world of humanity, God undergoes a transformation from the "immutable" to the mutable. This divine self-emptying, or kenosis, is a pivotal aspect.[53]

From an African perspective, Jesus of Nazareth represents not only an individual who exemplified the African ancestral ideal to its fullest extent but also someone who elevated this ideal to an entirely new level. Through his "sayings and deeds," Jesus infused life and vital strength in abundance (John 10:10). In seeking the essence of the African Christ, one discovers an African nomenclature for him: Christ, the Ancestor. In Christ, the Ancestor, "African identity is most authentically realized through identification with Christ, who epitomizes blackness."[54]

The call is evident for a theology of inculturation to progress, thereby advancing the decolonization of Christology. This process opens the gateway to exploring various facets of Christ, creating a multifaceted and versatile portrait, embracing multiple cultural dimensions while fostering a truly multicultural face.

---

52. Bujo, *African Theology*, 83.
53. Bujo, *African Theology*, 82.
54. Nyamiti, "African Christologies Today," 6.

Conclusion

Christianity has long been synonymous with European culture, overshadowing its deep roots in Semitic and African traditions, along with documented Asian influences. The rich diversity within Christian tradition has been obscured, giving rise to a Eurocentric and monocultural version of the faith, aligning with a project of modern civilization's dominance. Consequently, Christ's integration into African and Afro-diasporic spirituality has been challenging, often associating Christ with oppressive religion and foreignness, requiring theological reflection to convey hope in African terms.

Examining the intersection of political theology and inculturation theology, as proposed by theologian Charles Nyamiti, we must recognize that true and comprehensive inculturation theology is inherently political and liberating, and vice versa. A political theology understands that liberation necessitates a therapeutic dimension that transcends relief from suffering or eradication of hunger. It encompasses these aspects but goes beyond, fostering a transformation of the world. The existing system fails to bring about genuine liberation, relying on the alienation of others for survival.

For an African perspective, authentic liberation promises fullness of life, entailing a political connection with ancestors and contemporary relational dimensions. Pursuing black liberation must encompass this holistic approach, wherein changes in political and economic structures must be accompanied by reimagining African cultural paradigms, bolstering self-esteem, and fostering the inculturation of theological thought.

References

Brighenti, Agenor. *Por uma evangelização inculturada: Princípios pedagógicos e passos metodológicos*. São Paulo: Paulinas, 1998.
Bujo, Bénézet. *African Theology in Its Social Context*. Translated by John O'Donohue. Faith and Cultures Series. Maryknoll, NY: Orbis, 1992.
Caldeira, Cleusa. "Decolonialidade e experiência religiosa da 'dupla pertença': Um olhar a partir da subjetividade fronteiriça." *REVER* 23 (2023) 247–63.
———. "Theoquilombism: Black Theology Between Political Theology and Theology of Inculturation." *Perspectiva Teológica* 53 (2021) 137–59. https://doi.org/10.20911/21768757v53n1p137/2021.
Césaire, Aimé. *Discurso sobre o colonialismo*. Lisboa: Augusto Sá da Costa, 2006.
Fanon, Frantz. *Pele negra, máscaras brancas*. Salvador: EDUFBA, 2008.
Faustino, D. M. "Frantz Fanon: Capitalismo, racismo e a sociogênese do colonialismo." *SER Social Brasília* 20 (2018) 148–63.
Fasholé-Luke, Edward W. "Veneration and the Communion of Saints." In *New Testament Christianity for Africa and the World: Essays in Honour of Harry Sawyerr*, edited by Mark E. Glasswell and Edward W. Fasholé-Luke, 209–21. London: SPCK, 1974.

Gordon, Lewis R., ed. *Existence in Black: An Anthology of Black Existential Philosophy.* New York: Routledge, 1997.
Grosfoguel, Ramón. "El concepto de 'racismo' en Michel Foucault y Frantz Fanon: ¿Teorizar desde la zona del ser o desde la zona del no-ser?" *Tabula Rasa* (2012) 79–102. https://doi.org/10.25058/20112742.112.
———. "Negros marxistas o marxismos negros?" *Tabula Rasa* 28 (2018) 11–22.
L'Espinay, François de. "A religião dos orixás—outra palavra do Deus único?" *Revista Eclesiástica Brasileira* 47 (1987) 639–50. https://doi.org/10.29386/reb.v47i187.3250.
Kabasélé, François. "Christ as Ancestor and Elder Brother." In *Faces of Jesus in Africa*, edited by Robert J. Schreiter, 116–26. Faith and Cultures Series. Maryknoll, NY: Orbis, 1991.
Maldonado-Torres, N. "Sobre la colonialidad del ser: Contribuiciones al desarrollo de un conpecto." In *El giro decolonial: Reflexones para una diversidad epistémica más allá del capitalismo global*, edited by Santiago Castro-Gómez and Ramón Grosfoguel, 127–67. Bogotá: Siglo del Hombre, 2007.
Mashau, D. T., and M. T. Frederiks. "Coming of Age in African Theology: The Quest for Authentic Theology in African Soil." *Exchange* 37 (2008) 109–23.
Mbembe, Achille. "A universalidade de Frantz Fanon." *ArtAfrica* [Lisboa] 39 (2012) 16–21. https://www.epedagogia.com.br/materialbibliotecaonine/2894A-universalidade-de-Frantz-Fanon.pdf.
———. *Sair da grande noite: Ensaios sobre a África descolonizada.* Petrópolis: Vozes, 2019.
Nyamiti, Charles. "African Christologies Today." In *Faces of Jesus in Africa*, edited by Robert J. Schreiter, 3–22. Faith and Cultures Series. Maryknoll, NY: Orbis, 1991.
———. *Christ as the Ancestor: Christology from an African Perspective.* Gweru, Zimbabwe: Mambo, 1984.
Okpaleke, Ikenna Paschal, and Cleusa Caldeira. "Ancestor Christology: Re-Assessing Bénézet Bujo's Contribution to African Theology." *Horizonte* 20 (2022) e206314. https://doi.org/10.5752/P.2175-5841.2022V20N63E206314.
Patterson, Orlando. *Slavery and Social Death: A Comparative Study.* Cambridge: Harvard University Press, 1982.
Pires, J. M. "O Deus da vida nas comunidades afro-americanas e caribenhas." In *Teologia afro-americana: II Consulta Ecumênica de Teologia e Culturas Afro-Americana e Caribenha*, edited by Antônio Aparecido da Silva, 17–33. São Paulo: Paulus, 1997.
Potgieter, Raymond, and Christopher Magezi. "A Critical Assessment of Bediako's Incarnational Christological Model as a Response to the Foreignness of Christ in African Christianity." *In die Skriflig/In Luce Verbi* 50 (2016) 21–36.
Quijano, A. "Colonialidade do poder y clasificación social." In *El giro decolonial: Reflexiones para una diversidad epitémica más allá del capitalismo global*, edited by Santiago Castro-Gómez and Ramón Grosfoguel, 93–126. Bogotá: Siglo del Hombre, 2007.
Schreiter, Robert J., ed. *Faces of Jesus in Africa.* Faith and Cultures Series. Maryknoll, NY: Orbis, 1991.
Souza, N. S. *Tornar-se negro ou As vicissitudes da identidade do negro brasileiro em ascensão social.* Rio de Janeiro: Graal, 1983.
Vasconcelos, Aparecida Maria de, and Manuel Hurtado. "Descolonizar a cristologia." *Perspectiva Teológica* 48 (2016) 463–89.

Villa, Ernell, and Wilmer Villa. "Sociogénesis en las víctimas de la trata del mercado cautivo: Una orientación existencial de vidas negadas." *Tabula Rasa* 28 (2018) 163–94.

Wanamaker, C. A. "Jesus the Ancestor: Reading the story of Jesus from an African Christian Perspective, South Africa." *Scriptura* 62 (1997) 281–98.

Walsh, Catherine. *Pedagogías decoloniales: Prácticas insurgentes de resistir, (re)existir y (re)vivir.* 2 vols. Pensamiento decolonial. Quito: Abya Yala, 2013.

— Section Three —

The Story of Christianity Encounters Twenty-First-Century Issues

10

Christian Unity and Reconciliation: A Latin American Decolonial Contribution[1]

RAIMUNDO C. BARRETO JR.

A Divided Christianity in a Divided World

IN CONVERSATION WITH THE World Council of Churches' Eleventh Assembly theme "Christ's Love Moves the World to Reconciliation and Unity," in this chapter I reflect on the understanding of mission, unity, and reconciliation in the twenty-first century, engaging the conversation through a decolonial lens. By taking a decolonial approach, not only do I bring a Latinx/Latin American perspective to the discussion of Christian unity and reconciliation, but I also dislodge the narrative of the modern ecumenical movement, bringing what used to be the margins to the center of the conversation, and thus challenging hegemonic historiographical approaches to ecumenism.

Unity and reconciliation have been at the core of the ecumenical movement since its inception. Michael Kinnamon states that the call for peace and reconciliation of the world, on one hand, and for Christian unity, on the other, are not only deeply interconnected; they are central ecumenical concerns. Citing German educator Ernst Lange's affirmation that the ecumenical movement is a movement for peace, Kinnamon links the ecumenical emphasis on unity with the centrality of the Christian witness for peace in the world.[2]

---

1. This revised essay is reprinted with permission from the World Council of Churches (WCC). A previous version of this chapter appeared as Barreto, "Challenge for Christian Unity."

2. Lange, *And Yet It Moves*, quoted in Kinnamon, *Can a Renewal Movement*, 77.

Peace and reconciliation are at the heart of ecumenism, especially because the contemporary ecumenical movement was shaped in an age of major international conflicts. As Kinnamon recalls, the Life and Work movement was born amid the debris of World War I and the process of the inception of the WCC itself was deeply impacted by World War II.[3] Likewise, the Cold War also impacted the ecumenical movement in significant ways. Amid these and other political and military conflicts, twentieth-century ecumenism provided a witness for peace and reconciliation and a profound sense of relatedness. The day the Russian Orthodox Church joined the WCC on the eve of the Cuban mission crisis in 1961, for instance, is an excellent example of that witness for peace in a gravely fractured world. In the dawn of the third decade of the twenty-first century, it is important, once again, to reflect on the significance of the connection between unity and reconciliation as a key aspect of Christian witness.

Unfortunately, after more than a century of concerted ecumenical efforts,[4] both the world and the Christian churches remain deeply divided. By the time of the writing of this chapter, there were nearly thirty active armed conflicts and situations of political tension and instability around the world and a total of 70.3 million people displaced by conflict worldwide, according to the Center for Preventive Action of the Council of Foreign Relations.[5] As the chapter enters production, in addition to all those conflicts, the Russian invasion of Ukraine and the war that has been waged there for three years, and Israel's bloody military campaign in the Gaza strip in response to Hamas's attack on Israel that killed 1,200, have contributed to tens of thousands of deaths added to the toll of wasted human life in the recent past, and continue to threaten the possibility of peace in the region.

In the past few years, we have also seen an intensification of attacks on democratic institutions and an accelerated growth of authoritarianism and nationalism.[6] Bigotry, racism, xenophobia, anti-Semitism, Islamophobia, misogyny, homophobia, transphobia, and other forms of discrimination and intolerance remain widespread.

In addition to militarized conflicts, socioeconomic inequalities continue to be a major cause of death and exclusion affecting hundreds of millions across the globe. As the world continues to face the prolonged impact of a pandemic that killed more than 5.7 million people, economic inequality

---

3. Kinnamon, *Can a Renewal Movement*.

4. If we take the 1910 World Missionary Conference in Edinburgh as the event that sets in motion the development of the structures of the modern ecumenical movement.

5. See https://www.cfr.org/global-conflict-tracker/about.

6. For a recent article on the rise of Christian nationalism in Brazil and in the US, see Barreto and Chaves, "Christian Nationalism Is Thriving."

has increased since then to an obscene level. According to a recent Oxfam report titled *Inequality Kills*, "the wealth of the 10 richest men has doubled, while the incomes of 99% of humanity are worse off, because of COVID-19."[7] The report draws attention to the pernicious connection between inequality and death, which the pandemic only exacerbated. Among the many lives wasted during the pandemic, many died because they did not have access to vaccines or because they lacked access to essential hospital care or oxygen. Many others perished in connection with the loss of livelihood and hunger. The Oxfam report shows that a large number of the COVID-19 victims "were already likely to be more disadvantaged: more likely to live in low- and middle-income countries, to be women or girls, to belong to socially discriminated-against groups, to be informal workers."[8]

The world where Christians are called to work for unity and reconciliation today is as fractured as ever. However, the circumstances and nature of the prevailing conflicts of these days have changed. We are now living in a digital era, where social media has become a megaphone for hatred, amplifying extremist discourses and facilitating the spread of misinformation. Truth, which is said to be the first casualty of any war, has taken a serious hit in this new reality. Social media algorithms create artificial bubbles that reinforce distortions and speed up conspiracy theories.

If the *oikoumene*, the inhabited world, in general, remains so seriously divided and wounded, the over two billion Christians living in such a world are likewise not less fragmented. While doctrinal differences continue to be an obstacle for reconciliation and unity communion, especially among Western churches, Christians around the world are increasingly divided by culture, race/ethnicity, views on sexuality, and socioeconomic conditions. It is not that this sort of division did not exist earlier but that they are now more widespread than ever, impacting a larger number of Christians worldwide. As the late British historian Andrew F. Walls anticipated, the new configurations of the kind of differences that separate most Christians around the world today challenge us to move beyond ecumenical criteria based on "confessional comprehensiveness" toward those based on "ethnic, cultural, and geographical comprehensiveness."[9]

Indian theologian Felix Wilfred, in his turn, reminds us that the demographic shift we have seen in world Christianity in the last fifty years or so is not simply a shift "from the West to the South, but a shift of Christianity from the rich and middle classes to the poor." Accordingly, one of the

---

7. Ahmed, *Inequality Kills*, 10.
8. Ahmed, *Inequality Kills*, 4.
9. Walls, *Cross-Cultural Process*, 57.

critical barriers hindering Christian unity these days is a scandalous socioeconomic abyss. Wilfred reminds us that "those with below $500 dollars as annual income are the ones who will be, if not already, the most numerous Christian disciples in our world."[10] The shocking reality of forced poverty that most Christians (and most people around the world) experience today must be challenged, among other things, as standing in contrast with the gospel's message of reconciliation.

A broken world Christianity represented by more than nine thousand Christian denominations, thirteen thousand people groups, and thousands of languages and dialects is charged with the mission of promoting peace and reconciliation in a conflicted world.[11] This situation is further complicated by the fact that many among the large masses of impoverished people around the world are growing increasingly aware of how their lives and histories are impacted by coloniality—"the all-encompassing residual web of colonizing processes, tendencies, and practices and its ongoing manifestation, especially in present capitalist, globalizing, neoliberal systems."[12] Coloniality, says Lee Cormier, not only "regulates how we understand the world, and conditions all our relations" but also advances a racialized ideology of superiority "in which the church, the empire, and the notions of what was 'civilized' were understood to be inseparable."[13]

The interconnection between church and empire has deep historic roots. As Walter Mignolo shows, even someone who is often lauded as a champion for his defense of the rights of the indigenous people, like Bartolomé de Las Casas, perceived "all those who are outside the (Christian) Roman Empire" as barbarians; i.e., all those "who are beyond the Universal Church, since beyond the Universal Church there is no Empire."[14] In other words, in his view, the *oikoumene* was limited to the boundaries of the empire, which also coincided with the universal church. The universal church was necessarily linked to the expansion of empire, and "all non-Christian empires," including the Amerindian peoples and black Africans, were seen as barbarians. That kind of worldview would also inform the lines of distinction between church and mission in the following centuries, and the way the history of Christianity and even Christian theology were studied. Disciplinary, field, or subfield distinctions such as church history and mission studies

10. Wilfred, "Christianity Between Decline and Resurgence," 31.
11. For the statistics, see https://worldchristiandatabase.org/.
12. Cormier, "Decoloniality," 22.
13. Cormier, "Decoloniality," 22.
14. Mignolo, *Idea of Latin America*, 422.

or systematic and contextual theologies, for instance, still reflect lingering imperial specters.

Remapping Christianity, Ecumenism

As a globalized ideology that permeated the European and North American colonial projects, and whose ramifications continue to condition the current world order, the coloniality of power, knowledge, and being continues informing modern understandings of mission and unity. Thus, concepts of Christian unity, reconciliation, and mission must be continuously interrogated through the lenses of the victims of colonial "entangled global hierarchies . . . based on class, labor, military, race, gender, sexuality, religion, knowledge, language, etc."[15]

In the Americas, the most impoverished people are those whose ancestors experienced colonial genocide and slavery. It was in the context of such violence that a large number of the indigenous population and enslaved Africans were Christianized. The underlying assumption in that process of evangelization was that those "saved" souls in racialized bodies would mimic Western ways of life, but even when they did so they continued to be treated as "marginal elements of the new society."[16]

The renewed awareness of the oppressive circumstances of the evangelization of Latin America, which became more visible particularly by the time of the commemorations of five hundred years of the first evangelization in 1992, has forced many Christians in the region to rethink notions of unity, reconciliation, and mission from the bottom up. The theological and philosophical developments coming out of that new awareness have a particular contribution for a renewed envisioning of the *oikoumene*.

The world in which the modern ecumenical movement was shaped was drastically different than the reality in which unity and reconciliation need to be understood and lived out today. The rise of modern ecumenism coincided with the period that Eric Hobsbawn classified as "the age of empire."[17] One needs to consider that context when affirming that the ecumenical movement was "the outgrowth of the missionary movement."[18] The drive for unity among the Christian communions in the nineteenth and twentieth centuries largely stemmed from the success of the modern

---

15. Cormier, "Decoloniality" 23. These entangled global hierarchies comprise what decolonial scholars call "the Eurocentric colonial power matrix."
16. Dussel, *History of the Church*, 42.
17. Hobsbawn, *Age of Empire*.
18. Latourette, "Ecumenical Bearings."

missionary enterprise and its ingrained imperial memories. The missionary movement contributed significantly to an unprecedented geographical expansion of Christianity. Considering Christianity's territorial extension during that period, by the beginning of the twentieth century, it was possible to speak of Christianity as a world religion. Those memories and aspirations informed the inception of the modern ecumenical movement.

As Irvin notes, the modern ecumenical movement emerged in the beginning of the twentieth century under the influence of powerful "lingering memories of Christendom East and West."

> The churches or communions that formed the Ecumenical Movement in the 20th century . . . were mostly the descendants of Protestant communions that had formed along state lines in Europe and, although disestablished, continued to align themselves with the dominant culture and its political and social life, in North America.[19]

As such, Irvin continues, it was haunted by "the specter of Constantine," mirroring the spirit of the times. In contrast with that, Irvin points toward a new ecumenism, which began to rise particularly in the second half of the twentieth century, resembling now "the fluid assemblages and cross-border flows of globalization and exile."[20] Such ecumenical reimagination took shape side by side with the reconfiguration of world Christianity, also a terminology and approach to the study of Christianity shaped in particular in the final decades of the past century. At the time the 1910 World Missionary Conference met in Edinburgh, most Christians lived in Europe and the United States. In the course of the twentieth century, though, that situation took a drastic turn. As Wesley Granberg-Michaelson puts it,

> Christianity's geographic pilgrimage took the most pronounced, dramatic, and decisive change in direction in all its history. It rapidly accelerated its turn toward the south, and then also toward the east, and by 1980 there were more Christians in the global South than in the North for the first time in 1,000 years, and its center of gravity was in Africa.[21]

It is not, therefore, a mere coincidence that the drastic demographic, cultural, and epistemic changes in the study of world Christianity mirrored the concerted efforts to reimagine the world that were seeking to reshape the world order—including the struggles for independence among

---

19. Irvin, "Specters of a New Ecumenism," 17.
20. Irvin, "Specters of a New Ecumenism," 25.
21. Granberg-Michaelson, *From Times Square to Timbuktu*, 7–8.

formerly colonized peoples, the rise of the Third World movement, and the contributions from postcolonial and decolonial movements for indigenous autonomy. As I have shown elsewhere, the significant changes in world Christianity in the second half of the twentieth century were much more than a demographic shift.[22] They also represented a change in the racial, cultural, gender, and socioeconomic makeup of Christianity worldwide. After centuries of Eurocentric hegemony, the study of Christianity was now embracing new historiographical and anthropological approaches that allowed for a multiplicity of faces, voices, and knowledges in a variety of social and cultural loci of enunciation to be taken into account more thoroughly.

Justo González has described such a historiographical pivoting as the rise of both a new cartography and a new topography in Christian history.[23] The change in the cartography of Christianity refers to the emerging of newly enlarged world Christian maps that portray an increasingly polycentric Christianity, as compared to the modern Christian cartography that predominantly placed the North Atlantic at its center and the global South at its margins. For González, that is only a part of the story, though. He also draws attention to the importance of the topographic change that took place simultaneously, turning increased attention to the subjectivity of those who are now retelling the Christian story from those multiple loci of enunciation, emerging Christian voices that irrupt as producers of new histories and theologies.[24]

According to Mario Aguilar, the retelling of that enlarged story of Christianity is at the root of the resubjecting of Christian theologies.[25] New subjects whose voices had been previously silenced are now reshaping the ecumenical agenda, bringing new themes, concerns, perspectives, and social locations to the table of ecumenical dialogue. Among those voices are indigenous peoples, women, racialized communities, sexual- and gender-minoritized groups, and the economically poor. What does this new topography of world Christianity mean for the twenty-first-century ecumenical agenda? More than anything else, it demands that previously silenced voices be the ones most eagerly heard—prioritized—in ecumenical conversations.

The meaning of unity, reconciliation, and mission nowadays cannot be discerned apart from the recentering of those voices and realities. It is not merely a matter of inclusion of previously excluded subjects but an imperative to dislodge the Christendom mentality prevalent in the early modern

---

22. Barreto, "Epistemological Turn."
23. González, *Changing Shape of Church History*, 12.
24. González, *Changing Shape of Church History*, 19.
25. Aguilar, "Public Theology from Periphery."

ecumenical movement and recenter those voices that were once silenced.[26] In other words, it means that contemporary ecumenists are challenged to rethink ecumenism through a decolonial lens.[27]

The burgeoning field of world Christianity can help that process by adding methodological and theoretical tools that can help ecumenists engage the plurality of Christian experiences, expressions, and relational networks around the world. The "Christianities" blossoming in the global South can no longer be seen as mere extensions of Western missionary enterprises. They are instead faith expressions born and conceived in a variety of cultural and epistemological locations, as the Bible and Christian tradition are being read on different terms than they were read within a modern/colonial frame. Yet, world Christianity scholars cannot limit themselves to think only in terms of the distinctive "Christianities" shaping up in different cultures and contexts. They must also interrogate the plurality of "worlds" in world Christianity. As we revisit the idea of unity and reconciliation in ecumenical perspective in the twenty-first century, it is important to take into account the pluriversal nature of the contemporary world—a "world of many worlds."[28]

Interrogating Unity and Reconciliation in Latin American Perspective

Despite all good intentions, the early ecumenical understanding of unity and reconciliation emerged in connection with a view of missionary expansion haunted by imperial aspirations, the specter of Constantine, to borrow Irvin's analogy. In the course of the twentieth century, however, new theological subjects from the Asia-Pacific, Africa, and Latin America-Caribbean began to challenge those assumptions more prominently. It became increasingly clear that North Atlantic perspectives on mission and theology could no longer be universalized, nor could the worldwide geographical presence of Christianity be interpreted exclusively through the lenses of Western experiences. In other words, a globalized Eurocentric Christian narrative needs to be contextualized—put in its modern/colonial context—whereas

---

26. Irvin, "Ecumenical Dislodgings."

27. As Nelson Maldonado-Torres puts it, "The Decolonial Turn is about making visible the invisible and about analyzing the mechanisms that produce such invisibility or distorted visibility in light of a large stock of ideas that must necessarily include the critical reflections of the 'invisible' people themselves" ("On Coloniality of Being," 262).

28. Blaser and Cadena, "Pluriverse."

other previously invisible local histories must be made visible along with their contributions to an enlarged world Christian map.

Some initial efforts made to dislodge the Eurocentric dominance of the world order, especially those in connection with the decolonization process in the post-WWII world, influenced the subsequent southward and eastward turn in world Christianity. In particular, the Third World conferences that gathered in Bandung (1955), Cairo (1961), and Havana (1966) were key to giving voice to a growing desire on the part of the peoples of the majority world to be heard. Such a shared sentiment spreading throughout former colonies was felt within Christian circles. In the corridors of Vatican II, in the early 1960s, for example, Brazilian bishop Helder began to explicitly talk about the need for a "Christian *Bandung*," meaning the creation of a coalition of "Third World" Christians to stand in solidarity with the poor and oppressed of the world.[29] Similar aspirations led to the formation of the Ecumenical Association of Third World Theologians, a forum for dialogue among African, Asian, and Latin American theologians, which seeks to discern together new ways of being church and doing theology in ways that are more meaningful to their specific contexts and experiences.[30] Ecumenical initiatives from the underside of history—or from modernity's darker side[31]—have advanced an alternative logic, an ecumenism from below, which points to the possibility not only of another possible church but also of another possible world.[32]

A more recent example of how those aspirations have shaped up can be seen in the final document of the Amazon Synod, "The Amazon: New Paths for the Church and for an Integral Ecology,"[33] which encompasses three years of conversations between bishops in the Amazonia and local peoples and movements, and Pope Francis's post-synodal apostolic exhortation *Querida Amazonia*, his response to the synod, which articulated some possibilities for a new church and a new world, based on the sustained dialogue with the indigenous people of the Amazon, peasants, Afro-descendants, migrants,

---

29. Luz Marques, "Circulares conciliares," 68. For more on Câmara's articulation of this vision during the Second Vatican Council with representatives of the conferences of bishops in Asia and Africa in the council, see Barreto, "Vatican II."

30. The fact that this coalition included the phrase "Third World" in its title and has kept it ever since is a sign of how aligned its founders and participants were to the idea of a "Third World movement." See Torres and Fabella, *Emergent Gospel*, 2.

31. Mignolo, *Darker Side of Western Modernity*. Coloniality is modernity's darker side and is inseparable from it, even though its logic is often invisible, "disguised by the lights of modernity's progressive mission" (Mignolo, "Prophets Facing Sidewise," 112).

32. Cormier, "Jesus of History."

33. Segreteria Generale del Sinodo, "Amazon."

young people, and city and river dwellers that characterized the synod. In his apostolic exhortation, Francis expressed his vision for a renewed relationship with the people of the Amazon using the analogy of four dreams: a social dream, a cultural dream, an ecological dream, and an ecclesial dream. While this chapter does not examine the content of those dreams or follow the structure of *Querida Amazonia*, in what follows, I draw on Pope Francis's expressed dreams to address the ecumenical concern with unity and reconciliation at the dawn of the third decade of this new millennium from a Latin American perspective.

Reconciling Racialized Socioeconomic Disparities

As indicated earlier, one of the main walls of separation in the current moment of our history is the huge economic disparities that dehumanize the majority of the inhabitants of earth, including the majority of Christians around the world. According to the World Bank, in December of 2020 one quarter of the world population lived below the Society Poverty Line, an index that combines the USD$1.90-a-day line of absolute poverty with the level of income in a particular country, offering a better view, especially, of poverty in high-income economies.[34]

The forced impoverishment of hundreds of millions around the world divides the world population along the line of the human, since it forces millions to live under dehumanizing conditions and naturalizes the waste of human lives in those contexts. The fact that the mass impoverishment mentioned above in a world with plenty of natural resources to feed everyone cannot be considered natural was at the core of the rise of Latin American liberation theologies, which denounced the indifference toward the collective suffering of the masses and the systemic manufacturing of poverty as sin and idolatry. Franz Hinkelammert, in particular, denounced the systems of thought used to justify such a glaring injustice as "the ideological weapons of death."[35] The most significant move Latin American liberation theologians made in response to such a situation was to think theologically not simply in solidarity with the poor but from the heat of their struggle for liberation. Whereas such a move has often been interpreted as polarizing—as if by siding with the poor, liberation theologians were themselves creating a separation that already existed—in hindsight one can see how what they did was indeed a radically inclusive social and epistemological move, shifting the theological locus of enunciation from self-proclaimed

---

34. Schoch et al., "Quarter of the World."
35. Hinkelammert, *Armas ideológicas de la muerte*.

centers to the peripheries of the world. Encouraging compassion—suffering with—and the encounter of the incarnated Christ in the poor, liberation theologians have contributed to the resubjecting of Christian theology that Aguilar suggests.[36] Gustavo Gutiérrez, for instance, interpreted such an immersion in the practice of liberation as a sign of the irruption of the poor in history.[37] The move toward unity and reconciliation with the poor, then, was not only one based on inclusion but also one implying repentance and a demand for conversion—a change of course in the history of Christianity and the world. It called for the reinvention of the church, an ecclesiogenesis of the church as seen in the base communities formed by the Latin American poor;[38] or for the rediscovery of the church in the modern diaspora.[39] In either case, the idea that the church was being reinvented beyond (and even outside) the confines of known ecclesiastical institutions sounded paradoxically threatening and promising. Regardless of whether the signs that people like Leonardo Boff and M. Richard Shaull saw at that time were fully materialized later or not, both of those authors (among many others) were pointing to the fact that God was not imprisoned in the modern institutions of the Christian churches, and that in the Spirit's freedom to act in the world, new forms of Christian communities—particularly among the poor—were emerging. That phenomenon could be described as the irruption of the poor in the Third World—and its diasporic communities—as Gutiérrez had anticipated. As Ivone Gebara puts it, "The poor called the institutional church into question and brought about a new movement in theology."[40]

The abundance of Christian communities and expressions that the burgeoning world Christianity scholarship has drawn attention to in the past few decades seems to be in line with the renewal of Christian koinonia, at the same time enriching and complicating our understanding of Christian

36. Boff and Boff, *Introducing Liberation Theology*, 2–3.

37. For him, it meant a new presence of those who had been absent from both our society and from the church. What he meant by absent was that their voices and expressions, their sufferings, their comaraderies, their plans, their hopes were not central to the life of both church and society (Gutiérrez, *Theology of Liberation*).

38. The nature of that shift is evident in his description of what Boff saw happening in the 1970s: "We are not dealing with the expansion of an existing ecclesiastical system, rotating on a sacramental, clerical axis, but with the emergence of another form of being church, rotating on the axis of the word and the laity. We may well anticipate that, from this movement, of which the universal church is becoming aware, a new type of institutional presence of Christianity in the world may now come into being" (*Ecclesiogenesis*, 67).

39. Shaull, "Form of the Church."

40. Gebara, "Movement of May 1968," 265.

unity in the twenty-first century. Despite the challenges this reinvention of the church brings to existing ecumenical structures and conversations, it has a tremendous potential to recenter twenty-first-century world Christianity on the basis of the expansive experience of the collective poor, who, not long ago, were absent as constitutive makers of ecumenical praxis and thought.

The first generation of Latin American liberation theologians, however, was slow to realize that material poverty was only one face of oppression. It took another generation to show that white supremacy and heteropatriarchy, for instance, are other important facets of the colonial matrix of power that imposes hierarchical divisions among human communities, separating between those whose humanity is acknowledged and those who are not perceived as fully human, thus contributing to the creation of "expandable populations in massive proportions."[41]

Above all, one cannot ignore, as most first-generation Latin American liberation theologians did, that the political, cultural, and economic global hierarchies forming the colonial matrix of power define the line of the human and the nonhuman in racialized terms.[42] Due to their initially exclusive dependence on classic Marxist categories to interpret the historical structural causes of socioeconomic poverty,[43] it took a while for the first Latin American liberation theologians to understand the centrality of race and gender in that equation.

Reconciling Cultural and Epistemic Divides

Most of the economically impoverished masses around the world are black, indigenous, and people of color, reflecting the globalized hierarchies discussed above. Racism, therefore, is not simply a "contextual" evil that affects only particular societies. Instead, racism is a globalized phenomenon and can be overcome only if its globalized structural nature is taken into consideration. As Ramón Grosfoguel puts it, racism "is a global hierarchy of superiority and inferiority along the line of the human . . . produced and reproduced for centuries by the institutions of the 'capitalist/patriarchal western-centric/Christian-centric modern/colonial world-system.'"[44] The colonial matrix of power not only racially classifies people and regions of the world but also regulates gender and sexuality through economic, political,

---

41. Blaser and Cadena, "Pluriverse," 2.
42. Grosfoguel, "What Is Racism," 10.
43. Boff and Boff, *Introducing Liberation Theology*, 27.
44. Grosfoguel, "What Is Racism," 11.

and cultural norms.⁴⁵ The association of Christianity and whiteness with a superior morality and/or spirituality is also a dimension of that racialization of the world.

All these examples demonstrate the limits of an exclusively socioeconomic approach to the privileging of the poor as promoted at the origins of Latin American liberation theologies. As the complexity of systemic oppression becomes increasingly clearer, one can see how the people placed below the line of the human—i.e., those whose humanity is often questioned or negated—are not only violated on the basis of their civil, political, or economic rights, but also on the level of the denial of "the recognition of their subjectivities, identities, spiritualities and epistemologies."⁴⁶ Racism and cisheteropatriarchy have been key weapons in the controlling of both knowledge-construction and (in)validation across gender and racial lines. Policies of inclusion, therefore, are not sufficient to overcome colonial oppression. As Mignolo explains,

> Inclusion is a one-way street and not a reciprocal right. In a world governed by the colonial matrix of power, he who includes and she who is welcomed to be included stand in codified power relations. The locus of enunciation from which inclusion is established is always a locus holding the control of knowledge and the power of decision across gender and racial lines, across political orientations and economic regulations.⁴⁷

Shifting the locus of enunciation, therefore, is a critical decolonial move. The modern/colonial understanding of unity, and its companion—universal truth—end up imposing one civilization—the modern West—and a truth over all others. Modern Christian views on unity and universally valid truth claims have "usually accompanied the history of power and colonization and ha[ve] been all too frequently legitimized by these."⁴⁸ In that sense, the Western missionary enterprise was an arm of civilizatory processes aimed at the creation of a monocentric and monochrome world order. By contrast, the decolonial option is necessarily polycentric and pluriversal, thus requiring an "epistemic democratization."⁴⁹ This is not a project that gives up on truth but one that engages with concurrent truth claims, which, emerging from particular cultural and religious systems,

---

45. Mignolo, *Darker Side of Western Modernity*.
46. Grosfoguel, "What Is Racism?" 13.
47. Mignolo, *Darker Side of Western Modernity*, 45.
48. Espín, *Idol and Grace*, 237.
49. Mignolo, *Darker Side of Western Modernity*, 66.

may have universal relevance—something that can be realized only through consistent decolonial intercultural praxis and dialogue.[50]

In the past few decades, Latin America has seen the rise of ecofeminist, Amerindian, black, indecent/queer, and other forms of liberative theologies and philosophies offering discursive and praxeological alternatives for the construction of a reconciliation from the margins. Ivone Gebara's ecofeminism, for instance, highlights the fact that most of the economically poor in Latin America are women. A liberative theology that takes the daily suffering of marginalized women in a capitalist and patriarchal society seriously must, therefore, be informed by the daily life and perspectives of women in their search "for concrete solutions to daily-life problems."[51] Gebara rightly understands theologies as cultural products. And since "official theologies are cultural products of our hierarchical and masculine philosophies and ideologies,"[52] they end up reproducing the hegemonic dehumanization of the patriarchal and capitalist order. For Gebara, therefore, liberation is not simply about the inclusion of women in this hierarchical and unjust social structure. Rather, acknowledging the plurality of utopias (of possible worlds), she advances the possibility of new relationships that draw on a plurality of feminist theories and practices to rebuild new utopias, new forms of hope.[53]

Similarly, indigenous and black theologies have emerged in Latin America in response to centuries of cultural and epistemic genocide; i.e., of concerted efforts to erase "the knowledge and cultures of these populations, their memories and ancestral links and their manner of relating to others and to nature."[54] Prominent Brazilian scholar and political activist Abdias do Nascimento described such a discursive effort to erase Afro-Brazilian culture, morals, religion, and demographics as a politics of extermination or "the genocide of black Brazilians."[55] Likewise, Guillermo Cook called the underlying racism and cultural superiority of the Christian evangelization that attempted to eliminate indigenous ways of life considered superstitious and idolatrous a "cultural genocide."[56] The late Latin American historian and philosopher Enrique Dussel also reinforced that view by highlighting

---

50. Espín, *Idol and Grace*.
51. Gebara, "Ecofeminism," 95.
52. Gebara, "Ecofeminism," 98.
53. Gebara, "Ecofeminism," 101.
54. Sousa Santos, "Epistemologies of the South," 18.
55. Nascimento, *Genocídio do negro brasileiro*, 42.
56. Cook, "Introduction," 15.

how the exploitation of the indigenous people by the Iberian colonizers and missions targeted "the basic foundations of the indigenous cosmology."[57]

In spite of the genocidal violence perpetrated against indigenous and black Latin Americans and their traditions, which unfortunately persists to this day,[58] indigenous and African-derived religious traditions and spirituality have not only survived throughout the region but have even experienced a revitalization in the past decades. For a long time, Latin America was considered by many as a "Christianized: continent. During the colonial era, there was little room for the public practice of other religions. However, even in such a suppressive religious environment, the religious practices of immigrants, merchants, enslaved Africans, and Amerindians persisted. Not only did they survive, but they have contributed to reshaping Latin American Christianity, giving birth to multiple branches of popular religion.

Indigenous peoples and Afro-descendants in Latin America have never relinquished their agency as moral, cultural, political, and religious subjects. However, they have been often forced to face the paradox of an imperial religion that legitimizes the domination of colonized peoples in the name of the gospel of the Crucified, posing as the prototype of human culture and promoting a fetishized universality that denies other cultures their claims of access to truth.[59] In response to that, the colonized have over the centuries creatively found ways to coexist with that dominant imperial religion, despite the asymmetric conditions imposed by colonial conditions. In Brazil, enslaved Africans learned to navigate the fine line between keeping honoring their ancestors and deities while also remaining Christian—at least in appearance—to avoid punishment and suspicion. Thus, identifying those ancestors and deities with Catholic saints and performing their rituals before Catholic altars became both an act of creativity and inclusion (of the other) and a survival strategy. In one way or another, such practices contributed to the rise of a dark-skinned popular Catholicism that remains one of the most widespread religious devotions in the country.[60]

By contrast, Catholic confraternities or *irmandades* that emerged as spaces for Christian devotion on the part of free and enslaved Afro-Brazilians were especially significant for the preservation of African-derived religious traditions. In the *irmandades*, black Brazilians celebrated annual festivals, mourned their dead, and helped one another. The *irmandades* functioned as cradles for the formation of racial consciousness and as

57. Dussel, *History of the Church*, 421.
58. See, for instance, Barreto, "COVID-19 Pandemic."
59. Dussel, "Epistemological Decolonization of Theology."
60. Hoornaert, *Cristianismo moreno do Brasil*.

forums where different ethnic identities reinvented themselves. As such, they contributed to the preservation of African traditions that would later give birth to both *terreiros de candomblé* and the reinvention of the Catholic faith as black and Brazilian.[61]

Other Ways of Knowing, Other Ways of Connecting

As Graciela Chamorro reminds us, cultural and religious realities are not finished products. They are dynamic and complex.[62] Despite all the power asymmetry and attempt at assimilation, indigenous and African-derived religious traditions and spirituality have persisted and continue to influence Christian discourse in Latin America, the Caribbean, and beyond. The terms in which discourses on Christian unity and reconciliation were conceived in Eurocentric and Protestant-oriented ecumenical structures formed in the first half of the twentieth century must be expanded and even reinvented, since they can no longer meaningfully speak to a reality in which most Christians live, especially in the global South, where theological discourse has been deeply impacted by new subjects and voices whose experiences were not fully considered when the terms of that conversation were first developed.

Not only world Christianity has drastically changed since then, but the world in which Christians live today is also radically different than that in which the ecumenical movement was originally conceived. In this new world, truth claims can no longer be taken at face value as universally valid. The construction of universally relevant truth claims—which are important for unity and reconciliation to be possible—demand an attitude of mutual listening and epistemic humility. Western Christianity no longer has the final word in those conversations, and the universalization of its truth claims is now confronted with the unavoidable contextualization of the world that produced it, including the Western Christian historical participation in the coloniality of power, being, and knowledge that privileges Eurocentric and Christian-centric claims.

The success of a renewed Christian call for the reconciliation of the world, therefore, depends on how well Christians can listen to the subjects and cultures the colonial matrix of power made invisible, and to their opening up to that which indigenous voices in Latin America call *otros saberes*—other ways of knowing and forms of knowledge. Such a posture is in line

---

61. For more on this topic, see Nogueira Negrão, "Pluralismo"; Barreto, "Brazil's Black Christianity."

62. Chamorro, "Indigenous Religions and Cultures," 16.

with the idea of mission from the margins advanced in the Tenth WCC Assembly in Busan, which affirms "the agency of those who are marginalized, participating in their struggles and sharing their hopes, overcoming the marginalizing tendencies, and resisting and confronting forces of marginalization and exclusion in our specific contexts of the world."[63]

Likewise, this posture reaffirms Pope Francis's emphasis in *Querida Amazonia* on the need for an authentic option for the poor and abandoned, which takes on an Amazonian (indigenous) face, humbly engages their wisdom, and learns from them, especially their understanding of *buen vivir* (good living) and their deeply interconnection and interdependence with the whole of creation. Pope Francis's dream of a church with an Amazonian face responds to the call for an integral ecology on the part of the participants of the Amazon Synod, which involves sustained dialogue with the indigenous peoples and other minoritized communities. Considering the urgency of the world's ecological crisis, Pope Francis reverberates the synod's call for Christians around the world to listen and learn from the wisdom for the ecological coexistence of the Amerindian peoples.[64]

Chiquitano Bolivian missiologist Roberto Tomichá Charupá highlights the importance of reencountering, listening to, and living together (*convivir*) with those who are different—in particular those most impacted by the hegemonic face of modernity—for the reconciliation of the world. Such a move implies an openness to "incorporate other ways of knowledge and other logics as integral parts of living an authentic Christianity."[65]

The contemporary ecumenical task, therefore, necessarily includes the unlearning of colonial understandings of mission, unity, and reconciliation, and delinking from the logic of coloniality.[66] Acknowledging the entanglement of modern Western Christianity with colonial logic is an important step for repentance and conversion. Such an attitude is at the root of the epistemic humility needed to learn new grammars of *convivencia* with others in an enlarged and multifaceted world—a world made of multiple worlds.

The call for reconciliation at this point in history thus begins with the acknowledgment of the irreducible plurality of coexisting worlds, which leads to intercultural practices leading to the reframing of social, cultural,

---

63. World Council of Churches, "Mission from the Margins," para. 3.

64. See Tomichá Charupá, "Convivir ecológico-nomádico."

65. Tomichá Charupá, "Toward a Church," 25. Christine J. Hong similarly calls for the need to incorporate intercultural and interreligious intelligence into theological education (*Decolonial Futures*).

66. Mignolo, "Delinking."

and religious borderlands.⁶⁷ However, while listening to wounded and conflicted subjects—as co-wounded bodies and communities—is crucial for the possibility of healing and reconciliation, this is only the first step to that end. The following step is the need to "see through" our cultural conditioning and envision potential bridges that can help us move beyond internalized and exteriorized conflicts.⁶⁸ As Irvin reminds us, the modern/colonial difference has created borders that cut "through every region, every nation, every culture on the face of the earth."⁶⁹ Decolonial thinkers such as Walter Mignolo and Gloria Anzaldúa call us to move beyond our comfort zones to inhabit the borderlands.

Borderlands, which are at first glance places of exclusion, separation, and control can alternatively become sites of creativity and reinvention. Recovering the Nahuatl word *nepantla*, Anzaldúa has offered important insights to turning the existence between different races, beliefs, traditions, and social conditions into a mestiza/o/x locus of enunciation that shows great tolerance for contradictions and ambiguity.⁷⁰

Whereas the urge for intercultural dialogue has been around for decades, the most significant recent development in intercultural relations is that the global South is now claiming a protagonist role in designing new methods and setting the agenda for intercultural dialogue.⁷¹ The initiatives seen in Latin American and Latinx scholars such as Ivone Gebara, Roberto Tomichá Charupá, Graciela Chamorro, and Gloria Anzaldúa, as discussed above—and also present in Pope Francis's *Querida Amazonia*—are examples of important efforts to move beyond the Eurocentric "'I' which, by virtue of its colonial memories, has asserted itself as the universal standard" of humanity's thinking and being.⁷² Ecumenical efforts for unity and reconciliation, therefore, must critically engage with a burgeoning decolonial body politic of knowledge, which points to the possibility of new ways of reconnecting with one another (and with the world) and coexisting. This is crucial if we are to resist and reverse the inversions and distortions of colonial Christendom, thus moving toward overcoming its persisting impact on Christian and human relations in the contemporary world.⁷³

67. Hong, *Decolonial Futures*, 129–36.
68. See Anzaldúa, *Light in the Dark*.
69. Irvin, "World Christianity," 14.
70. Anzaldúa, *Borderlands*, 101.
71. Dussel, "Agenda for South-South," 3.
72. Dussel, "Agenda for South-South," 3.

73. For Dussel, Christianity, which started as the faith of the Jewish messianic community, formed around the life and story of the Nazarene Jesus, which appealed to subaltern peoples in the Hellenistic-Roman empire, underwent two drastic inversions.

Bibliography

Aguilar, Mario I. "Public Theology from the Periphery: Victims and Theologians." *International Journal of Public Theology* 1 (2007) 321–37.

Ahmed, Nabil. *Inequality Kills: The Unparalleled Action Needed to Combat Inequality in the Wake of COVID-19*. Oxfam Briefing Paper. Oxford: Oxfam International, 2022. https://oxfamilibrary.openrepository.com/bitstream/handle/10546/621341/bp-inequality-kills-170122-en.pdf.

Anzaldúa, Gloria. *Borderlands/La frontera: The New Mestiza*. 25th anniv. 4th ed. San Francisco: Aunt Lute, 2012.

———. *Light in the Dark/Luz en lo Oscuro: Rewriting Identity, Spirituality, Reality*. Edited by Analouise Keating. Durham: Duke University Press, 2015.

Barreto, Raimundo, and João B. Chaves. "Christian Nationalism Is Thriving in Brazil: Bolsonaro's Faith-Based Enablers." *Christian Century* 138 (2021) 22–25. https://www.christiancentury.org/article/critical-essay/christian-nationalism-thriving-bolsonaro-s-brazil.

Barreto, Raimundo C., Jr. "Brazil's Black Christianity and the Counterhegemonic Production of Knowledge in World Christianity." *Studies in World Christianity* 25 (2019) 71–94.

———. "The Challenge for Christian Unity and Reconciliation Today from a Decolonial Perspective." *International Review of Mission* 111 (2022) 70–87.

———. "The COVID-19 Pandemic and the Ongoing Genocide of Black and Indigenous Peoples in Brazil." *International Journal of Latin American Religions* 4 (2020) 417–39.

———. "The Epistemological Turn in World Christianity: Engaging Decoloniality in Latin American and Caribbean Christian Discourses." *Journal of World Christianity* 9 (2019) 48–60.

———. "Vatican II, Medellin, and Latin American Ecumenism: A Brazilian Protestant Perspective." *Journal of World Christianity* 9 (2019) 187–202.

Blaser, Mario, and Marisol de la Cadena. "Pluriverse: Proposals for a World of Many Worlds." In *A World of Many Worlds*, edited by Marisol de la Cadena and Mario Blaser, 1–22. Durham: Duke University Press, 2018.

Boff, Leonardo. *Ecclesiogenesis: The Base Communities Reinvent the Church*. Translated by Robert R. Barr. Maryknoll, NY: Orbis, 2012. Kindle.

Boff, Leonardo, and Clodovis Boff. *Introducing Liberation Theology*. Translated by Paul Burns. Maryknoll, NY: Orbis, 1987.

Chamorro, Graciela. "Indigenous Religions and Cultures: Apropos an Intercultural Public Theology." In *Public Theology in Brazil: Social and Cultural Changes*, edited by Eneida Jacobsen et al., 7–24. Theology in the Public Square/Theologie in der Offentlichkeit 6. Zurich: LIT, 2013.

Cook, Guillermo. "Introduction: Brief History of the Maya Peoples." In *Crosscurrents in Indigenous Spirituality: Interface of Maya, Catholic and Protestant Worldviews*, edited by Guillermo Cook, 11–31. Studies in Christian Mission 18. Leiden: Brill, 1997.

The first, in the fourth century, changed it into a triumphalist imperial religion. The second, in the sixteenth century, turned it into a colonial Christendom, the Christianity that the Abya Yala peoples first encountered ("Epistemological Decolonization of Christianity").

Cormier, Lee. "Decoloniality: A Conceptual Introduction." In *Decoloniality and Justice: Theological Perspectives*, edited by Jean-François Roussel, 19–24. São Leopoldo, Brazil: Oikos, 2018.

———. "Jesus of History, Christs of Faith, and Hope That Another World Is Possible." Paper presented at International Theological Commission of the Ecumenical Association of Third World Theologians, Sri Lanka, 2007.

Dussel, Enrique. "Agenda for a South-South Philosophical Dialogue." *Human Architecture* 11 (2013) 3–18.

———. "Epistemological Decolonization of Christianity." In *Decolonial Christianities: Latinx and Latin American Perspectives*, edited by Raimundo Barreto and Roberto Sirvent, 25–42. New Approaches to Religion and Power. New York: Palgrave MacMillan, 2019.

———. "The Epistemological Decolonization of Theology." *Concilium: International Journal of Theology* 2 (2013) 21–31.

———. *A History of the Church in Latin America: Colonialism to Liberation, 1492–1979*. Translated by Alan Neely. Grand Rapids: Eerdmans, 1981.

Espín, Orlando O. *Idol and Grace: Traditioning and Subversive Hope*. Maryknoll, NY: Orbis, 2014. Kindle.

Francis. "Querida Amazonia." Vatican, Feb. 12, 2020. https://press.vatican.va/content/salastampa/en/bollettino/pubblico/2020/02/12/200212c.html.

Gebara, Ivone. "Ecofeminism: A Latin American Perspective." *Crosscurrents* 53 (2003) 93–103.

———. "The Movement of May 1968 and Theology in Latin America: The Third World in the Theology of Liberation." *Ecumenical Review* 70 (2018) 264–71.

González, Justo L. *The Changing Shape of Church History*. St. Louis: Chalice, 2002.

Granberg-Michaelson, Wesley. *From Times Square to Timbuktu: The Post-Christian West Meets the Non-Western Church*. Grand Rapids: Eerdmans, 2013.

Grosfoguel, Ramón. "What Is Racism?" *Journal of World-Systems Research* 22 (2016) 9–15.

Gutiérrez, Gustavo. *A Theology of Liberation*. 15th anniv. ed. Maryknoll, NY: Orbis, 2019. Kindle.

Hinkelammert, Franz J. *Las armas ideológicas de la muerte: El discernimiento de los fetiches, capitalismo y cristianismo*. San José: Editorial Universitaria Centroamericana, 1977.

Hobsbawn, Eric. *The Age of Empire, 1875–1914*. New York: Vintage, 1989.

Hong, Christine J. *Decolonial Futures: Intercultural and Interreligious Intelligence for Theological Education*. Postcolonial and Decolonial Studies in Religion and Theology. Lanham, MD: Lexington, 2021.

Hoornaert, Eduardo. *O cristianismo moreno do Brasil*. Petrópolis: Vozes, 1991.

Irvin, Dale T. "Ecumenical Dislodgings." *Mission Studies* 22 (2005) 187–205.

———. "Specters of a New Ecumenism: In Search of a Church 'Out of Joint.'" In *Religion, Authority, and the State: From Constantine to the Contemporary World*, edited by Leo D. Lefebure, 3–32. New York: Palgrave Macmillan, 2016.

———. "World Christianity: An Introduction." *Journal of World Christianity* 1 (2008) 1–26.

Kinnamon, Michael. *Can a Renewal Movement Be Renewed? Questions for the Future of Ecumenism*. Grand Rapids: Eerdmans, 2012. Kindle.

Latourette, Kenneth S. "Ecumenical Bearings of the Missionary Movement and the International Missionary Council." In *1517–1948*, edited by Ruth Rouse and Stephen C. Neill. Vol. 1 of *A History of the Ecumenical Movement*. 3rd ed. Geneva: World Council of Churches, 1986.

Luz Marques, Luiz Carlos. "As circulares conciliares de Dom Helder." In *Dom Helder Camara: Circulares conciliares*, edited by Luiz Carlos Luz Marques and Roberto de Araujo Farias, 1:52–70. Recife, Brazil: Pernambuco, 2008.

Maldonado-Torres, Nelson. "On the Coloniality of Being." *Cultural Studies* 21 (2007) 240–70.

Mignolo, Walter D. *The Darker Side of Western Modernity: Global Futures, Decolonial Options*. Latin American Otherwise. Durham: Duke University Press, 2011.

———. "Delinking: The Rhetoric of Modernity, the Logic of Coloniality and the Grammar of De-Coloniality." *Cultural Studies* 21 (2007) 449–514.

———. *The Idea of Latin America*. Wiley-Blackwell Manifestos. Hoboken, NJ: Blackwell. Kindle.

———. "Prophets Facing Sidewise: The Geopolitics of Knowledge and the Colonial Difference." *Social Epistemology* 19 (2005) 111–27.

Nascimento, Abdias do. *O genocídio do negro brasileiro: Processo de um racismo mascarado*. Rio de Janeiro: Paz e Terra, 1978.

Nogueira Negrão, Lísias. "Pluralismo e multiplicidades religiosas no Brasil contemporaneo." *Sociedade e Estado* 23 (2008) 261–79.

Schoch, Marta, et al. "A Quarter of the World Lives in Societal Poverty." World Bank Blogs, Dec. 2, 2020. https://blogs.worldbank.org/opendata/quarter-world-lives-societal-poverty.

Segreteria Generale del Sinodo. "The Amazon: New Paths for the Church and for an Integral Ecology." Segreteria Generale del Sinodo, n.d. http://secretariat.synod.va/content/sinodoamazonico/en/documents/final-document-of-the-amazon-synod.html.

Shaull, Richard. "The Form of the Church in the Modern Diaspora." *PSB* 57 (1963) 3–18.

Sousa Santos, Boaventura de. "Epistemologies of the South and the Future." *From the European South* 1 (2016) 17–29. https://www.fesjournal.eu/numeri/archivi-del-futuro-il-postcoloniale-litalia-e-il-tempo-a-venire/epistemologies-of-the-south-and-the-future/.

Tomichá Charupá, Roberto. "El convivir ecológico-nomádico de los pueblos amerindios: Una narrativa profética, simbólica y mística." *Concilium: Revista Internacional de Teología* 378 (2018) 87–96. https://www.revistaconcilium.com/wp-content/uploads/2019/pdf/378.pdf.

———. "Toward a Church with an Indigenous Face: Some Premises and Urgent Challenges." In *The Church and Indigenous Peoples in the Americas: In Between Reconciliation and Decolonization*, edited by Michel Andraos, 13–29. Studies in World Catholicism Book 7. Eugene, OR: Cascade, 2019. Kindle.

Torres, Sergio, and Virginia Fabella, eds. *The Emergent Gospel: Theology from the Underside of History*. Maryknoll, NY: Orbis, 1976.

Walls, Andrew F. *The Cross-Cultural Process in Christian History: Studies in the Transmission and Appropriation of Faith*. Maryknoll, NY: Orbis, 2001.

Wilfred, Felix. "Christianity Between Decline and Resurgence." In *Christianity in Crisis?*, edited by Jon Sobrino and Felix Wilfred, 27–37. Concilium 2005.3. London: SCM, 2005.

World Council of Churches. "Mission from the Margins." World Council of Churches, n.d. https://www.oikoumene.org/what-we-do/mission-from-the-margins.

11

The Indigenous Church: The Changing Face of Liberation Christianity in Latin America[1]

GRACIELA CHAMORRO[2]

THE VISIBILITY THAT THE indigenous peoples of Abya Yala have gained in recent decades is related, among other things, to the leading role that many of their leaders have played in the sphere of the church and theology. The age-old wisdom of these peoples and the notoriety achieved by their representatives in the religious field are also echoed in areas such as anthropology, ecology, and politics. This chapter deals with the origin of indigenous churches and the theological reflection that accompanied the movement. For that, whenever possible, sources written by indigenous people and oral testimonies of indigenous people who collaborated with this research are used.

First Attempts

Juan F. Gorski seeks to find the deepest roots for an indigenous church and an indigenous theology in the actions of some Catholic missionaries between 1955 and 1960, in the Andean and Mesoamerican region, where 90 percent of the population indigenous to the continent is concentrated.[3] In

---

1. *Kuna*, meaning "mature land," is the word used by indigenous intellectuals to designate the entire American continent.

2. Translated by Stephen Di Trolio. Thanks to Roberto Tomichá Charupá, Sofía Chipana Quispe, Laura Vicuña Pereira Manso, Vânia Pereira, and Izaias Silva Pataxó for their invaluable collaboration in the research and writing of this text.

3. Gorski, "Desarrollo histórico," 10–11.

his assessment, these new missionary agents from the middle of the last century resorted to training indigenous catechists and ended up drinking from the native wisdom found in the language, culture, and religion of these original peoples.

Then, Gorski highlights the positive impact of the Second Vatican Council on non-Christian religions as a powerful stimulus for reflection on indigenous religious experiences, led mainly by people linked to ecclesial institutions in Mexico, Guatemala, Ecuador, Peru, and Bolivia.

Chiquitano Roberto Tomichá Charupá, OFM, from Bolivia, echoing the words of Gustavo Gutiérrez, writes that the Second Vatican Council (1962-65) was a true "sign of the times" for the church in Latin America and the Caribbean, for having fostered a dialogue with the contemporary world and for having enabled the recognition of the alterity and sociocultural and religious diversity of indigenous peoples, among others.[4]

In the footsteps of this remarkable event, several attempts were made to recover and value the culture of the original peoples in the churches. Initially, the attempts were led by indigenists and later by the indigenous people themselves. The Missions Department of the Latin American and Caribbean Episcopal Council (Consejo Episcopal Latinoamericano y Caribeño, CELAM), created in 1966, played a very important role in raising awareness, promoting, recognizing, and disseminating cultural diversity through the organization of indigenous pastoral meetings, the first six of which were held in Ambato (Ecuador, April 24-28, 1967), Melgar (Colombia, April 20-27, 1968), Caracas (Venezuela, September 14-19, 1969), Xicotepec de Juárez, Puebla (Mexico, January 25-28, 1970), Iquitos (Perú, March 21-27, 1971), and Manaus I (Brazil, June 20-25, 1977).[5]

Tomichá Charupá points out that the first two meetings, the one in Ambato and the other in Melgar, were more consistent with the decisions of the Second Vatican Council than with the second conference of CELAM, held in Medellín, Colombia, in 1968. The meetings in Medellín still insisted on the traditional view of seeing indigenous peoples as recipients and not as agents of evangelization. Contrary to the meetings in Melgar, there in Medellín, indigenous people were not recognized or valued in themselves. In Ambato and Melgar, particular emphasis was placed on the diversity of indigenous languages, cultures, religions, and customs. In Melgar, there was a profound recognition of peoples' plural and complex cultural reality—in the ways of occupying and inhabiting specific spaces; in their perception of the world, their languages, traditions, and rituals. The indigenous cultures

---

4. Tomichá Charupá, "Teologías amerindias," 367.
5. Tomichá Charupá, "Teologías amerindias," 367-69.

and those of African origin were treated and placed alongside the dominant Western culture. In these meetings these various cultures were seen as constitutive elements on the continent. This gap was recognized, realizing that their cultural reality was not sufficiently known or coherently treated within the church. In Melgar, the theological category "seeds of the Word" was applied to indigenous peoples, thus echoing the *Ad Gentes* decree of the Second Vatican Council and recognizing the need to understand the history of indigenous peoples as part of the broader universal history of salvation.

The gatherings of Ambato and Melgar also surpassed the third conference of Puebla of CELAM (1979), which portrayed indigenous peoples as still needing evangelization, however, stating that they have some values to contribute to the world, especially in terms of the ecological discussion. At the threshold of commemorations of the five hundredth anniversary of the conquest, a lack of awareness of the history of the Americas and the indigenous peoples began to "affect the generalized theological awareness in Latin America." In this context, the fourth conference of Santo Domingo (1992) recognized the multiethnic and multicultural constitution of the continent, asking for respect for the indigenous church and the different theological approaches of native peoples.[6]

The fifth conference in Aparecida (2007) rediscovered and recognized indigenous peoples as the "seeds of the Word," which "facilitates" that indigenous peoples "find" what they have always silently "desired," Christ. The document of Aparecida speaks of indigenous peoples as vital subjects in society and in the church who want to be recognized in "their individual and collective rights, within Catholicism with its worldviews, their values, and their particular identities, to live a new ecclesial Pentecost," and of the church at a moment that values indigenous people, for "their respect for nature and love for mother earth as a source of food, common home and the altar of human sharing."[7]

Tomichá Charupá points out that, from the point of view of its institutionality, CELAM, at the request of the Congregation for the Doctrine of the Faith, organized four Latin American symposia, from 2002 to 2011, intended for bishops and theologians, to accompany the processes of inculturation of the gospel among the indigenous peoples of the continent and acquire adequate doctrinal discernment of *teologia índia*. These workshops were held in Mexico (1990), Panama (1993), Bolivia (1997), and Paraguay (2003).

---

6. Gorski, "Desarrollo histórico," 12.
7. Tomichá Charupá, "Teologías amerindias," 370.

The themes addressed in these meetings were about the names of God, Christology, and creation from the perspective of indigenous peoples. In the more popular sphere of ecclesial communities made up of indigenous peoples, from 1990 to 2020, the Latin American Ecumenical Coordinating Group for Indigenous Pastoral Care, in its various national training centers, organized seven workshops on *teologia índia* with the participation of pastors, theologians, and laypeople, "creating very favorable and open environments for the exchange of life experiences among the participants."[8]

Among the entities that participated or actively participate in the promotion of indigenous theology are the National Center for Assistance to Indigenous Missions (in Mexico), the Peruvian Institute of Arbitration, the International Institute for Democracy and Electoral Assistance, the Amazonian Center for Anthropology and Practical Application (in Peru), the Missionary Council for Indigenous Peoples (in Brazil), Universidade da Assunção (in Brazil), the Pastoral Land Commission (in Bolivia); Editorial Abya Yala (in Ecuador), and the Ecumenical Association of Third World Theologians and the Latin American Council of Churches, among others.[9]

Indigenous Church Projects

The first attempts for form an indigenous church are in line with the meetings between Ambato and Melgar, which intended to create a mobilization to form such an indigenous church. Two projects stand out: Chiapas in Mexico and Riobamba in Ecuador. Below is a summary of Tomichá Charupá's retrospective on those projects.[10]

One of the projects took place in the diocese of Dom Leonidas Proaño (1910–88). Bishop in Riobamba for thirty-one years, he had the clear objective of moving from a pro-indigenous pastoral program to an indigenous one, which in his vision would be carried out by indigenous people in the role of pastoral agents, catechists, missionaries, leaders, nuns, and bishops. Since in indigenous pastoral care, awareness and evangelization are always linked, he believed that people would end up organizing themselves. Thus, in 1986, Proaño presented to the Ecuadorian Episcopal Conference the "National Indigenous Pastoral Plan," with two general objectives: "The transformation of indigenous people into a people that contributes to the transformation of Ecuadorian society and the construction of an indigenous church that would contribute its own values to enrich local churches

---

8. Tomichá Charupá, "Teologías amerindias," 371.
9. Gorski, "Desarrollo histórico," 12–14.
10. Tomichá Charupá, "Teologías amerindias," 371–74.

and the Universal Church." The plan intended, in short, "the formation of an indigenous people with its own identity, but also open to authentic and fair integration with the non-indigenous Ecuadorian people." To this end, Proaño founded the organization Servidores de la Iglesia Católica de las Nacionalidades Indígenas del Ecuador (SICNIE, Servants of the Catholic Church for the Indigenous Nationalities of Ecuador) in 1988, which would be in charge of continuing process of gestation of an indigenous church in Ecuador.

The other project highlighted is that of Chiapas, located in the diocese of Dom Samuel Ruiz. Bishop of the Diocese of San Cristóbal de las Casas from 1960 to 2000, Dom Samuel trained indigenous catechists, taking advantage of the cultural contribution of these indigenous peoples for evangelization in their own languages, cultures, and worldviews. In the diocesan catechist schools, permanent indigenous deacons were trained, who would participate actively and creatively in the life of the church.

The church model Samuel Ruiz envisioned was that of an indigenous church, which attempts to live the gospel of Jesus Christ based on the social, cultural, economic, political, and religious reality of indigenous peoples. To this end, in 1988 he founded the human rights center Fray Bartolomé de Las Casas, which receives reports of human rights violations from various social sectors. Samuel Ruiz was also a mediator in the dialogues between the federal government of Mexico and the Zapatista National Liberation Army (Ejército Zapatista de Liberación Nacional, EZLN), which emerged in Chiapas in 1994.

For Tomichá Charupá, these bishops led unique experiences on the continent in the effort to create a church with an indigenous face, thought, and heart. They presented God as someone close to humans, committed to the life and liberation of marginalized and excluded sectors of society; and using the "see, judge, and act" method, they led these social sectors to become aware of reality and to appropriate tools of social and ecclesiastical organization, thus becoming subjects of their own liberation processes.

Development of the Indigenous Churches

The objective formulated by Proaño of an indigenous church that establishes a foothold in society, politics, culture, and economy, among other aspects of real life, included, for example, organizations founded by Proaño himself, such as La Ecuador Runakunapak Rikcharimui (a movement of the indigenous people of Ecuador), with its own leaders trained by the Catholic Church. These organizations contributed greatly to the sociopolitical and cultural participation and affirmation of indigenous people in Ecuador. The critical training of indigenous leaders, men and women, was fundamental in the Ecuadorian social process.[11] These indigenous leaders were and are at the base of the national indigenous movement that forced the Ecuadorian state to review its commitments to indigenous rights and the environment.

In 1986, through the newly created Confederation of Indigenous Nationalities of the Ecuadorian Amazon (Confederación de las Nacionalidades Indígenas de la Amazonia Ecuatoriana, CONFENIAE), the movement began to present its political demands regarding land, environment, health, and culture. Still in that decade, CONFENIAE became a national movement, gradually imposing the indigenous agenda on government decisions. From 1990 onwards, CONFENIAE carried out a major uprising in the country, a moment in which the indigenous issue in Ecuador caught the attention of the international community. The critical discourse about the continental commemorations of the conquest led to the consolidation of a national political party: the Pachakutik Plurinational Movement, which in 1996 obtained 21 percent of the votes in the presidential elections and actively participated in the drafting of the constitutional text. The constitution was promulgated in 1998 and is the most advanced in Latin America. In it, Ecuador is recognized as a multicultural and multiethnic state, two innovative concepts in the Magna Carta. One of its chapters is dedicated to the collective rights of indigenous and Afro-Ecuadorian peoples. The constitutional text interweaves "very current discussions in modern sociology and philosophy about gender, the right to difference, identity and communitarianism, but also ecological and legal anthropology."[12]

The mission of the indigenous church within the church itself created and strengthened ministries, celebrations, lifestyles, and theology. At the ministerial level, a sign of progress was the formation of *llacta michic* (servants of the people), lay leaders responsible for looking after the local community. This ministry later disappeared, along with the indigenous seminary of Riobamba. Proaño managed to get the Ecuadorian Episcopal Conference to create the Department of Indigenous Pastoral in 1985, but this was also suppressed in recent years in the process of restructuring the conference. The most visible national organization of indigenous pastoral care that continues to this day appears to be SICNIE. But Proaño's legacy lives on in some congregations of consecrated indigenous women and indigenous priests, both religious and diocesan.

---

11. Email from Roberto Tomichá Charupá to author, July 18, 2023.
12. Figueroa, "Povos indígenas versus petrolíferas," 57.

From the point of view of the hierarchy, Proaño's legacy remained alive for a while, but later it waned and completely receded. Dom Leonidas's successor, Dom Víctor Corral, was a moderate in matters of indigenous pastoral care. He was succeeded by a liberal, who imprinted on the diocese a style that was more "indigenist" than indigenous, with paternalistic actions and neocolonial stances—a setback in the indigenous church project in Ecuador.[13]

As in Ecuador, in Chiapas the indigenous movement developed at a time of great political ferment. In 1991, the "believing people" movement was born, comprised of several Christian religious entities and groups that coordinated joint actions to denounce injustices and defend the rights of indigenous peoples. The Mayan people grew in capacity for action on the eve of the commemorations of the conquest of America, in 1992, and on the eve of the entry into force of the North American Free Trade Agreement, in 1994. The EZLN, supported by national and international civil society, declared war on the Mexican government against the treaty. The "believing people" and indigenous movements supported the Zapatista army. Indigenous groups identified with Zapatismo, as it also fought for land, dignity, democracy, and recognition of indigenous rights. Many Catholic catechists from the diocese of São Cristóvão joined the EZLN, and Bishop Samuel Ruiz had to face the Catholic hierarchy in Mexico and Rome several times. The Fray Bartolomé de Las Casas human rights center, founded in 1988, fulfilled its role in receiving reports of human rights violations. Those movements remain active, facing growing difficulties in past decades.

Indigenous-Christian Theological Reflection

The indigenous church is accompanied by a theological reflection that in the 1990s came to be called *teología india, teología indígena,* or *teología amerindia*. "This theology aims," according to J. F. Gorski, "to elaborate a new indigenous expression of the Christian faith based on the rediscovery, appropriation and appreciation of the experiences and religious and cultural expressions of the original peoples of the Americas."[14] In order to safeguard these new subjects of theological work and refute accusations, Gorski states that it is not fair to consider the protagonists of *teología india* as a sectarian or parallel group opposed to the episcopal magisterium.[15]

---

13. Email from Roberto Tomichá Charupá to author, July 18, 2023.
14. Gorski, "Desarrollo histórico," 9.
15. Gorski, "Desarrollo histórico," 15.

To develop this topic, we turn to Zapotec Catholic priest Eleazar López, who has proposed a theology at the church level since the 1990s, an indigenous-Christian theology, following in the footsteps of Bishop Samuel Ruiz. For López, *teología india* has existed for millennia; what happened, in 1992, in Santo Domingo, was simply its "official" launch.[16] Along the same lines, the Kuna indigenous theologian Aiban Wagua states that it was through this ancient reflection that indigenous peoples conceived their life projects and integrated the traumatic experiences of centuries of conquest and mission into their lives.[17] Eleazar López calls *teología india* the "collection of religious practices and popular theological wisdom, which members of indigenous peoples use to explain the new and ancient mysteries of life. Therefore, it is not something new or properly ecclesiastical, but an ancient reality that has survived the ravages of history."[18]

The novelty, according to López, is in the notoriety that indigenous peoples have gained in society, in the sympathy and commitment they have achieved in sectors of the churches.[19] This encourages them, continues Gorski, to come out of hiding, to celebrate their defeats and hopes, to rescue them, and to seek dialogue with other social actors.[20]

Theology of Which Indigenous People?

The more than five hundred indigenous peoples of Abya Yala are distinguished by their languages, the natural resources at their disposal, their means of subsistence, their histories of interethnic contact, their historical projects and achievements, and so on. In the case of theology, they also distinguish themselves by the degree of connection they keep with the churches and the way in which they are inserted in the production and reproduction of knowledge in their group. For Eleazar López, it is necessary to differentiate the indigenous people who buried their ancient beliefs forever from those who adjusted their beliefs to the possibilities that their status as defeated peoples allowed them.[21] The Zapotec relates the former to the indigenous groups that today cultivate their Christian faith as something irreconcilable with their original religious practices.

---

16. López, *Teología india*, 104, 106–7.
17. López, *Teología india*, 291.
18. López, *Teología india*, 11.
19. López, *Pueblos de la esperanza*, 190.
20. Gorski, "Desarrollo histórico," 15.
21. López, *Pueblos de la esperanza*, 191–92.

The second group is comprised of those who kept their old practices and schemes of understanding God and life alive, reworking them in an environment increasingly dominated by Christian symbols. For López, this group includes the ancestors of *teología india*.[22] Their descendants no longer want to be treated as children or as property of the church but as members who have something to say to the church that they integrate and shape. They want to strengthen the indigenous base of their communities, indigenize their Christianity, integrate themselves into the liberating discourse, and reconnect with their religious roots hidden by the religion that colonized them. Most of this chapter deals with this second group of Christian indigenous peoples.

The third group is the one that passes through the churches, but without effective adherence, which joins only strategically, depending on the benefits that the churches bring to them. They soon move away, because deep down they understand that the church is a threat to indigenous identity and autonomy.

The fourth group is made up of indigenous people from evangelical churches, with a Pentecostal evangelical theology, from churches that call themselves "indigenous churches." In Brazil, they are grouped in organizations such as the National Council of Evangelical Indigenous Pastors and Leaders (Conselho Nacional de Pastores e Líderes Evangélicos Indígenas, CONPLEI), which celebrated its thirty-seventh anniversary in its July 2023 congress.[23] In one of the forums at this congress, the council had forty-seven indigenous and nonindigenous missionary agencies present.

CONPLEI brings together thousands of indigenous people engaged in the mission of converting other indigenous people and opening "a genuinely indigenous church in each ethnic group." The Trans-Amazonian Network of Indigenous Christian Leaders is one of many CONPLEI initiatives.[24] The network operates in Bolivia, Venezuela, Colombia, Ecuador, Peru, Brazil, Paraguay, and Guyana, evangelizing indigenous peoples to free them from protectionism, paternalism, and isolationism, which, according to these churches, were introduced by policies of respect for diversity and cultural preservation.

Finally, the fifth group is made up of indigenous people, mainly from the Amazon, but also from the Cerrado and the Atlantic Forest, who live in relative autonomy of ritual, thought, and spiritual practice. The body of wisdom of this group is presented as "theology" mainly by nonindigenous

---

22. López, *Teología india*, 48.
23. See https://www.conplei.org.br/.
24. CONPLEI, "Movimentos paralelos no exterior."

people. Ethnicities speaking languages from the Guarani group, due to their conception of "word," are particularly attractive to Christian theologians. The writings of Bartomeu Meliá and Graciela Chamorro serve as examples.[25] Likewise, we know about the spirituality of Amazonian peoples with little or no contact with churches through ethnological or collaborative writings, such as *The Falling Sky*, written by Yanomami Davi Kopenawa, the shaman-narrator, and Bruce Albert, the ethnologist-writer.[26] The Amazonian peoples are subjects and the founding themes of the Ecclesial Conference of the Amazon (Conferência Eclesial da Amazônia, CEAMA), which I will consider later.

Indigenous Protagonism in Theology

Many writings state that the protagonism of indigenous theology belongs to indigenous collectives (groups or communities), warning that individuals, indigenous or not, should not supplant these collectives nor plunder their thoughts.[27] This concern is understandable in the ritual and experiential field of theology, as it is well known that written theology, as a rule, is authorial—including among indigenous people—as one can see in the bibliography of this text. There is a community moment of collaborative theological experience and reflection, where protagonism is shared and is more egalitarian. There is another, where the group's "spokespersons," in many cases priests, are tasked with formulating the people's theological reflection in writing. At this moment, there is obviously a tendency to reproduce existing inequalities in churches and society.

From the historical experience with the states that colonized them, indigenous peoples learned that, in general, these states do not integrate ongoing nation projects. Faced with this, they often claim that they have their own projects, that their identity was forged not only from experiences of defeat and contempt but also from their capacity for resistance and their dreams of liberation. So it makes sense to say that their theology is their life project, one of the most ambitious of which is the multiethnic state with some autonomy.

---

25. Meliá, "Experiencia religiosa de los Guaraní"; Chamorro, *Terra madura, yvy araguyje*.

26. Kopenawa and Bruce, *A queda do céu*.

27. López, *Teología india*, 261–63.

A "Theology" About the People and Their Life Project

Does the term "theology" fit? There are reservations regarding the application of this word to indigenous religious reflection. The ecclesiastical hierarchy considers the indigenous gnosiological instrument insufficient for a "true" theological task, says López.[28] Only in 2019, in the "Final Document of the Special Synod for the Amazon," did the Catholic Church officially recognize "Indian theology" or "Indian theologies" as having the same status as other emerging theologies.[29]

Despite the obstacles presented by the ecclesiastical hierarchy and the reticence of some indigenous intellectuals regarding the inadequacy of the term for the way of producing and communicating indigenous religious knowledge, the term "theology" is already in common use, not as a reflection on God, in the strict sense, but as a reflection that accompanies, explains, and guides the journey of indigenous peoples. It is "a theology about the people and their life project."[30] Yet, that is precisely where God is, maintaining and recreating the utopian hopes of the people.[31]

In indigenous Mesoamerica, according to López, "theology" is created based not only on the divine word uttered by specialists, but also through the interpretation of everyday people, through songs, mythical stories, and prayers.[32] The function of theology is not only to handle the word; it is also to discover the destiny of the people, interpret the calendar, "hold the sky," advise people, be an inspiration, be an eagle to reach the sky and a serpent to enter the earth or be experienced in the cosmic human and divine, contemplate nature, discern the signs of the times, decipher dreams as a way of analyzing reality, and narrate and update the history of the people's salvation. In other words, the theological reflection that underlies this practice, or that this practice raises, seeks to respond to concrete situations in the life of the community. God is in life, which is why theology must contemplate life, savor it, bathe in its mysteries. The paths to this understanding are the religious and cultural codes of each people. When theology is intended for base communities, it is done following the logic of oral and ritual tradition; when it is intended for the "external market" or for theological training institutions, writes López, it is written down.[33] The newness of indigenous theol-

---

28. López, *Teología índia*, 95.
29. Holy See Press Office, "#SinodoAmazonico," §§54, 158.
30. López, *Teología índia*, 8.
31. López, *Teología índia*, 8–9.
32. López, *Teología índia*, 94–103.
33. López, *Teología índia*, 106–7.

ogy seems to lie precisely in sharing this knowledge in new environments, in theology workshops, for example, and also through writing.

This certainly distinguishes indigenous groups from many nonindigenous groups. For the latter, the word is often everything, while for an indigenous person it is not. They need silence and the ritually lived word to recognize "a radical approach," to be touched more deeply and to be able to release mobilizing energy.[34]

Among the themes central to his work, indigenous Mexican priest Porfirio Méndez García highlights the land as a source of life and place of encounter with God, healing therapies, customary rights of people, alternative projects, right to difference, family, community, authority, service, autonomy, justice, reconciliation, symbolism, life and death, indigenous spirituality, and ministries in indigenous churches. Updating the history of the Mesoamerican peoples, López traces the itinerary of indigenous faith as a life option. Let us take a look at some of these themes.

Earth

López highlights the nomadic period as the longest day in history and as the cradle of indigenous people's spiritual culture, surviving to this day in myths and symbols of the time. Mother Earth, New Fire, Hurricane Wind, Source of Water, and Protective Hill are some of the names given to God in this period.

The Mesoamerican myth, as presented by López, is summarized as follows. From the body of Cipactli—the original energy of life, symbolized in fire, the jaguar, and the serpent in movement—caves, hills, rivers, and trees emerged. Many people still imagine the cave as their place of origin and center of dispersion. Before they dispersed, they lived together as siblings and spoke the same language. Native eschatology foresees the return of all groups to the original matrix.

However, earth/nature is not only a provider of life; it can also destroy and kill, which is why the relationship with it is mediated by rite. By asking permission from the owner of the mountain to cut down a tree or hunt an animal, this ancient custom that ritualizes human dependence on the land is perpetuated. Nagualism is also a legacy of the nomadic era. It consists of the belief that each human being has their animal counterpart, *nagual*, in nature. Supposedly, what happens to the nagual automatically happens to its human counterpart. If that one dies, this other will also die.

---

34. López, *Teología india*, 9.

Human Beings

With the settlement of peoples, the axis of cultural formation became anthropocentric. López, by contrast, draws attention to the founding myth of time, referring to a story widespread throughout Mesoamerica, according to which the sky fell on the earth.[35] The deities Quetzalcoatl, from the east, and Tezcatlipoca, from the west, were unable to lift it. Four human beings were created to help them. Two by two they entered from the north and south. They found the eastern and western deities in the center of the earth. Tezcatlipoca turned into a huge tree. Quetzalcoatl used his crown, and the four humans used Tezcatlipoca's branches to rebuild the sky. The myth is periodically ritualized by the Voladores de Papantla, a fertility dance. It is worth remembering that in the center of the Mayan altar, the roots of a huge ceiba tree penetrate the earth while its crown reaches into the sky, holding it and uniting it with the earth. The fact that God is presented as someone who needs human beings makes them cocreators of nature, because through their work and their effort the world becomes a more favorable place for humans.

Other myths try to compensate for some people's apparent disadvantage. The poor, the sick, foreigners, the disabled, and albinos, among others, are considered to be sent by God and receive special attention. Food produced by the community becomes symbols of God's presence. The planting, harvesting, and consumption of domesticated vegetables in the region became ritualized. Corn became so crucial in the region that it became part of the myth of the origin of human beings. These are made of corn, and there is as much variety of them as there is of corn. Flourishing cultures, subsequently, emerged in the region and with them the worldview inspired by Quetzalcoatl.

In it, Cipactli, the original energy of life, is represented by two braided serpents, which, when separated from each other, formed heaven and earth. Life appeared. Quetzalcoatl's task is to keep each being in its place, transforming the space between them into a matrix of life. In a Quetzalcoatlic society there should be, according to López, "communal appropriation of land, adequate productive technology, but not aggressive, for the sake of nature, exercise of political power as a service and religiosity centered on God, which is concerned with the flourishing of people's lives."[36] In these theocratic cities, structured and self-sufficient populations emerged, autonomously governed by wise civil and religious leaders. The empowerment of

---

35. López Bac, "Altar maya," 36–39.
36. López, *Teología índia*, 38.

the person and the people was one of the mechanisms for exercising power in defense of life.

Thirst for Power

With the decline of the theocratic cities led by the priests of Quetzalcoatl, López continues, Mesoamerican societies began to be guided mainly by the warrior ideal, which intensified when they submitted to the Aztecs.[37] To justify human sacrifices, the latter transferred Quetzalcoatl's virtues to Huitzilopochtli, god of war, saying that he was born with a shield and a bow of arrows in his hands to defend himself from the entities that conspired to kill him. Thus, the image of a warrior God prevailed, symbolized by the Sun who rose every morning bathed in blood and fought during the day until he died. As the resolution of conflicts demanded greater power, the idea of God and human beings became increasingly linked to the conquest. By intensifying agriculture, trade, and warfare, the Aztecs exerted violent pressure on nature and other human beings. Symbolically, this social transformation is represented in the eagle (sky) that devours the serpent (earth) perched on a nopal, a kind of cactus. Quetzalcoatl left for the east, promising to return. This mythical-historical narrative shapes the faith of many people to this day in Mesoamerica.

The Return

According to Eleazar López, the indigenous groups that today call themselves sons and daughters of the moon or of the earth keep alive the tradition of nonurban agricultural villages that were affected by the power of Tenochtitlán in the past. The myth of Xólotl, in the oral tradition of the Huastecs, expresses the struggle that this people, "the people of the Moon," faced with the Aztecs, "the children of the Sun."

According to the story, because of his daily struggle against the stars, the warrior Sun needed to feed on the blood and hearts of the gods immolated to him by the priests. Once, the Day Star asked that Xólotl, the god of the lagoon, who had the shape and loyalty of a dog, be sacrificed to him. He was an ownerless dog, who played with children, butterflies, and other animals. The priest who promised to fulfill the Sun's request approached Xólotl and told him that the Sun wanted to drink his blood to defeat the

---

37. López, *Teología india*, 41–42.

stars. "I don't want to die, I shouldn't die!" was his reaction. "You will die, because the Sun wants it," replied the priest.

The tears that rolled down Xólotl's face turned into dew, which wet all the grass in the place. But the Sun, with his heat, sucked away the moisture. He persisted in his unhealthy desire to drink blood. Xólotl ran to deceive the priests, who made the glassy obsidian of their knives shine. Cornered, he disappeared from the sight of his tormentors. He once turned into a corn plant; on another occasion, into a maguey pie; and, in the end, into a fish and ended up being caught. When Xólotl was about to be sacrificed, the Sun sent a ray with the message: "Let the little dog free . . . I don't want any more sacrifices!" Then Xólotl became a dog again: guide of the blind, friend of creatures and painted butterflies.[38]

"Return" and "dispersion" are frequent theological motifs in indigenous discourse. In the Andean highlands, the return of the ancient deity Viracocha, who introduced the domestication of plants and animals to the Andes, is awaited. For many Amazonian peoples, "white people" did not arrive in Brazil in 1500; they returned to Brazil that year, after many years of traveling around the world learning new techniques.

We now turn to the Amazonian peoples, who are both the subjects and, at the same time, the fundamental theme of the Ecclesial Conference of the Amazon.

The Ecclesial Conference of the Amazon (CEAMA)

CEAMA was organized as a permanent episcopal body on June 29, 2020, to promote synodality in the Amazon region. It outlines the Amazonian face of the church and looks for new paths for the evangelizing mission. It has the participation of CELAM, the Latin American and Caribbean Secretariat of Caritas, the Latin American and Caribbean Confederation of Religious Men and Women, the Pan-Amazonian Ecclesial Network, and representatives of the Indigenous Peoples of the Amazon.[39]

For its executive secretary, the Colombian Jesuit Alfredo Ferro Medina, in order to respond to the calls and signs of hope in the Amazonian territory, "a process of personal and institutional conversion is needed . . . ; it is necessary to persist in a synodal, ecological, pastoral and cultural journey of conversion."[40] The objectives of the conference, continues Ferro Medina,

---

38. Fr. José Barón Larios compiled this story in Huejutla, Hidalgo. López, *Teología india*, 42–47.

39. Holy See Press Office, "#SinodoAmazonico."

40. Da Silva, "CEAMA," para. 31.

require a predisposition to the new, opening oneself to the Spirit; recovering the history of Amazonia and the people who inhabit it; getting to know the cultures that developed and exist there; becoming aware of reality; understanding territoriality as interconnection; living an ecological spirituality exposed to the elements; working in networks and alliances; promoting the defense of life and human rights; influencing political decisions; crossing borders; promoting alternative socioeconomic, energy, and environmental proposals; cultivating personal habits that embrace a healthy and simple life; and decentralizing the ecclesiastical structure.

CEAMA arises in the context of an unprecedented environmental crisis. The Amazon is a vast territory of seven million km^2, which covers nine countries: Bolivia, Peru, Ecuador, Colombia, Venezuela, Brazil, Guyana, Suriname, and French Guiana. The conference extends through the vastness of the Amazon and understands that its mission is to ensure that the different paths that shelter this territory meet in the common purpose of saving the planet and humans from an ecological catastrophe.

The Amazonian population is estimated at 33,600,000 inhabitants, of which at least two million are indigenous, speaking 240 languages, belonging to 390 ethnicities, of which 145 are in voluntary isolation. The Amazon is essential for the distribution of rainfall in the various regions of South America and contributes to large air movements across the planet. Currently, it is the second most vulnerable area in the world concerning climate change caused by humans.[41]

Of the total Amazonian inhabitants, 70 percent are in urban areas and 30 percent in rural areas, which shows the brutal consequence of migration and requires the church to search for new paths for an integral ecology that speaks to both the countryside and the city. CEAMA understands that, starting in the Amazon, the church is called to a mission that is Samaritan, merciful, supportive, ecumenical, interreligious, and cultural.[42] The challenge of interreligious dialogue in the Amazonia with indigenous and African-derived religions requires that Christians understand these matrices of spirituality in their own expressions and in their relationship with the forest and Mother Earth.[43] For this reason, the "Final Document of the Synod" states that it is necessary to generate greater missionary momentum among native vocations; so that the Amazon is evangelized by Amazonians.[44] Currently, the church has the historic opportunity to differentiate itself from the

41. Holy See Press Office, "#SinodoAmazonico," §6.
42. Holy See Press Office, "#SinodoAmazonico," §§21–22.
43. Holy See Press Office, "#SinodoAmazonico," §25.
44. Holy See Press Office, "#SinodoAmazonico," §26.

new colonizing powers.⁴⁵ Sister Laura Vicuña Pereira Manso, indigenous to the Kariri people and vice-president of CEAMA, understands that there are already many paths taken in this mission, but there are many more paths to be followed. But the paths already taken and the ongoing experiences need to be made more visible.

Final Considerations

Leonidas Proaño and Samuel Ruiz were visionary pastors. Roughly speaking, it can be said that the objectives of the indigenous pastors that they represent seem to have flourished more in the organization of indigenous people in civil society, in denouncing rights violations, and in the fight for rights, than in the church itself.

The church hierarchy apparently cannot accept the discomfort of indigenous people with the fact that they are seen again and again as objects of evangelization. This difficulty is linked to the church's inability to understand its own multicultural constitution and relativize its truths, which have been constructed from the site of a dominant culture and a dominating power. This difficulty has led indigenous religious people to break with the church in order to meet the demands of their people in a more integral and coherent way.

However, despite the ups and downs and contradictions, the experience of Riobamba—like that of San Cristóbal de Las Casas in Chiapas—was and continues to be a beacon of hope on the path of indigenous peoples, which also illuminates other churches regarding the real possibility of an "indigenous church." Among the contributions that these experiences can teach other churches and peoples, it can be indicated that (1) the entire cosmo-creation lives and endures in the environment and in each of its elements; (2) there is a strong communal sense of inclusive reciprocity (*ayllu-ayni*), including everything that exists, such as ancestors and protective beings, a cosmic synodality, in the words of Roberto Tomichá Charupá; (3) one lives from a daily-relational spirituality and martyrdom, in constant creative, resilient, and proactive movement; (4) it is necessary to overcome all types of dualities and exclusive dichotomies, whether personal, relational, interior, gender-based or spiritual; and (5) it is necessary to take care of "Mother Earth" as a concrete and symbolic expression of life.⁴⁶

---

45. Holy See Press Office, "#SinodoAmazonico," §15.
46. Email from Roberto Tomichá Charupá to author, July 18, 2023.

Some of these contributions can be exemplified in the "Mayan altar" by Ernestina López Bac, a Kaqchikel Mayan from Guatemala.[47] López Bac interprets the Mayan altar as an ecocentric altar. The cross is a meeting of four paths. This interpretation of the cross is an invitation to ecumenical and interreligious openness. The altar integrates spiritual knowledge and ritual practices based on the 260-day lunar calendar, in which each day has a meaning. The response that this Guatemalan thinker presents indicates that a reception of indigenous spiritualities by Christian churches implies, at the very least, a cosmological interpretation of Christ.

The idea of "complementarity" is a key contribution to the conceptual field. The Aymara theologian Sofía Chipana presents it as a fundamental element of the Andean cosmovision, which can be assumed as a regulating principle of balance and harmony.[48] Thanks to this principle, many Christian elements were integrated into the Andean world. The reception of this concept in Christianity could open the possibility for churches to recognize themselves as multicultural and recognize the interculturality of biblical texts.

This chapter ends by pointing out that the indigenous church and theology represent changes comparable to liberation Christianity, as they, even using the same method as liberation theology, ended up emphasizing other aspects of reality. For indigenous peoples, liberation is deeply marked by a feeling of community and the solidarity experienced in the community in rituals and sharing, and in mobilizations of denunciation and the struggle for rights, as exemplified in Mexico and Ecuador. In the movements led by indigenous Christians and others in these countries, the historical strength of faith emerges, challenged to drive radical decisions in favor of life.

The central problem of indigenous peoples in Abya Yala is the lack of guarantee to live on their lands in accordance with what they understand to be their "natural rights." In their life project, the land is the center of their attention, concern, celebration, and theological reflection. "Mother Earth" is the ground beneath our feet and everything that exists and sustains existence. Aiban Wagua speaks of "cosmo-sentiment" to express that other beings in nature are linked to humans by family ties and can only be understood within this relationship. Thus, *paba* and *nana* can be translated only as "papa" and "mama," not as god or goddess.[49] Other indigenous groups translate the names of supernatural beings as Our Father, Our Mother, Our Grandfather, and Our Grandmother, among other terms.

47. López Bac, "Altar maya," 34–38.
48. Chipana, "Biblia," 44–49.
49. López, *Teología india*, 292–93.

In this sense, indigenous theology is critical of other theologies and of every form of knowledge and power that is sustained by violence and oppression over social sectors in situations of vulnerability and insecurity. It is critical of the power exercised by the state, society's elites and churches, when they reproduce the violence that emerged in the big cities in the history of humanity. Mesoamerican Indian theology, in the "history of salvation" presented by Eleazar López, recovers theological perspectives prior to that time, as they were more humanizing.[50] The poor, like Xolotl, then occupied the center of the expectation of Quetzalcoatl's return. It was not against "power" but against "power through death" that the children of the moon raised their voices in history. For indigenous theology, it is not the Sun-Supreme-Being that is sustained by human blood that should be revered; it is the Life-Sustaining-Sun that must be revered. As in the time of the eagle and the serpent, indigenous people speak out theologically against the aggressive actions that the state or any oppressive sector of society or church enacts against indigenous groups and other poor people. They thus counteract, in symbolic and ritual ways, the proclivity to submit and convert others to dominant practices and thoughts.

Bibliography

Chamorro, Graciela. *A espiritualidade guarani: Uma teologia ameríndia da palavra.* Teses e dissertações 10. São Leopoldo: Sinodal, 1998.
———. *Teología guaraní.* Iglesia, pueblos y culturas 61. Quito: Abya Yala, 2004.
———. *Terra madura, yvy araguyje: Fundamento da palavra guarani.* Dourados: Editora UFGD, 2008.
Chipana, Sofia. "La Biblia en los procesos andinos de descolonización e interculturalidad." *Concilium: Revista Internacional de Teología* 382 (2019) 41–53.
CONPLEI. "Movimentos paralelos no exterior." CONPLEI, n.d. https://www.conplei.org.br/movimentos-paralelos-no-exterior/.
Da Silva, Jonas Jorge. "CEAMA: Conversão e caminhada sinodal com a igreja ministerial amazônica." Instituto Humánitas Unisinos, Aug. 10, 2021. https://www.ihu.unisinos.br/categorias/160-cepat/611861-ceama-conversao-e-caminhada-sinodal-com-a-igreja-ministerial-amazonica.
Figueroa, Isabela. "Povos indígenas versus petrolíferas: Controle constitucional na resistência." *Sur, Revista Internacional de Direitos Humanos* 3 (2006) 48–79. https://doi.org/10.1590/S1806-64452006000100004.
Gorski, Juan F. "El desarrollo histórico de la teología india y su aporte a la inculturación del evangelio." In *Desarrollo histórico de la teología india*, 9–34. Iglesia, pueblos y cultura 48–49. Quito: Abya Yala, 1998.

---

50. López, *Teología índia*, 46–47.

Holy See Press Office. "#SinodoAmazonico—Final do documento do Sinodo dei Vescovi ao Santo Padre Francesco." IHU, Oct. 26, 2019. https://www.ihu.unisinos. br/images/ihu/2019/Eventos/Landing_Sinodo/Documento_Final.pdf.

Kopenawa, Davi, and Albert Bruce. *A queda do céu: Palavras de um xamã Yanomami*. São Paulo: Letras, 2015.

López, Eleazar. *Los pueblos de la esperanza frente al neoliberalismo: Pastoral indígena*. Edited by Articulación Ecuménica Latinoamericana de Pastoral Indígena et al. Iglesia, pueblos y cultura 44–45. Quito: Abya Yala, 1996.

———. *Teología india: Antología*. Evangelio y culturas 3. Cochabamba: Universidad Católica Boliviana Editorial, 2000.

López Bac, Ernestina. "'Altar maya' como experiencia teológica e interreligiosa." *Concilium: Revista Internacional de Teología* 382 (2019) 31–39.

Meliá, Bartomeu. "La experiencia religiosa de los Guaraní." In *El rostro indio de Dios*, edited by Manuel M. Marzal, 355–421. Lima: Pontificia Universidad Católica del Perú Editorial, 1991.

Tomichá Charupá, Roberto. "Teologías amerindias, balances y tareas pendientes." *Miscellanea Francescana* 113 (2013) 365–89.

12

Latin American Pentecostalism as Popular Religion

ÁNGEL D. SANTIAGO-VENDRELL

TODAY PENTECOSTALISM IS CONSIDERED the fastest-growing branch of Christianity in the world, comprising about one-fourth of the total Christian population. In Latin America, the fire of Pentecostalism spread from the beginning of the twentieth century, and since the 1960s, the region has witnessed dramatic growth in numbers. This chapter considers to what extent Pentecostalism is a popular religion in Latin America. First, the chapter identifies and describes the term "popular religion" as used by Roman Catholics. Second, it addresses how Latin American Pentecostalism is a form of popular religion, using the descriptive definitions of the study of primal religions and orality. Third, Pentecostalism as popular religion offers an experience of a direct encounter with God through preaching the word, reading the Bible, and songs as theological sources. Fourth, Pentecostalism as popular religion is expressed in practices such as exorcisms and mission outreach. Finally, the role of Pentecostals in politics is described and analyzed using a case study from Vieques, Puerto Rico.

Popular Religion in Latin American Roman Catholicism

In Roman Catholic statements, syncretism usually is associated with the religion of the people or popular religion. By *popular religion*, Roman Catholics mean "the whole complex of underlying beliefs rooted in God, the basic attitudes that flow from these beliefs, and the expressions that manifest them."[1] Christianity in Latin America has over five hundred years of his-

---

1. "Third General Congress (Puebla, 1979)," in Scherer and Bevans, *Basic Statements*, 105.

tory. When the Spaniards and Portuguese conquistadors invaded and colonized the Caribbean and Latin America, the indigenous populations had their own religious worldviews. In the imagination of the conquistadors, the indigenous populations were idolaters and without a true religion. The natives were persecuted and their religions demonized. They were forced to convert, and their places of worship were destroyed. Even though the indigenous populations were forced to convert to Christianity and their sites of worship were destroyed, the religiosity of the natives and later of African slaves cohabitated with Roman Catholic practices, especially the devotion to saints and virgins.

The religious cosmovision of the natives and Africans continued to coexist through the liturgical and ecclesial symbols of Roman Catholicism and its devotion to the saints, processions, and festivals. In this historical crossroads, the preservation and tensions of the encounter of cultures and religions created spaces for new formulations of the sacred. This formulation of the sacred that incorporates some aspects of African or indigenous cosmovision is what people refer to as *popular religion*. The faith of the people is intrinsically tied up with the cultural parameters that surround the practitioners and the socioeconomic norms that shape their existence. In this matrix of religious experiences, popular religion is popular because its protagonists are the marginalized, poor, and excluded in any society, as opposed to the elites and producers of knowledge, be it political or religious.[2] However, this pejorative understanding of popular religion when compared to official religion based on notions of syncretism and power places popular Catholicism as underdeveloped and superstitious. When the sacramental roles of priests and bishops in the Roman Catholic Church are contrasted with the roles of laypeople in popular Catholicism, there is also a classist understanding that laypeople lack the necessary education to understand what they are doing in their practices. The first generation of Latin American liberation theologians were critical of the alienating aspects of popular Catholicism for its fatalism and the ease of potential reactionary political ideologies to hijack the movement.[3] More recently, popular Catholicism has

---

2. Espín, "Pentecostalism and Popular Catholicism." I want to make a clear distinction between popular Catholicism, and Santeria, Espiritismo, Umbanda, and Candomblé. The African religions in the diaspora borrowed the imagery of Roman Catholics saints to perpetuate their own religion. Even though popular Catholicism is the religion of the people, it is tied with the mother Holy Roman Catholic Church. In Cuba, an image of Saint Barbara in the house of a Catholic represents the real virgin in the mind of the follower. Not so in Afro diaspora religions. When a follower of any of these religions has a statue of Saint Barbara, they are communicating with Shango, the god of thunder in Santeria.

3. Miguez Bonino, "Popular Piety," 148–58.

gained adepts among liberation theologians who defend the practices of the people and the liberating potential of the masses.[4] In other words, popular Catholicism in Latin America can be both liberating and alienating.

Latin American Pentecostalism as Popular Religion

Today the Pentecostal movement in Latin America is considered as an autochthonous and contextualized form of Christianity. Even though there is a direct link between North American and European Pentecostal missionaries to Latin America, there is another stream of native Pentecostals preaching to their own people in the early twentieth century. The cases of Juan Lugo in Puerto Rico and Maria de Los Angeles Rivera in Mexico are examples that corroborate not just the contextualized nature of Pentecostalism but also its development among the urban poor and rural peasantry. For example, Lugo converted in Hawaii, was discipled in the United States, and was commissioned a missionary to his own people in Puerto Rico. When Lugo arrived in Puerto Rico on August 30, 1916, the island had changed drastically regarding religious liberties since its five hundred years of Spanish colonial rule and the religious monopoly of the Roman Catholic Church. His message of divine healing, transformation of the human condition, and a direct encounter with the Holy Spirit enthralled the masses, who flocked to hear him preach. From the city of Ponce, his ministry extended to the rural towns of Adjuntas, Juana Diaz, Orocovis, Villalba, Barranquita, and Coamo. This placed Lugo's ministry among the poorest sectors of Puerto Rican society in urban and rural areas.[5]

The same can be said about the ministry of Maria de Los Angeles Rivera. From 1926 to 1931, Rivera established preaching posts and groups of new converts in Obregon, Hermosillo, Santa Ana, and Nogales, locating the headquarters for her evangelistic crusades in Obregon.[6] Rivera is considered the mother of modern Mexican Pentecostalism because of her evangelistic zeal in spreading the gospel. She was also a divine healer. Rivera's message of divine healing attracted people by the hundreds to hear her speak. In a place like Sonora—where life expectancy was thirty years at the time, there were very few doctors, and the health care service was in ruins—Atkinson's message of divine healing was more than popular among low-income people who needed medical assistance. People in Mexico were attracted to her message of divine healing because of the scarcity of those services for

---

4. Vidales, *Práctica religiosa*.
5. Lugo, *Pentecostés en Puerto Rico*, 78–79.
6. Avalos, "María Atkinson."

poor people but also because people were seeking for an experience with the divine. For people who did not have access to medical care, the Pentecostal experience offered an antidote, a cure. Healing and salvation were collapsed into each other as part of a single action of God.

The first converts in Latin America to Pentecostalism were among the lowest class, who were attracted by the offering of a direct experience with the divine. This direct experience with the divine was different than both popular Catholicism and Afro-Caribbean religions, which need mediators to communicate with the divine. In popular Catholicism there are the officially trained professionals and the saints, and in Afro-Caribbean religion, believers are in a transactional relationship with the orishas through sacrifices and offerings, but Pentecostals have direct access to the Spirit, as the Spirit dwells in believers. In this sense, it could be said that Latin American Pentecostalism is a form of primal spirituality.

The term *primal religion* is a rather new term that is used to identify people of oral traditions.[7] Primal religions are expressions of tribal people who have never been in contact with a major religion; and contrary to the belief that they have no religion, they have a religion full of symbols and codes impregnated with the divine. Walter Hollenweger, emeritus professor of mission and leading expert on global Pentecostalism at the University of Birmingham, argues that the reason for Pentecostal expansion lies in its black roots of oral tradition. He states, "Today, Pentecostalism is strongest in those countries of the Third World where an oral mode of communication is almost the only way to spread the gospel."[8] Quentin J. Schultze, professor of communications at Calvin College, argues, "The primacy of oral over literate culture among poor Latin Americans nearly guarantees that any existing Protestant impulses will move these people toward old-style Pentecostalism. Oral cultures are predicated on the primacy of the spoken word."[9]

Direct Experience of the Divine Through Preaching, Reading the Bible, and Singing

Latin American Pentecostals are experts on the primacy of the spoken word through the preaching of the word of God. They enchant their audiences with an eloquence that speaks to the heart and emotions more than modern forms of rationalization or doctrinal sermons based on some propositional

---

7. Turner, "Primal Religions," 28.
8. Hollenweger, *Pentecostalism, Origins and Developments*, 20.
9. Schultze, "Orality and Power," 67.

truth. The enchanters captivate their audiences with the immediacy of the spoken word, becoming playwrights by embellishing the biblical record with their own experiences narrated in the language of the people. The first Latin American Pentecostals did not attend Bible college or professional theological seminaries but created their own education structures for laypeople called *institutos biblicos*. By memorizing the Bible and using the language of the poor and interpreting their reality as a cosmic war against the forces of evil, Latin American enchanters invite the congregation to be participants of the biblical drama of redemption.

Latin American Pentecostals understand the authority of Scriptures not as an order of propositional truths but rather as an experiential encounter with the Holy Spirit. The truth of Scripture is revealed through an internal process bringing about the liberation of human beings. In other words, the enchanters cast a spell powerful enough to transform the lives of believers from simple poor people to new creatures in Christ. Perhaps one of the most popular practices among Latin American Pentecostals is welcoming the new believer into the family of God. The new believers cease to be of this world and become citizens of a new world order with Jesus Christ as Lord and the Spirit as the giver and guide of the new life.

Pentecostal orality is characterized by the immediacy of God in the community. In the rationalization of religion, orality could be seen as the biggest expression of the Pentecostal religious service, in which everything happens through verbal expression: prayers, songs, testimonies, exorcisms, Bible readings, and speaking in other tongues.[10] Latin American Pentecostals experience their faith as a living encounter with the Spirit of life. God is perceived as a reality in their communities and daily lives that can be touched and that responds to their individual needs. They experience God through their prayers, in which they open their hearts to the living God with the assurance that their cries are heard. They experience the nearness of God when God's Spirit is poured into the believer, creating a dynamic participation with the divine.[11] Perhaps one of the most crucial moments in Latin American Pentecostal *cultos* is the worshipping experience.

Popular religion is expressed by symbols and rituals. The context of the *culto* provides Latin Americans a place to encounter God. The Pentecostal worship service or *culto* can take place either in the regular Sunday service, a special service in the ghetto, or a hospital visit. One of those experiences with the divine is through the medium of *coritos*. *Coritos* are simple songs or choruses that the Latin American Pentecostal sings unto God. They are

---

10. Santiago-Vendrell, "Popular Religion."
11. Shaull and Cesar, *Pentecostalism and the Future*, 160–64.

popular because they were transmitted through oral tradition, and even today, many of the songs do not have an original author to be named. For example, every Latin American Pentecostal knows the *corito* "Alabaré," but no one knows its author. Nonetheless, the *corito* invites believers to worship God with an eschatological certainty that if John (not sure which John, the Baptist or the beloved disciple) is there rejoicing with multitude of people, they should do likewise.

> Alabaré alabaré alabaré a mi Señor
> alabaré alabaré alabaré a mi señor
> Juan vio el número de Redimidos
> y todos alababan al Señor
> unos cantaban otros oraban
> y todos alababan al señor
> alabaré alabaré alabaré a mi señor.

However, there are also theological distortions in *coritos* in popular Pentecostalism such as "El rubio de Galilea" (The blond from Galilee):

> El hombre de Galilea, va pasando va,
> Y déjalo que te toque,
> Y déjalo que te toque y recibe la bendición
> Y déjalo que te toque,
> Y déjalo que te toque y recibe la bendición.

The depiction of Jesus as a blond man from Galilee is in the psyche of every Pentecostal child, youth, and adult, as it is one of the most famous *coritos* in Latin American Pentecostalism. This racialization of Jesus as a blond man had helped with the notion of whitening Puerto Rico since its colonial times, which has contributed to racist tendencies in Puerto Rican society. Whitening was the most effective source to acquire the honor and privileges of the white ruling elites. Whitening was accomplished through marriage or "illicit" relationships, as white came to represent honor, prestige, and social standing. The fruits of this process would not be for the first generation, but with time the process of whitening would provide future generations with a new identity rooted in becoming white.[12]

There is always an alienating aspect in popular Pentecostalism that if not corrected becomes oppressive and dehumanizing. It is well known that after the Azusa Street Revival of 1906, where black, Latinx, Asian, and white Christians worshipped together, the movement divided by racial tensions a few years later. The Assemblies of God, the biggest Pentecostal denomination in the world, is a direct by-product of the Pentecostal schism that

---

12. Santiago-Vendrell, "Constructing Race in Puerto Rico," 162–66.

took place at Azusa. Nonetheless, the worship experience in Latin American Pentecostalism is a liberating encounter with God in which believers are cleansed by the powerful source of sound beats. The songs of the *coritos* are the same, but the same song sounds very different from place to place, as Puerto Rican *salsa* music is quite different than Mexican *rancheras*, or Dominican *merengue* than Colombian *cumbia*. The beauty of the Latin American worship experience is that each culture instrumentalizes the song according to its rhythms. Every believer who knows how to play an instrument is invited to participate with his/her talent for the enjoyment of the congregation and the glory of God.

Exorcists and Evangelists

One important characteristic of primal spirituality is its relation with transcendent powers. The relationship with transcendent powers is the belief that humans can enter a relationship with the divine. This relationship is built upon the conviction of human weakness and the supernatural. In their weakness, humans need good spirits for protection against evil. This relationship is accomplished through rituals and sacrifices offered to the divinities, but in popular Pentecostalism the primal experience is directed by the Holy Spirit. This aspect is reflected in a holistic cosmovision wherein there is no division between the physical and the spiritual. Everything is related to everything in the sense that all our bodies were made to raise us to the divine.

In this primal experience, the rationality constructed by Pentecostals is not influenced by the philosophical paradigm of the Enlightenment.[13] Reality for Latin American Pentecostals is not limited to what is visible, tangible, and material but encompasses everything visible and invisible. The religious world of the poor is likewise conceived in another realm, the realm of the Spirit. In this context, the worldview of Latin American Pentecostals assumes that the world is a battleground between the forces of good against evil. The world as they know it is full of demons that are constantly plotting against humanity. But they also know that God is present in their midst as someone who will overcome all the demonic forces around them.

Most Latin American Pentecostals have a unified response when it comes to religious others: other religion is demonic. For them, indigenous, Afro-Cuban, and Afro-Brazilian religions are syncretistic expressions of falsehood and should be rejected as such. Many preachers correlate demonic possessions to mental illness as practitioners clear their minds to

13. Shaull, "From Academic Research."

be filled with psychosomatic illnesses produced by demons. Satan and his demons are astute imitators of God by performing healing miracles under a Christian umbrella.[14] The *espiritista* in Puerto Rico opens the service with a prayer to the Holy Trinity and a prayer to Jesus. Then he proceeds to sing hymns such as "Alone with Jesus." This is followed by a cleansing ritual with herbs and plant roots digested by the seeker/client. Latin American Pentecostals see this type of syncretism as opposed to the Holy Spirit. Preachers strongly encourage Christians not to participate in or flirt with any aspect of the occult, as Satan is waiting for any opening to destroy human beings, as Christians are not exempt from being possessed by demons. The Pentecostal position is clear. There should be no interaction between Christians and adherents of other religions other than to exorcise them because other religions are categorized as deceitful and evil in nature.

In Brazil Pentecostalism rejects and calls for discontinuity with the Afro-Brazilian worldviews of Candomblé, Macumba, Umbanda, and Roman Catholic popular religiosity. The demons that had captivated the poor and made them prisoners of illnesses, sexual impotence, drug addiction, alcoholism, and other maladies are perceived by Pentecostals as representing the Afro-Brazilian religions.[15] For example, when demons are exorcised in Pentecostal services, preachers tend to ask the name of the demon, and the demons respond by identifying themselves as Exu Tranca-Rua, Maria, Shango, or other names of the Yoruba pantheon or popular Catholicism.[16] In this sense, the real origin of the demons is the Afro-Brazilian religions or Roman Catholicism. Thus, to suggest that Brazilian Pentecostalism did not entirely break with the traditions of popular religion but continues them through a process of acculturation and appropriation is to miss the point on the spiritual warfare that goes on for the acquisition of power in both forms of religions.

Mission as Transformation and Empowerment

Pentecostals consider social problems such as poverty, exclusion, exploitation, marginalization, diseases, and addictions to be inflicted by the demonic. They believe that God can help the poor, who face these maladies, to overcome those obstacles and give them victory amid despair. In this sense, Latin American Pentecostalism makes an immediate connection with the world of the poor because it demonstrates that the power of God

---

14. Calderón, "Espiritismo, un caos espiritual."
15. Macedo, *Orixás, caboclos e guias*, 19.
16. Ruuth and Rodrigues, *Deus, o demônio*, 68.

is available to transform the present conditions of human existence with a gracious and compassionate experience of divine grace. This is clearly seen in the evangelistic efforts of Latin American Pentecostals to convert drug addicts. For Latin American Pentecostals, drug addiction has its origins in demonic forces that want to destroy humanity through vices. In the case of drug addicts, their human dignity is shattered, but Latin American Pentecostals believe that the power of the Spirit is more than capable to transform lives. The only churches that dare enter the drug-infested ghettos of Puerto Rico are the Pentecostal.

The autobiographical work of Cookie Rodríguez presents a case study on how a Pentecostal popular religiosity of evangelization is constructed amid oppression. One of the first Latina Pentecostals who dedicated her life to the holistic ministry of converting female drug addicts to Christ was Cookie Rodríguez. Rodríguez is an ex-addict and prostitute born in Caguas, Puerto Rico, and reared in the Bronx, New York. She tells the story of overcoming the "demon" of drug addiction in her autobiography *Lord! Please Make Me Cry*. As a result of her encounter with Jesus Christ, Rodríguez founded New Life for Girls in 1972. New Life for Girls is a faith-based, residential substance abuse treatment program for women with seven locations in the US. New Life for Girls is open to all women who struggle with addictions, Latinas, African Americans, Asian Americans, Native Americans, and Caucasians. The gospel as preached by Latina Pentecostals such as Rodríguez is manifested not by words alone or a pie in the sky that serves as opium but is a transformational gospel with all the social implications of rescuing people from drug addiction.

Another example of Pentecostal popular religion is the testimony of Piri Thomas, a Puerto Rican reared in the Bronx, New York. In 1967, Piri Thomas published *Down These Mean Streets*, a chronicle of his youth. In this autobiography he describes his life on the streets, his experiences with sex, drugs, and crime, and his quest toward dignity. In his second book, *Savior, Savior, Hold My Hand*, he continues his autobiographical narrative, focusing on his religious conversion to Pentecostalism and concluding with a description of his present commitment to people rather than institutionalized forms of religion after having served a seven-year sentence in prison for armed robbery. He describes the challenges of working within Pentecostal structures that tended to place a straitjacket on his ministry of preaching to drug addicts and gang members. Thomas's departure from institutionalized Pentecostalism made his literary career a form of popular Pentecostalism, as it unveils a strong criticism of the fallouts of organized religion and the racism of denominational leaders, and Thomas decided to dedicate his life to helping people overcome their addictions.

The Pentecostals are the only religious group that dares to enter the housing projects of Puerto Rico. When Pentecostals arrive at any housing project with a high concentration of drug business, the drug dealers stop dealing and retreat to obscurity until the Pentecostals are gone. The housing project becomes a sanctuary where the Holy Spirit is operative in the whole service. One of the most popular *coritos* that is sung in the projects is "Christ can break your chains of sin and give you security. How can I live without my Jesus, if you are the foundation of my life, you [God] delivered me from hell and death, how could it be possible to live without Jesus":

> Cristo rompe las cadenas,
> Las cadenas del pecado.
> Cristo rompe las cadenas
> Y nos da seguridad.
> Como es posible yo vivir sin mi Jesús,
> Si el fundamento de mi vida eres Tu.
> Tú me libraste del infierno y de la muerte,
> Como es posible yo vivir sin ti Jesús.

One important aspect of the Pentecostal service in the housing project is that the official pastor of any congregation seldom preaches. Instead, lay members who had previously been part of the world of drug addiction are the ones given the sermon. The ex-drug addict knows the people in the projects and can testify of the transforming power of the Spirit because his own life becomes a symbol of liberation. The preacher offers salvation in the name of Jesus who has rescued him/her from the same condition. "If it happened to me, it could happen to anyone" is a constant phrase in the Pentecostal sermon because the changed life of the preacher validates the reality of the transformative power of the Holy Spirit to change lives. Every believer in Latin American Pentecostalism becomes a new messenger of the good news to others. Therefore, Latin American Pentecostalism, which appears to be centered in the otherworld or the realm of the Spirit, makes possible an experience of transcendence that becomes the motivating factor in all aspects of the daily struggle to survive in the here and now.

Pentecostals and Politics

There is a growing amount of recent scholarship about the relationship between Pentecostals and politics in Latin America. Today Pentecostals in Latin America are not just voting but creating their own political parties and exercising tremendous power in the process. The case of Puerto Rico is different than the rest of Latin America and the Spanish Caribbean because of its status as a commonwealth or a colony of the US. After more than a century, the Puerto Rican people are still struggling to understand their relationship with the US. The history of US relations with Puerto Rico has been understood in three different perspectives. These three opinions are most clearly seen in the three major political parties in the Island. El Partido Nuevo Progresista, which favors statehood for the island, sees the US as empowering the Puerto Rican people through technological advances, education, civilization, urbanization, and liberal institutions. El Partido Popular Democratico wants to maintain the status quo and keep the current relationship of Puerto Rico with the US as a commonwealth state or *estado libre asociado*. The third political alternative is represented by the Partido Independentista de Puerto Rico. This group wants complete control of the destiny of Puerto Rico with no interference from the US. These three divergent political positions, which are always colliding with each other, came to unity when an "errant" five-hundred-pound bomb killed David Sanes Rodríguez on April 19, 1999, in the Isla Nena de Vieques.

The ministry of one Pentecostal pastor, Wilfredo Estrada Adorno, channeled the inner pain of a people beaten down by the colonial domination of an alien oppressor. Estrada Adorno was one of the main players in the acts of civil disobedience against the war machine of the US on the island of Vieques.[17] Estrada Adorno's participation in the struggle for the liberation of Vieques was prompted by his understanding of the Judeo-Christian faith as one that sought to accompany the poor, the widows, and the marginalized of society. Even though Estrada Adorno was a Pentecostal pastor with the Church of God (Cleveland, Tennessee), the Pentecostal leadership of that denomination did not support him publicly, and no official church endorsed him. Pentecostals of the Church of God were conspicuous by their near absence in the process of liberating Vieques despite the recognition that one of them was the leader of the movement. Pentecostal denominational leaders opted to abstain from criticism against the Partido Nuevo Progresista, a political party that had delivered great results for them. Pentecostals catapulted Pedro Rosello to victory in the elections of 1992 and 1996. During his administration, Pentecostals became unofficial advisers in policies related to religious freedoms and morality. Rosello implemented policies that favored Pentecostals over Catholics and mainline Evangelicals, such as a weekly breakfast on Mondays, legalization of naturopathy, the

---

17. Barreto, *Vieques, the Navy*.

policy of five minutes of meditation in the mornings in public schools, and land lots for erecting churches for one dollar.[18]

In an act of defiance against all odds, Estrada and an ecumenical coalition organized a mass demonstration to try to sway the Clinton/Rosello deal that would allow the navy to continue their exercises with live ammunition. This civic march was a march for the peace of Vieques. Governor Rosello saw the proposal as a political attack against his administration and against the US. Nevertheless, the ecumenical coalition continued with its plan to have a mass demonstration for the peace of Vieques. On February 21, 2000, more than two hundred thousand Puerto Ricans marched peacefully from the Americas Expressway to the Roberto Clemente Sports Complex.[19]

Pentecostal believers were involved as independent individuals, even going against denominational and political leaders who advised them against participating in the demonstrations, for the liberation of Vieques. Perhaps the march could be interpreted as a form of popular Pentecostal religiosity in which Christians dismissed the religious establishment's demands and opted to follow their own conscience. The Pentecostal individuals who participated in the demonstration and procession were guided by the Spirit of God, who requires from them to act justly and to love mercy and to walk humbly with God (Mic 6:8). In the prophetic tradition of Micah, the prophet was called by God to tell kings and kingdoms about the oracles of God. To act justly in this instance meant to denounce the US Navy as agents of death. It was a moral obligation for them to accompany the people of Vieques in their quest for justice. As thousands of people marched together, they were singing *coritos* of liberation to the Lord.

The ecumenical call from Adorno's coalition included sectors from all religious creeds in Puerto Rico. The Methodist Church of Puerto Rico was represented by Bishop Juan Antonio Vera Méndez; Monseñor David Alvarez and Monseñor Roberto González Nieves represented the Episcopal Church; the Roman Catholic Church was represented by Monseñor Alvaro Corrada del Rio; and Rev. Francisco Soza represented Lutherans. This ecumenism of the Spirit is not interested in doctrinal agreements, structural compromises, or any creedal confession, but rather it is a communion of brothers and sisters praying and singing, working, protesting, and giving testimony to the world that Christians can work together to mend this broken world. It is the ecumenism of the Spirit that calls Latin American Pentecostals to engage the world with all its complexities and strive for justice and peace. As the famous *corito* says, "It does not matter the denomination to which you

---

18. Martínez-Ramírez, "Pentecostal Expansion," 129–30.
19. Vega, "Día que los angeles."

belong; if you are covered by the cross, if your heart is like mine, let's shake hands, and my brother you will be":

> No me importa la iglesia que vayas
> Si detrás del calvario tú estás
> Si tu corazón es como el mío
> Dame la mano y mi hermano serás

The transforming experience of the Spirit calls Pentecostals out of the world of vices, marginalization, and emptiness, and into a new world in need of redemption in which faith is a living encounter with God. Latin American Pentecostals want to see the world as Jesus sees the world, and Jesus saw the lost world with compassion. "When he saw the crowds, he had compassion on them, because they were harassed and helpless, like sheep without a shepherd" (Matt 9:36). In this sense, Pentecostals themselves experienced the oppression of the US Navy in Puerto Rico and were moved to compassion. They had compassion for the victims but denounced the oppressor.

Conclusion

When popular religions, popular Catholicism, and Latin American Pentecostalism are compared in their symbols and methodology there are similarities and some differences. A similarity is that all forms of religion offer a way to experience the sacred, but the ways to get there are quite different. In African religions in the diaspora, the orixás are the intermediaries between believers and Olodumare; in popular Catholicism the mediation comes from saints and local virgins like Guadalupe in Mexico, Our Lady of Providence in Puerto Rico, and Our Lady of Charity in Cuba, just to mention some. The Pentecostal experience offers a direct path to God by the divine mediation of the Holy Spirit. This mediation is so intense that the living God dwells in believers. The baptism with the Holy Spirit is not an initiation or rite of passage but a gift that produces reconciliation with God. I would prefer to use the term "primal" Pentecostalism instead of "popular" because the term presents a methodological conundrum.

There is no doubt that the beginnings of Pentecostalism in Latin America were among the poor and oppressed masses in rural areas and in the ghettos in urban centers. In Puerto Rico, these masses were mostly rural, as Roman Catholicism and mainline Evangelicalism did not engage the rural areas in the beginning of the twentieth century and decided to dedicate all their energies to the coastal town Ponce and the San Juan area. However, Pentecostals adapted to the changing conditions of their contextual realities.

The boom of Pentecostalism in Puerto Rico took place in an economic environment of new opportunities in the 1950s and 60s that brought to the island rapid social changes due to industrialization and major educational and economic improvements.

Today Pentecostalism in Latin America is not solely the religion of the poor, as it has been accepted by the middle and upper classes. Does it continue to be popular when more opulent members of society join the movement? An affirmative answer is still possible because the rich and powerful also participate in popular culture, but the risk of manipulation is always there. That said, Latin American Pentecostalism has shown the capacity to change the course of history as in the case of Vieques. It has also contributed to some of the most horrendous political crimes as in the case of Guatemala and the dictatorship of Efraín Ríos Mott. When this happens, Pentecostalism becomes anti-popular or against the aspirations of the poor or a cause like Vieques. Estrada Adorno and the ecumenical coalition's biggest critics were Pentecostal brothers and sisters. Perhaps Jorge Rashke was one of the biggest names criticizing the march for peace and Pentecostals for collaborating with Roman Catholics through his immense Clamor a Dios broadcast network. Whether Latin American popular Pentecostalism is liberationist or alienating remains to be seen.

Bibliography

Avalos, Jose. "María Atkinson and the Rise of Pentecostalism in the U.S.-Mexico Borderlands." *Journal of Religion and Society* 3 (2001) 1–20.

Barreto, Amílcar Antonio. *Vieques, the Navy, and Puerto Rican Politics*. Gainesville: University of Florida Press, 2002.

Calderón, Wilfredo. "El espiritismo, un caos espiritual." *Evangelio* 28 (1973) 8–10.

Espín, Orlando. "Pentecostalism and Popular Catholicism: The Poor and Traditio." *Journal of Hispanic/Latino Theology* 3 (1995) 14–43.

Espinoza, Gastón. *Latino Pentecostals in America: Faith and Politics in Action*. Cambridge: Harvard University Press, 2014.

Hollenweger, Walter J. *Pentecostalism, Origins and Developments Worldwide*. Peabody, MA: Hendrickson, 1997.

Lugo, Juan L. *Pentecostés en Puerto Rico o la vida de un misionero*. San Juan: Puerto Rico Gospel, 1951.

Macedo, Edir. *Orixás, caboclos e guias: Deuses ou demônios?* Rio de Janeiro: Universal, 1990.

Martínez-Ramírez, Héctor M. "Pentecostal Expansion and Political Activism in Puerto Rico." *Caribbean Studies* 33 (2005) 113–47.

Miguez Bonino, Jose. "Popular Piety." In *Popular Religion, Liberation and Contextual Theology: Papers from a Congress (January 3–7, 1990, Nijmegen, the Netherlands) Dedicated to Arnulf Camps OFM*, edited by Jacques Van Nieuwenhove and Berma

Klein Goldewijk, 148–58. Kerk en Theologie in Context—Church and Society in Context 8. Kampen: KOK, 1991.

Rodriguez, Cookie. *Lord! Please Make Me Cry.* Pittsburgh: Whitaker, 1974.

Ruuth, Anders, and Donizete Rodrigues. *Deus, o demônio e o homen.* Lisboa: Colibri, 1999.

Santiago-Vendrell, Angel D. "Constructing Race in Puerto Rico: The Colonial Legacy of Christianity and Empires, 1510–1910." In *Can White People be Saved? Triangulating Race, Theology, and Mission*, edited by Love Sechrest et al., 150–73. Downers Grove, IL: IVP Academic, 2018.

———. "Popular Religion as a Unifying Factor in the Latino/a Religious Community: A Pentecostal Proposal in US Latino/a Ecumenical Theology." *Journal of Pentecostal Theology* 12 (2003) 129–41.

Shaull, Richard. "From Academic Research to Spiritual Transformation: Reflections on a Study of Pentecostalism in Brazil." *Penuma* 20 (1998) 71–84. https://doi.org/10.1163/157007498X00063.

Shaull, Richard, and Waldo Cesar. *Pentecostalism and the Future of the Christian Churches: Promises, Limitations, Challenges.* Grand Rapids: Eerdmans, 2000.

Scherer, James A., and Stephen B. Bevans, eds. *Basic Statements, 1974–1991.* Vol. 1 of *New Directions in Mission and Evangelization.* Maryknoll, NY: Orbis, 1992.

Schultze, Quentin J. "Orality and Power in Latin American Pentecostalism." In *Coming of Age: Protestantism in Contemporary Latin America*, edited by Daniel R. Miller, 65–85. Lanham, MD: University of America Press, 1994.

Thomas, Piri. *Down These Mean Streets.* New York: Knopf, 1967.

———. *Savior, Savior, Hold My Hand.* New York: Bantam, 1973.

Turner, Harold. "The Primal Religions of the World and Their Study." In *Australian Essays in World Religions*, edited by Victor C. Hayes, 27–37. Adelaide: Australian Association for the Study of Religions, 1977.

Vega, Ana Lydia. "El día que los angeles marcharon" [The day that the saints marched]. *El Nuevo Dia*, Feb. 29, 2000.

Vidales, Raul. *Práctica religiosa y proyecto histórico: Hipótesis para un estudio de la religiosidad popular en América Latina.* Lima: Centro de Estudio y Publicaciones, 1975.

13

Christianity, Gender, and Ecology in Abya Yala*

SANDRA DUARTE DE SOUZA

ANTHROPO-ANDROCENTRISM THAT HAS ORIENTED and framed forms of being, living, knowing, and believing in Latin America produced human disidentification with nature and, simultaneously, the identification of human with a specific type of subject—male, white, heterosexual proprietor. The history of the colonization of this plural continent intended its subjugation and therefore the erasure of its traditions, knowledges, and experiential place in the name of a Christianity that had sex, race, and class—and that shared the colonial ideal of land possession and exploration. Intended, because it was never fully achieved. That which we now call "world Christianity" demonstrates the survival and resurgences that call into question the asepsis that colonial Christianity aspired to.[1] This means that discussing the history of Christianity in Latin America is discussing amalgamated experiences, redesigned beliefs, indigenized and Africanized theologies, and religious experiences far beyond the monolithic Christianity prevalent in mainstream academic approaches.

We want to consider the relations between Christianity, gender, and ecology in Latin America from this perspective. This discussion is possible only if we strip ourselves of universal narratives and occupy the often subalternate epistemic places of women and their ways of doing religion. The Christianity that arrived on the continent legitimized land expropriation and human disidentification with nature as well as with other humans.

---

1. *This text is part of the project called "New Theoretical Approaches to the Religious Phenomenon in Latin America," funded by the FAPEG Program to Support Stricto Sensu Graduate Programs (Edital 01/2024).

Barreto, "Decolonialidade e interculturalidade."

It produces a theology that is lethal to women, the most dispossessed among the dispossessed, silencing their knowledges and shattering communal life—which are fundamental for their survival. However, women's communal experience in the struggles for land has been redesigning the Christianity that was planted here as monoculture. We will observe this in the experiences of evangelical women that are part of the Landless Workers Movement (LWM) in Brazil. They revisit the Bible not to justify land and people exploitation but to strengthen themselves in the struggle for a land that belongs to all—a land that engenders life and does not admit hunger. They theologize way, way beyond the boundaries of their religious confessions—and so oftentimes they *do not fit* into the sterility of their surrounding churches.

Naming and Dominating

The ways in which we know and name a people, their culture, their experiences, and their territory affect our perception of them—and conceal processes of resistance against colonial taxonomy itself. The erasure of the memories of indigenous peoples has occurred in many ways throughout the history of this vast continent, so-called Latin America.[2] This homogenizing classification—in which honoring a European traveler prevailed—was imposed to a continent that houses diverse and countless peoples, cultures, and cosmovisions. One of the many erasures inflicted to consolidate this colonial version of the history of our continent is the following: renaming its lands after their invader's name and calling its people "Indians"—thus ignoring its natives' forms of naming themselves. This version tells the history of a continent from its invasion, calling it "discovery," thus negating other existences that inhabited here with their traditions and cosmologies before that. This is retold throughout the years, paradoxically perpetuating itself as the single history of a plural land. As Françoise Vergès puts it,

> We are fighting against a system that has dismissed scientific knowledge, aesthetics, and entire categories of human beings as non-existent. Although the European world never succeeded in being completely hegemonic, it appropriated without hesitation

---

2. The name of this continent is attributed to the Italian navigator and cartographer Américo Vespúcio. This traveler, who participated in two Portuguese expeditions into the continent (in 1501 and 1503), concluded that what Christopher Columbus had named Índias was, actually, a New World. Later, in 1507, a cartographer called Martin Waldseemüller rechristened the region with the name America, in explicit homage to Américo Vespúcio.

or shame the knowledge, aesthetics, techniques, and philosophies of the people it enslaved and whose civilizations it denied.[3]

Underneath this name/notion of Latin America that was defined at the end of the nineteenth century[4] lies the native people's ethnical, linguistic, economic, and political plurality, which refuses to be erased—starting with the plurality of names attributed to the regions inhabited by these different peoples. The Tupi-Guarani named it Pindorama (Land of palm trees); the Mexica (who predated the Aztecs) called it Anahuac (Close to water). The Inca Empire, which was constituted around the thirteenth century, named the region under their dominion Tawantinsuyu (Realm of the four parts). There were certainly many other names for regions inhabited by native peoples that were forcefully turned into colonial properties. As a way of resisting this pasteurized designation that conceals the abundance of life that existed prior to colonization, native peoples have adopted the Kuna expression *Abya Yala*—which means "Land in its full maturity/Land of vital blood." This is a way of affirming a sense of belonging without, however, reinforcing the narrative of a single continental identity. We adopt the expression Abya Yala to consider "Latin America" from a decolonial perspective, where life pulses and diversity resists any homogenizing designs of domination.

Christianizing and Civilizing

The history of Christianity in Abya Yala is, forcibly, the history of the colonial invasion of our continent. The self-referential, exploitative, slaveholding, racist, and misogynistic Christianity that moored and anchored in Latin America is ravenous in its devouring lust.

The invention of race and racism, products of the European economic expansion projects in the sixteenth century, offered ideological support for colonial domination. Even today, they ground relations of domination in capitalist societies. Their skin-color marker would determine a colonizer's "natural" superiority, empowered by a Christianity that is white, patriarchal, and greedy for riches. Whiteness is taken here as both world producer and organizer. In the words of Willie Jennings, "Whiteness emerges, not simply as a marker of the European but as the rarely spoken but always understood organizing conceptual frame."[5]

---

3. Vergès, *Feminismo decolonial*, 31.
4. Ardao, *Génesis de la idea*.
5. Jennings, *Christian Imagination*, 26.

Colonial action aimed at the physical and symbolic extermination of the other. It involved invisibilizing and negating worlds other than the European. It was necessary to erase them, bury them into the unspeakable, or else "monstrify" them, turn them into "sinners," creating narratives that would present them as vile and "uncivilized."[6] Diverse worlds were erased via this generic classification of Europeans vs. "non-Europeans," that is, "Indians" and Africans. It was necessary to pasteurize them: hijacking their diversity, history, culture, and the world itself. Cosmocide walked hand in hand with epistemicide. The (unsuccessful) attempt to erase indigenous and African knowledges was also an attempt to relegate them to a condition of nonexistence. A world that was never a world.

Genocide, epistemicide, cosmocide, and ecocide were the strategies employed to enforce the modern-colonial enterprise, which laid the bases for the development of capitalism.[7] The devouring lust of the colonial engine spared no people, no knowledge, no land, no forest, and no water on the continent they invaded. In the invaders' narrative, subalterns have no say. This is how all this predatory and bloodthirsty violence during the colonization of Abya Yala becomes the history of a heroic, civilizing achievement—one of rescuing "bestial people" and saving "lost souls." The colonized had their human status denied, and hierarchy was constituted based on European references—therefore, installing a kind of ontological racism that endures even today in how one relates to this continent. This constitutes an ideological weapon in the service of domination.[8]

Quijano argues that this colonial project of domination is based in a taxonomy that establishes the

> codification of the differences between conquerors and conquered in the idea of "race," a supposedly different biological structure that placed some in a natural situation of inferiority to others. The conquistadors assumed this idea as the constitutive, founding element of the relations of domination that the conquest imposed. On this basis, the population of America, and later the world, was classified within the new pattern of power.[9]

---

6. Ronaldo Vainfas refers to the discomfort Jesuit priests had with indigenous women's nudity: "To the eyes of Jesuits, always complaining about the difficulties with catechism, with the climate, and with the lack of resources, sexual frenzy raged on, chiefly, among Indians: always nude, polygamic, incestuous" ("Moralidades brasílicas," 232).

7. Quijano and Wallerstein, "Americanity as a Concept."

8. Moura, "Racismo como arma ideológica."

9. Quijano, *Cuestiones y horizontes*, 770.

Quijano makes explicit the active colonial role in the production of a legitimizing justification for the domination of the people of Abya Yala, from those classified as "Indians" to those who were forcefully brought into our continent as slaves and classified as "negroes." Self-classified "white" Europeans sat at the top of the hierarchy they had produced and presented themselves as paradigms for culture and civilization, as the measure of what is human. In short,

> The context of bourgeois commercial expansion and renaissance culture opened the doors for the construction of modern philosophical ideas which would later transform European men into *universal men* (important: mind the gender), and all peoples and cultures which did not match European cultural systems into less evolved variations.[10]

Religion is integral to what is understood as the European cultural system. Caravels brought this "universal man"—European!—who came ashore with sword and cross. This evangelizing project was, for autochthonous people, one of ethnic disidentification. Christian mission in Abya Yala played a fundamental role in the de-indigenization and the de-Africanizing of enslaved peoples and the very denial of their humanity.

Disidentify and dehumanize to dominate. No wonder the long debates over whether autochthonous people had soul or not. Granted, Pope Paul the III's papal bull *Sublimis Deus*, proclaimed in 1537, affirmed the humanity of Indians.[11] But the *padroado*/patronage system[12] held the Catholic Church both as hostage and as accomplice to the interests of the Spanish and Portuguese Crowns and, therefore, subjected to their goals of domination. Father Antônio Vieira demonstrates his affinity to the crown regarding black slavery, calling slavery a "means of salvation." That is, through toil in the land,

---

10. Almeida, *Racismo estrutural*, 18; emphasis added.

11. We must understand that, previously, in 1452, the *Dum Diversas* bull by Pope Nicholas V authorized the enslavement of the so called "enemies of Christ." Besides the goal of religiously legitimizing war on Muslims (Saracens) in the African continent and justifying their perpetual servitude, the document gave the Portuguese Crown the right to extend their domination to other peoples, limitlessly. Therefore, the enslavement of both the autochthonous people of Abya Yala and Africans had the church's seal of approval.

12. Agreement between the Church and monarchies dating back to the tenth century. In the colonial period, the institution of *padroado*/patronage refers to the agreement between the Spanish and Portuguese Crowns and the Catholic Church, which granted monarchs the right to interfere on ecclesiastical matters such as appointing priests and bishops, creating bishoprics, conducing ecclesiastic court investigations, authorizing or not the establishment of religious orders, etc. Patronage even allowed disobedience of papal bulls, if the Iberian monarchs thought the documents conflicted with their interests.

enslaved people could attain the salvation of their souls and ensure their entrance into the kingdom of God.[13]

Christianity's approval of slavery was also constituted upon the bodies of women—both Indians and black. Female enslavement was doubly important to the colonial process. Women labored as slaves subjected to excessive workdays. They were also used to breed new slaves, being recurrently violated to satisfy the lust of their masters—and to spin the wheels of slaveholding economy, as the children of colonial rape were slaves themselves. In nineteenth-century Brazil, the application of the doctrine of *partus sequitur ventrem* defined whether a child was a slave or not in their mother's womb.[14] Slave mother, slave children. An example of the religious legitimizing of such doctrine can be found in Father Antônio Vieira's sermon 20, titled "Maria Rosa Mística" (Mystical Rose Mary):

> Know ye why the Virgin Mary recognized and confessed herself a slave before she conceived the Son of God? The reason why, and highest Mystery, was that birth, according to law, does not follow the condition of the father, but that of the mother: *Partus sequitur ventrem*—our Lady desired, via this advance declaration, that the Son, which would be hers, as the Son of a slave woman, also be born our slave. As the Son of his Father, he is Lord of men; but, as the Son of his Mother, the same Mother wanted that he were also a slave to men.[15]

Thus, slavery from the womb was religiously justifiable in the equivalence between enslaved women and Mary, as well as the enslaved fetus to Jesus himself. There were times when priests did not overly concern themselves with the elaboration of religious excuses for the slavery of children—they understood it as natural and necessary for colonial economy and society. It sufficed that slave owners understood the importance of domesticating slaves' bodies and minds to the point of willingly contributing to this very system. Father André João Antonil tried to guide slaveholders in the proper treatment of slaves, so slaves would not rebel against their masters and question their enslavement. His book titled *Cultura e opulência do Brasil* (Culture and opulence in Brazil) makes evident the objectifying outlook on slaves this Jesuit had. Regarding pregnant slaves, he affirms:

---

13. Hoornaert, *Formação do catolicismo brasileiro*, 35.

14. Doctrine originated in Roman law, applied in the English Crown's colonies during the seventeenth century. Later, in the nineteenth century, it was incorporated into the colonies of the Spanish and Portuguese Crowns.

15. Vieira, "Sermão XX," 143–44.

> Slaves are the hands and feet of sugar mill owners, for in Brazil, without them, it is impossible to make, retain, and increase estate, nor keep the mill running. Their fitness or unfitness for labor depends on how you treat them. . . . Seeing their masters being kind enough to gift their little children anything that overflows from their tables makes slaves serve them with goodwill and rejoice in making their servants multiply. On the contrary, some slaves deliberately seek abortions, only to keep the children of their wombs from suffering what they suffer.[16]

Despite the efforts to naturalize and sacralize the status of a slave, and despite the historical erasure of resistance against slavery, especially so resistance by women, there are important records of slaves' key participation in actions to liberate themselves from this regime—such as organizing uprisings against slavery, planning escapes, organizing and managing *quilombos*, care for those that had escaped and were in need of shelter, and planning and executing the assassination of colonial masters. They were also unbowed by the *partus sequitur ventrem* doctrine. It was not rare that enslaved women used their medicinal knowledge to abort fetuses—or to commit infanticide so as not to submit their children to slavery. They often paid with their lives. The history of Delfina, registered by a police precinct in the state of Ceará in 1870, shows the agency black women had to resist slavery:

> The pregnant slave Delfina, from the district Frade, was on the verge of giving birth when her master Manoel Bento da Costa sent for a midwife to assist her. Instead of waiting, Delfina locked herself into a room where, after delivering her own baby, she proceeded to kill it, and to lock the tiny body into a box, the keys to which she deliberately misplaced.[17]

Resistance often led to being marked for death but also translated the desire for freedom by all those who did not accept the colonial yoke and the destruction it represented. Accounts of abortions provoked by slaves depict one of the most important means by which enslaved women in Brazil resisted—whether Indian, African, or African descendant.

Coloniality, Ecocide, and Gender Domination

If we can agree that nowadays it is no longer about colonization and evangelization in terms of metropolis-colony relations of domination, coloniality still persists overtly to maintain domination. This requires that we make

16. Antonil, *Cultura e opulência do Brasil*, 111.
17. Santos, "Slave Mothers," 468.

explicit and criticize geography, color, sex, religion, and the grammar of power.

This European project of civilizing and exploring, in the names of modernity and of the Christian faith, arrogated itself the right to submit the land and peoples of Abya Yala to its cravings for riches and power. Communal goods were expropriated under the pretext of presenting the Christian God to all people. In the name of God and for the salvation of people, it was necessary to expand the frontiers of Christianity and Western cosmovision, to which all people should convert. Ethical and religious justification for the invasion of land, domination of its people, stealing of its riches, and denial and repression of their knowledges and systems of meaning was laid out.

"America" was "christened and colonized." This project of power produced an economic model that Quijano and Wallerstein call the "modern-colonial capitalist world-system." The world economy, which aims at maximizing profit, uses the ideology of success to push forward its death policies and the affirmation of capitalism as a universal economic model. As Wallerstein so well points out,

> Historical capitalism is a patently absurd one. One accumulates capital in order to accumulate more capital. Capitalists are like white mice on a treadmill, running ever faster in order to run still faster. In the process, no doubt, some people live well, but others live miserably.[18]

This modern-colonial capitalist world-system rooted itself upon racialization, genderization, hierarchizing, and exploitation of the people and natural riches from peripheral capitalism countries. The so-called Latin America was invented to meet the politico-economic demands of its colonizers. In its predatory obsession, capitalism constitutes itself as a kind of idolatrous religion, a violent religious system that demands worship, conversion, human and planetary sacrifices.[19] A system that invades lands and bodies, especially the body-territory of women.

When Maria Mies discusses the process of accumulation and its relation to patriarchy, she draws attention to violence as a mechanism for the domination of colonies, women, and nature—which was fundamental to what has been conventionally called *modernization*: "necessary" violence

---

18. Wallerstein, *Historical Capitalism*, 40.

19. This perspective was extensively worked on by the DEI, Departamento Ecumênico de Investigações (ERD, Ecumenical Research Department). The DEI was founded in 1977 by Franz Hinkelammert, Hugo Assmann, and Pablo Richard. It became an important center for the discussion of Latin American liberation thinking. It has been dedicating itself to the study of the relation between theology and Marxism.

from dominators' viewpoint. This is why violence, even today, is "the secret of modern capitalist patriarchal civilization,"[20] a patriarchal civilization that is based upon war and conquest as their "most 'productive' modes of production."[21]

This system's genetic coding considers nature a "subaltern space." We understand nature "both as biophysical reality (its flora, its fauna, its human inhabitants, its ecosystems' diversity) and as its territorial configuration (the sociocultural dynamic that significantly articulates those ecosystems and landscapes)."[22] Subordination of nature implies subordination of everything associated with it. Therefore, subordination of women is the immediate consequence of such logic. The gender of domination is male. The patriarchal foundational paradigm was built upon hierarchical dualisms, which led to the simultaneous disidentification of humans to nature, to non-whiteness, and to women. The measure of modern humanness classifies beings and knowledges based on their color, sex, and religion, demanding that everything and everyone submit to its mythic-ritual system—colonizing cosmovisions, both producing and teaching its "cosmoagony" as the single, universal truth.

Modern cosmogony, which I have just called "cosmoagony," insists on the denial and disqualification of knowledges that do not align with dominant knowledges. It brushes aside collective knowledges and ways of doing, and invalidates perspectives that do not match with binarism, such as human/nature, black/white, man/woman, rational/irrational, etc. It is in this sense that Catherine Walsh refers to a fourth type of coloniality—besides methodological, epistemological, and ontological coloniality:

> It is the cosmogonic coloniality or coloniality of Mother Nature, which is related to the vital-magical-spiritual power of the existence of African descendant and indigenous communities, each with their own historic particularities. It is rooted in the Cartesian binary distinction between man/nature, categorizing as non-modern, "primitive," and "pagan" the sacred and spiritual relations that connect the above and under worlds to the land, and to the ancestors as living beings.[23]

The colonial attempt to apply its domination technologies, bury cosmovisions, impose belief systems, and invalidate life systems did not account for

20. Mies, *Patriarchy and Accumulation*, xxi.
21. Mies, *Patriarchy and Accumulation*, 74.
22. Alimonda, *Naturaleza colonizada*, 22.
23. Walsh, "Interculturalidad crítica," 3.

the agency of colonized peoples. The survival of cultic, medicinal, alimentary, idiomatic, and relational characteristics of indigenous and African peoples—strongly female driven—fracture this allegedly homogenous system, which is supposedly immune to contact with others. That is, a system presenting itself as impervious to meeting/confronting the other. In the case of Christianity upon Latin American soil, such fractures can be seen both in the ways by which different groups organize and institutionalize themselves and in their communitarian practices—not necessarily institutionalized—that develop at the margins and despite organizations.

As affirmed by Raimundo Barreto, "colonial Christianity was subverted in the process, giving rise to new popular religious expressions that continued to express important elements from indigenous and African matrix cultures."[24] This "subversion" is noticeable in the ways self-declared Christian women have been constructing different ways of living and believing, not infrequently disobeying their tradition's rigid and misogynistic theologies and doctrines in order to obey other knowledges, especially those learned from lived life and contact with other women. They disobey to obey themselves, their sisters, in a sororal community much wider than what hegemonic Christianism wants or even *can* admit.

LWM Pentecostal Women: Toward a Theology That Delegitimizes Latifundia

The modern-colonial capitalist world-system has been increasing the vulnerability of Latin American women. This exploiting and spoliating action is not experienced without resistance. An example of resistance is the way some evangelical women have been resignifying their own faith—reading the Bible and theologizing communally from their experience of the struggle for land ownership.

The notorious participation of women in the most important movement that struggles for land in Brazil, the LWM, makes explicit what ecofeminism and decolonial feminism have been emphasizing: there is a close relation between dominating nature and dominating women. In a televised interview, Lucineia Freitas, LWM's gender sector national leader, criticized agribusiness's predatory violence:

> Agribusiness has been encroaching on territories, expelling women from the countryside, from waters, and from forests. This encroachment engenders hunger and violences against

---

24. Barreto, "Decolonialidade e interculturalidade," 128.

women, against countryside inhabitants and also engenders hunger in cities. Therefore, in defense of dignified life, to confront hunger, women have been denouncing agribusiness.... LWM stood out, during the last period [COVID pandemics], for its actions of solidarity. These actions of solidarity are possible because we produce food, but to produce food, this territory had to be occupied, negotiated, and settlement and production policies for these areas had to be implemented. So, there is this integration between the struggle for land and the process of production, production of food, production of other goods that enable dignified life. It is essential that this process is driven by women, as women are the most impacted by the way agribusiness has been encroaching. This production model engenders hunger and violence, and to confront hunger and violence, from violence against territory to violence against our bodies, we must enable an agrarian reform policy that starts reorganizing Brazil's land structure through settlements and demarcation of territories.[25]

Lucineia Freitas speaks about an economic system that takes over the land to produce hunger, that expels women "from the countryside, from waters, and from forests," which denies the generation of life by engendering death. For LWM's women, being a part of this movement is reclaiming that which was expropriated from them as well as from their families. They have been paying with their lives for the claim for the right to live.

This is the case of Luiza Ferreira, an important LWM leader in northeastern Brazil, in the state of Pernambuco. She was assassinated due to leading occupations in that region. The settlement in the municipality of São Lourenço da Mata (state of Pernambuco) is named after this woman who was murdered in the struggle for land. Field research in this settlement was undertaken by Fábio Alves Ferreira and Milene Almeida. Ferreira and Almeida ascertained that women are the majority in this location. At the time of research, there were 136 families settled there. The authors found out that 80 percent of people settled there claimed to be Pentecostal and a part of the Assemblies of God. Out of these, around 70 percent were women.[26] This is significant, considering that this church is usually very refractory to female leadership.

Twelve women were interviewed by the authors. They verified that women operate religion as a legitimation mechanism for their struggle for land, a struggle understood as the "fulfillment of God's promise," a

---

25. Durao Coelho, "Mulheres são as mais afetadas," para. 27.
26. Ferreira and Almeida, "Mulher pentecostal na luta," 133.

"prophecy" that "will not be fulfilled without struggle."²⁷ These women produce "their own hermeneutic in which there is not an institution telling the meaning of life. Those women interpret life and produce meaning from a synthesis of religious and political discourses."²⁸

Rodrigo Cardoso interviewed a woman whose name is Elisabeth Costa. She is also a member of the Assemblies of God in the same settlement. Her theologizing is very assertive: "When God created the world, he gave everyone land. He did not wish that a group lived in the *favelas* [slums]."²⁹ Distinct from the God of *latifundia*—who is male, white, and elitist—this God is in the lips of many LWM evangelical women, who are mostly black. He is present in their daily experiences of confronting the violent and diabolical modern-colonial capitalist-patriarchal world-system.

If colonization expropriated in the name of the Christian God, and if coloniality has been finding justification in the affirmation and reproduction of this anthropophagic deity, these peasant women have been reimagining the Christian God out of their experiences in the struggle for land. They drift away from religious orthodoxy and from the sterile hermeneutics that are disconnected from the lives of those that suffer. In their reflections and practices, they evoke a kind of theologizing that will not fit into their churches' institutional constraints. The criterion of experience is understood here as the source for all hermeneutics, as knowledge incarnated.

Ivone Gebara refers to this theology constructed from daily experience as "ordinary life epistemology,"³⁰ a dynamic knowledge, relationally constructed, which transforms itself from the interpolations of daily life. The daily corporeal experience of being woman in a colonial-patriarchal society calls into question the "asepsis" of a theology that presents itself as untouchable by the concreteness of life. Therefore, these women's theologizing is effectively a "lifelogizing,"³¹ a *vithalogue*.³² They know and teach from

---

27. Ferreira and Almeida, "Mulher pentecostal na luta," 132.
28. Ferreira and Almeida, "Mulher pentecostal na luta," 138.
29. Cardoso, "Evangélicos ocupam o MST," para. 7.
30. Gebara, "Epistemologias teológicas," 33.
31. I borrow this notion from Ivone Gebara. Gebara referred to women's theological doing as *vidalogia* (lifeology) in an event to promote her book *Caminhos para compreender a teologia feminista* (Ways to understand feminist theology).
32. I gladly welcome this terminology, suggested to me by my English translator, Carlos Guilherme Fagundes da Silva Magajewski. *Vithalogue* intends to weave together the notions of life (subsumed in the Latin root *vita*), vital (understood as both essential/ necessary and full of life/lively), and theology (hence the *th*). Last, instead of the suffix "-ize" (as in theologize, patronize) as indicative of making/acting the thing denoted by the noun/adjective, we chose to use "-logue," as in dialogue.

life, not just from private life but from a collective of women that lies at the margins.

The way these women from the settlement understand their struggle and the restoration of a place to live, plant, harvest, and share reclaims the communal weave and reaffirms the interdependence between all beings. Célia Xakriabá, an indigenous woman, translates this interdependence in terms of the autochthonous peoples' conception of nature: "We are the extensions of the land's body. If it is sick, our body also is.... Healing the land is healing the food, the seed, the fruit, the river, the head, the thought, the spirit... Healing humanity itself."[33] We are interdependent beings. Processes of life and death, of sickness and healing, cannot be disconnected from this reality, as "reestablishing and reconstituting the communion between nature and people is an act of decolonizing and liberation for society as a whole."[34] Such an act of decolonizing turns Abya Yala into that which is the very power of its name: a land permanently blooming.

Bibliography

Alimonda, Hector. *La naturaleza colonizada: Ecología política y minería en América Latina*. Buenos Aires: CLACSO, 2011.
Almeida, Silvio Luiz de. *Racismo estrutural*. São Paulo: Pólen, 2019.
Antonil, André João. *Cultura e opulência do Brasil*. Belo Horizonte: Itatiaia/Edusp, 1982. http://www.educadores.diaadia.pr.gov.br/arquivos/File/2010/literatura/obras_completas_literatura_brasileira_e_portuguesa/ANDRE_ANTONIL/CULTURA/CULTURA_TEXTO.HTML.
Ardao, Arturo. *Génesis de la idea y el nombre de América Latina*. Caracas: Centro de Estudios Latinoamericanos Romulo Gallegos, 1980.
Barreto, Raimundo. "Decolonialidade e interculturalidade no chistianismo mundial: Uma perspectiva latino-americana." In *Ciências da religião e teologia: Epistemologia, identidade e relações*, edited by Sandra Duarte de Souza, 115–48. São Paulo: Recriar, 2022.
Cardoso, Rodrigo. "Os evangélicos ocupam o MST." Istoé, 2014. https://istoe.com.br/383339_OS+EVANGELICOS+OCUPAM+O+MST/.
Durao Coelho, Rodrigo. "Mulheres são as mais afetadas pelo agronegócio, diz dirigente do MST." Programa Central do Brasil, Mar. 7, 2023. https://www.brasildefato.com.br/2023/03/07/mulheres-sao-as-mais-afetadas-pelo-agronegocio-diz-dirigente-do-mst).
Ferreira, Fábio Alves, and Milene Almeida. "A mulher pentecostal na luta por terra: Uma análise do assentamento Luiza Ferreira." *Aceno* 3 (2016) 125–40.
Gebara, Ivone. "As epistemologias teológicas e suas consequências." In *Epistemologia, violência e sexualidade: Olhares do II Congresso Latino-Americano de Gênero e*

---

33. Xakriabá, "Curar a terra," para. 26.
34. Walsh, "Interculturalidad, decolonialidad," 215.

Religião, edited by Elaine Neuenfeldt et al., 31–50. São Leopoldo: Sinodal/EST, 2008.

———. *Caminhos para compreender a teologia feminista*. São Paulo: Recriar, 2023.

Hoonaert, Eduardo. *Formação do catolicismo brasileiro, 1500–1800*. Petrópolis: Vozes, 1994.

Jennings, Willie James. *The Christian Imagination: Theology and the Origins of Race*. New Haven: Yale University Press, 2011.

Mies, Maria. *Patriarchy and Accumulation on a World Scale: Women in the International Division of Labour*. Critique Influence Change. New York: Zed, 1998.

Moura, Clóvis. "O racismo como arma ideológica de dominação." *Revista Princípios* 34 (1994) 28–38.

Quijano, Aníbal. *Cuestiones y horizontes: De ladependencia histórico-estructural a lacolonialidad/descolonialidaddel poder*. Ciudad Autónoma de Buenos Aires: CLACSO, 2014.

Quijano, Aníbal, and Immaneul Wallerstein. "Americanity as a Concept or the Americas in the Modern World-System." *International Social Science Journal* 134 (1992) 549–57.

Santos, Martha S. "'Slave Mothers,' *Partus Sequitur Ventrem*, and the Naturalization of Slave Reproduction in Nineteenth-Century Brazil." *Tempo* 22 (2016) 467–87. dx.doi.org10.20509/TEM-1980-542X2016v224106.

Vainfas, Ronaldo. "Moralidades brasílicas: Deleites sexuais e linguagem erótica na sociedade escravista." In *História da vida privada no Brasil: Cotidiano e vida privada na América Portuguesa*, edited by Laura de Mello e Souza, 221–74. São Paulo: Letras, 1997.

Vergès, Françoise. *Um feminismo decolonial*. São Paulo: UBU, 2020.

Vieira, Antônio. "Sermão XX—Maria Rosa Mística." In *Sermões do Padre Antônio Vieira*, 14:31–39. Lisboa: Seabra & Antunes, 1857.

Wallerstein, Immanuel. *"Historical Capitalism" and "Capitalist Civilization."* London: Verso, 1996.

Walsh, Catherine. "Interculturalidad crítica y pedagogía de-colonial: Apuestas (des) de el in-surgir, re-existir y re-vivir." Red de Interculturalidad, Feb. 2014. https://redinterculturalidad.files.wordpress.com/2014/02/interculturalidad-crc3adtica-y-pedagogc3ada-decolonial-walsh.pdf.

———. "Interculturalidad, decolonialidad y el buen vivir." In *Interculturalidad, estado, sociedad: Luchas (de)coloniales de nuestra época*. Quito: Universidad Andina Simón Bolívar Editorial, 2009.

Xakriabá, Célia. "Curar a terra é curar a nós mesmos." YAM, 2020. Interview with Martina Medina. https://yam.com.vc/sabedoria/791662/celia-xakriaba-curando-a-terra-curamos-a-nos-mesmos.

14

Christianity on the Move:
Migratory Christianity in and from Latin America

João B. Chaves

IN THIS CHAPTER, I address ways in which Christianity and migration interact in Latin America and in other regions (particularly the United States) where large numbers of Latin American migrants live. Because I focus primarily on the late twentieth and twenty-first centuries, I begin by providing a brief historical background that will help to situate the contemporary context. After outlining the historical background, I present examples of migratory Christianity in Latin America, showing how the continuous presence of imported forms of Christianity shapes local religiosities. Finally, I show examples of migratory Christianity from Latin America, mentioning migrant groups in Europe but focusing primarily on the US.

I draw heavily on my research among Brazilian immigrants in the US, using the story of Brazilian Baptist immigrants as a case study that highlights two important characteristics of migratory Christianity: (1) its roots in migration to and mission in Latin America, and (2) aspects of one of the most potent examples of Latin American transnational religious networks, namely, the creation of what Oosterbaan et al. call lusospheres. *Lusospheres* are groupings of religious communities worldwide whose success the transnational appeal of Brazilian religions and culture as well as the agency of migrant religious entrepreneurs facilitated.[1] The Brazilian Baptist case illustrates how the broader creation of lusospheres takes place in the US,

---

1. Oosterbaan et al., "Lusospheres."

exemplifying ways in which migratory Christianity from Latin America develops in the US, the most popular destination for Latin America immigrants.[2]

Although the "in" and "from" distinction provides a valuable framework for understanding Latin American migratory Christianity, it is crucial to qualify the distinction by recognizing the complex ways in which religion and migration have interacted among Latin Americans. Different forms of Christianity established themselves in Latin America due to the continuing and overlapping migration flows over the centuries. Countries in the region continue to receive migrants and their religions today, ensuring the continuation of Christianity's reshaping by new iterations of border-crossing dynamics. Unlike previous times, however, the complex place of Christianity in Latin America today also entails an increasing role of transnational dynamics that help sustain relationships between local individuals and institutions and foreign-based initiatives. The growing influence of communication technologies, including social media, strengthens such relationships. In other words, foreign forms of Christianity affect Latin American groups today and are, in turn, affected by Latin Americans in unprecedented ways even without physically crossing borders as communication technologies continue to strengthen contemporary hypoconnectivities.

The place of Pentecostalism and charismatic movements in the region exemplifies the complexity of placing sharp distinctions between migratory Christianity "in" Latin America and "from" Latin America. The cases of Brazil and Argentina illustrate this well. After being influenced by the Chicago awakening of the early twentieth century, Italian immigrant Luigi Francescon and Swedish-born Daniel Berg and Gunnar Vingren migrated from the US to South America, where there were also enclaves of Italian and Swedish immigrants. There, Francescon started churches in Brazil and Argentina, while Berg and Vingren started what would become one of the largest Pentecostal denominations in the world, the Assemblies of God in Brazil.[3] Today, Latin American immigrants to the US and Europe bring with them forms of Pentecostalism that European migrants who became Pentecostal in the US introduced before arriving in the region.[4]

Charismatic sensibilities also crossed borders multidirectionally. In the Baptist case, for example, Southern Baptist missionary Rosalee Mills Applebee was responsible for mentoring locals who became charismatic in the 1960s via her influence. One of those mentees pastored a church that

2. Rocha and Vásquez, "Introduction," 3–9.
3. Palma, *Grassroots Pentecostalism*, 25–52.
4. Lin, *Prosperity Gospel Latinos*; Madrazo, *Predicadores*.

now has branches in the US, branches that actors and politicians visiting the US on business or for leisure attend. The church, Igreja Batista da Lagoinha, is also considered a major global player in the Latin American contemporary Christian music industry. Migration "in" and "from" happen simultaneously, including the flows and exchanges created by missionaries, labor migrations, spiritual tourism, media consumption, social media connectivity, and geopolitical interests.[5]

Historical Background

The geographical region commonly known today as Latin America does not have an easily identifiable, single identity. Rather, the region is thoroughly diverse, complex, and multilayered. The term Latin America was largely "invented" only in the second half of the nineteenth century as, at best, a relatively adequate descriptor of this geographical region whose common general contours and shared geopolitical interests changed over time.[6] However, despite the differences between (and within) Latin American countries, the region's nations share a history of European colonialism and US imperialism that helped not only to decimate indigenous populations but also to brutalize Afro-diasporic peoples enslaved to work in the region.[7]

Religion, of course, had been an element of the lives of what we now call Latin American peoples before indigenous populations had contact with European colonizers. The original inhabitants of the Américas developed a complex web of civilizations and cultures long before European colonizers arrived in the late fifteenth century. Although the distinction between "religious" and "secular" realms is mostly a late European development, the Inca, Mayas, Aztecs, and Yanomami (to cite only a few native groups) had what could be categorized as religious practices and beliefs deeply embedded into their way of life.[8] Native groups also migrated throughout the region, often changing their cultural traditions due to migratory experiences.[9] However, the arrival of European colonizers was a watershed moment with worldwide impacts that are difficult to overstate. Christianity was an integral part of the

---

5. Rocha, "How Religions Travel," 23–28.
6. Gobat, "Invention of Latin America," 1345–49.
7. Gabbert, "Longue Durée," 256–59.
8. For examples, see Davies, *Incas*, 131–32; Bassett, *Fate of Earthly Things*, 27–44; Baron, *Patron Gods*, 46–51; Jokic, *Living Ancestors*, 51–58.
9. In the case of the Yanomami, for example, scholars debate where their predecessors lived before the late eighteenth century and have claimed that the Yanomami are solitary remnants of migrants who settled in their present location. For more, see Jokic, *Living Ancestors*, 27–39.

apparatus of European colonization in Latin America, although the explicit alignment of church officials with colonial enterprises varied with the particular time and place.[10]

The complex introduction of Catholicism by Spanish and Portuguese colonizers and local appropriations and translations of the religion were significantly successful. After the arrival of the Spanish and Portuguese colonizers, the forms of migration and types of Christianity in Latin America continued to diversify. European and American missionaries significantly shaped the later infusion of Protestantism in the region, finding fertile ground there particularly after the second half of the nineteenth century.[11] Indigenous actors subverted forms of colonial Christianity, often as acts of resistance, cultural preservation, and survival.[12] Enslaved and free Afro-diasporic peoples engaged in Christian practices and helped shape aspects of Latin American Christianity.[13] Latin Americans developed theologies that denounced oppressive systems that affected both locals and foreigners.[14] Authoritarian regimes co-opted Christian symbols and doctrines to implement particular theo-political agendas.[15] As a result of its thriving and creative journeys in Latin America, Christianity has been the majority religion in the region for centuries, with over 90 percent of the population identifying as Christian and projections suggesting that the vast majority of Latin Americans will continue to be Christian for the foreseeable future.[16] Furthermore, Latin American forms of Christianity have not been confined to the region but have traveled worldwide as locals migrated and shaped several contexts, especially in Europe and the US.

Different forms of migration heavily informed the infusion of Christianity in the region and its global dissemination, and thus the patterns of migratory flows involving Latin America were multilayered. Generally speaking, three primary migration patterns have characterized Latin America: migration to Latin America from several countries, interregional migration, and migration from Latin America to developed countries. As a

---

10. González and González, *Christianity in Latin America*, 40–63. See also Schwaller, *History of Catholic Church*, 52–70; Lynch, *New Worlds*, 185–90; and Prien, *Christianity in Latin America*, 356–65.

11. See Chaves, *Global Mission*; Hartch, *Rebirth*, 40–41.

12. Lindenfeld, *World Christianity*, 1–30; Hanks, *Converting Words*, 16–22.

13. O'Toole, "(Un)Making Christianity."

14. See Barreto, *Protesting Poverty*; Kirkpatrick, *Gospel for the Poor*; Zegarra, *Revolutionary Faith*.

15. For the Brazilian and Guatemalan cases see, respectively, Cowan, *Moral Majorities*; Garrard-Burnett, *Terror in the Land*.

16. Zurlo, "Demographic Profile," 3–6, 16.

result of these migration patterns, religions have shaped and been shaped by people on the move and the contexts they created, contexts directly affected by migrations to, within, and from Latin America over centuries. Religious movements and institutions informed by migratory dynamics also affect those who have not moved.[17] From festivals to labor markets and the arts, the religious practices of migrant groups have shaped host nations profoundly.

Moreover, technologies that allow for stronger transnational interaction, which facilitates "multiple belongings" and helps maintain relationships across cultures, languages, and borders, continuously inform migrant practices, religious and otherwise.[18] As Peggy Levitt has argued, "Transnationalization globalizes religion, and once they are in place, transnational religions contribute to globalization."[19] The radically complex reality of overlapping migratory patterns and fluctuating transnational relationships continuously configure and reconfigure individual and communal identities of migrants from Latin America and nonmigrants worldwide.[20] The religious practices of migrants are at the heart of this reconfiguration of identities, which has happened continuously throughout the past centuries, thus informing the complex web of interconnections that characterize contemporary cartographies of transnational networks.

Migratory Christianity in Latin America

Catholic and Protestant missions from Europe and the US were two significant agents of the dissemination of Christianity in Latin America.[21] However, local and indigenous appropriation, translation, and dissemination were indispensable for the success and diversity of the religion throughout the region.[22] Locals and foreigners traveled to and within Latin America for several reasons and cross-pollinated ideas and imaginations, religious and otherwise. The presence of foreigners from the US, Europe, Africa, Asia, and other Latin American countries in several Latin American nations has historical and contemporary relevance as people continue to migrate to and within the region. Since the global economic crises of 2008 and 2012, Latin

17. Fredericks, "Religion, Migration, and Identity," 10.
18. Chaves, *Migrational Religion*, 92–94.
19. Levitt, "Two Nations Under God," 160.
20. Richlin, *In the Hands of God*, 10.
21. Hartch, *Rebirth*, 167–70.
22. For examples of the inculturation and adaptations of Christianity in Latin America, see Garrard, *New Faces of God*, 35–72; Barreto, "Beyond Contextualization."

American countries have received more than one million migrant families, and are thus being significantly inserted in transnational migration routes.[23] Brazil, Argentina, and Ecuador have been primary recipients of such refugees and economic migrants, who often marry locals and form multifaith families.[24]

Approximately 16.5 percent of Latin American and Caribbean migrants worldwide are in other countries of the region. Migration in Latin America, however, is an important element of the region's dynamics, and the role of religion in interregional migration is significant. For example, the influx of Haitian, Bolivian, and Colombian immigrants in Brazil underscores the presence of groups for whom religiosity is an important means of adaptation. High levels of ethnic solidarity, the tendency to concentrate in particular neighborhoods, and engagement in religious practices that help to maintain ethnic identity characterize such groups.[25] Venezuelan migration to Colombia and Brazil also grew significantly in the last decade. In the Venezuelan case—as in the case of Cubans who migrated to Latin American countries—religion in general and Roman Catholicism in particular often helped to mediate adaptation in host countries.[26] The role religion played in the lives of migrants in Latin America is thus similar to that played by religion in the lives of Latin American migrants in the US and Europe. Religion—particularly Christianity—helps mediate the migrants' adaptation in host countries. The US and Europe host around 83 percent of Latin American and Caribbean migrants, with the majority living in the US, thus being a more significant site for studying Latin American migrant religiosity.

Migratory Christianity from Latin America

A significant number of Latin American immigrants live in the US and Europe—and practice their religion in host countries with cultural and linguistic patterns different than theirs. The US has by far the greatest number of Latin American immigrants in the world, most of them concentrated in metropolitan areas.[27] According to 2015 UN estimates, there are around thirty-six million Latin American and Caribbean immigrants worldwide—twenty-four million (66.2 percent) of them living in the US.[28] Spanish is

23. Uebel and Abaide, "Migrantes e famílias," 47–49.
24. Uebel and Abaide, "Migrantes e famílias," 50–51.
25. Bosenbecker and Monsma, "Empresários binacionais," 171–76.
26. Uebel and Abaide, "Migrantes e famílias," 62–63.
27. Budiman, "Key Findings."
28. Bayona-i-Carrasco and Avila-Tàpies, "Latin Americans," 202–3.

the most widely spoken of all foreign languages in the US, and Portuguese is ninth. Together, Spanish and Portuguese speakers account for over 62 percent of foreign language speakers in the US, with an overwhelming number being Spanish speakers.[29] Europe has approximately five million immigrants from Latin American and Caribbean countries (13 percent of Latin American and Caribbean migrants worldwide). Most Latin American migrants to Europe went to the countries of southern Europe—particularly Spain, Italy, and Portugal. The United Kingdom, the Netherlands, France, and Germany were also popular destinations for Latin American migrants. However, almost half of all Latin American and Caribbean immigrants in Europe settled in Spain.[30]

In the US, Latin American immigrants attend a wide array of churches, and this for several reasons. Different patterns of church attendance and religious affiliation inform and are informed by the shape of the adaptations of migrant groups into US society.[31] The fact that Latin Americans and Latine groups in the US take different pathways of societal engagement problematizes the mistaken notion that Latin American immigrants and US-born Latines form a pan-ethnic monolith. Religious communities inform such pathways as they often subscribe to a variety of visions of ethnic identity and welcome parishioners into distinct, and often conflicting, notions of pan-ethnicity.[32] In other words, an understanding that such mediation is not uniform in intent, reception, or employment must accompany the general recognition that churches mediate immigrant living in host countries.

There are, however, significant overlaps among otherwise diverging immigrant religious groups. At a basic level, broad ethnic solidarity and contextualization of theological convictions and ecclesial practices together characterize the dispositional core of the churches of Latin American immigrants in the US. Ethnic solidarity, however, does not mean that such churches are immune to incorporating forms of US structural racism into their beliefs and practices.[33] Nevertheless, it does mean that in immigrant contexts a core attractiveness of churches shifts to include the possibility of reinforcing ethnic (and national) identity—which is rarely an explicit element of religious practices in churches in Latin America created to serve locals.

---

29. Ward and Batalova, "Frequently Requested Statistics."
30. Bayona-i-Carrasco and Avila-Tàpies, "Latin Americans," 200–206.
31. Calvillo, *Saints of Santa Ana*, 87–107.
32. Calvillo, "Diverging Latinidades," 419–21.
33. Serrão, "Transmitting Racism Through Religion."

Baptists and Migratory Christianity in and from Latin America: A Case Study

The transnational connections Baptists have created are multilayered, and the history of Baptists in Latin America highlights the importance of migration in and from the region. Migration resulting from geopolitical dynamics, climate-related occurrences, and individual efforts all shaped the history of Baptists in Latin America. Consequently, the history of Baptists (as well as other denominations) in the region aligns with the growing body of research indicating that migration, not traditional missionary endeavors, is the primary catalyst for the spread of Christianity in its various forms. However, the underlying migration patterns that influenced the development of Latin American Baptists were diverse and varied.

Brazil and Mexico, for instance, witnessed the emergence of Baptist communities through the settlement of former Confederates from the southern US.[34] A combination of push-and-pull factors similarly motivated cohorts of immigrants from Switzerland, Belgium, Germany, Russia, and Wales to settle in Argentina during the late nineteenth century. After establishing themselves in their new homeland, French-speaking colonists from Belgium and Switzerland took the initiative to invite Baptist pioneer Pablo Besson to Argentina.[35] Additional instances of migration roots in the history of Baptists in Latin America include German Baptist settlers in Chile and Paraguay, Caribbean migrants in Colombia and Panama, enslaved Afro-descendants transported to Costa Rica from other Latin American nations, Scandinavian immigrants who influenced Baptist missions, and Eastern European groups that formed ethnic Baptist associations in the region.[36]

The reasons and paths of migration for these groups and others were diverse. However, their arrival as immigrants significantly affected Baptist development and influenced various Latin American nations. Some Baptists initially came to Latin America with roles such as Bible salespeople, school teachers, transnational religious or education entrepreneurs, or colonists. Examples include W. D. T. MacDonald in Chile, the Gervin family and Victor Mura in Paraguay, Júlio Malves and Solomon Ginsburg in Brazil, the Westrup family in Mexico, James Thomson in multiple countries, and Archibald Reekie in Bolivia. While some of these eventually became associated with Baptist missionary institutions, traditional Baptist missionary

---

34. Wahlstrom, *Southern Exodus to Mexico*, 4–5; Chaves, *Global Mission*, 38–49.

35. Cancicli, *Pablo Besson*, 65–86; Anderson, *Evangelical Saga*, 183.

36. Johnson, *Global Introduction*, 173; Ronis, *Epopéia de fé*, 299–308; Moore, *Evangélicos en marcha*, 71–73; and Anderson, *Historia de los bautistas*, 396–98, 421.

appointments did not facilitate their initial presence in Latin America. However, missionary enterprises played a vital role in expanding and organizing Baptist work once mission agencies entered different countries, often continuing to shape the religious paths established by earlier immigrant influences. Such enterprises facilitated pathways for the insertion of migrant religious communities in the US.

The case of Southern Baptist Convention (SBC) missionaries in Brazil and Brazilian Baptist Convention (BBC) immigrant churches in the US illustrates this dynamic particularly well. Already from the early years of the denomination, Southern Baptists considered Brazil a potential mission field. Still, it was not until 1881 that Southern Baptist missionaries began to arrive in Brazil consistently. Over time, these missionaries distanced themselves from the attitudes of traditional Confederate exiles who initially hosted them because the churches of former Confederates showed little concern for evangelizing the locals. In 1882, SBC missionaries began planting churches designed to convert Brazilians to the Baptist faith.[37] The Baptist denomination in Brazil not only grew in numbers but also adopted the Southern Baptist model of organization. With the invaluable assistance of local leaders, the missionaries first formed individual churches, followed by regional and state conventions, and eventually, in 1907, a national convention.

Moreover, the missionaries founded theological seminaries and denominational publications, exerting control over these and other central denominational institutions for a significant portion of Baptist history in Brazil.[38] When the BBC reached its centenary in 1982, it had established Baptist missions in various countries, including Chile, Portugal, Bolivia, Paraguay, Mozambique, Angola, Azores, Uruguay, Argentina, Rhodesia, Venezuela, France, Spain, Canada, South Africa, Peru, and Ecuador. Furthermore, and perhaps rather surprisingly to some readers, it had a mission in the US, the birthplace of the SBC.[39]

Indeed, while immigrants and missionaries from the US were pursuing their objectives in Brazil, Brazilians were also migrating to the US in response to the influence of missionaries and their connections established in Brazil. Two main reasons explain why individuals who had been introduced to Protestant Christianity by immigrants and missionaries in Brazil came to the US. First, the missionaries believed it was necessary to send Brazilian converts to the US for theological and ministerial training. Second, US denominations wanted to enlist Brazilians in their efforts to convert and

---

37. Parsons and Chaves, *Remembering Antônia Teixeira*, 13–28.
38. Chaves, "Brazilian Migrational Christianity."
39. Chaves, *Migrational Religion*, 165.

minister to European immigrants and Spanish-speaking communities in the US. The Baptist example illustrates broader dynamics in this context, as other denominations, particularly Methodists and Presbyterians, engaged in similar endeavors.[40]

In the 1980s, a noticeable emergence of churches consisting mainly of undocumented Brazilian parishioners became a regular feature in the religious landscape of the US. We can trace this development traced back to the BBC, which was influenced by the SBC and dispatched a missionary to target the Iberian Portuguese population residing on the American East Coast. The influx of Portuguese and Azorean migrants to the US, initially driven by the whaling industry's demands, influenced immigration patterns in New England and California between the 1870s and 1920s. Another wave of migration in the second half of the twentieth century further increased the Portuguese and Azorean immigrant populations in these regions.[41] At the outset, it was primarily this Iberian Portuguese population that the BBC had in mind when sending a missionary to the US.

Nevertheless, Brazilian migration to the US experienced significant growth in the later decades of the twentieth century. With thousands of Brazilian Evangelicals making their way to the US, numerous Brazilian churches were established to cater to these immigrants. As immigrant churches, these faith communities faced constant pressure to adapt to their swiftly changing environment. Initially, their leaders—male pastors seeking to replicate the communities from which they hailed—conceived of these churches as extensions of their denomination in Brazil. However, the challenges associated with immigrant life gradually pushed these church communities in a direction that surpassed their traditional role in Brazil.[42]

The history of Brazilian immigrant churches highlights how immigrant theologies emerge within faith communities under pressure to adapt to new environments. The firsthand migrant experiences of Brazilian parishioners are the primary catalyst for the theological distinctiveness in their religious communities. Generally speaking, leaders of immigrant faith communities rarely engage with academic theologians' writings on migration, even if those theologians have lived experiences within such communities. Academic works often engage in scholarly conversations of little interest to the average immigrant Christian. Though a few leaders have

---

40. Chaves, *Migrational Religion*, 25–45.

41. Leal, "Migrant Cosmopolitanism," 233–34.

42. It is important to emphasize that other national and religious groups whose histories can be traced to Latin America share similar characteristics with Brazilian Baptist immigrants in the US. For examples, see Lin, *Prosperity Gospel Latinos*; Madrazo, *Predicadores*; Calvillo, *Saints of Santa Ana*; Richlin, *In the Hands of God*.

expressed some interest, they typically view contextual theologies as validations of their existing beliefs or dismiss them as excessively radical. The most influential sources of theological innovation arise from the migration experiences of immigrant leaders and their congregants. Consequently, it is sociological realities that guide transnational religious networks, rather than those networks fitting neatly into formal theological frameworks, and this leads to dynamic theological and ecclesiological creativity. Leaders and members of immigrant communities are not preoccupied with formulating their theological convictions into rigid formulas; instead, they seek to develop practical tools and a language that effectively addresses the challenges of immigrant life.

One aspect of this situation is the "transient syndrome" one can observe among Brazilian immigrants, which refers to the tendency of most Brazilian immigrants in the US to view themselves as "target earners" who plan to return to Brazil. While in the US, they often move between states for better employment opportunities. This characteristic challenges Brazilian immigrant churches as they struggle to project their future and address the fact that many of their members do not regard long-term membership in a particular US church as possible. This dynamic creates a distinct sense of a "church on the move" unique to immigrant congregations. These faith communities cannot assume their survival beyond the first generation. Although strategies are in place to sustain the community's mission for future generations, such as appealing to non-Brazilians and using more English to engage younger individuals, many of these churches' efforts and creativity are dedicated to caring for transient parishioners. Consequently, measuring the impact of specific immigrant churches becomes challenging since sheer numbers do not account for the substantial number of immigrants who benefit from church services but eventually leave for various reasons.

Another significant contextual challenge lies in the role of Brazilian immigrant churches in facilitating the adaptation of immigrants to the US. Unlike churches primarily comprised of Anglo-Americans, Brazilian immigrant churches hold a prominent position in the lives of immigrants, who view these churches as means of obtaining religious, social, and legal assistance directly related to their immigrant status, particularly for undocumented immigrants. For instance, a pastor who has served churches in Brazil and the US described the distinction between ministering to Brazilian immigrants and Brazilians residing in Brazil as completely distinct experiences. He further explained that much of this disparity can be attributed to the alienation that Brazilian migrants experience due to being far away from their homeland. Another pastor emphasized that the primary functions of these churches are to facilitate integration, provide emotional support, and guide individuals into the American culture and job market while catering to their spiritual needs. Recognizing the significance of aiding undocumented immigrants in this process, Brazilian immigrant churches perceive their role as an explicit mediating structure, even as they seek to expand their influence beyond their Brazilian congregants.

Furthermore, Brazilian immigrant churches exemplify a keen awareness of their specific circumstances, adroitly navigating between two distinct realms: Brazilian Evangelicalism and the immediate US environment. Their existence entails a continuous negotiation between these interconnected yet separate realities. However, the primary factors that influence theological change within Brazilian immigrant communities through migration dynamics are three: First, the substantial presence of undocumented congregants; second, the rapid pentecostalization of Brazilian immigrant Baptists, resulting from an influx of immigrants from a Pentecostal background; and third, the form of women's leadership within these communities.

The emerging immigrant theologies, which both the significant number of undocumented members in Brazilian immigrant churches and also the increasing influx of Pentecostal adherents and the acceptance of women's ordination fostered, are a compelling testament to the adaptable nature of pastoral theological reflection. In a relatively short period, Brazilian immigrant pastors have transitioned from a tendency toward legalistic views on immigration issues, similar to those held by many political candidates supported by the SBC, to embracing theologically justified advocacy for immigrant rights. Such developments are a testament to the creativity and adaptive potential of forms of migratory Christianity developed by Latin American transnational religious networks.

Conclusion

Migratory Christianity in and from Latin America therefore informs several complex dynamics. The intricate relationship between Christianity and migration in the region and its impact on other regions, particularly the US, continues to grow in strength and significance. Religious practices in Latin America, shaped by European colonialism and US imperialism, influenced the dissemination of Christianity in the region and the globalization of migratory Christianity in Europe and the US. Although native groups in Latin America have rich religious traditions, the success of Catholic and Protestant missions from Europe and the US, as well as the local appropriation and translation of the religion, guaranteed the success of Christianity in the region. Migrants from various countries within Latin America and outside the region have played a significant role in shaping religious practices and beliefs through the cross-pollination of ideas. The interregional migration within Latin America has also contributed to the diversity of religious traditions and the mediation of ethnic identity through religion. Furthermore, migratory Christianity from Latin America has had a profound impact on the US and Europe, where a significant number of Latin American immigrants reside. These migrants engage in religious practices to host countries with different cultural and linguistic patterns that function as means of adapting and maintaining ethnic identity.

The case study of Brazilian Baptists exemplifies the complexity of migratory Christianity. The history of Baptists in Latin America shows the influence of migration from different regions, such as the settlement of former Confederates from the southern US in Brazil and Mexico. Migrant communities played a crucial role in establishing and developing Baptist churches in Latin America, often surpassing traditional missionary endeavors in importance. The history of such groups emphasizes the simultaneous nature of migration "in" and "from" Latin America, highlighting the continuous interplay between religion and migration. It acknowledges the role of transnational dynamics—including communication technologies and social media—in sustaining relationships between Latin American migrants and their religious communities. Overall, the complexity of migratory Christianity in and from Latin America, and its effect on the region and other parts of the world, will likely remain an essential aspect of world Christianity. The continuous interconnection between religion and migration contributes to the formation of transnational networks and the global dissemination of Latin American forms of Christianity. Both in and outside Latin America, Christianity thus serves as a mediator of adaptation for migrants, maintaining ethnic identity and shaping their pathways in host countries.

Bibliography

Anderson, Justice C. *An Evangelical Saga: Baptists and their Precursors in Latin America.* Maitland, FL: Xulon, 2005.

———. *Historia de los bautistas.* Commemorative ed. El Paso: Mundo Hispano, 2015.

Baron, Joanne P. *Patron Gods and Patron Lords: The Semiotics of Classic Maya Community Cults.* Denver: University Press of Colorado, 2016.

Barreto, Raimundo. "Beyond Contextualization: Gospel, Culture, and the Rise of Latin American Christianity." In *World Christianity as Public Religion*, edited by Raimundo Barreto et al., 97–117. World Christianity and Public Religion. Minneapolis: Fortress, 2017.

Barreto, Raimundo C., Jr. *Protesting Poverty: Protestants, Social Ethics, and the Poor in Brazil.* Translated by Stephen Di Trolio. Waco: Baylor University Press, 2023.

Bassett, Molly H. *The Fate of Earthly Things: Aztec Gods and God-Bodies*. Austin: University of Texas Press, 2015.
Bayona-i-Carrasco, Jordi, and Rosalia Avila-Tàpies. "Latin Americans and Caribbeans in Europe: A Cross-Country Analysis." *International Migration* 58 (2020) 198–218.
Bosenbecker, Patrícia, and Karl Monsma. "Os empresários binacionais da imigração: Uma discussão histórica." *Mediações* 23 (2018) 170–92.
Budiman, Abby. "Key Findings About U.S. Immigrants." California-Mexico Studies Center, Aug. 20, 2020. https://www.california-mexicocenter.org/key-findings-about-u-s-immigrants-pew-research-center/.
Calvillo, Jonathan E. "Diverging Latinidades in Latinx Churches." *PRSt* 49 (2022) 419–32.
———. *The Saints of Santa Ana: Faith and Ethnicity in a Mexican Majority City*. New York: Oxford University Press, 2020.
Canclini, Santiago. *Pablo Besson: Un heraldo de la libertad cristiana*. Buenos Aires: Convención Evangélica Bautista, 1957.
Carneiro, Maria Luiza Tucci. "Literatura de imigração e literatura de exílio: Realidades e utopias." *Revista de Crítica Literaria Latinoamericana* 23 (1997) 67–80.
Chaves, João B. "Brazilian Migrational Christianity in North America." In *Latin American and Latinx Religions in North America: An Introduction*, edited by Lloyd D. Barba, 247–62. Bloomsbury Religion in North America. London: Bloomsbury, 2023.
———. *The Global Mission of the Jim Crow South: Southern Baptist Missionaries and the Shaping of Latin American Evangelicalism*. Macon: Mercer University Press, 2022.
———. *Migrational Religion: Context and Creativity in the Latinx Diaspora*. Waco: Baylor University Press, 2021.
Cowan, Benjamin A. *Moral Majorities Across the Américas: Brazil, the United States, and the Creation of the Religious Right*. Chapel Hill: University of North Carolina Press, 2021.
Davies, Nigel. *The Incas*. Denver: University Press of Colorado, 1995.
Fredericks, Martha. "Religion, Migration, and Identity: A Conceptual and Theoretical Exploration." In *Religion, Migration and Identity: Methodological and Theological Explorations*, edited by Martha Fredericks and Dorotta Nagy, 9–29. Theology and Mission in World Christianity 2. Leiden: Brill, 2016.
Gabbert, Wolfgang. "The Longue Durée of Colonial Violence in Latin America." *Historical Social Research* 37 (2012) 254–75.
Garrard, Virginia. *New Faces of God in Latin America: Emerging Forms of Vernacular Christianity*. Oxford: Oxford University Press, 2020.
Garrard-Burnett, Virginia. *Terror in the Land of the Holy Spirit: Guatemala Under General Rios Montt, 1982–1983*. Religion and Global Politics. Oxford: Oxford University Press, 2009.
Gobat, Michel. "The Invention of Latin America: A Transnational History of Anti-Imperialism, Democracy, and Race." *American Historical Review* 118 (2013) 1345–75.
González, Justo L., and Ondina E. González. *Christianity in Latin America: A History*. Cambridge: Cambridge University Press, 2007.
Hanks, William F. *Converting Words: Maya in the Age of the Cross*. Berkeley: University of California Press, 2010.

Hartch, Todd. *The Rebirth of Latin American Christianity*. Oxford Studies in World Christianity. Oxford: Oxford University Press, 2014.

Jokic, Zeljko. *The Living Ancestors: Shamanism, Cosmos and Cultural Change Among the Yanomami of the Upper Orinoco*. New York: Berghahn, 2015.

Johnson, Robert E. *A Global Introduction to Baptist Churches*. Introduction to Religion. Cambridge: Cambridge University Press, 2010.

Kirkpatrick, David C. *A Gospel for the Poor: Global Social Christianity and the Latin American Evangelical Left*. Philadelphia: University of Pennsylvania Press, 2019.

Leal, João. "Migrant Cosmopolitanism: Ritual and Cultural Innovation among Azorean Immigrants in the USA." In *Cosmopolitanism in the Portuguese-Speaking World*, edited by Francisco Bethencourt, 233–49. European Expansion and Indigenous Response 27. Leiden: Brill, 2017.

Levitt, Peggy. "Two Nations Under God? Latino Religious Life in the United States." In *Latinos Remaking America*, edited by Marcelo M. Suárez-Orozco and Mariela M. Paéz, 150–67. Berkeley: University of California Press, 2008.

Lin, Tony Tian-Ren. *Prosperity Gospel Latinos and Their American Dream*. Chapel Hill: University of North Carolina Press, 2020.

Lindenfeld, David. *World Christianity and Indigenous Experience: A Global History, 1500–2000*. Cambridge: Cambridge University Press, 2021.

Lynch, John. *New Worlds: A Religious History of Latin America*. New Haven: Yale University Press, 2012.

Madrazo, Tito. *Predicadores: Hispanic Preaching and Immigrant Identity*. Waco: Baylor University Press, 2021.

Marchi, Regina M. *Day of the Dead in the USA: The Migration and Transformation of a Cultural Phenomenon*. New Brunswick, NJ: Rutgers University Press, 2009.

Moore, Robert C. *Los evangélicos en marcha . . . en América Latina*. El Paso: Bautista, 1959.

Oosterbaan, Martijn, et al. "Lusospheres: The Globalization of Brazilian Religion." In *Global Trajectories of Brazilian Religion: Lubospheres*, edited by Martijn Oosterbaan et al., 1–20. Bloomsbury Studies in Religion, Space and Place. London: Bloomsbury, 2020.

O'Toole, Rachel Sarah. "(Un)Making Christianity: The African Diaspora in Slavery and Freedom." In *The Oxford Handbook of Latin American Christianity*, edited by David Thomas Orique et al., 101–19. Oxford Handbooks. Oxford: Oxford University Press, 2015.

Palma, Paul J. *Grassroots Pentecostalism in Brazil and the United States: Migrations, Missions, and Mobility*. Cham, Switz.: Palgrave MacMillan, 2022.

Parsons, Mikeal, and João B. Chaves. *Remembering Antônia Teixeira: A Story of Missions, Violence, and Institutional Hypothesis*. Grand Rapids: Eerdmans, 2023.

Prien, Hans-Jürgen. *Christianity in Latin America*. Translated by Stephen Buckwalter. Religion in the Americas 13. Leiden: Brill, 2012.

Richlin, Johanna Bard. *In the Hands of God: How Evangelical Belonging Transforms Migrant Experience in the United States*. Princeton: Princeton University Press, 2022.

Rocha, Cristina. "How Religions Travel: Comparing the John of God Movement and a Brazilian Migrant Church." In *Global Trajectories of Brazilian Religion: Lubospheres*, edited by Martijn Oosterbaan et al., 23–36. Bloomsbury Studies in Religion, Space and Place. London: Bloomsbury, 2020.

Rocha, Cristina, and Manuel A. Vásquez. "Introduction: Brazil in the New Global Cartography of Religion." In *The Diaspora of Brazilian Religions*, edited by Cristina Rocha and Manuel A. Vásquez, 1–42. International Studies in Religion and Society 16. Leiden: Brill, 2013.

Ronis, Osvaldo. *Uma epopéia de fé: História dos batistas letos no Brasil*. Rio de Janeiro: Batista, 1974.

Schwaller, John Frederick. *The History of the Catholic Church in Latin America: From Conquest to Revolution and Beyond*. New York: NYU Press, 2011.

Serrão, Rodrigo. "Transmitting Racism Through Religion? Ethnic Transcendence and Colorblind Racism in Latina/o Congregations." *PRSt* 49 (2022) 385–401.

Uebel, Roberto Rodolfo Georg, and Jalusa Prestes Abaide. "Migrantes e famílias transnacionais na América do Sul: Tendências contemporâneas." *Século XXI Revista de Ciências Sociais* 8 (2018) 47–74.

Wahlstrom, Todd W. *The Southern Exodus to Mexico: Migration Across the Borderlands After the American Civil War*. Lincoln: University of Nebraska Press, 2015.

Ward, Nicole, and Jeanne Batalova. "Frequently Requested Statistics on Immigrants and Immigration in the United States." Migration Policy Institute, Mar. 14, 2023. https://www.migrationpolicy.org/article/frequently-requested-statistics-immigrants-and-immigration-united-states-202.

Zegarra, Raúl E. *A Revolutionary Faith: Liberation Theology Between Public Reasons and Public Religion*. Stanford, CA: Stanford University Press, 2023.

Zurlo, Gina A. "A Demographic Profile of Christianity in Latin America and the Caribbean." In *Christianity in Latin America and the Caribbean*, edited by Kenneth R. Ross et al., 3–16. Edinburgh Companions to Global Christianity. Edinburgh: Edinburgh University Press, 2022.

Timeline: Latin America and the Caribbean

Brett Knowles

American church historian Martin Marty has aptly commented that (in religion as elsewhere) "both hurricanes and glacial forces leave altered landscapes."[1] The "hurricane" represents sudden, drastic change, the product of clearly identifiable catalytic events such as, for example, the Second Vatican Council from 1962 to 1965. By contrast, the "glacier" represents a process of gradual, subtle change, which may not be attributable to any specific causative event or series of events. These "glacial" forces therefore symbolize slow, cumulative progressions of attitudes and orientations. This is a metaphor particularly applicable to Latin America, where change has usually emerged through long-standing processes, rather than through catalytic events that can be placed within a timeline of dates.

Nevertheless, this timeline contains entries from Latin America and the Caribbean covering the period from 1492 (Columbus's discovery of America) up to the present day. Country locations are placed in bold type at the end of each entry and are derived from the United Nations, Department of Economic and Social Affairs, Statistics Division website.[2] Continental entries, with no specific country location, are cited as [**Latin America and the Caribbean**].

---

1. Marty, "Introduction," 1.
2. United Nations Statistics Division, "Methodology," s.vv. "Geographic Regions."

Year and Event

1492 Christopher Columbus discovers the Americas on behalf of Ferdinand II of Aragón and Isabella I of Castile, making his first landfall in the Bahamas. [**Bahamas**]

1493–94 Pope Alexander VI issues the bull *Inter Caetera* in 1493, allocating all discoveries in the New World west and south of a line drawn west of the Azores to Castile; this line is moved 270 leagues westward in the Treaty of Tordesillas between Castile and Portugal the following year, thereby inadvertently including Brazil (but not other New World territories) in the Portuguese, rather than the Spanish, sphere of influence. [**Brazil**]

1500 The Portuguese explorer Pedro Álvares Cabral discovers Brazil and makes friendly contact with the local inhabitants; men from his ship build a Christian altar and celebrate the first Mass in Brazil four days after his arrival. [**Brazil**]

1501 The Spanish Franciscan priest Francisco Garcia de Padilla OFM arrives in Santo Domingo as the first bishop in Hispaniola (the name given to the island now comprising Haiti and the Dominican Republic). [**Dominican Republic, Haiti**]

1505 The Spanish Crown begins the formal colonization of Puerto Rico and the forceful evangelization of its inhabitants. [**Puerto Rico**]

1510 The first Dominicans arrive in Hispaniola, followed by a party of 2500 settlers the following year. [**Dominican Republic, Haiti**]

1511 The Dominican priest Antonio de Montesinos preaches against the encomienda (entrusting) system, requiring groups of Indians to render tribute and services to individual adventurers; Montesinos insists that the cruel and unjust treatment of the Indians under this system is tantamount to slavery. [**Dominican Republic, Haiti**]

1512–13 King Frederick II of Aragón and his daughter, Queen Joanna I of Castile, pass the Laws of Burgos protecting the rights of the natives and regulating the settlements in the Americas; however, these regulations were not always observed. [**Dominican Republic, Haiti**]

1512–13 Bartolomé de Las Casas becomes a priest and, as such, the first person to be ordained in the Americas; the following year he develops an increasing opposition to the oppressive encomienda system and thereafter devotes himself to the defense of the Indians. [**Dominican Republic, Haiti**]

1513 The Spanish monarchy orders the mandatory reading of the *Requerimiento* (Requirement): a statement, in Spanish, of Spain's right to conquest) to the natives on a first encounter; this included their obligation to allow preaching to them by Catholic missionaries. [**Dominican Republic, Haiti**]

1513 Vasco Nuñez de Balboa views the Pacific Ocean from the Isthmus of Panama, the first European to do so. [**Panama**]

1523 Following his conquest of the Aztecs in Mexico in 1519–21, Spanish conquistador Hernán Cortés de Monroy y Pizarro Altamirano receives a letter from the Spanish Crown forbidding the oppression of the Indians in the Americas. [**Mexico**]

1524 Twelve Franciscan missionaries arrive in Mexico and begin work, followed by twelve Dominicans the following year. [**Mexico**]

1531 Juan de Zumárraga, the first bishop-elect of Mexico, reports that he had presided over the demolition of five hundred temples and twenty-six thousand idols; this report might have been an attempt to justify his activities as bishop and protector of the Indians, since he had not yet been consecrated. [**Mexico**]

1531 Spanish prelate Diego Alvarez de Osorio serves as the first bishop-elect in Nicaragua, although he is never actually consecrated into this office. [**Nicaragua**]

1531 Visions of Our Lady of Guadalupe, fusing Indian indigenous and European elements, appear to two Nahuatl peasants. [**Mexico**]

1537 Spanish priest Vasco de Quiroga becomes the bishop of Michoacán and sets up a utopian community for the Indians in his diocese. [**Mexico**]

1537 The papal bull *Sublimis Deus* of Pope Paul III defends the rights of the Indians in the Americas, but this decree is ignored by the Spanish conquistadors. [**Latin America and the Caribbean**]

1541 The ambivalence of attitudes to forcible evangelization in Latin America is exemplified by the Spanish conquistador Pedro Gutiérrez de Valdivia, who founds Santiago (later to be Chile's capital), embarks on the conquest of the country, and seeks to compel the conversion of its inhabitants; however, monks accompanying Valdivia also begin a process of peaceful evangelism. [Chile]

1542 The Spanish government passes two laws reforming the whole system of encomienda (which had resulted in the abuse of the native populations); these new laws prohibit their enslavement and grant Native Americans specific protections. [**Latin America and the Caribbean**]

1549 The Portuguese king João III sends the first Jesuit mission to Brazil under the leadership of Father Manuel da Nóbrega. [**Brazil**]

1550–51 The Dominican missionary friar Bartolomé de las Casas, by now the bishop of Chiapas in southern Mexico, debates with the Spanish humanist scholar Juan Ginés de Sepúlveda in Valladolid, Spain, on the issues of colonialism and the welfare of the Indians; Casas follows this up two years later with the publication of a vigorous attack (*A Short Account of the Destruction of the Indies*), detailing the abuses committed by some Spaniards against the Indians. [**Mexico**]

1552 The first Council of Lima decides to withhold the Eucharist from Indian believers, apparently due to concerns over the perceived superficiality of their conversion (although racial prejudice might also have been a factor). [**Peru**]

1555 Nicolas Durand de Villegaignon and Jean de Cointac set up a short-lived French Calvinist Protestant (Huguenot) colony in Rio de Janeiro. [**Brazil**]

1555 The first Council of Mexico recommends that Indians, mulattoes, and mestizos should not be ordained, although the ordination of half-castes and illegitimate sons is later allowed by Pope Gregory XIV in 1576. [**Mexico**]

1570 An extensive network of Catholic bishoprics develops throughout Latin America, linked to the metropolitan sees in Mexico City and Lima. [**Mexico, Peru**]

1578 King Philip II of Spain orders that the Indians in South America be taught the gospel in their own languages, rather than in Spanish; although this became the practice for some decades, a synod of bishops in Buenos Aires in 1655 reversed it, imposing a rule of teaching being conducted only in Spanish. [**Argentina, Chile**]

1587 The Jesuits arrive in Paraguay to begin work, although their mission to the Indians does not start in earnest until 1609. [**Paraguay**]

1599 Peruvian Amerindian Martin de Porres becomes a lay Dominican friar in Lima, and famous for his holiness and care of the sick (including the working of miracles); he dies in 1639 and is canonized in 1962. [**Peru**]

1606 Under orders from the Spanish monarch Felipe III, the governor of Hispaniola, Antonio de Osorio, engages in the forced depopulation of the northern and western parts of the island and the relocation of its inhabitants to Santo Domingo in the southeast; this eviction, known as *las devastationes de Osorio* (the devastations of Osorio), was an attempt to regain Catholic hegemony in the area and to eliminate both Protestantism and free trade (which was seen as piracy). [**Dominican Republic, Haiti**]

1609 The Spanish Crown gives the Jesuits control of Paraguay and of large parts of inland South America, leading to the formation of a creative network of thirty mission colonies or "reductions" (from Spanish *reducciónes*) for the Guaraní Indians. [**Argentina, Brazil, Paraguay, plurinational state of Bolivia, Uruguay**]

1615 Incan convert Felipe Guáman Poma de Ayala sends a handwritten illustrated manuscript to King Philip III of Spain, describing the Indians' plight under the conquistadors and calling for greater justice for them. [**Peru**]

1641 The king of Portugal bars the access of his subjects to the Jesuit settlements in La Guayra to protect their Indian inhabitants from the depredations of colonists and from bands of Portuguese Indian half-castes who are carrying them away into slavery. [**Paraguay**]

1652 The Jesuit orator, writer, and missionary Antonio Vieira argues for the removal of the Indians of Brazil from the jurisdiction of the Portuguese colonial governors to prevent their exploitation. [**Brazil**]

1652 Philip IV of Spain recognizes the abuses of the conquistadors, ordering the end of military operations and the establishing of Christian missions to pacify the Indian population, thus beginning the Catholic missionary network in Venezuela. [**Venezuela**]

1671 Pope Clement X canonizes the ascetic Dominican lay tertiary Isabel Flores de Oliva (known as Saint Rose of Lima) fifty-four years after her death in 1617 at the age of thirty-one; as the first American-born saint, she is venerated as the patron saint of Peru, all South America, the West Indies, and the Philippines. [**Peru**]

1687 Following a powerful 8.4–8.7 magnitude *terremoto* (earthquake) that devastates Lima and other parts of Peru, and kills more than five thousand people, the Jesuits introduce the three-hour service, a prayerful meditation on Jesus's last seven words from the cross, into Catholic liturgies for Good Friday. [**Peru**]

1712 Governor Christopher Codrington bequeaths his two Barbados estates to the Anglican Society for the Propagation of the Gospel in Foreign Parts as the foundation of a college. [**Barbados**]

1799 The French corsair *Grande Buonaparte* brings a captured ship, owned by the London Missionary Society (LMS), to the port of Montevideo; its passengers include thirty Protestant families en route to the South Pacific, and although these missionaries are forced to return to London, they conduct the first known Protestant meetings in Uruguay while anchored in Montevideo. [**Uruguay**]

1804 Jean Jacques Dessalines leads the only successful slave revolt in history, which results in the proclamation of Haiti's independence from France and the permanent abolition of slavery, as well as the massacre of many French colonists and the expulsion of the Catholic clergy; however, Catholicism is restored to favor three years later, becoming the state religion of Haiti. [**Haiti**]

1808–26 After more than a century of tension between the Creoles (American-born Spanish colonists, who sought greater autonomy) and the *peninsulares* (Iberian-born colonists, who were unwaveringly loyal to the Spanish Crown), revolutions begin in the northern viceroyalty of New Granada (Venezuela, Colombia, Ecuador, and Panama) in 1809–10, followed a few months by others in the southern viceroyalty of the Río de la Plata (Argentina, Uruguay, Bolivia, and Paraguay); these revolutions are both political and religious, targeting the dominance of the Spanish Crown and the privileged position of peninsular Spanish priests and clergy, and by 1826 all of Latin America, except for Cuba and Puerto Rico, had gained political independence while remaining loyal to the Catholic Church. [**Latin America and the Caribbean**]

1810 The *Grito de Dolores* (Cry of Dolores), proclaimed by the Creole Catholic priest Miguel Hidalgo y Costilla, marks the beginning of the Mexican

War of Independence, ultimately leading to Mexico's liberation from Spain in 1821. [**Mexico**]

1812–20 After Belize passes from Spanish control in 1798, becoming a British colony in all but name, St. John's Anglican Cathedral is erected in Belize Town, sparking a wave of church building and school constructing throughout the country. [**Belize**]

1816 The interconnection between political and religious elements in the Latin American revolutions is exemplified in the Congress of San Miguel de Tucumán, which passed a declaration of Argentina's autonomy from Spanish rule; eleven of its twenty-nine members are Roman Catholic clerics. [**Argentina, Uruguay, plurinational state of Bolivia**]

1823 The antislavery LMS missionary John Smith dies in prison, apparently of ill health, while awaiting execution after aiding a slave revolt in Demerara; his death reinforces the movement to abolish slavery. [**Guyana**]

1824 The arrival of hundreds of African American Protestant immigrants in the Dominican Republic forces the redefining of religious liberty as their rights to worship are recognized by the state. [**Dominican Republic**]

1826–30s Many newly independent liberal South and Central American governments suppress the Catholic religious orders (dominated by loyalist Spanish priests) throughout Latin America; this reinforces the exodus of many *peninsulares* (priests identified with Spanish interests) after independence. [**Latin America and the Caribbean**]

1836–56 The Peruvian priest and liberal scholar Francisco de Paula González Vigil writes two multivolume defenses of the authority of governments and bishops against what he calls the "pretensions" of the Roman Curia; these works challenge the authoritarianism of the Catholic Church in both the political and religious spheres. [**Peru**]

1838 Britain abolishes slavery in the British Caribbean, which (despite the Slavery Abolition Act of 1833) had continued as a six-year "apprenticeship" system forcing slaves to remain on their plantations. [**Trinidad and Tobago**]

1843–69 Successive constitutions enshrine the privileged position of Catholicism in Ecuador: that of 1843 institutionalizes Roman Catholicism as the official state religion and the 1861 constitution, although guaranteeing freedom of thought, retains its status as the only legal religion in the country; the 1869 constitution extends this by making Roman Catholicism a requirement for citizenship. [**Ecuador**]

1857 As part of the major reforms introduced under its minister of justice, Benito Pablo Juárez Garcia, the new liberal government of Mexico temporarily deposes Catholicism as the state religion. [**Mexico**]

1860–75 Ecuador's president Gabriel Garcia Moreno presides over one of most staunchly Catholic administrations in Latin American history; his reformist dictatorship is based upon the premise that Ecuador's political and economic difficulties would be resolved by the application of moral principles by a powerful leader. [**Ecuador**]

1867 The Mexican government, led by the anti-Catholic reformer Benito Pablo Juárez Garcia, overthrows the Second Mexican Empire, executes Maximilian I (briefly the emperor of Mexico), and re-implements the anti-clerical laws previously passed in the 1850s. [**Mexico**]

1872 The *questão religiosa* (religious question) erupts when a Brazilian bishop attempts to expel Freemasons from Catholic lay fraternities; this challenges both the prime minister, Baron Rio Branco (who is himself a Masonic Grand Master), and the Brazilian emperor Pedro II, who had previously forbidden the promulgation within Brazil of a papal decree banning Catholic participation in Masonic associations. [**Brazil**]

1889–91 The fall of the Brazilian Empire and the deposition of Emperor Pedro II in 1889 brings about a republican regime and, two years later, the enactment of a constitution separating church and state, removing the status of official religion and disestablishing the Catholic Church; however, although the country has been secular ever since, the Catholic Church remained influential until the 1970s, and a strong Catholic, evangelical, and Pentecostal constituency continues among the Brazilian population. [**Brazil**]

1896 Brazilian federal troops suppress the "Born Jesus" millennialist movement, led by miracle worker Antônio Conselheiro, in a bloodbath at his community of Canudos; more than fifteen thousand people lose their lives in the massacre. [**Brazil**]

1898 Spain's defeat in the Spanish-American war ends its colonial rule in Puerto Rico and the alliance between the Catholic Church and the government; the ceding of the island to the US in the Treaty of Paris in the same year leads to numerous American missionary agencies beginning cooperative and systematic Protestant church planting. [**Puerto Rico**]

1899 The Colegio Pio Latino-Americano Pontificio (Pontifical Latin American College) hosts the Plenary Council for Latin America at the Vatican, calling for reforms in the Latin American Catholic Church; this is the first major council of Latin American bishops presided over by their own archbishops. [**Latin America and the Caribbean**]

1909 Pentecostalism emerges in the Valparaiso congregation of Methodist Episcopal missionaries Willis and Minnie Hoover through the influence of Indian Pentecostal pioneer Pandita Ramabai's book *The Baptism of the Holy Ghost and Fire*; the Hoovers are also influential in fostering the beginnings of Pentecostalism in Argentina later that year. [**Argentina, Chile**]

1910 The quasi-religious Mexican Revolution under Emiliano Zapata and others leads to the end of a thirty-year dictatorship and to the establishment of a constitutional republic, but this revolution also contributes to further repression of the Catholic Church in Mexico. [**Mexico**]

1910s Republican anticlericalism in Cuba and Uruguay leads to the disestablishment of the Catholic Church in these countries. [**Cuba, Uruguay**]

1917 The British colonial government passes the Shouters Prohibition Ordinance prohibiting the charismatic practices of the Spiritual Shouter Baptists; the noise generated by these Shouter practices (which include shouting, clapping, loud singing, and the ringing of bells) were held to disturb the peace, being described by the then attorney general, Sir Henry Gollam, as an "unmitigated nuisance."[3] [**Trinidad and Tobago**]

1921 A missionary conference in Chichicastenango creates the Protestant Indian League to foster indigenous-language evangelism in Guatemala and Southern Mexico, and to translate the Bible into Kaqchikel and Quiché; this league would become a precursor of well-known missionary translation agencies such as Wycliffe Bible Translators and the Summer Institute of Linguistics. [**Guatemala**]

1923–24 Cardinal Juan Bautista Benlloch y Vivó, archbishop of Burgos, tours South America urging Hispanidad (Spanishness), i.e., the rooting of Latin American identity in Spanish Catholicism. [**Latin America and the Caribbean**]

1925 Most Chilean Catholics accept the State's decision to disestablish the Catholic Church under the constitution of 1925. [**Chile**]

---

3. *Trinidad and Tobago Guardian*, "Ring the Bell," para. 7.

1929 Following the end of the Cristero War (1927–29), the incoming president, Emilio Cándido Portes Gil, lifts the restrictions against the Mexican church, although tensions between church and state continue until the 1940s. [**Mexico**]

1941 The Catholic Church, with the support of President Élie Lescot, launches Operation Nettoyage (Operation Cleanup) to purge vodou (voodoo) from Haiti; however, vodou survives and receives recognition as an official religion in 2003. [**Haiti**]

1946–64 An intense Liberal-Conservative political feud results in more than two hundred thousand deaths over an eighteen-year period known as La Violencia (the Violence); because Protestants are identified with the Liberals, they bear the brunt of this violence and cruelty, although anti-Catholic riots also erupt following the assassination of a Liberal leader. [**Colombia**]

1955 A conference of Roman Catholic bishops in Latin America, CELAM I, sets up a general secretariat with the approval of the Vatican. [**Colombia**]

1956 Five young evangelical American missionaries (Jim Elliot, Pete Fleming, Ed McCully, Nate Saint, and Roger Youderian) are killed on the Curaray River while attempting to contact an isolated Stone Age tribe, the Aucas; Elisabeth Elliot's accounts of their mission work and martyrdoms helps to inspire a worldwide missionary movement, embodied in groups such as Youth with a Mission (YWAM), over the next two decades. [**Ecuador**]

1959 Cuba falls to communist revolutionaries led by Fidel Castro, becoming the first communist dictatorship in Latin America; the party's insistence on Marxist-Leninist principles (including atheism), together with the rejection of communism by the Cuban Catholic hierarchy, leads to discrimination and the severe restriction of religious practice in Cuba, although there is no overtly systematic persecution of Christians. [**Cuba**]

1961 Uruguayan Jesuit theologian Juan Luis Segundo begins teaching his *cursos de complementación Cristiana* (courses of Christian complementation) in Montevideo, analyzing political, social, and economic problems in the light of the Catholic faith. [**Uruguay**]

1964–85 Hélder Camara, the archbishop of Olinda and Recife, speaks out against the Brazilian government as part of a clergy critique of the military regimes for neglecting justice and abusing human rights; in response, the government dispatches several assassination squads attempting to silence him. [**Brazil**]

1966 Christian base communities (i.e., relatively autonomous grassroots Christian lay communities, based on worship and study of the Bible, as well as on social and political engagement) are formed in several locations in Nicaragua and elsewhere; like liberation theology, these communities reflect the volatility and renewal that has characterized Latin American Catholicism since the early 1960s. [**Nicaragua**]

1966 Socialist Catholic priest Camilo Torres Restrepo leaves his academic post to join the revolutionary Ejército de Liberación Nacional (National Liberation Army) as a Marxist-Christian chaplain but dies in his first guerrilla skirmish. [**Colombia**]

1968 A crucial meeting of Catholic bishops in Medellin (CELAM II), opened by Pope Paul VI during the first-ever papal visit to Latin America, declares that the church will stand on the side of the poor. [**Colombia**]

1970 Marxist politician Salvador Guillermo Allende Gossens becomes the democratically elected president of Chile, but an authoritarian military coup d'état under General Augusto Pinochet overthrows him three years later; Pinochet's régime then engages in the widespread imprisonment, torture, and killing of opponents, which paradoxically fosters the growth of Evangelicalism throughout the country both directly and indirectly. [**Chile**]

1971 Peruvian Dominican priest and theologian Gustavo Gutiérrez publishes his foundational text *Teología de la liberación (A Theology of Liberation)*, calling for Christian solidarity with the poor and oppressed, and emphasizing the duty of churches to aid them through civic and political involvement, and by changing existing institutions to promote social justice. [**Peru**]

1974–84 The Argentine military conducts the Dirty War of state terrorism to suppress a left-wing insurgency and sets up a repressive dictatorship; despite many Christians (including Catholic priests) being tortured and killed, the Catholic hierarchy, through its support for anachronistic social systems, fails to immediately condemn this violence. [**Argentina**]

1978 More than nine hundred members of the California-based Peoples' Temple cult commit suicide at the bidding of their charismatic leader, Jim Jones, at the utopian Jonestown agricultural commune in Guyana. [**Guyana**]

1979 Pope John Paul II condemns the excesses of liberation theology in his address to the third general conference of the Latin American Catholic bishops (CELAM III), held at Puebla, Mexico. [**Mexico**]

1979–90 The Sandinista uprising leads to the formation of a Marxist regime in Nicaragua (despite the attempts of the American CIA-backed Contras militia to overthrow this); the uprising provides the context and the impetus for the liberationist Nicaraguan Church of the People. [**Nicaragua**]

1980 An assassin shoots Óscar Arnulfo Romero y Galdámez, the archbishop of San Salvador and a zealous campaigner for social justice, at the altar during his celebration of Mass in a hospital chapel. [**El Salvador**]

1980 Four female American Catholic members of a humanitarian aid mission (Maryknoll Sisters Maura Clarke and Ita Ford, Ursuline nun Dorothy Kazel, and lay missionary Jean Donovan) are apprehended, beaten, raped, and murdered by five members of the El Salvador National Guard; public outrage forces the Salvadorian regime to investigate the murders. [**El Salvador**]

1984 Pope John Paul II takes issue with liberation theology by approving Cardinal Ratzinger's "Instruction on Certain Aspects of the 'Theology of Liberation'" and reiterates his opposition during his papal visit to Lima the following year. [**Peru**]

1985 An agreement is signed between the Haitian state and leaders of the Protestant denominations, recognizing the legality of Protestant churches, which up to this time had been only de facto entities with no legal standing. [**Haiti**]

1986 El Salvador's Christian Democrat administration, under CIA-backed José Napoleón Duarte, declares its reluctance to accept earthquake relief from Catholic agencies, due to the clergy's alleged support of the leftist insurgency over the past six years; some of Duarte's generals also refuse to permit the Red Cross to deliver humanitarian aid to civilian victims of El Salvador's civil war. [**El Salvador**]

1989 The Spanish Jesuit liberation theologian Jon Sobrino narrowly escapes a military assassination squad that kills six of his fellow Jesuits for their opposition to the El Salvadorian Civil War. [**El Salvador**]

1991 A new Colombian constitution is promulgated but is opposed by the Catholic Church because it disestablishes state (i.e., Catholic) religion and guarantees freedom of religion. [**Colombia**]

1992 The Paraguayan constitution recognizes the pervasiveness of Guaraní (the indigenous language spoken by most of the population), giving it equal footing with Spanish as a national language; its survival since the Spanish conquests of the sixteenth century is partly due to the fostering of the language in the Jesuit mission communities (*reducciónes* [reductions]), which had safeguarded the Guaraní Indians from colonial oppression and enslavement. [**Paraguay**]

2005–7 Tensions develop between the Marxist government of Hugo Chavez and some sections of the Christian church, with Chavez criticizing bishops who have opposed him and accusing New Tribes missionaries of espionage; meanwhile, American televangelist Pat Robertson suggests assassinating Chavez. [**Venezuela**]

2013 The papal conclave, convened to elect a successor to Pope Benedict XVI following his resignation (the first such papal renunciation since that of Gregory XII in 1415), elects the Argentinian cardinal Jorge Mario Bergoglio of Buenos Aires as Pope Francis I; Francis's accession also creates numerous firsts, since he is the first Latin American and Southern Hemisphere pope, the first Jesuit pope, and the first non-European pope since the Syrian Pope Gregory III in 741. [**Argentina**]

Bibliography

Cleary, Edward J. "The Transformation of Latin American Christianity, c. 1950–2000." In *World Christianities c. 1914–c. 2000*, edited by Hugh McLeod, 366–84. Cambridge History of Christianity 9. Cambridge: Cambridge University Press, 2006.

Hill, Jonathan, ed. *Zondervan Handbook to the History of Christianity*. Oxford: Lion, 2006.

Jenkins, Philip. *The Next Christendom: The Coming of Global Christianity*. 3rd ed. Future of Christianity Trilogy. Oxford: Oxford University Press, 2011.

Johnson, Todd M. "Christianity in Global Context: Trends and Statistics." Pew Research, n.d. https://www.pewresearch.org/wp-content/uploads/sites/7/2005/05/051805-global-christianity.pdf.

Korschorke, Klaus, et al., eds. *A History of Christianity in Asia, Africa, and Latin America, 1450–1990: A Documentary Sourcebook*. Grand Rapids: Eerdmans, 2007.

Lamport, Mark A., ed. *Encyclopedia of Christianity in the Global South*. 2 vols. Blue Ridge Summit, PA: Rowman & Littlefield, 2018.

Marty, Martin E. *The Christian World: A Global History*. New York: Modern Library, 2009.

———. "Introduction: Religion in America 1935–1985." In *Altered Landscapes: Christianity in America 1935–1985*, edited by David W. Lotz et al., 1–16. Grand Rapids: Eerdmans, 1989.

McManners, John, ed. *The Oxford Illustrated History of Christianity*. Oxford: Oxford University Press, 1995.

Neill, Stephen. *A History of Christian Missions*. Edited by Owen Chadwick. 2nd ed. Pelican History of the Church 6. Harmondsworth, UK: Penguin, 1986.

Ratzinger, Joseph. "Instruction on Certain Aspects of the 'Theology of Liberation.'" Vatican, Aug. 6, 1984. https://www.vatican.va/roman_curia/congregations/cfaith/documents/rc_con_cfaith_doc_19840806_theology-liberation_en.html.

Roberts, J. M. *The Penguin History of the World*. Rev. ed. Harmondsworth, UK: Penguin, 1995.

Salinas, J. Daniel. "The In-Roads of Evangelical Theology and the Evangelical Movement in Latin American Spanish-Speaking Countries." *Evangelical Review of Theology* 34 (2010) 307–12.

Trinidad and Tobago Guardian. "Ring the Bell of Freedom." *Trinidad and Tobago Guardian*, Mar. 30, 2020. https://www.guardian.co.tt/opinion/ring-the-bell-of-freedom-6.2.1089093.2de1dc6245.

United Nations Statistics Division. "Methodology: Standard Country or Area Codes for Statistical Use (M49)." United Nations Statistics Division, n.d. http://unstats.un.org/unsd/methodology/m49/.

Indes of Names and Subjects

Abya Yala, 167, 170, 174, 184, 204, 205, 206, 209, 214
Ad Gentes decree, 169
Adjuntas, 189
Adorno, Wilfredo Estrada, 197, 198, 200
Africa, 220, 208
African Americans, 195
African Christology, 134–35
African Methodist Episcopal Church, 82
African, 188
  descendant, 208, 210
  matrix cultures, 211
  peoples, 211
Africanized theologies, 202
Africans, 205
Afro-Brazilian, 193, 194
Afro-Caribbean, 190
Afro-Cuban, 193
Afro-diasporic peoples, 218
Afro-Ecuadorian peoples, 172
agglutinating dimension, 95
Aguas, Manuel, 82
Aguilar, Mario, 151, 155
Aguilera, Sanchez, 10–11
Alamán, Lucas, 75
Alberdi, Juan Bautista, 83
Albert, Bruce, 176
Alcántara, Rojas, 8, 10
Alexander, Pope, 57
Alianza Bolivariana para los Pueblos de Nuestra América, 98
Almeida, Milene, 212
Althusserian, 99
Álvares, Domingos, 54–55

Alvarez, David, Monsenor, 198
Amazon Synod, 153, 161
Amazon, 175, 181, 182
"Amazon: New Paths for the Church and for an Integral Ecology, The," 153
Amazonia/Amazonian, 176, 181, 182
Amazonian Center for Anthropology and Practical Application, 170
Ambato, Ecuador, 168, 170
America, 173, 209. *See also United States.*
  Americas, 169, 173
American Bible Society, 85, 86
American East Coast, 225
Americas Expressway, 198
Américas, original inhabitants of, 218
amulets, 55
Anahuac (Close to water), 204
Andean, 167, 181, 184
Anderson, Arthur J. O., 8
Anglo-Americans, 226
Angola, 224
annexationists, 88
Anton, Ferdinand, 40
Antonil, Father André João, 207
Anzaldúa, Gloria, 162
Applebee, Rosalee Mills, 217, 221, 223, 224
aprismo (student movement), 98
Arce Dr., 43–44
Archicofradia del Santísimo Sacramento y Caridad, 25

248 INDES OF NAMES AND SUBJECTS

Arte y vocabulario mexicano
(A Nahuatl vocabulary), 6
Asia, 220
Asian Americans, 195
Asian, 192
Assemblies of God, 193, 212, 213
    in Brazil, 217
assimilationists, 88
Atkinson, Maria, 189
Atlantic Forest, 175
Atzaqualco Pictorial Catechism, 11
Aymara, 184
Azorean migrants to the US, 225
Azores, 224
Aztec, 180, 204, 218
Azusa Street Revival of 1906, 192–93

Bac, Lopez, 184
Baptist, 216, 217, 223, 224, 225, 228
    Brazilian, 216, 228
    churches in Latin America, 228
    faith, 224
    missionary, 217, 223
    missions, 224
    Southern, 224
Barranquita, 189
Barreda, Gabino, 72
Barreto, Raimundo, 211
Bastian, Jean-Pierre, 87
Baudot, George, 8
Bautista, Juan, Friar, 6
Becoming Sinners, 123
Belgium, 223
benzedeira, 123
Berg, Daniel, 217
Besson, Pablo, 223
Betto, Frei, 105
Bible salespeople, 223
Bible, 187, 190, 191, 203, 211
"Black Holocaust," 126, 134
black liberation theology (Afro-Brazilian theology), 126
"Black Skin, White Masks," 128
Bloch, Maurice, 121
Boff, Leonardo, 105, 155
Bolívar, Simón, 73–74
Bolivia, 168, 169, 175, 182, 223, 224

Bolivian immigrants in Brazil, 221
Bourbon Reforms, 66–68
Braga, Erasmo, 79
Brazil, 175, 181, 182, 194, 207, 208, 211, 212, 215, 217, 221, 223, 224, 225, 226, 228
    immigrants in, 221
    land structure, 212
    northeastern, 212
    Pernambuco, 212
    Venezuelan migration to, 221
Brazilian Baptist, 216, 228
    Brazilian Baptist Convention (BBC), 224, 225
Brazilian, 217
    churches in the US, 227; e
    evangelicals, 225, 227
    immigrants in the US, 225, 226
    parishioners, 225
    pentecostalism, 194
Brazilians, 224
British and Foreign Bible Society, 85, 86
Bronx, New York, 195
Bruckmann, Mónica, 97
Bujo, Bénézet, 139
Burkhart, Louise M., 3–4, 8–9, 11–13

cabildos, 53, 57
Cabral, Pedro Alvares, 112
Caetano da Silva Coutinho, Dom José, 81
Caguas, Puerto Rico, 195
California, 225
Calvin College, 190
Câmara, Helder, 153
Canada, 224
Candomblé, 113–20, 123, 136
    abiã, 120–22
    fundamento, 116–17
    mae de santo, 113
    Olorum, 114
    orixás, 114–15, 116, 118–19, 120, 136
    pai de santo, 113
    terreiros, 114, 116, 120–22, 133, 160

INDEX OF NAMES AND SUBJECTS 249

Candomble, 194
Cantares mexicano, 46–47
Caracas, Venezuela, 168
Cardoso, Rodrigo, 213
Caribbean, 168, 188
  immigrants, 221
  immigrants in Europe, 222
  migrants, 221, 222, 223
Carrasco, Davíd, 41
Carta atenagórica, 41
Cartesian binary distinction, 210
Catholic Church, 171, 206, 227
  missions to Latin America, 220
Catholic/Catholicism, 167, 169, 173, 189, 190, 194, 197, 199, 219
Caucasian, 195
CEAMA, 176, 181, 182, 183
Ceará, 208
CELAM, 168, 169, 181
Center for Preventive Action of the Council of Foreign Relations.146
Central American Mission, 89
Cerrado, 175
Césaire, Aimé, 128
Chamorro, Graciela, 160, 162, 176
Charles IV, King, 67
Charupá, Roberto Tomichá, 161, 16
Charupa, Roberto Tomicha, 168, 169, 170, 171, 183
Chiapas, Mexico, 170, 171, 171, 173
Chicago awakening, 217
Chile, 223, 224
Chipana, Sofia, 184
Christ, 169, 184, 191, 195
  "the Ancestor," 139
Christensen, Mark, 13
Christian, 219, 225
  contemporary music, 218
  God, 209, 213
  faith, 209
  identifying as, 219
  mission in Abya Yala, 206
  women, 211
Christianism, hegemonic, 211
Christianity, 173, 174, 175, 176, 182, 184, 187, 188, 189, 192, 194, 198, 202, 203, 209, 216, 217, 218, 219, 220, 227
  approval of slavery, 207
  colonial, 202, 211
  from Latin America, 217
  in Abya Yala, 204
  in Latin America, 202, 211, 216, 217, 219
  mission, 206
  spread of, 223
  world, 202
Christology, 170
  of the ancestors, 137
Church of God, Cleveland Tennessee, 197
Cipactli, 178, 179
Clamor a Dios, 200
Coamo, 189
Colegio de las Niñas de Nuestra Señora de la Caridad, 25, 27–28, 30–31
Colombian
  colonial Christianity, 211
  immigrants in Brazil, 221
  Venezuelan migration to, 221
colporteurs (itinerant booksellers), 84–85
Columbia/Columbian, 175, 182, 193
Comisión Económica para América Latina y el Caribe, 99
Confederate immigration, 83
Confederates, US southern, 223, 224, 228
CONFENIAE, 172
configurations of the religious, 97
confraternities, 59–60
Congregation for the Doctrine of the Faith, 169
CONPLEI, 175
convivencia, 161
Cook, Guillermo, 158
Cordoba, Argentina, 98
Cormier, Lee, 148
Corral, Dom Victor, 173
Costa Rica, 223
Costa, Elisabeth, 213
COVID pandemics, 212
Creoles, 66–67, 69, 76

Cuba, 199
Cubans, 221
Cultura e opulência do Brasil, 207
Culture and opulence in Brazil, 207
Cunha, Welthon R., 117, 118

da Costa, Manoel Bento, 208
Day Star, 180
de Alba, Klor, 4
de Alva, Bartolome, 12
de Aquino, Fabian, 10
de Aquino, Nahua Fabian, 13
de Bingen, Hildegard, 35
de Casterón y Trigo, Doña Ana Margarita, 26
de Escalona, Alonso, 10
de ganho, 115
de Gaona, Juan Father, 6
de Guadalupem Sor Maria *see* de Pevedilla, Doña María
de Jesús, Úrsula, 59
de la Cruz, Abelardo, 8
de la Cruz, Sor Filotea, 42
de la Fuente, Agustín, 6
de Las Casas, Bartolomeu, 130
de Mier, Servando Teresa, 69
de Molina, Alonso, Friar, 6
de Pevedilla, Doña María, 30–31
de Rivas, Hernando, 6
de Sahagún, Bernardino, Friar, 10–11, 41
de San Alberto, Juana Esperanza, 59
de San Martín, José, 73–74
de San Pedro, Catarina, 30
de Sandoval, Alonso, 57
de Santa Cruz, Manuel Fernández, 41
de Santillana, Doña Isabel Ramírez, 38
de Uría, Don Nicolás, 26
de Vega, Ana, 54–55
de Vetancurt, Agustín, Friar, 13
de-Africanizing, 206
decolonial/decolonization, 145, 153, 157–58, 162
del Castillo, Bernal Díaz, 41
Delfina, 208

Department of Indigenous Pastoral, 172
Diálogos de la paz y tranquilidad del alma (Dialogues of peace and tranquility for the soul), 6
Díaz, Porfirio, 75–76
Diocese of San Cristobal de las Casas, 171
Dion, Michel, 119–20
"*Discourse on Colonialism*," 128
Dominican, 193
Dos Santos, Theotonio, 97
Down These Mean Streets, 195
Dussel, Entrique, 158

Ecclesial Conference of the Amazon, 181
Ecofeminism, 36, 42
economic nationalism, 74
Ecuador, 221, 224
Ecuador/Ecuadorian, 168, 170, 171, 172, 173, 175, 182, 184
Ecuadorian Episcopal Conference, 170, 172
Ecularization, 70
Ecumenical Association of Third World Theologians, 153, 170
El Colegio de Santa Cruz de Tlatelolco (The Holy Cross of Tlatelolco College), 6–7
El divino Narciso, 40
El Partido Independentista de Puerto Rico, 197
El primero sueño, 36–38, 40
El rubio de Galilea, 192
El sueño, 46–48
Ellacuría, Ignacio, 103
encosto, 123
Enlightenment, 193
Episcopal Church, 198
epistemic democratization, 157
epistemic genocide, 158
Espejo divino (Divine mirror), 6
Estrada, 198
Europe, 217, 219, 220, 221, 222, 227, 228
    Latin American migrants to, 221

INDES OF NAMES AND SUBJECTS   251

migrant groups in, 216
missions to Latin America, 220
Pentecostal, 189
European!, 206
European, 204, 205, 206
   colonialism, 218
   colonization in Latin America, 218–19
   cultural system, 206
   economic expansion projects, 204
   immigrants, 225
   migrants, 217
   missionaries, 219
   project, 209
   traveler, 203
Evangelicals/Evangelicalism, 197, 199
Exu Tranca-Rua (demon), 194
EZLN, 173

faith missions, 89
Falling Sky (The), 176
Fanon, Frantz, 128–29, 131–33
Fasholé-Luke, Edward, 138
Fenn, Richard, 115
Ferdinand VII, 67, 69, 71
Ferreira, Fábio Alves, 212
Ferriera, Luiza, 212
Fifth Conference in Aparecida, 169
Final Document of the Special Synod for the Amazon, 177, 182
Fletcher, James, 86
Frade district, 208
France, 222, 224
Francescon, Luigi, 217
Francis, Pope, 153–54, 161–62
Francisco de Vitória, 130
Francisco del Paso y Troncoso, 12
Françoise d'Eaubonne, 36
Fray Bartolome de Las Casas, 171, 173
Frederiks, M. D., 134
Freitas, Lucineia, 211, 212
French Guiana, 182
French-speaking colonists, 223

Gaillemin, 11
Galarza, 11
Galilee, 192
Gallicanism, 81–82
Garcia, Porfirio Mendez, 178
Gasda, Élio, 102
Gebara, Ivone, 213
Gebara, Ivone, 37, 155, 157, 162
General History of the Things of New Spain, 41
German Baptist settlers, 223
Germany, 222, 223
Gervin family, 223
Ginsburg, Solomon, 223
Global Christianity, ix;
   entanglement in, xiv
God, 170, 171, 175, 177, 179, 180, 187, 190, 191, 193, 194, 195, 196, 198, 199, 209, 212, 213
   kingdom of, 207
   of latifundia, 213
   Son of, 207
God's promise, fulfillment of, 212
Goldstein, Warren, 96
González, Colom, 72
González, Justo, 151
Gonzalez, Roberto, Monsenor, 198
Gorski, Juan F., 167, 168, 173, 174
Granberg-Michaelson, Wesley, 150
Grosfoguel, Ramón, 127, 156
Guadalupe, 199
Guarani Group, 176
Guatemala/Guatemalan, 168, 184, 200
Guerra de dioses: Religión y política en América Latina, 101
Gutiérrez, Gustavo, 155, 168
Guyana, 175, 182

Habermas, Jürgen, 100
Haitian, immigrants in Brazil, 221
Harding, Rachel E., 115
Hawaii, 189
Hermosillo, 189
heteropatriarchy/cisheteropatriarchy, 156
Hinkelammert, Franz, 154
Hobsbawn, Eric, 149

Hollenweger, Walter, 190
Holy Spirit, 189, 191, 193, 194, 196, 199
Holy Trinity, 194
homo africanus, 13
Huastecs, 180
Huehuetlatolli, 10
Huitzilopochtli, 180
Hurricane Wind, 178

Iberian Portuguese, 225
idealogical weapons of death, 154
Igreja Batista da Lagoinha, 218
Igreja Universal do Reino de Deus, 113, 122–24
immigration (Brazil), 80–84
Inca, 204, 218
Indian(s), 203, 205, 206, 207, 208
Indigenous Peoples of the Amazon, 181
Inequality Kills, 147
International Institute for Democracy and Electoral Assistance, 170
International Missionary Council, 79
intrinsic religious-theological potency, 104
Iquitos, Peru, 168
irmandades, 159
Irvin, Dale T., 150, 151–52, 162
Isla Nena de Vieques, 197
Italian immigrants, 217
Iztaccíhuatl, 39

Jansenism, 81–82
Jennings, Willie, 204
Jesuit(s), 207, 57, 70–71
Jesus Christ, 171, 191, 194, 195, 199, 207
Johnson, Paul C., 114, 116–17, 120, 121
José Caetano da Silva Coutinho, 81
Juan de Mijangos, 6
Juana Diaz, 189
Judeo-Christian, 197

Kabasélé, François, 138

Kalley, Robert, 86
Kardecism, 117
Kariri, 183
Kinnamon, Michael, 145, 146
Kopenawa, Yanomami Davi, 176
Kuna, 174, 204

L'Espinay, François de, 136
la Caridad *see* Colegio de las Niñas de Nuestra Señora de la Caridad
la Cruz. Juana Inés de, Sister, 34–35
La Ecuador Runakunapak Rikcharimui, 171
La respuesta, 36, 39–43
La vision de los vencidos, 4
Lancasterian method, 85
landless movement (MST—Brazil), 102, 106
Landless Workers Movement (LWM), in Brazil, 203
Lange, Ernst, 145
Las Casa, Bartolomé de, 148
Latin America, 202, 204, 204, 209, 216, 218, 219, 220, 224, 227; Baptist churches in, 223, 228; Christianity in, 202, 211, 216, 217; immigrants, 217; interregional migrants, 228
Latin America/American, 168, 169, 172, 187, 188, 189, 190, 191, 193, 197, 199
Latin American and Caribbean Confederation of Religious Men and Women, 181
Latin American and Caribbean Secretariat of Caritas, 181
Latin American Council of Churches, 170
Latin American Ecumenical Coordinating Group for Indigenous Pastoral Care, 170
Latin American
 Baptists, 223
 contemporary Christian music, 218

countries, 220
immigrants, 222
immigrants in the US and Europe, 221
migrant religiosity, 221
migrants, 216
Pentecostalism, 187, 190, 191, 193, 194, 195, 196, 200
women, 211
Latin Americans, 217, 219, 222
Latinas, 195
Latines, US-born, 222
Latinx, 192
Leeming, 10
Léon Hippolyte Denizart Rivail, (Allen Kardec), 117
Leonidas, Dom, 173
León-Portilla, Miguel, 4, 41, 45
Levitt, Peggy, 220
Liberation theology, 101–3
Life and Work movement, 146
limitations of political-state institutionality, 95–96
Llacta michic, 172
Lockhart, James, 8
Lopez, Eleazar, 174, 175, 177, 178, 179, 180, 185
Lord of men, 207
Lord! Please Make Me Cry, 195
Lord, 191, 198
Loving Mystery, 135
Löwy, Michael, 101
Lugo, Juan, 189
Lutheran, 83, 198
LWM (Landless Workers Movement), 203, 211, 212, 213
women, 211, 212

Maafa (Black Holocaust), 134
MacDonald, W. D. T., 223
Mackin, Robert, 102
Macumba, 194
Maduro, Otto, 101
Magna Carta, 172
Malê uprising, 60
Malves, Júlio, 223
Manaus I, Brazil, 168

Manichean opposition, 106
Manoel da Conceição, José, 82
Manso, Laura Vicuna Pereira, Sister, 183
Manuscrito 1492 (Manuscript 1492), 10
Marcos, Sylvia, 37
Maria (demon), 194
Maria Rosa Mistica, 207
María, Madre Francisca, 26
Marín-Guadarrama, 10
Mary, 207
Mashau, D. T., 134
Mayan Alter, 184
Mayan,(s) 173, 179, 184, 218
Mbembe, Achille, 128, 129
Mbiti, John S., 138
McNair, Stuart, 89
Medellin, Colombia, 168
Medina, Alfredo Ferro, 181
Medina, Martin, 41
Melgar, Columbia, 168, 169, 170
Melia, Bartomeu, 176
Mendez, Juan Antonio Vera, Bishop, 198
Mennonite, 82
Mercosur, 98
Mesoamerica/Mesoamerican, 167, 177, 178, 179, 180, 185
Methodist Church of Puerto Rico, 198
Methodists, 225
Mexica, 204
Mexican/Mexico, 168, 169, 171, 173, 184, 189, 190, 193, 199, 223, 228
  Declaration of Independence, 73
  Pentecostalism, 189
  Revolution (1910–21), 7, 75, 98
Mexican-American War (1846–48), 74
Meyer, Jean, 71
Micah, 198
Mies, Maria, 209
Mignolo, Walter, 148, 157, 162
misanthropic skepticism, 130
Missionary Conference of Jerusalem (1928), 79

Missionary Council for Indigenous
    Peoples, 170
missionary enterprise, 84
Mitologia dos orixás, 115
Monroe, James, 74
Montoya, Dávila, 10
Monzon, Christina, 13
Morales, Evo, 100
Mother Earth, 178, 182, 183, 184
Mother Nature, 210
Mother Stella de Oxossi, 115, 117
Mother, 207
Mott, Efrain Rios, 200
Mozambique, 224
Mura, Victor, 223
Muriel, Josephina, 23
Mystical Rose Mary, 207
mysticism as nourishment, 105–6

Nabokov, Isabelle, 118, 119, 121, 124
Nabokov, Peter, 121
Nagualism, 178
Nahuatl Christianity in Performance,
    12
Napoleon Bonaparte, 66
Nascimento, Abdias do, 158
National American Free Trade
    Agreement, 173
National Center for Assistance to
    Indigenous Missions, 170
National Indigenous Pastoral Plan,
    170
Native Americans, 195
natural rights, 73
Neocolonialism, 74
Nepantlism, 4
Netherlands, 222
New England, 225
New Fire, 178
New Life For Girls, 195
new workers, 98
Nicaraguan Sandinismo, 98
Nogales, 189
non-Europeans, 205
North American, 189
Nyamiti, Charles, 138, 140
Nyctímene, 47

Obregon, 189
Ogun, 56
oikoumene, 147, 148, 199
Oosterbaan, 216
Organization of American States, 99
Orocovis, 189
Orokaiva children's initiation, 121
otros saberes, 160
Our Father, 184
Our Grandfather, 184
Our Grandmother, 184
Our Lady of Charity, 199
Our Lady of Providence, 199
Our Mother, 184
Oxfam, 147

Pachakutik Plurinational Movement
    172
Panama, 169, 223
    Canal, 74
Pan-Amazonian Ecclesial Network,
    181
Paraguay, 169, 175, 223, 224
Parker, Cristián, 101
Partido Nuevo Progresista, 197
partus sequitur ventrem doctrine,
    207, 208
Pastoral Land Commission, 102,
    170
Patterson, Orlando, 111–12, 115–16,
    131
Paul III, Pope 206
Paz, Octavio, 46
Pellicer, Dora, 13
Pentecost/Pentecostal, 169, 175, 187,
    189, 190, 192, 193, 194, 195,
    196, 197, 198, 199, 211, 212,
    217, 227, 187, 192, 217
Penzotti, Francisco, 85–86
performance of political identities,
    95–96
Pernambuco, 212
Peronism, 98
Peru, 168, 175, 182, 224
Peruvian Institute of Arbitration,
    170
Phelan, John Leddy, 8

INDEX OF NAMES AND SUBJECTS 255

Pindorama (Land of palm trees), 204
Pires, José Maria, 133
Plymouth Brethren, 89
Ponce, 189, 199
Portugal, 188, 222, 224
Portuguese
  colonizers, 219
  crown, 206
  Iberian, 225
  language, 222
  migrants to the US, 225
  speakers, 222
power relation, 111
Prada, Manuel González, 72
Prandi, Reginaldo, 115
prefigurative dimension, 97
Presbyterians, 225
primal religion, 187, 190
Proano, Don Leonidas Bishop, 170, 171, 172, 173, 183
Protective Hill, 178
Protestant/ Protestantism, 71, 190, 219, 224, 227
  missions to Latin America, 220
Proto-Ancestor, 139
Psalmodia christiana, 8
Puerto Rico/Rican, 189, 192, 193, 194, 195, 196, 197, 198, 199
Pui-lan, Kwok, 106–7

Querida Amazonia, 153–54, 161, 162
Quetzalcoatl, 179, 180, 185
Quijano, Anibal, 130, 205, 206, 209

Rashke, Jorge, 200
Recogimiento de San Miguel de Belém, 26, 28
recogimiento, 20–31; de mujeres, 27
Reed, Jean-Pierre, 96
Reekie, Archibald, 223
Reis, João José, 83
"Religion of the Orixás—Another Word of the One God?, The," 136
religious racism, 130
Ress, Judy, 36–37

restoration (Catholic) program, 91
Rhodesia, 224
Ricard, Robert, 3
Rieger, Joerg, 106
Rio de la Plata, 90
Riobamba, Ecuador, 170, 172, 183
Rituals of Blood, 115–16
Rivera, Maria de Los Ángeles, 189
Robbins, Joel, 123
Roberto Clemente Sports Complex, 198
Roca, Suarez, 8
Rodriguez, Cookie, 195
Rodriguez, David Sanes, 197
Roman Catholic/Catholicism, 187, 188, 189, 194, 198, 199, 200, 221
Rome, 82, 91, 173
Rosello, Pedro, 197, 198
Ruiz, Dom Samuel, Bishop, 171, 173, 174, 183
Russia, 223
Russian Orthodox Church, 146

San Cristóbal de Las Casas in Chiapas, 183
San Juan, 199
Santa Ana, 189
Santo Domingo, 169, 174
Sao Cristovao, 173
Sao Lourenco da Mata, 212
São Paulo, 82, 83
Satan, 194
Savior, Savior, Hold My Hand, 195
Schultze, Quentin J., 190
Schwaller, 13
Scriptures, 191
Second Vatican Council, 168, 169
Sell, 12
Sepulveda, Juan Ginés de, 130
Sermones en mexicano (Sermons in Mexicano), 10
Shango, 194
Shaul, M. Richard, 155
SICNIE, 171, 172
Siekmeier, 72, 76
Slavery and Social Death, 111–12
Smith, Christian, 102

social death, 111–12, 131–32
Social movements (SM)
   approaches and frameworks, 99–100
   emergence, 96–97
   histories, 97–98
   political-social currents, 101
societies of thought, 87
Society Poverty Line, 154
sociogeny/sociogenesis, 132–33
Son of a slave woman, 207
Son of God, 207
Son of his Father, 207
Son of his Mother, 207
Sonora, 189
Soto, Oscar, 97
Source of Water, 178
South Africa, 224
South America, 182, 217
Southern Baptist Convention (SBC), 217, 224, 225, 227
Southern Cone, 83, 85, 86, 88
Souza, Neusa Santos, 131
Soza, Francisco, Rev., 198
Spain, 222, 224
Spanish/Spaniards, 188
   Caribbean, 197
   colonizers, 219
   crown, 206
   language, 221
   speakers, 222, 225
Spanish-American War (1898), 74
specter of Constantine, 150, 152
Spirit (the), 182, 190, 191, 193, 195, 196, 198, 199
Spirit of God, 198
Spirit of Life, 191
Stedile, João Pedro, 106
storytelling components, ix, xiv; history, contexts, and communities, x; migration and global diaspora, xv; movement, xv; public theologies, xv; translation, xv
Sublimis Deus, 206, 234
Sun, 180, 181
   Sun-Supreme Being, 185

Sung, Jung Mo, 107
Supreme Ancestor, 138
Suriname, 182
Swedish immigrants, 217
Switzerland, 223

Tavárez, David, 13
Tawantinsuyu (Realm of the four parts), 204
Taylor, Mark Lewis, 105
Tenochtitlan, 38, 41
Teologia India, 170, 173, 174, 175
Teresa of Ávila, 35
Terraciano, 8
Terreiro Ilé Axé Opô Afonjá, 117
The Florentine Codex, 41
theologies for political power, especially in Africa and the Americas, xvi; influence of evangelicalism, liberation theologies, and Pentecostal practices for, xvi
theology of the multitude, 106–7
theoquilombism, 127, 133
Thérèse of Lisieux, 35
Third World, 190
   conferences, 153
   priests' movement, 102
Thomas, Piri, 195, 196
Thomson, James "Diego," 85, 223
tlamatinimes, 45
Torres, Nelson Maldonado, 130
Trans-Amazonian Network of Indigenous Christian Leaders, 175
Treaty of Tordesillas, 1494, 57, 233
Tupi-Guarani, 204
type of utopian ideal, 103

Umbanda, 113, 117–20, 194
Union Católica, 87
Unión de Naciones Suramericanas, 98
United Kingdom, 222
United States (US), 189, 195, 197, 198, 216, 217, 218, 219, 220, 221, 222, 224, 225, 226, 227
   Brazilian migration to, 225

Brazilian churches in, 227
Confederates, 223
imperialism, 218, 227
Latin American immigrants to, 217, 221
Latine group in, 222
migrant religious communities in, 224
missionaries from, 224
missions to Latin America, 220
southern Confederates, 223
structural racism, 222
Universal Church, 171
Universidade da Assuncao, 170
University of Birmingham, 190
Uruguay, 224
US Navy, 198
US-born Latines, 222
utopian inspiration, source of, 97

Varguismo, 98
Vatican II, 153
Vendepatrias, 75
Venezuela, 175, 182, 224
Venezuelan migration to Colombia and Brazil, 221
Vergès, Françoise, 203
Via crucis en mexicano, 13
Vieira, Antonio, 42
Vieira, Father Antônio, 206, 207
Vieques, Puerto Rico, 187, 197, 198, 200
Villalba, 189
Vingren, Gunnar, 217
Viracocha, 181
Virgin Mary, 207
vodoun, 60–61
Voladores de Papantla, 179

Wagua, Aiban, 174, 184
Waldensians, 82

Wales, 223
Wallerstein, 209
Walls, Andrew F., 147
Walsh, Catherine, 210
Walsh, Robert, 81
Wanamaker, Charles A., 137
War of Gods: Religion and Politics in Latin America, 101
Weber, Max, 111
Western cosmovision, 209
Westrup family, 223
Wilfred, Felix, 147–48
Wolf, Eric, 4
Words and Worlds Turned Around, 3
world Christianity versus global Christianity, xi
World Council of Churches, 145, 147, 161
World Missionary Conference (1910), 150
World Social Forum (Porto Alegre), 98
Wycliffe Bible Translators, 89

Xakriabá, Célia, 214
Xicotepec de Juarez, Puebla, Mexico, 168
Xolotl, 180, 181, 185

y Costilla, Miguel Hidalgo, 69
y Pavón, José Morelos, 59
Yanomami, 218
Yoruba, 194
Yturri, Doña Margarita, 25–26

Zapatismo, 173
Zapatista National Liberation Army, 171, 173
Zapotec, 174
Zibechi, Raúl, 101

www.ingramcontent.com/pod-product-compliance
Lightning Source LLC
Chambersburg PA
CBHW021943240426
43668CB00037B/603